Chinese Business

It is difficult to overstate the importance of China to the world economy, and yet the majority of books either look at Chinese business by applying Western frameworks or models to the context of China or focus on a particular aspect of business in China.

Authored by an academic expert on China, this new, completely revised edition of *Chinese Business* offers its readers a comprehensive and systematic body of knowledge of Chinese business. It has taken a holistic perspective, intending to achieve a balance between the academic and practical, between theory and practice and between traditional and current (Internet-based) industry. The framework of this book subsumes all the major factors that should be taken into consideration when Western companies contemplate a China strategy, including history, philosophy, ancient military classics, strategy and marketing, innovation, Internet business and human resources. The discussion of these factors is supplemented with insightful case studies.

Chinese Business, Second Edition, can be used as a textbook for undergraduates and postgraduates at business schools and as a useful reference for researchers, senior executives, consultants and government officials involved in Chinese business.

Hong Liu is Founding Director of the China Business Centre at Manchester Business School, University of Manchester, UK.

Chinese Business

Landscapes and Strategies

Second Edition

Hong Liu

Routledge
Taylor & Francis Group

LONDON AND NEW YORK

Second edition published 2018
by Routledge
2 Park Square, Milton Park, Abingdon, Oxon, OX14 4RN

and by Routledge
711 Third Avenue, New York, NY 10017

Routledge is an imprint of the Taylor & Francis Group, an Informa business

© 2018 Hong Liu

First edition published by Routledge 2009

British Library Cataloguing-in-Publication Data
A catalogue record for this book is available from the British Library

Library of Congress Cataloging-in-Publication Data
A catalog record for this book has been requested

ISBN: 978-1-138-91824-5 (hbk)
ISBN: 978-1-138-91825-2 (pbk)
ISBN: 978-1-315-68864-0 (ebk)

Typeset in Bembo
by Apex CoVantage, LLC

To my beloved wife, Xu Ying, and daughter, Angela

To my mom, Dong Ming

Contents

Tables

Figures

Boxes

About the author

Having been awarded a bachelor's degree in engineering from Beijing University of Science and Technology, a master's degree in economics from Renmin University of China and a national scholarship prize for the best academic performance of the year in marketing management, Hong Liu acquired a doctorate in business administration from Warwick Business School.

He has taught full-time MBA, executive MBA and senior executive programmes at Manchester Business School for over 20 years. Having served as a board member of The 48 Group Club, he has been consulted by the Chinese, British, Polish and Bruneian governments and by a number of multinationals such as EADS, Volvo Trucks and AstraZeneca as well as China's Yangtze River Pharmaceutical Group.

As the Founding Director of the China Business Centre at Manchester Business School, he has directed management development programmes for several hundreds of Chinese senior officials and executives. Having delivered lectures and speeches to senior executives of various multinationals and banks, as well as lawyers and public organisations, he has published numerous papers on marketing and strategies in China, and is the author of *The Chinese Strategic Mind* (Edward Elgar Publishing, 2015).

Acknowledgements

I would like to thank Xu Ying, my wife, for her wholehearted support during the process of writing up this book. As a successful senior executive in a large Chinese company, she has provided me with both moral support and invaluable feedback on Chinese ways of doing business.

My thanks go to Xu Jingren, Chairman and CEO of the Yangtze River Pharmaceutical Group, for his candid discussion with me about his management philosophy and approaches, which are embedded in Chinese tradition.

I am grateful to Stephen Perry, Chairman of The 48 Group Club, for his encouragement and insightful discussion about various aspects on doing business in China. His views on Chinese business from a Western perspective with a deep understanding of Chinese culture have proved to be inspiring and thought-provoking.

I am also indebted to Robin Wensley, Andrew Leung, Elaine Ferny, Nigel Banister, Nigel Campbell, Peter McGoldrick, Lars-Uno Roos, Terry Clague, Nigel Hubbell, Feng Xiaodong, Rui Ying, Hua Xiong, Lai Ting, Qing Xinling, Hong Xia and Luo Jing.

Preface

This book is intended to deliver a systematic body of knowledge about Chinese business, being concerned with any business that involves dealings with Chinese companies, in terms of competition or collaboration, and Chinese 'stakeholders' including the Chinese government, consumers, banks and other institutions in a working relationship. The book addresses two major aspects of Chinese business: (a) how Chinese companies manage and organise their businesses in China and/or elsewhere and (b) how foreign companies should manage their strategies and organisations effectively either in China or elsewhere, whether in competition or cooperation with Chinese companies, or more generally work with other Chinese stakeholders. It has the following characteristics:

(1) It provides a framework or knowledge system for understanding Chinese business, including factors that critically influence the behaviour and competitiveness of Chinese companies.
(2) It explains and analyses Chinese strategy and management, mainly from a Chinese perspective, with a view to helping Western readers/businesses to develop their strategies and manage their businesses effectively.
(3) The knowledge system consists of two parts: (a) elements of Chinese history, philosophy and ancient military classics that are deemed to have an effect on Chinese decision-makers and (b) Chinese and Western literature that is concerned with theories and best practices in the context of doing business in China. My selection of literature is guided by over 20 years' experience of teaching, research and consulting on Chinese business.
(4) Its target audience includes university undergraduates and postgraduates, practitioners or senior executives and academics who have an interest in doing business in China.

As Chinese businesses exert a growing influence on the global economy, there has been a mushrooming of publications to examine issues about how Western companies should compete against or cooperate with their Chinese counterparts. Other books either look at Chinese business from a Western perspective by applying Western frameworks or models to the context of China or focus on a particular aspect of business in China, such as Confucianism/Taoism, Sun

Tzu's *Art of War*, successful Chinese companies or Chinese innovation. Few provide a systematic framework to synthesise the factors that affect how and why Chinese executives manage and organise their businesses in a particular way, with a view to dealing with them effectively.

Designed and structured from a holistic perspective, the framework of this book subsumes all the major factors that should be taken into consideration when Western companies contemplate a China strategy, including philosophy, history, ancient military classics, strategy and marketing, innovation, the Internet and human resources. Particularly and uniquely discussed are the effects of the *I Ching*, Chinese innovation, Internet-based businesses and human resource management (HRM) on the landscape and strategies of Chinese business. The *I Ching* is the cornerstone of Chinese philosophy, yet it has received inadequate attention in other writings on Chinese business. It is particularly notable that Chinese e-business and m-businesses, as latecomers to the game, have grown about 15–20 per cent faster than those in Western developed economies, with far-reaching strategic implications for Western companies. Western companies taking full consideration of all of these factors shaping the competitiveness of Chinese companies might be in a better position to make and give full effect to sound strategic and managerial decisions.

The book has benefited from over twenty years' experience of teaching the topic of doing business in China in full-time and executive MBA programmes and senior executive development programmes. My research and consulting experience and the feedback I have had from students and executives have convinced me that it is essential for foreign executives to be equipped with multidisciplinary knowledge to be able to develop sustainable businesses in China. Given how few books to date have delivered such a knowledge system, I believe that this one is ideally placed to fulfil an urgent need.

Taking a perspective that balances between the academic and practical, the Chinese and Western and the traditional and Internet-based industries, the book can be used as a textbook for undergraduates and postgraduates at business schools and as a reference for senior executives, consultants and government officials who are involved in Chinese business. In addition, Chinese wisdom will provide readers with substantial food for thought to enrich the pool of their strategic, managerial and organisational knowledge.

1 The nature of Chinese business

To know that we know what we know, and to know that we do not know what we do not know, that is true knowledge.

– Nicolaus Copernicus

To know what you know and what you do not know, that is true knowledge.

– Confucius

The beginning of thought is in disagreement – not only with others but also with ourselves.

– Eric Hoffer

Perspectives on doing business in China: Western versus Chinese

Why in the West do we need special books or university courses on doing business in China, the volume of which has increased greatly over the past decade (although not all academic members of staff at universities agree with the necessity of running such special courses)? Why has the volume of such books or courses not been matched by those about 'American business', 'German business' or 'French business'? When I was teaching an in-house corporate strategy programme on Chinese business to senior executives of a major multinational corporation, a participant once asked: 'Why should we study Chinese ways of doing business? Why shouldn't Chinese executives learn our Western culture and practices?' This reflects a mentality apparently typical of many Western senior executives, as well as policy-makers and academics.[1] Thus it was that the chairman of a Western company once advised me that in order to bridge cultural gaps between the West and China, I should write for Chinese senior executives, in order to help them to understand how Western businesspeople think about and make their strategic decisions, as the top executives of Western multinational corporations would be unlikely to be willing to study Chinese strategic thinking. It is necessary for Chinese executives to make their communications and intentions understood by Western counterparts in order to engage in fair competition and to forge cooperation on a win–win basis. Any Western senior executives who suffered from failing to understand Chinese strategies or behaviour would simply avoid doing business with Chinese companies, with resultant losses for both sides. Many Western companies, such as eBay, The Home Depot, Best Buy and Tesco, have failed to establish a strategic foothold in China, just because they have failed to overcome cultural barriers and so have responded inadequately to the needs and wants of Chinese consumers. In 2003, for instance, eBay, a leading global Internet company, entered China's e-commerce market by acquiring a Chinese company, EachNet, and thus a 90 per cent share of China's e-commerce market. Within three years, it was outdone by a Chinese newcomer, Alibaba's Taobao, and drifted into oblivion in China. The reason for this failure is summarised as follows:

> eBay's biggest mistake was in getting the culture wrong. A 'leave it to the experts' attitude demoralized the original EachNet team in Shanghai, as eBay executives were parachuted in from headquarters in San Jose or other parts of the eBay empire. No matter how skilled the new arrivals, most spoke no Chinese. They faced a steep learning curve to understand the local market.[2]

Chinese executives do indeed also need to have a better understanding of Western culture and strategic and managerial practices in order to pursue globalisation strategies successfully. Since the Chinese government announced a 'go global' policy in 1999,[3] Chinese cross-border mergers and acquisitions (M&As) have increased dramatically.[4] For instance, the following UK brands are now owned by Chinese companies: Weetabix by China's Bright Foods, Manganese Bronze by Geely, Sunseeker by Dalian Wanda, Pizza Express by Hony Capital, House of Fraser by Sanpower and Silver Cross by Fosun. However, a majority of Chinese cross-border M&As have ended up failing or underperforming, one of the main reasons being that Chinese companies have been unable to follow or understand Western M&A procedures and practices.[5] At an early stage of Alibaba's development involving an international dimension, its founder, Jack Ma, confessed that 'managing a multinational organization is no easy task with the language and cultural gaps.'[6]

There are two things that Western senior executives or readers who take an interest in Chinese business should understand:

(1) China's political weight and economic influence have become so significant in the international arena that Western companies, whether they like it or not, must inevitably do business or compete with Chinese ones. From 1985 to 2015, the annual growth of China's GDP averaged 9.4 per cent,[7] making China the world's largest economy based on the measure of purchasing power parity (PPP) in December 2014, according to the International Monetary Fund (IMF), and the world's largest recipient of foreign

direct investment, with the world's largest foreign reserves.[8] The dominant role played by China in chairing the G20 meeting in Hangzhou, China, in September 2016 has reaffirmed China's economic and political position and impact in the world. Meg Whitman, the former CEO of eBay, has asserted: 'Whoever wins China, will win the world.'[9] A 2016 PwC survey of 1409 CEOs in 83 countries denotes that the USA (39%) and China (34%) remain the countries from which their growth will come from.[10]

(2) Chinese culture and tradition and thus strategic behaviour are markedly different from those of the West. Misreading or misunderstanding the behaviour of Chinese decision-makers or consumers would potentially lead to losses both financially and strategically. A 2016 article in *Fortune* magazine asserts: 'Indeed, China is an incredibly complex market that differs culturally, politically, and economically from the United States.'[11] Chinese and Western cultures have distinctively different roots: Western culture can trace its origins to Classical Greece, while Chinese culture has its foundation in ancient Chinese civilisation,[12] with the *I Ching*, Confucianism and Taoism being seen as moulding Chinese behaviour across the centuries. The scope for misreading and miscomprehension between the Chinese and Western people remains wide.[13] Different traditions and values tend to result in divergent expectations or interpretations, fostering misjudgements and miscalculations in a cross-cultural setting.

There is an underlying assumption in the West that all companies should aggressively pursue technological innovation and seek to lead the world in the industries in which they operate, emulating Apple or Google/Alphabet.[14] This may not be entirely true in China from a philosophical or cultural point of view. Chinese philosophy, including the *I Ching*, Taoism and Confucianism, has principles that explicitly contradict such assumption or actions.[15] For instance, in the first hexagram of the *I Ching*, one is emphatically advised:

> The Dragon
> Lies hidden.
> Do not act.

This is explained as follows:

> The Master said:
> He possesses Dragon Power,
> But stays concealed.
> He does not Change
> For the World's sake,
> Does not crave success or fame.
> He eschews the World.
> Neither oppressed by solitude,
> Nor saddened by neglect,

In Joy he Acts,
In Sorrow stands aside.
He is never uprooted.
This is the Hidden Dragon
In lowly place;
This is Yang Energy
Concealed in the deep.
The True Gentleman acts
From Perfection of Inner Strength.
His Actions are then visible daily.
Here he is Concealed,
He is
Not yet visible,
His conduct is not yet
Perfected.
He does not
Act.[16]

This has been found to typify the practice among Chinese-run companies[17] in both the USA, China and elsewhere, in that they prefer to keep a low profile and purposely stay behind their leading competitors.[18] For instance, when Thomson Reuters published its list of Top 100 Global Innovators in 2015, Huawei was not among the top 20; nor was it among the top 20 in the 2015 Global Innovation 1000 study undertaken by PwC. On the other hand, Huawei filed 3898 PCT applications in that year, ranking the highest in the world, and has maintained the top position since 2013. In 2015, Huawei licensed 769 patents to Apple, which was ranked as the world's most innovative company, but received only 98 patent licences from the US firm in return. There are indications that Huawei deliberately keeps a controlled pace, not the fastest, in pursuit of the most advanced technological innovation, because of its founder's 'Middle Way' philosophy.[19] It is the founder's conviction that too much innovation is as bad as too little. Jujitsu, NEC and Motorola are examples of companies whose overambitious innovations have exceeded market demand and brought about disastrous failures. For instance, Motorola invested $2.6 billion to develop the Iridium satellite system, the deployment of which in the late 1990s resulted in the bankruptcy of the Iridium Corporation, as the market could not afford such an expensively innovative system.

If we look at Huawei from a Western perspective, we may conclude that the company's R&D capability is still a long way short of that of Western companies. However, from Huawei's viewpoint, this appears to be a strategy like that of a long-distance runner, following the leader while waiting for the right moment to sprint for the line. For those who are familiar with Chinese culture, there is a well-known Chinese tradition that the grand masters of Chinese martial arts tend to go to great lengths to hide themselves, not showing their muscles or physically fighting with others, unless and until it is absolutely necessary.

Many books have been written on Chinese business under different headings, dealing with various aspects of business strategy and management in China. They are all intended to help international readers to develop or manage their businesses in China, with a view to improving their chances of success. Some are based on empirical studies of successful foreign companies in China, some on the application of Western management and organisational theories to the context of China and some on a combination of Chinese philosophies and practices with Western theories or models. More and more are now looking into how Chinese companies such as Huawei, Lenovo, Alibaba and Haier have become successful internationally. Four questions arise:

- How do our existing frameworks and models explain the behaviour of Chinese executives?
- Are the practices of successful foreign companies in China replicable by other companies?
- To what extent is the success of foreign companies in China attributable to an adaptation to unique Chinese factors?
- How can Western companies benefit from an understanding of Chinese best practices or ancient wisdom?

Research suggests that US management theories may not be shared by European and Asian countries.[20] On the other hand, the managerial practices of Chinese business leaders are influenced by Confucianism, Taoism, Mohism, Legalism and even Communism.[21] Gordon Redding (1980) writes:

> That there are fairly large-scale differences in cognitive processes is often a matter of surprise to Westerners viewing Oriental people and vice versa. The problem is an inherent inability to step outside one's own world view and see the possibility of an alternative. And yet the literatures in psychology, philosophy and anthropology which examine the Chinese are full of references to such a difference, and references moreover which are consistent.[22]

Language is one of the most important parts of any national culture. The Chinese language system, having developed independently of the Indo-European languages, significantly differs from them, giving rise to great discrepancies in cognition and philosophy between the Chinese and Western peoples. Notwithstanding the existence of diverse derivatives, the basic form of the Chinese writing system is pictography. The contrast with alphabet-based Indo-European languages underlies differences in other social dimensions:

- The Chinese people have a different form of logic compared with Westerners as a result of the divergent development of their language systems.[23] The 'Chinese did not develop any formal systems of logic. There was a conspicuous lack of discussion of forms of inference, as the Chinese failed to develop anything either like an Aristotelian syllogism or a Nyaya syllogism.'[24] The difference in logic results in the possibility of misconception, misunderstanding and miscommunication between Westerners and Chinese.

- Chinese people are inclined towards imaginative and holistic thinking, while Westerners are prone to abstract and analytical thinking. The former often consider the part as the whole and pay less attention to detail than the latter. It is evident that e-commerce has developed much faster in China than in Western developed economies. One reason for this is that the development of e-commerce requires holistic thinking, affording Chinese companies some advantage.[25]
- The Chinese language has shaped the nature of ancient Chinese philosophies such as Confucianism, Taoism, Legalism and Mohism, infusing them with the characteristics of practicality, holism, simplicity and stability.[26]

The distinctive and fundamental difference in cognitive logic between Chinese and Western cultures has been recognised by social psychologists.[27] Western logical thinking is characterised by analytic cognition, which is defined as 'involving a detachment of the object from its context, a tendency to focus on attributes of the object to assign it to categories, and a preference for using rules about the categories to explain and predict the object's behaviour'.[28] It is based on the laws of non-contradiction and the excluded middle. The law of the excluded middle states that something is either 'A' or 'not A'. In practice, Western managers tend to categorise problems, breaking them down into their component parts and seeking to resolve stepwise, which requires a sharper focus on details than is attempted by their Chinese counterparts. In contrast, Chinese logical thinking is manifested in holistic cognition, which is defined as 'involving an orientation to the context or field as a whole, including attention to relationships between a focal object and the field, and a preference for explaining and predicting events on the basis of such relationships'.[29] Peng and Nisbett write:

> At the deepest level of Chinese philosophical thinking, 'to be or not to be' is not the question because life is a constant passing from one stage of being to another, so that to be is not to be, and not to be is to be ... Because reality is dynamic and flexible, the concepts that reflect reality are also active, changeable, and subjective rather than being objective, fixed, and identifiable entities.[30]

In practice, Chinese managers have a greater tendency than Western managers to be generalists, developing broad knowledge involving many different areas of expertise and function, with an overall concern for the final outcome as a result of the integration of the different areas.

Let us examine three illustrative examples.

(1) Huawei, a leading Chinese multinational in telecommunications and smartphones, has formed a strategic partnership with Vodafone, whereby engineers from both companies have worked together. It is notable that the

Vodafone engineers have quite sharply focused and in-depth knowledge in specific fields, while those from Huawei have much broader knowledge, enabling them to deal with issues involving different fields and finding solutions for technical problems. Such cognitive differences are reflected in many Chinese and Western technological products, as noted by Western media: 'Chinese companies also approach the internet in a different way. In the United States, tech firms emphasize simplicity in their apps. But in China, its three major internet companies – Alibaba, Baidu and the WeChat parent Tencent – compete to create a single app with as many functions as they can stuff into it.'[31] With a background in the teaching of English, Jack Ma ventured into a high-tech business in April 1999, founding Alibaba, which is now one of the world's largest Internet companies by capitalisation. At the Web 2.0 Conference in 2006, he stated: 'I'm 100 percent "made in China". I learned English myself, and I know nothing about technology. . . . One of the reasons why Alibaba survived is because I know nothing about computers. I'm like a blind man riding on the back of a blind tiger.'[32] In another speech, delivered at Stanford University in 2013, he further confessed, 'Even today, I still don't understand what coding is all about, I still don't understand the technology behind the Internet.'[33] In contrast, most Western high-tech entrepreneurs have a technological background and some kind of high-tech expertise or knowledge.

(2) A prestigious Hong Kong educational foundation once set up special scholarships for the best students from universities in Hong Kong, Taiwan and mainland China in 54 fields of natural science and social studies, including pharmacology, immunology, American literature, sociology, international economics and engineering thermophysics, to pursue their studies at universities in North America and Europe. Selection was carried out through an examination administered by a committee of distinguished scholars from top universities in mainland China, Hong Kong and Taiwan. In the area of marketing, the exam subjects included English, (macro and micro) economics, international business law and marketing. As few universities had programmes covering all of these in depth, it would be extremely challenging for candidates to excel in all of them. Clearly, the committee's requirements reflected a philosophy quite different from that of higher education in the West, favouring a holistic cognition with a requirement for a much broader scope of knowledge. Eventually, only 38 scholarships were awarded, as not a single candidate was identified to be qualified in the other 16 areas.

(3) Consider the differences between Western medicine and traditional Chinese medicine (TCM): under the Western diagnostic and therapeutic approach, a physical disorder is often recognised by symptoms and signs such as headache or stomach pain or skin rash, examined directly with scientific instruments and tests (e.g. blood or urine tests), then treated with drugs, surgery, physiotherapy, plaster or salve. Following the traditional Chinese remedial approach, by contrast, a doctor would normally first seek the cause of the symptoms by taking a holistic view, that is generally employing

four diagnostic methods: interrogation, inspection, auscultation and olfaction and pulse-taking and palpation.[34] The condition is then often treated using methods such as herbal medicine, cupping, breathing technique therapy, plaster, acupuncture and massage. The herbal prescription for treating a particular complaint normally consists of about ten different herbs, each of which addresses a separate dimension of the complaint. A condition characterised by symptoms affecting the head, say, will frequently be treated through putting needles into meridians elsewhere, such as on the neck, arms or foot, with no direct connection to the symptomatic area. Although TCM has been practised for several millennia, with proven effectiveness for many complaints and illnesses, it has not been fully integrated with Western medicine; it has to coexist and work in its own way, and will continue to do so in the foreseeable future.

How would these differences influence the strategies and managerial practices of Western companies? Or how should Western companies take these differences into consideration in their strategy, management and organisation? Sun Tzu (544–496 BC), one of the most globally influential of Chinese strategists, once wrote:

> Know the enemy and know yourself; in a hundred battles you will never be in peril. When you are ignorant of the enemy but know yourself, your chances of winning or losing are equal. If ignorant both of your enemy and of yourself, you are certain in every battle to be in peril.[35]

Knowing Chinese competitors or collaborators and consumers is a necessary condition for foreign firms to succeed in China.

Most existing books on Chinese business have been written from a Western perspective, applying Western strategic or analytical frameworks to business in China. This book is intended to provide Western readers with an in-depth understanding of the nature of Chinese business: its strategic, managerial and organisational logic. This knowledge may grant foreign firms an improved chance of success in China because a better understanding of their Chinese counterparts will facilitate their market entry and enhance their operational strategies in China. As China's growing economic influence is increasingly reshaping the configuration of the global economy, more and more books have addressed aspects of doing business in China and with Chinese companies. This one is designed to help Western readers to perceive businesses in China from a Chinese perspective and through the lens of Chinese logic, the better to understand the behaviour of Chinese companies and particularly of Chinese executives and consumers, allowing them to formulate a more adaptive strategy for their dealings with Chinese businesses.

Some limitations of academic research and journals in the business field should be mentioned in terms of providing applied guidelines for practitioners. In the West, research in the natural sciences has led to great success in the development of technology and industry, bringing about the prosperity of Western economies. As a result, academic business research has also become ever more analytical, quantitative and mathematical, widening the gap between such research and the requirements of practitioners, including in the area of international (and Chinese) business. It is notable that following the development of science and rationality in the West during the eighteenth-century Age of Enlightenment, ideas and ideals were increasingly characterised by 'reason' and 'scientific method', emphasising empirical observations with quantitative and multivariate statistical approaches. The academic field of strategy and management began to witness the influence of scientific thinking in the 1950s, when

> the renewed emphasis on scientific thinking and scientific rigour . . . sought once again to reduce uncertainty. As a consequence, people began applying scientific thinking, and especially mathematical calculation, to anything and everything. . . . Knowledge can only be considered to be 'proper' knowledge if can be scientifically proven and expressed in mathematical form.[36]

Quantitative research generally addresses 'what' and/or 'how many/much' issues, but does not ask 'how' or 'why', these being mostly pursued by qualitative research. Undoubtedly, quantitative or 'scientific' business research has great value for the understanding of the business world and particularly for meeting macro-objectives of a general nature. However, quantitative research may not provide substantive recommendations on how to do things to generate positive performance. Clausewitz was the first to note the limitations of the Enlightenment approach in developing the theory of warfare or (military) strategy in the West:

> The science of warfare had begun to concentrate on the art of making weapons, constructing fortifications, and organizing armies, and the ways to get the latter to move as was required. It had thus shifted from siege strategy and military tactics toward an increasingly elaborate art of mechanics. When it attempted to systematize the material data, it either reduced superiority in warfare simply to numerical data (thereby making warfare simply depend on mathematical laws) or else it proceeded by way of a geometrification of one of the crucial factors.[37]

Readers who are interested in Chinese business may pay more attention to a number of major journals that are practitioner-orientated, such as *Harvard Business Review*, *Sloan Management Review* and *California Management Review*, and particularly those that are published by consulting firms, such as *McKinsey Quarterly* and *Strategy + Business*. From time to time, these publications issue insightful papers on a particular aspect of doing business in China. In addition, it appears that some changes are taking place in academic journals in that some have started to accept and publish qualitative research papers, with the aim of reducing the gap between practitioners' requirements and academic output.

There has been the recognition that more high-quality indigenous research is called for in the fields of Asian and international business.[38]

Academic business research tends to be driven by economic development, rather than the reverse. As Western economies, particularly the UK and the USA, have become leading economic forces in the world since the nineteenth century, many areas of social science have been dominated by developments in these countries. In the fields of strategy and management, for instance, the universal 'Western cognition' or typical 'analytic thinking' has prevailed. 'Most strategy research, by its very nature, is more atomistic than holistic, focusing on just a few variables at once.'[39] 'The analysis based on economic power also sheds light on why Chinese management research, including context-sensitive research, often assumes a Western perspective,'[40] according to an Asian researcher. Still, the same author notes the absence of 'any significant trend to require research and theories developed in the U.S. context to take into account their relevance and applicability in other cultural contexts'.[41]

During the period of the Japanese economic miracle, which followed World War Two and lasted until the late 1980s, there was a proliferation of academic papers on just-in-time manufacturing, total quality management, the 'Japanisation' of manufacturing and Japanese management and marketing. From the 1960s to the 1990s, the economies of the Asian 'Four Tigers', namely Hong Kong, Singapore, South Korea and Taiwan, caught the attention of the world, because of their rapid growth, resulting in a mushrooming of academic publications on Asian factors and the role of Confucian society in attempt to explain their competitive advantage. As China increasingly stands out as the world's economic growth engine, it is not surprising increasing numbers of publications focus on or re-examine factors such as Chinese strategic thinking and cultural traditions such as the *I Ching*, Confucianism, Taoism and Internet Plus. The seeds of this change are already beginning to sprout among Chinese senior executives and entrepreneurs, and Western academics.

This book includes extensive discussion and analysis of areas such as history, philosophy and ancient military classics, seemingly unrelated to business, but which are extremely important for understanding Chinese business. They can help readers to understand the factors underpinning the behaviour of Chinese executives and consumers (why they behave and do things in particular ways) and to grasp the business logic of Chinese companies (how management is performed within Chinese companies and how successful Chinese businesses are organised in certain ways and why). Therefore, the book aims to convey the fundamental knowledge of Chinese management and organisation that the reader will need in order to see Chinese business through the eyes of an insider, in addition to vital aspects of business logic and strategy in China. When Joseph Needham, a renowned sinologist, studied and wrote on science and technology in China, his starting points were Chinese culture, geography and history, as knowledge of these fields is considered the basis of science and technology.

Strategy versus management and organisation

Notably, there are numerous books on doing business in China or internationally. As explained previously, because of the Western analytical mode of thinking, many of these tend to focus on a particular topic or issue, such as human resource management in China, leadership in China, *guanxi* strategy and management or marketing management in China. As this book provides a knowledge system for those doing business in China, it covers a number of disciplinary areas, including not only indigenous knowledge such as Chinese history, military classics and philosophy, but also strategy and management/ organisation. A reasonable question may be raised by readers: What would be the relationships between strategy, management and organisation? This might be easily answered by those with knowledge of the fields of strategy and organisational studies, but it would not be straightforward for non-specialists. Therefore, it is necessary to discuss these relationships before we explore various managerial and organisational aspects of doing business in China.

Let us take a look at a Chinese multinational, Huawei, a leading player in world markets for telecom equipment and smartphones. In the area of strategy development, the company's founder, Ren Zhengfei, strongly accentuates 'Chinese characteristics', calling for strategic inputs from ancient Chinese wisdom, including military and historical literature,[42] and de-emphasising the role of Western strategic theories, models or frameworks. For instance, in the process of drafting its Basic Law of Huawei, a document providing strategic guidelines and fundamental policies for the company, having carefully considered potential consulting service providers, Huawei chose a group of professors from Renmin University of China over major multinational consulting firms, including McKinsey, BCG, A.T. Kearney and PwC, to deliver the firm's strategic blueprint. The rationale for this decision was that these Chinese professors have both in-depth knowledge of Chinese tradition and culture and working experience in Western countries, enabling them to combine Chinese wisdom with Western best practices. Huawei's strategy often reflects the teachings of Mao Zedong, the late founder of the People's Republic of China, or his deeds during the period of Chinese civil war. Nevertheless, in the areas of management and organisation, the company has cooperated widely with international consulting firms such as IBM, Hays, PwC and Accenture. For instance, in 1998, Huawei commissioned IBM to develop an integrated product development system for the company, involving about 70 consultants from IBM over a span of ten years. At a cost of $48 million, the project revolutionised Huawei's R&D process, resulting in a dramatic improvement in corporate performance. The company has employed about 1400 foreign nationals in its 20 R&D centres worldwide. One might be surprised to know that a retired member of the Toyota board of directors led a group of experienced Japanese consultants who worked for Huawei for 10 years and that a group of senior German engineers also helped the company for over a decade. In other words, strategically, the company tries to follow Chinese tradition and tread a Chinese-style path, but managerially and organisationally, it endeavours to learn from or incorporate Western best practices.

A similar pattern can be observed in other major Chinese companies. For instance, the development of Alibaba, which is listed on the NASDAQ with the largest IPO in world history, is considered a product of Chinese wisdom combined with Western operations. CEO Jack Ma's management philosophy 'includes being more international than domestic enterprises and being more domestic than international enterprises'.[43] In the process of restructuring Alibaba, he appointed to his top executive team various men imbued with US corporate values, including Joe Tsai (who formerly worked for a US law firm and Swedish investment bank) as CFO, John Wu (a former Yahoo executive) as CTO and Savio Kwan (a former GE executive) as COO; yet he borrowed from Mao Zedong an approach known as the 'rectification movement' when steering the company in a new direction.[44] It appears that while Jack Ma has driven the adoption of strategy with Chinese characteristics, the company has fully utilised Western managerial and organisational theories and best practices.

This phenomenon is embedded in the relationship between 'strategy' and 'structure'. It has been noted that many other Chinese entrepreneurs and business leaders, such as Liu Chuanzhi (Lenovo), Zhang Ruimin (Haier), Zhang Chaoyang (Sohu), Zong Qinghou (Wahaha), Ma Yun (Alibaba) and online game giant Shi Yuzhu, have all studied and applied the writings of Mao Zedong, which can be seen as having crystallised Chinese strategic wisdom.[45] For instance, when Haier started its internationalisation process in the mid-1990s, its founder, Zhang Ruimin, adapted a strategy that Mao Zedong successfully applied during the Chinese civil war, that is 'the encirclement of cities from the countryside', or to effect 'the encirclement of developed economies from developing countries'.[46]

In his 1962 seminal work, *Strategy and Structure*, Alfred D. Chandler first proposed that 'structure follows strategy',[47] which has been supported by a number of studies.[48] Strategy is 'the determination of the basic long-term goals and objectives of the enterprise and the adoption of courses of action and the allocation of resources necessary for carrying out these goals', while structure is 'the design of organization through which the enterprise is administered'.[49] Generally, strategy deals with issues in the following areas: business policy,[50] organisational performance,[51] the external environment,[52] internal resources[53] and strategy implementation.[54] In other words, strategy tends to determine the effectiveness of an organisation, concerning 'doing the right thing', while structure is about how the company operates and organises itself efficiently, involving 'doing things right', with the aim of implementing the strategy.

Strategy plays an important role in setting the direction of an organisation, outsmarting its rivals, or at least enabling it to be flexible in coping with a hostile environment. If an organisation's strategy is 'right', although it may make some tactical errors or start from a weaker position, it can still come out as a winner. Furthermore, 'strategy is needed to focus effort and promote coordination of activity.'[55] Without strategy, the organisation would be a collection of individuals all doing things their own way and unable to take collective action, which is the essence of organisation. Therefore, binding individual actors together is significant and crucial through the provision of a sense of direction.[56]

Understandably, if an organisation heads in the wrong direction, attempts to achieve an inappropriate goal or adopts a poor position, then the more efficient it is, the worse it will perform. When the organisation changes its strategy, it must alter its structure to fit or follow the new strategy. Conversely, it has been suggested that there are cases where strategy follows structure.[57] One view of the strategy-structure relationship is that a proactive organisation tends to have a pattern of structure following strategy while in a reactive one strategy tends to follow structure. One way or another, strategy and structure are closely interrelated. If a company has a strategy with Chinese characteristics, its structure must accommodate these characteristics somehow, although it may also incorporate many Western 'scientific' elements. Strategy and management are both seen as art and science. As far as the Chinese context is concerned, it may be said that strategy is 80 per cent art (uniqueness) and 20 per cent science (commonality), while in management, there is a 50:50 per cent balance.

Framework of the book

Figure 1.1 shows the framework on which the book is based, showing that Chinese management and organisation (CMO) follows Chinese (business) strategy. The ultimate goal of the book is to help readers to understand CMO

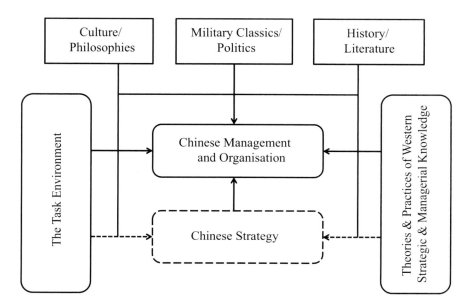

Figure 1.1 A framework for Chinese management and organisation

by offering a balanced perspective: academic versus practitioner, Western versus Chinese, and traditional versus 'new' (Internet) industry. The aim is that counterstrategies and alternative structures may be effectively deployed. The book does not deal directly with the relationship between Chinese strategy and influences on it, which is why dashed lines are used in the lower part of the diagram.[58] As shown in the figure, CMO is influenced by firms' business strategy, by Western theories and practices and by the task environment, that is competition, suppliers, distributors and customers. This book addresses the Chinese factors, such as culture/philosophy, military classics and history/literature, which have an important effect on CMO, providing major inputs into it.

The discipline of Western business management has over a century of history during which it has gradually developed into a complete system that covers every aspect of business and organisation. Frederick Taylor, who is considered as the father of work study, published his book titled *Principles of Scientific Management* in 1911,[59] addressing some managerial tasks such as scientifically selecting, training and motivating workers and production planning and control. Five years later, French mining engineer and executive Henri Fayol, in his book *Industrial and General Administration*, elucidated six primary functions of management: forecasting, planning, organising, coordinating, commanding and controlling, together with fourteen 'principles of management'.[60] Since then, publications on management and organisation in the West have proliferated, resulting in the theories and principles of management and organisation being systemised, itemised and globalised. For instance, research has generated substantial publications in each of these business areas or functions: nature of management, nature of organisation, leadership, strategic management, human resource management, marketing management, technology (R&D) management, supply chain management, international business, e-commerce/e-business strategies, Internet marketing, corporate responsibility and corporate governance.

As indicated previously, Western theories and practices of business management and organisation may be applicable in China, and strategy is closely intertwined with structure, suggesting that Chinese management and organisation should also, to some extent, adapt to the Chinese environment. These connections are illustrated in Figure 1.2.

On the whole, the theme of teaching and research activity has followed the framework of the business system in the West, with emphasis on the differing nature of market and economic relationships. In practice, many new types of enterprises characterised by market-driven behaviour have developed in China due to the disintegration of the past unitary and centrally controlled enterprise structure. The degree to which state-owned enterprises (SOEs) have been controlled by state bodies has varied considerably from sector to sector, from region to region, and from enterprise to enterprise. As a result, a plethora of publications in the West have discussed enterprise behaviour, market structure and enterprise control.[61]

During the period from 1978 to 1997, publications on Chinese management and organisation focused mainly on two types of firms: family businesses

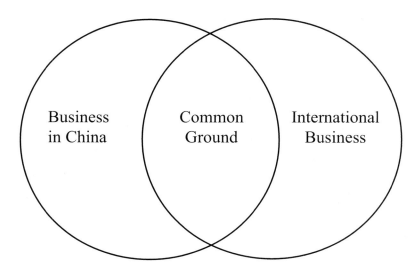

Figure 1.2 Nature of Chinese business

in Southeast Asia and SOEs in mainland China.[62] As a result of the influence of Sun Tzu's *Art of War*, management and organisation in regional firms were distinctive and bewildering to outsiders.[63] The Chinese family businesses overseas were quite influential in Southeast Asia, with two typical types of managerial practices: (1) networking with an attachment to different business groups linked by trust[64] and (2) diversification involving a number of (often unrelated) businesses to achieve economies of scope.[65]

Research has identified a number of management problems in those businesses, including a centralised decision-making style,[66] the stifling of creativity by the prevalence of a culturally embedded respect for authority and age,[67] and failure to utilise professional managers to lead business development.[68] Mainland SOEs mainly addressed challenges or bottlenecks and the dynamic business environment surrounding the enterprises. The emphasis of their managerial practices was on strategic alliances and the development of *guanxi*.[69] The period witnessed the emergence of non-SOEs such as private firms, collective enterprises and township and village enterprises, which also primarily adopted network- and *guanxi*-building approaches.[70]

Major publications reporting empirical research on business and management in China for the period from 2000 to 2005 deal mainly with issues in the following categories:

(1) joint ventures and strategic alliances in China;
(2) firms' strategy and behaviour; and
(3) human resource management in China.[71]

However, although research on management and organisation in Asia has increased significantly, 'there continues to be reliance on simply extending existing theory to a new context and not the development of sufficient insight to the specifics of the Asian setting.'[72]

Since 2004, when the problem of a lack of research with sufficient insights into Asian-specific management issues was recognised,[73] management scholars have endeavoured to carry out research with an indigenous approach. For example, management research has witnessed the taking of a *yin-yang* perspective,[74] the development of a scale measuring the five key schools of Chinese cultural traditions[75] and the exploration of a definition and a typology of Chinese indigenous research.[76] However, there has still been no 'significant trend to require research and theories developed in the U.S. context to take into account their relevance and applicability in other cultural contexts'.[77]

It would be reasonable to say that existing knowledge of the conduct of business in China would fall mainly into the middle and right circles of Figure 1.2, predominantly based on the application of Western theories and frameworks to business in China, with a trend towards expanding into the left circle. Since China has had only three decades of the development of a market-based economy, systematic theories of management and organisation have yet to be developed. Before we embark on a journey to lay out Chinese business management and organisation, the left circle, the following questions should be addressed:

(1) Is there distinctive knowledge about Chinese management and organisation?
(2) If yes, what would be the idiosyncrasies of Chinese management and organisation?
(3) What would be the main sources of knowledge about Chinese management and organisation?

This book is structured to provide answers to these three questions. An overview of what Chinese entrepreneurs and business leaders have done, after we remove the elements of Western management and organisation, may reveal the teachings, principles and practices embedded in Chinese history, literature, philosophy and military classics. The remaining section of this chapter discusses the nature of some of non-business areas that have exerted a strong influence on Chinese entrepreneurs and business leaders.

Philosophy

Research and practice have indicated that the managerial thinking and decisions of Chinese political and business leaders are profoundly influenced by Chinese philosophy. A major difference between Chinese and Western philosophies is that since its origins in ancient Greece with philosophers such as Thales of Miletus, Pythagoras, Socrates, Empedocles, Plato and Aristotle, Western philosophy has constantly developed into various schools and numerous philosophical sub-disciplines, which have greatly influenced relevant areas of the natural and social sciences. By contrast, Chinese philosophy has, since antiquity, continued to be dominated by a few classics such as the *I Ching* and Confucianism, and to a lesser degree Taoism and Buddhism, with limited development of other influential schools of philosophy.

Notably, ancient Chinese philosophy, particularly in the form of Confucianism, Taoism and Buddhism, has been tied much more closely to the daily activities of the populace than Western philosophy, exerting a significant influence on political, social and commercial behaviour.

> In Confucian philosophy, one could never successfully separate and understand a 'moral' portion independent of the larger philosophical context. Implicit in Confucius' teachings is the belief that personhood is not and cannot be compartmentalized: the self is at once social, moral, political, and intellectual.[78]

This is because Chinese philosophy is characterised as 'world transcending', having both 'this-worldly' and 'other-worldly' aspects, that is it is concerned with the conduct of everyday life in society while also dealing with the highest sphere to be reached, separate from the plane of common activity.[79] Guided by this-worldly philosophy, people are encouraged to cultivate themselves to achieve 'sageness within and kingliness without' (one who becomes a sage through self-cultivation or conformance with the law of nature will attain a natural power in the world, regardless of any official position held). Following other-worldly philosophy, one should endeavour to rid oneself of all common temptations such as money, power and sex, in order to live a sublime life that separates one from common people. As a Taoist view puts it: 'Life is an excrescence, a tumour, and death is to be taken as the breaking of the tumour.'[80] While advising people on how to attain Tao, the highest of realms to be aimed at, Taoist teachings also afford guidelines or wisdom in many fields of the social domain, such as politics, diplomacy, government, economics, commerce/business, the military and health care. For instance, about 20 of the 81 chapters of the *Tao Te Ching* involve discussions that have implications for military strategies and tactics.[81]

> Chinese philosophy has one main tradition, one main stream of thought. This tradition is that it aims at a particular kind of highest life. But this kind of highest life, high though it is, is not divorced from the daily functioning of human relations. Thus it is both of this world and of the other world, and we maintain that it 'both attains to the sublime and yet performs the common tasks.' What Chinese philosophy aims at is the highest of realms, one which transcends the daily functioning of human relations, although it also comes within the scope of this daily function.[82]

This explains why Chinese philosophy has a more direct and stronger influence on the life and behaviour of the Chinese people than Western philosophy does on the Western populace.

The first and foremost book that has shaped Chinese thinking and behaviour is the *I Ching* or *Book of Changes*. It may be seen as an ancient authoritative encyclopaedia of Chinese culture, in particular laying the foundations of Chinese cosmology and philosophy and making invaluable contributions to Chinese history and literature. The Chinese word *i* means both 'change' and 'easy'. The essential idea of the *I Ching* is that in the beginning, there was '*tai ji*' or the Great Ultimate, which engendered two forces, *yin*, the passive or female component, and *yang*, the positive or male element, whose interactions give rise to multiplicity. The two forces are intertwined and intermingled, changing constantly. The universe is seen as the realm of perpetual activity, where the interactions of *yin* and *yang* change cyclically and progressively, leading to the development of society, morality and civilisation, or anything else for that matter.[83]

A treatise by the well-known Chinese historian Sima Tan, whose son Sima Qian wrote the *Records of the Great Historian* (*Shiji*), discusses six schools of thought: Confucianism, Taoism, Mohism, Legalism, the 'School of Names' and the 'School of *Yin* and *Yang*' (*yin-yang jia*)[84], which treatise has profoundly influenced the development of Chinese philosophy ever since its appearance.

> It is, in fact, considered by some to be a primordial and quintessential expression of the 'Chinese mind.' Any reader of Marcel Granet might indeed regard it as the central stream of the entire Chinese 'structure of thought.' Others have discerned in it something like the expression of the Chinese Jungian 'collective subconscious.'[85]

The Confucian doctrine has for two millennia greatly influenced how Chinese people think, behave and lead their lives. It is represented by the Four Books and Five Classics written before 300 BC. The Four Books are *Great Learning*, *The Doctrine of the Mean*, *The Analects* and *Mencius*; and the Five Classics are the *Book of Poetry*, the *Book of Documents*, the *Book of Rites*, the *I Ching* or *Book of Changes*[86] and the *Spring and Autumn Annals*. These classics contain great Chinese wisdom, having had a significant effect on the realms of most social contexts in Chinese history.

Taoism, represented by *Lao Tzu* and *Zhuang Tzu*, plays a vital role in shaping the thought of Chinese people. Joseph Needham, a British scientist, historian and sinologist, states that 'a Chinese thought without Taoism is like a tree without roots'; Taoist influence in China has also been noted and emphasised by some Chinese philosophers.[87]

Buddhism as a philosophy[88] with profound and enlightened teachings has also been influential in China. It was founded by Siddhartha Gautama, a prince who was born in Nepal between 563 BC and 483 BC. It began to be disseminated into China in AD 67 during the Han dynasty (206 BC – AD 220). Buddhism teaches people how to end their suffering by cutting out greed, hatred and ignorance. When people do bad things, they suffer bad consequences, and when they do good things, the consequences are good. Good and bad things do not cancel out.

This cause-and-effect chain is reflected in the endless cycles of life, death and rebirth. Buddhists believe in reincarnation (rebirth). The ultimate goal is to reach a state of enlightenment (nirvana) and liberate oneself from endless reincarnation and suffering. Some see Buddhism as a religion, some as a philosophy, while for others it is a way of finding reality. Alternatively, there are those who think that it is unnecessary to label Buddhism at all.

Other sources of the philosophical ingredients of Chinese business can be found in Mohism or the School of Mo, founded by Mozi (470–391 BC), in Legalism or the School of Law, laid out by Han Feizi or Master Han Fei during the Warring States period, and in the *Book of Lord Shang*, by Shang Yang and Li Si of the Qin dynasty.

History

The importance of Chinese history in understanding Chinese business, politics, philosophy, sociology and military affairs can hardly be overemphasised. Chinese history has been meticulously recorded, both officially and privately, accumulated, examined and re-examined, disseminated and widely read. Therefore, it may be seen as an encyclopaedia of knowledge in China, particularly in the domains of political, military and business affairs. The following are some exemplary historical classics.

(a) The *Twenty-Four Histories*, a collection of official Chinese annals, is considered the most authoritative and comprehensive source of Chinese history. The collection covers a period from prehistory in 3000 BC to the end of the Ming dynasty in 1644. After imperial China came to an end in 1911, a book on the last (Qing) dynasty was added to the body, making the *Twenty-Five Histories*. A group of Chinese researchers has studied the *Twenty-Five Histories* and extracted stratagems used throughout Chinese history, resulting in the publication of a book of 893 pages presenting 94 different stratagems and identifying the 1560 events recorded in the historical classics where these were successfully employed over the 5000 years to 1911.[89]

(b) *Zizhi Tongjian (Comprehensive Mirror for Rulers)* was written during the Northern Song dynasty by the writer and politician Sima Guang (AD 1019–1086), who was determined to produce a book that would assist in making good law and warn against evil. Having finished a treatise covering the period from the Warring States to the Qin dynasty, he presented a copy to Emperor Ying Zhong of Song, who appreciated it and encouraged him, providing a number of historians including Liu Shu, Liu Ban and Fan Zuyu to assist him. The final work comprised 294 volumes and about three million Chinese characters. Covering 16 dynasties with a span of 1400 years and recording major historical incidents from 403 BC to AD 959, it took 19 years to complete. Organised chronologically, its emphasis is on politics, rather than culture, economics or literature. Sima Guang made it clear that his book was intended to provide princes and emperors with guidelines for righteous and sagacious rule. It has remained one of the favourite readings of Chinese politicians and businesspeople. Mao Zedong is reported to have read the book 17 times by the time of his death in 1976. The ordinary paperback copy that accompanied him throughout his life is still kept at Zhongnanhai, Mao's former residence.

(c)   *Zuo Zhuan* or *Tso Chuan* is a private historical and literary masterpiece which records in detail court politics, battles and wars between different states, featuring vivid descriptions of people and events with political and military implications in the period from 722 to 468 BC.[90] For instance, the book describes over 400 battles and wars, with an analysis of the factors leading to victories. It has often been used as a handbook for political and military strategies and tactics.

In addition to the above, there are a number of highly influential private history books, including the *Spring and Autumn Annals* (by Confucius), the *Strategies of the Warring States*, the *Bamboo Annals*, the *Discourses of the States, History of the Han Dynasty* and *History of the Three Kingdoms*. All of these historical writings offer their readers insights and principles concerning the wise governance of state affairs, the management of family and state businesses and the formulation of military strategy and tactics, as well as how to become a benevolent human being useful to society.

Ancient military classics

As a result of holistic thinking embedded in Chinese culture, military strategies and tactics have long been utilised by the Chinese people in different fields, such as politics, commerce, sports and social conflict. On the other hand, China constitutes an extensive reservoir of strategic ideas because of its long military history. In antiquity, China witnessed a great deal of warfare. It has been calculated that there were 1109 significant military conflicts between the Chinese and northern nomads from 215 BC to AD 1684 and 225,887 recorded armed rebellions between 210 BC and AD 1900.[91] Sawyer observes that 'virtually every year witnessed a major battle somewhere in China, significant conflicts erupted nearly every decade, and the nation was consumed by inescapable warfare at least once a century.'[92]

A high incidence of warfare gave rise to a substantial body of ancient Chinese literature on military strategies and tactics, with the earliest writings dating back over two millennia. The Spring and Autumn and Warring States periods witnessed a proliferation of military writings, but during the Qin dynasty, the emperor burned a large proportion of these in order to enhance his control over unorthodox thought and dissenting voices, historically known as 'burning Confucian books and burying Confucian scholars'. Despite this attempt at suppressing heterodoxy, a significant number of military books survived. For instance, the *Treatise on Literature* from the *Book of Han* indicates that at the beginning of the Han dynasty there were about 182 books. During the period of Emperor Cheng of Han (51–7 BC), a book was published entitled the *Seven Strategies*, including a volume entitled *On the Art of War*, which covered 63 schools of military methods.[93] A study has found that in antiquity, a total of 3380 books in 23,503 recorded volumes were written on various aspects of military strategy, tactics and organisation in ancient China.[94] From this huge volume of military literature, two emperors of the Song dynasty (AD 960–1279) ordered a compilation and chose seven of them as standard military textbooks, known as *The Seven Military Classics: Tai Gong's Six Secret Teachings, The Methods of the Sima, Sun Tzu's Art of War, Wu Tzu, Wei Liao Tzu, Three Strategies of Huang Shigong* and *Questions and Replies between Tang Taizong and Li Weigong*. These became compulsory texts at military academies, containing the standard knowledge required to qualify for senior military positions in ancient China. Of all the classics, Sun Tzu's work is seen as the most comprehensive and influential, but other thinkers and classics have also contributed to China's military literature. These military classics continue to have a profound influence on Chinese politics, sport, commerce and military affairs.

Literature

Among the many works recognised as Chinese literary classics are the *Romance of the Three Kingdoms*, the *Water Margins*, the *Journey to the West*, the *Romance of the Sui-Tang Dynasties* and the *Yue Fei Chronicles*. Also in this category are the biographies (and associated philosophies) of successful politicians, military commanders and those who were involved in running businesses, including Guanzi or Master Guan, a ministerial official in the state of Qi during the Spring and Autumn period, Zeng Guofan, a statesman and military general of the late Qing dynasty, and Hu Xueyan, a notable late Qing businessman.

These literary classics contain considerable wisdom that is useful for military strategy, state affairs and business management and organisation. For instance, the *Romance of the Three Kingdoms* is full of military and political strategies which are demonstrated to provide the key to winning battles, wars and power struggles. It is considered to deserve to be known as the encyclopaedia of Chinese political and military stratagems. One example is vividly illustrative. During the period of the Three Kingdoms, in a battle between the states of Wei and Shu, a detachment of the Wei army suddenly penetrated the Shu defences and appeared before the city where the Shu general, Zhuge Liang, resided. The Shu were unprepared and unable to defend the city conventionally, as there were few soldiers garrisoned there. Cunningly, the Shu general ordered the city gate to be left wide open and unguarded, except by a few old men clearing away tree leaves. Zhuge Liang himself sat atop the city wall and played on his zither. The too-obvious lack of military preparedness made the enemy believe that there was an ambush, so the attacking force chose to withdraw. This is the historically famous 'empty-city stratagem'. Henry Kissinger has noted that Mao Zedong showed great mastery of stratagem during the Chinese civil war.[95] His strategic thinking has since inspired countless Chinese military commanders, politicians, business leaders and entrepreneurs, as well as foreign military leaders.[96]

While Huawei's founder, Ren Zhengfei, has been a close follower of Mao Zedong, Alibaba's founder has been heavily influenced by Chinese historical literature, particularly the works of Hong Kong-born martial arts author (Louis) Cha Leung-yung, better known by his pen name Jin Yong. Jack Ma has even made a large number of colleagues and employees adopt a nickname from Jin Yong's novels or other martial arts novels; for instance, within Alibaba and as the name of his online persona, he is known as Feng Qingyang, a swordsman created by Jin Yong. Inspired by one of Jin Yong's novels, Jack Ma has codified the company's values as 'Six Vein Spirit Sword'.

> The sword he writes about is not an actual weapon, but the art of building up one's internal strengths in order to defeat any opponent. In Alibaba's case, the strengths that form the Six Vein Spirit Sword are akin to those outlined in the 'Mission, Vision, and Values' of Jack's favourite corporate guru, Jack Welch, the former CEO of General Electric.[97]

Concluding remarks

This book aims to convey a fundamental and systematic knowledge of Chinese business through the eyes of a Chinese insider. Incorporated are views from philosophy, history, ancient military classics and relevant sub-disciplines of business studies. When Joseph Needham, a renowned sinologist, studied and wrote on science and technology in China, he started with Chinese culture, geography and history, as knowledge of these fields is considered the basis of science and technology. I can state with certainty that most Chinese state leaders have a good command of philosophy, history and literature,[98] without which it would be extremely difficult for anyone to climb up the Chinese hierarchical ladder. The Chinese bureaucratic system is likened to a jungle whereby philosophy, history and (historical, literary and military) literature are compared to the maps for travellers to get through it to their desired destinations. Trying to understand Chinese business without knowing Chinese history, philosophical thought or military classics would be like studying the human body by examining only the skin, not the heart or brain.

The book is intended to offer a complete and comprehensive view of strategy, management and organisation with a balance between Chinese and Western perspectives, providing ingredients for Western companies to manage their operations and organisations that will maximise their chances of success. The underlying philosophy of the book is that readers should understand how businesses are managed and organised, so that they may combine this understanding with their own general 'Western' knowledge in order to optimise their strategy, management and organisation by planning from a dual insider-outsider perspective. It can be used, most appropriately, as a textbook for undergraduate, MBA and executive courses at business schools as part of a programme for international or Asian business studies and executive development, as it incorporates fundamental knowledge from different fields to give readers a comprehensive view of Chinese business. Since it takes both academic and practical perspectives, it should also appeal to practising managers and executives with responsibility for businesses in China and elsewhere in Asia.

Notes

1 Jacques, M. (2012), "Why Do We Continue to Ignore China's Rise? Arrogance," *The Observer*, Sunday, 25 March 2012. Pillsbury, M. (2014), "Misunderstanding China: How Did Western Policy Makers and Academics Repeatedly Get China So Wrong?" *The Wall Street Journal*, 17 September 2014.

2 Clark, D. (2016), *Alibaba: The House That Jack Ma Built*, New York: HarperCollins Publishers, p. 165.

3 Buckley, P.J., Clegg, J.L., Cross, A.R., Liu, X., Voss, H. and Zheng, P. (2007), "The Determinants of Chinese Outward Foreign Direct Investment," *Journal of International Business Studies*, 38, 499–518.

4 Williamson, P.J. and Raman, A.P. (2011), "How China Reset Its Global Acquisition Agenda," *Harvard Business Review*, 89 (4), 104–119. Weinland, D., Massoudi, A. and Fontanella-Khan, J. (2016), "China's Megadeals Fail to Offset Slowdown," *The Financial Times*, 29 June.

5 Williamson, P.J. and Raman, A.P. (2011), "How China Reset Its Global Acquisition Agenda," *Harvard Business Review*, 89 (4), 104–119.

6 Clark, D. (2016), *Alibaba: The House That Jack Ma Built*, New York: HarperCollins Publishers, p. 141.

7 Woetzel, J., Chen, Y., Manyika, J., Roth, E., Seong, J. and Lee, J. (2015), *The China Effect on Global Innovation*, Seattle: McKinsey Global Institute, McKinsey & Company, http://www.mckinseychina.com/wp-content/uploads/2015/07/mckinsey-china-effect-on-global-innovation-2015.pdf

8 Tung, R.L. (2016), "Opportunities and Challenges Ahead of China's 'New Normal,'" *Long Range Planning*, 49, 632–640. PwC (2015), "A Marketplace Without Boundaries? Responding to Disruption," *19th Annual Global CEO Survey*, www.pwc.com/gx/en/ceo-survey/2015/assets/pwc-18th-annual-global-ceo-survey-jan-2015.pdf, retrieved on 12 December 2016. PwC estimates that China's GDP will overtake that of both the USA and EU at market exchange rates just before 2030.

9 Clark, D. (2016), *Alibaba: The House That Jack Ma Built*, New York: HarperCollins Publishers, p. 165.

10 PwC (2016), "Redefining Business Success in a Changing World CEO Survey," *19th Annual Global CEO Survey*, www.pwc.com/gx/en/ceo-survey/2016/landing-page/pwc-19th-annual-global-ceo-survey.pdf, retrieved on 12 December 2016.

11 Salomon, R. (2016), "Why Uber Couldn't Crack China," *Fortune*, 7 August 2016, http://fortune.com/2016/08/07/uber-china-didi-chuxing/.

12 Nisbett, R.E. (2003), *The Geography of Thought: How Asians and Westerners Think Differently . . . and Why*, New York: Free Press, pp. 1–45.

13 Pillsbury, M. (2014), "Misunderstanding China: How Did Western Policy Makers and Academics Repeatedly Get China So Wrong?" *The Wall Street Journal*, 17 September 2014.

14 Christensen, C.M., Raynor, M.E. and McDonald, R. (2015), "What Is Disruptive Innovation?" *Harvard Business Review*, 93 (12), 44–53. Cheng, J.L.C. and Yiu, D. (2016), "China Business at a Crossroads: Institutions, Innovation, and International Competitiveness," *Long Range Planning*, 49, 584–588. Gassmann, O., Zeschky, M., Wolff, T. and Stahl, M. (2010), "Crossing the Industry-Line: Breakthrough Innovation Through Cross-Industry Alliances With 'Non-Suppliers'," *Long Range Planning*, 43, 639–654.

15 Liu, H. (2015), *The Chinese Strategic Mind*, Northampton, MA: Edward Elgar Publishing, pp. 110–116.

16 Minford, J. (2015), *I Ching (Yijing): The Book of Chang*, translated with an introduction and commentary by John Minford. New York: Penguin Books, pp. 14–16.

17 Including the companies founded and run by American Chinese.

18 Chen, M.J. (2001), *Inside Chinese Business: A Guide for Managers Worldwide*, Boston: Harvard Business School Press, pp. 104–110.

19 Liu, H. (2015), *The Chinese Strategic Mind*, Northampton, MA: Edward Elgar Publishing, pp. 186–187. There will be a more detailed discussion about this point in Chapter Three.

20 Hofstede, G. (1993), "Cultural Constraints in Management Theories," *Academy of Management Executive*, 7, 81–94.

21 Fernandez, J.A. (2004), "The Gentleman's Code of Confucius: Leadership by Values," *Organizational Dynamics*, 33 (1), 21–31. McDonald, P. (2012), "Confucian Foundations to Leadership: A Study of Chinese Business Leaders Across Greater China and South-East Asia," *Asia Pacific Business Review*, 18 (4), 465–487. Tsui, A.S., Wang, H., Xin, K., Zhang, L. and Fu, P.P. (2004), "'Let a Thousand Flowers Bloom': Variation of Leadership Styles Among Chinese CEOs," *Organizational Dynamics*, 33, 5–20.

22 Redding, G.S. (1980), "Cognition as an Aspect of Culture and Its Relation to Management Processes: An Exploratory View of the Chinese Case," *Journal of Management Studies*, 17 (2), 127–148.

23 Wagner, R.G. (1999), "Science and Civilisation in China, Volume 7, Part 1: Language and Logic by Christoph Harbsmeier; Kenneth Robinson Reviewed by R.G. Wagner," *The American Historical Review*, 104 (5), 1644–1645. Logan, R.K. (1986), *The Alphabet Effect: The Impact of the Phonetic Alphabet on the Development of Western Civilization*, New York: St. Martin's Press.

24 Liu, S.H. (1974), "The Use of Analogy and Symbolism in Traditional Chinese Philosophy," *Journal of Chinese Philosophy*, 1, 313–338.

25 This will be explained in detail in Chapter Seven.

26 Liu, H. (2015), *The Chinese Strategic Mind*, Northampton, MA: Edward Elgar Publishing, pp. 52–77.

27 Peng, K. and Nisbett, R.E. (1999), "Culture, Dialectics, and Reasoning About Contradiction," *American Psychologist*, 54, 741–754. Nisbett, R.E., Peng, K., Choi, I. and Norenzayan, A. (2001), "Culture and Systems of Thought: Holistic Versus Analytic Cognition," *Psychological Review*, 108 (2), 291–310. Norenzayan, A. and Nisbett, R.E. (2000), "Culture and Causal Cognition," *Current Directions in Psychological Science*, 9 (4), 132–135.

28 Nisbett, R.E., Peng, K., Choi, I. and Norenzayan, A. (2001), "Culture and Systems of Thought: Holistic Versus Analytic Cognition," *Psychological Review*, 108 (2), 293.

29 Ibid.

30 Peng, K. and Nisbett, R.E. (1999), "Culture, Dialectics, and Reasoning About Contradiction," *American Psychologist*, 54, 743.

31 Mozur, P. (2016), "China, Not Silicon Valley, Is Cutting Edge in Mobile Tech," *The New York Times*, 2 August, www.nytimes.com/2016/08/03/technology/china-mobile-tech-innovation-silicon-valley.html?smid=tw-nytimes&smtyp=cur, retrieved on 28 August 2016.

32 Erisman, P. (2015), *Alibaba's World*, New York: Palgrave Macmillan, p. 1.

33 Clark, D. (2016), *Alibaba: The House That Jack Ma Built*, New York: HarperCollins Publishers, p. 24.

34 Nowadays, hospitals and doctors specializing in traditional Chinese medicine in terms of diagnosis and treatment also rely on scientific instruments and methods such as X-rays and blood tests, in addition to the traditional four methods.

35 Griffith, S.B. (1963), *Sun Tzu: The Art of War*, Translated and with an Introduction by S.B. Griffith and Forward by B.H. Liddell Hart, Oxford: Oxford University Press, p. 125.

36 Witzel, M. (2012), *A History of Management Thought*, London and New York: Routledge, p. 184.

37 Jullien, F. (2004), *A Treatise on Efficacy: Between Western and Chinese Thinking*, translated by Janet Lloyd, Honolulu: University of Hawaii Press, p. 10.

38 Tsui, A.S. (2004), "Contributing to Global Management Knowledge: A Case for High Quality Indigenous Research," *Asia Pacific Journal of Management*, 21, 491–513. Li, P.P., Leung, K., Chen, C.C. and Luo, J.D. (2012), "Indigenous Research on Chinese Management: What and How," *Management and Organization Review*, 8 (1), 7–24.

39 De Wit, B. and Meyer, R. (2010), *Strategy Process, Content, Context: An International Perspective* (4th ed.), Hampshire, UK: South-Western, p. 6.

40 Leung, K. (2012), "Indigenous Chinese Management Research: Like It or Not, We Need It," *Management and Organization Review*, 8 (1), 2.

41 Ibid, p. 1.

42 He is personally a close follower of Mao Zedong, the founder of the People's Republic of China, whose ethos is predominantly based on Chinese wisdom and tradition.

43 Yip, G.S. and McKern, B. (2016), *China's Next Strategic Advantage: From Imitation to Innovation*, Cambridge, MA: MIT Press, p. 59.

44 Clark, D. (2016), *Alibaba: The House That Jack Ma Built*, New York: HarperCollins Publishers, pp. 142–143.

45 Liu, H. (2015), *The Chinese Strategic Mind*, Northampton, MA: Edward Elgar Publishing, pp. 151–172.

46 Fischer, B., Lago, U. and Liu, F. (2015), "The Haier Road to Growth," *Strategy + Business*, 27 April, www.strategy-business.com/article/00323?gko=c8c2a, retrieved on 27 April 2016.

47 Chandler, A.D. (1962), *Strategy and Structure: Chapters in the History of the Industrial Enterprise*, Washington, DC: Beard Books.

48 Amburgey, T.L. and Dacin, T. (1994), "As the Left Foot Follows the Right? The Dynamics of Strategic and Structural Change," *Academy of Management Journal*, 37 (6), 1427–1452. Paterson, B. (1988), "Still Plausible Stories: A Review of Chandler's Classics," *Academy of Management Review*, 13 (4), 653–656. Channon, D.F. (1973), *The Strategy and Structure of British Enterprise*, London: Macmillan Press.

49 Chandler, A.D. (1962), *Strategy and Structure: Chapters in the History of the Industrial Enterprise*, Washington, DC: Beard Books, pp. 13–14.

50 Learned, E.P., Christensen, C.R. and Andrews, K.D. (1965), *Business Policy: Text and Cases*, Homewood, IL: Richard D. Irwin.

51 Schendel, D. and Hofer, C.W. (1979), *Strategic Management: A New View of Business Policy and Planning*, Boston, MA: Little Brown.

52 Bracker, J. (1980), "The Historical Development of the Strategic Management Concept," *Academy of Management Review*, 5 (2), 219–224.

53 Jemison, D.B. (1981), "The Contributions of Administrative Behavior to Strategic Management," *Academy of Management Review*, 6 (4), 633–642.

54 Van Cauwenbergh, A. and Cool, K. (1982), "Strategic Management in a New Framework," *Strategic Management Journal*, 3 (3), 245–264.

55 Yavitz, B. and Newman, W.H. (1982), *Strategy in Action: The Execution, Politics, and Payoff of Business Planning*, New York: The Free Press, p. 26.

56 Mintzberg, H. (1987), "The Strategy Concept II: Another Look at Why Organizations Need Strategies," *California Management Review*, 30 (1), 25–32.

57 Hall, D.J. and Saias, M.A. (1980), "Strategy Follows Structure!" *Strategic Management Journal*, 1 (2), 149–163. Engdahl, R.A., Keating, R.J. and Aupperle, K.E. (2000), "Strategy and Structure: Chicken or Egg? Reconsideration of Chandler's Paradigm for Economic Success," *Organization Development Journal*, 18 (4), 21–31. Fredrickson, J.W. (1986), "The Strategic Decision Process and Organizational Structure," *Academy of Management Review*, 11 (2), 280–297.

58 Those readers who wish to know more about Chinese strategy are invited to consult Liu, H. (2015), *The Chinese Strategic Mind*, Northampton, MA: Edward Elgar Publishing.

59 Taylor, F. (1911), *Principles of Scientific Management*, New York: Harper.

60 Fayol, H. (1916), *Industrial and General Administration*, London: Pitman.

61 E.g. Holton, R.H. (1985), "Marketing and the Modernization of China," *California Management Review*, 27 (4) (Summer), 33–45. Vernon-Wortzel, H. and Wortzel, L.H. (1987),

"The Emergence of Free Market Retailing in the People's Republic of China: Promises and Consequences," *California Management Review*, 29 (3), 59–76. Walder, A.G. (1989), "Factory and Manager in an Era of Reform," *The China Quarterly*, June, 242–264.

62 Peng, M.W., Lu,Y., Shenkar, O. and Wang, D.Y.L. (2001), "Treasures in the China House: A Review of Management and Organizational Research on Greater China," *Journal of Business Research*, 52, 95–110.

63 Tung, R. (1994), "Strategic Management Thought in East Asia," *Organizational Dynamics*, 22 (4), 55–65.

64 Lasserre, P. (1988), "Corporate Strategic Management and the Overseas Chinese Groups," *Asia Pacific Journal of Management*, 5 (2), 115–131. Kao, J. (1993), "The Worldwide Web of Chinese Business," *Harvard Business Review*, March–April, 24–36.

65 Hoskisson, R. and Hitt, M. (1994), *Downscoping: How to Tame the Diversified Firm*. New York: Oxford University Press. Chen, M. (1995), *Asian Management Systems*, London: Routledge.

66 Tai, B. and Tai, L. (1986), "A Multivariate Analysis of the Characteristics of Problem Firms in Hong Kong," *Asia Pacific Journal of Management*, 3 (2), 121–127.

67 Chen, M. (1995), *Asian Management Systems*, London: Routledge.

68 Micklethwait, J. (1996), "The Limits of Family Values," *The Economist*, 9 March, 10–12.

69 Peng, M.W. (1997), "Firm Growth in Transitional Economies: Three Longitudinal Cases From China, 1989–1996," *Organization Studies*, 18 (3), 385–413. *Guanxi* is a characteristically Chinese form of networking or relationship-building involving the mutually beneficial exchange of favours or connections. Luo,Y. and Chen, M. (1997), "Does guanxi Influence Firm Performance?" *Asia Pacific Journal of Management*, 14, 1–16. Peng, M.W. (2000), *Business Strategies in Transition Economies*, Thousand Oaks, CA: Sage Publications.

70 Peng, M.W. (1997), "Firm Growth in Transitional Economies: Three Longitudinal Cases From China, 1989–1996," *Organization Studies*, 18 (3), 385–413. Peng, M.W and Tan, J.J. (1998), "Towards Alliance Post-Socialism: Business Strategies in a Transitional Economy," *Journal of Applied Management Studies*, 7 (1), 145–148. Xin, K. and Pearce, J. (1996), "*Guanxi*: Good Connections as Substitutes for Institutional Support," *Academy of Management Journal*, 39, 1641–1658.

71 Quer, D., Claver, E. and Rienda, L. (2007), "Business and Management in China: A Review of Empirical Research in Leading International Journals," *Asia Pacific Journal of Management*, 24, 359–384.

72 Bruton, G.D. and Lau, C.M. (2008), "Asian Management Research: Status Today and Future Outlook," *Journal of Management Studies*, 45 (3), 636–659.

73 Tsui, A.S. (2004), "Contributing to Global Management Knowledge: A Case for High Quality Indigenous Research," *Asia Pacific Journal of Management*, 21, 491–513. Meyer, K.E. (2006), "Asian Management Research Needs More Self-Confidence," *Asia Pacific Journal of Management*, 23, 119–137. Bruton, G.D. and Lau, C.M. (2008), "Asian Management Research: Status Today and Future Outlook," *Journal of Management Studies*, 45 (3), 636–659.

74 Fang, T. (2012), "Yin-Yang: A New Perspective on Culture," *Management and Organization Review*, 8 (1), 25–50. Li, X. (2012), "Can Yin-Yang Guide Chinese Indigenous Management Research?" *Management and Organization Review*, 10 (1), 7–27.

75 Pan,Y., Rowney, J.A. and Peterson, M.F. (2012), "The Structure of Chinese Cultural Traditions: An Empirical Study of Business Employees in China," *Management and Organization Review*, 8 (1), 77–95.

76 Li, P.P., Leung, K., Chen, C.C. and Luo, J.D. (2012), "Indigenous Research on Chinese Management: What and How," *Management and Organization Review*, 8 (1), 7–24.

77 Leung, K. (2012), "Indigenous Chinese Management Research: Like It or Not, We Need It," *Management and Organization Review*, 8 (1), 1–5.

78 Lai, K.L. (1995), "Confucian Moral Thinking," *Philosophy East and West*, 45 (2), 249–272.

79 Fung,Y.L. (1947), *The Spirit of Chinese Philosophy*, translated by E.R. Hughes, London: Routledge, pp. 1–2.

80 Ibid, p. 15.
81 Yao, J.M. (2012), *Laozi zhihui (Lao Tzu's Wisdom)*, Jinan, China: Shandong People's Publishing House, p. 171.
82 Ibid, p. 17.
83 Chan, W.T. (1963), *A Source Book in Chinese Philosophy*, translated and compiled by W.T. Chan, Princeton, NJ: Princeton University Press, pp. 262–263.
84 *Yin-yang jia* is also rendered into English as 'School of Naturalists', 'Interrelation of Heaven and Man' or 'Correlative Cosmology'.
85 Schwartz, B. (1985), *The World of Thought in Ancient China*, Cambridge, MA: Harvard University Press, p. 351.
86 There are different versions of the *I Ching*; this is the one written by Confucians to interpret the earlier versions, also known as *The Ten Wings*.
87 Peng, K., Spencer-Rogers, J. and Nian, Z. (2006), "Naïve Dialecticism and the Tao of Chinese Thought," in U. Kim, K. Yang and K. Hwang (ed.), *Indigenous and Cultural Psychology: Understanding People in Context*, New York: Springer, pp. 247–262.
88 Buddhism has also been regarded as a religion by many people, particularly by those in Central and East Asian countries.
89 He, J.J. (2003), *Ershiwu shi ji mou da quan (Complete Works of Stratagem From Twenty-Five Histories)*, Changsa: Yuelu Publishing House.
90 Ebrey, P.B. (1993), *Chinese Civilization: A Sourcebook*, New York: The Free Press, p. 14.
91 Deng, K.G. (2000), "A Critical Survey of Recent Research in Chinese Economic History," *Economic History Review*, LIII (I), 1–28.
92 Introduction to Liu, B.W. (1996), *One Hundred Unorthodox Strategies: Battle and Tactics of Chinese Warfare*, translated by R.D. Sawyer, Oxford: Westview Press, Inc., p. 1.
93 Ibid, p. 120.
94 Xu, B.L. (2002), *Zhong guo bing shu tong lan (An Overview of Chinese Military Books)*, Beijing: PLA Publishing House, pp. 20–21.
95 Ferguson, N. (2011), "Henry Kissinger's Prescription for China," *Newsweek*, 15 May 2011.
96 Elliott-Bateman, M. (1967), *Defeat in the East: The Mark of Mao Tse-tung on War*, London: Oxford University Press. Nixon, R.M. (1983), *Leaders*, New York: Simon & Schuster, pp. 247–248. Mohanty, M. (1995), "Power of History: Mao Zedong Thought and Deng's China," *China Report*, 31 (1), 1–14. Li, S. and Yeh, K. (2007), "Mao's Pervasive Influence on Chinese CEOs," *Harvard Business Review*, 85 (12), 16–17.
97 Clark, D. (2016), *Alibaba: The House That Jack Ma Built*, New York: HarperCollins Publishers, pp. 29–32.
98 Notably, many Chinese state leaders also excel at calligraphy, which crystallises Chinese culture.

2 History matters in Chinese business

He who does not forget the past is the master of the present.

– Sima Qian

History, we now know, is not merely, or even primarily, past politics; it is also past economics, past society, past religion, past civilization, in short, past everything.

– S.T. Bindoff

Misunderstanding of the present is the inevitable consequence of ignorance of the past.

– Marc Bloch

Significance and fixation: a Chinese phenomenon

Western readers may wonder what history could have to do with conducting business, as it is basically considered irrelevant or ignored in Western business, yet research shows that history continues to have a major impact on Chinese executives.[1] 'In the eighteenth century, China was the dominant world power until its prestige declined as a result of foreign invasions and pressures. The wound to national pride remains open, and its influence should not be underestimated.'[2] Knowledge of general Chinese history is essential for Western firms to understand Chinese thinking, attitudes and behaviour, while knowledge of particular Chinese history (political, commercial and military) is essential for them to understand Chinese wisdom if they are to develop and carry out effective business strategy and organisation in China.

As an advanced and ancient civilisation, China has a history that has outlived all other great empires in Eurasia, including the Egyptian, Roman, Byzantine, Arabian, Ottoman and Tsarist-Soviet.[3] Until 1880, China's industrial output accounted for 33 per cent of the world's total, against 22 per cent for the whole of Europe.[4]

Who are the Chinese? Where did they come from? How have they evolved? What are the histories of which the Chinese people have been proud? Why and how did China's relationships with Western nations become strained or indeed hostile during the nineteenth and early twentieth centuries? Addressing these questions is the first necessary step towards planting a foot in the door of Chinese affairs, whether political or commercial. France was one of the few Western countries that had recognised the newly founded People's Republic of China in January 1964, because its president, Charles de Gaulle, was knowledgeable about Chinese history. Richard Nixon was the first American president to break the ice of the Cold War by taking the historic step of forging a closer relationship with China, thus changing the world, as a result of his knowledge of Chinese history. If one examines Western businesses which have been successful in establishing a foothold in China, it becomes readily apparent that the strength of their position has a solid foundation in the intimate knowledge of Chinese history furnished by their consultants, advisors or employees.

The Chinese people take history much more seriously than their Western counterparts. History has been a major source of literature and a major component of Chinese culture. The contrast with India is notable:

> The Chinese are a people with a highly developed history-consciousness. Since 841 B.C. there have been continuous historical records of great events in a chronological order. The sheer bulk of the so-called Twenty-four Histories is overwhelming. This situation is in sharp contrast to that of the ancient Indian people, who could not care less about recording in a meticulous fashion what had happened in this mundane world.[5]

China's close attention to history and its implications has been observed by foreign statesmen, including Nixon:

> As with Russia, we can only hope to understand present-day China if we know something about its past. Even the changes now taking place have roots in the past, and in some respects are a return to tradition. More than most countries, China is a product of its past, and its history is unique. Other nations come and go, other empires rise and fall, but China endures; China is forever.[6]

Henry Kissinger also remarks:

> In no other country is it conceivable that a modern leader would initiate a major national undertaking by invoking strategic principles from a millennium-old event – nor that he could confidently expect his colleagues to understand the significance of his allusions. Yet China is singular. No other country can claim so long a continuous civilization, or such an intimate link to its ancient past and classical principles of strategy and statesmanship.[7]

It is often said that history is an important subject for political and business leaders, a bridge connecting the past to the present and a mirror to see into the future. Emperor Taizong of Tang (598–649) famously said: 'With a bronze mirror, one can see whether he is properly attired; with history as a mirror, one can understand the rise and fall of a nation; with men as a mirror, one can see whether he is right or wrong.'[8]

In ancient China, there were specially appointed officials whose responsibility was to record significant speeches, statements and events associated with the ruler and his dynasty. In earlier dynasties, there was a 'Left Historian', charged with recording the important speeches and utterances of emperors, and a 'Right Historian', whose task was to make a note of significant events. Later, the two positions were integrated and assumed by one person, known as the Grand Historian. 'The office of Grand Historian combined responsibility for astronomical observation and for the regulation of the calendar with the duties of keeping a daily record of state events and court ceremonies.'[9] Those who have contributed to the recording of history are well remembered and acclaimed. For instance, Sima Tan and Sima Qian (father and son) are well-known historians of the West Han dynasty (206 BC – AD 25). The latter was castrated by Emperor Wu of Han because he held a view that was contradictory to that of the emperor concerning the innocence of a Han general being held captive by an enemy. Despite this inhumane treatment, Sima Qian became one of China's most influential historians, laying out the framework for the *Twenty-Four Histories*.

The origin of the word 'China' is associated with an ancient Chinese empire, the first united Chinese dynasty of Ch'in[10] [ʧin] (221–206 BC). 'Chinas' initially appeared in the ancient Sanskrit literature, and later Marco Polo, a Venetian trader and explorer who visited China in the thirteenth century, referred to it as Ch'in, which came from the Persian. The word was then widely used by merchants on the trading route which passed through places including Akka (Acre) in Israel, the Persian Gulf, Iran, Amu Darya, the Pamir mountains, modern Sinkiang (a Uigur area), the Gobi Desert and Shangtu, a summer palace for the first Yuan emperor, Kublai Khan. English, German, Spanish and Portuguese have the same spelling of 'China' but with slightly different pronunciations: / ʧainə/, /çi:na/, /ʧina/ and /ʃinɐ/ respectively.

History has always tended to have a great impact on how Chinese people think and behave. Many great leaders, including ancient Chinese emperors and their strategic advisors, have been well versed in history. For instance, Mao Zedong, a great strategist and statesman and the founding father of the People's Republic of China, is known to have been proficient in Chinese history and to have been influenced by ancient strategic thinking such as the politics of imperial courts recounted in the *Twenty-Four Histories*, *Zizhi Tongjian*, *Zuo Zhuan* or *Zuo Chronicle* by Zuo Qiumin, *Zhan Guo Ce* or *The Strategies of the Warring States* by Liu Xiang, *Guoyu* or *The Discourses of the States* and the *Bamboo Annals*. The *Spring and Autumn Annals* was the first historical chronicle compiled by a private person, Confucius, a great Chinese thinker and educationalist; it occupies an important place in Chinese history.[11]

History can help Western businesspeople to understand certain Chinese attitudes and behaviour in business negotiation or dealings and to build close business or personal relationships, which is extremely important in certain areas for business success in China. The achievement of General Motors (GM) in launching Buick and matching the success in China of its long-entrenched arch competitor, Volkswagen, is partially attributable to the fact that the last Chinese emperor had a Buick. This historical legacy has been utilised to GM's competitive advantage.

One finds that a great deal may be learned from ancient Chinese wisdom. For example, China has had a large number of great strategists, among whom Sun Tzu has been particularly recognised throughout the world, and the works of other Chinese strategic thinkers may also be inspiring and enlightening. Considering the limited space and the issue of relevance, the present selection of historical information is based on two principles: (1) significance, that is events and people that have had a great impact on China (and often the world) and (2) association with administration, commerce, science and technology.

Box 2.1 presents a mini case which shows how history and historical literature have provided Mao Zedong with unlimited Chinese wisdom, making him the unchallengeable leader in China in the twentieth century.

Box 2.1   Effect of history and historical literature on Mao Zedong[12]

Although Mao Zedong was not a historian, having written no historical monographs, his knowledge of Chinese history was unparalleled. He was versed in almost all of the Chinese classics, including all Chinese classic (official and private) histories and literary works.[13] Mao Zedong told Edgar Snow that his familiarity with classic stories began

> while still very young, and despite the vigilance of my old teacher, who hated these outlawed books and called them wicked. I used to read them in school, covering them up with a Classic when the teacher walked past. So also did most of my schoolmates. We learned many of the stories almost by heart, and discussed and rediscussed them many times . . . I believe that perhaps I was much influenced by such books, read at an impressionable age.[14]

Stuart Schram (1967) writes: 'There is no doubt that these novels influenced him [Mao] profoundly, especially the historical *Romance of the Three Kingdoms*, and *Water Margin*.'[15] 'Mao Zedong was a voracious reader and prolific writer.'[16] His great knowledge of Chinese history is reflected in the *Selected Works of Mao Zedong*, which refer to all kinds of historical personages, including sages, emperors, chancellors, politicians, strategists, scholars, poets, rebels, historians, traitors and notorious eunuchs.[17] 'Nevertheless, if Mao "disliked" the classics, as he tells us, he learned to know them well, as his subsequent writings with their frequent classical references abundantly show.'[18] For instance, he had read the *Twenty-Four Histories*, the Four Books and the Five Classics[19] and *Zizhi Tongjian* (*History as a Mirror*).[20]

Harrison Salisbury (1985) writes:

> It was a village school, but in five years he [Mao] learned such classics as the *Analects of Confucius, Mencius* and *Zuozhuan*, the *Commentary by Zuo Qiuming on the Spring and Autumn Annals*. Many years later Mao deprecated his study of the Chinese classics. He told Robert Payne: 'I hated Confucius from the age of eight,' but the truth was he absorbed the Five Classics into his system and illuminated his writings with quotations from Confucius and Mencius.[21]

It can be said that Mao Zedong's strategic decisions and actions were far more often inspired by Chinese classics than derived from an 'orthodox' education. His obsessive reading of stories of rebellion, such as the *Yue Fei Chronicles*,[22] the *Water Margin*, the *Romance of the Sui-Tang Dynasties*, the *Romance of the Three Kingdoms* and the *Journey to the West*,[23] had left a permanent mark on what he would do, and how he would do it, in his future life.

Journey to the West inspired Mao with a rebellious spirit and a strong ability to fight with agility. The Monkey King, a main character in the novel, is a skilled and intrepid combatant, daring to defy the Jade Emperor and fight against the best warriors of Heaven. This classic features the device that the Monkey's individual hairs have the magical ability of being transformed into clones of the Monkey King himself and into various weapons, animals and other objects, totalling 72 transformations. In one of his writings, entitled 'On Contradiction,' Mao uses the Monkey King to make a point:

> In speaking of the identity of opposites in given conditions, what we are referring to is real and concrete opposites and the real and concrete transformations of opposites into one another. There are innumerable transformations in mythology, for instance . . . the Monkey King's seventy-two metamorphoses in Hsi Yu Chi.[24]

In another article, 'A Most Important Policy,' Mao Zedong writes:

> As for the question of how to deal with the enemy's enormous apparatus, we can learn from the example of how the Monkey King dealt with Princess Iron Fan. The Princess was a formidable demon, but by

changing himself into a tiny insect the Monkey King made his way into her stomach and overpowered her.[25]

The *Water Margin* instilled Mao with the idea that 'we are all brothers and sisters of the planet'. Stuart Schram (1967) explains:

> Liang Shan P'o was the name of the mountain fortress on which the bandit heroes of Mao's favourite novel *Water Margin* had established themselves to fight for justice and order in an unjust and disorderly world. Exactly ten years later, Mao was to mount the Chingkangshan [mountain] and begin an adventure not altogether dissimilar.[26]

Inspired by the spirit of brotherhood at Liang Shan, Mao promoted a policy of equality between officers and soldiers during the Yanan period (1935–1947). After the founding of the People's Republic, he abolished the existing military rank system and reinstated a policy of equality and unity between officer and soldier.

> In the novel *Shui Hu Chuan* [*Water Margin*], Sung Chiang thrice attacked Chu Village. Twice he was defeated because he was ignorant of the local conditions and used the wrong method. Later he changed his method; first he investigated the situation, and he familiarized himself with the maze of roads, then he broke up the alliance between the Li, Hu and Chu Villages and sent his men in disguise into the enemy camp to lie in wait, using a stratagem similar to that of the Trojan Horse in the foreign story. And on the third occasion he won.[27]

The *Romance of the Three Kingdoms* provided Mao with a strategy 'handbook', as noted by Stuart Schram: 'Mao also learned a great deal about the role of deception in warfare from his favourite novels, the *Romance of the Three Kingdoms* and *Water Margin*.'[28] Harrison Salisbury (1985) also comments on the effect of the literary classic on Mao Zedong:

> Mao committed to memory the tales of *Three Kingdoms and Outlaws* and to his final days read and reread these collections of slightly fictionalized episodes from China's history. He commented on them repeatedly and used them as textbooks for guerrilla warfare. When his enemies accused him of fighting in Jaingangshan or on the Long March in accordance with what he had learned from *Outlaws*, they were right and were paying him a practical compliment.[29]

It was Chinese historical literature that inspired Mao's conception of the crucial role of the peasantry in China's revolution, as Snow reports:

> I [Mao] continued to read the old romances and tales of Chinese literature. It occurred to me one day that there was one thing peculiar about such stories, and that was the absence of peasants who tilled the land. All the characters were warriors, officials, or scholars; there was never a peasant hero . . . I found that they all glorified men of arms, rulers of the people, who did not have to work the land, because they owned and controlled it and evidently made the peasants work it for them.[30]

As a result of these literary influences, Mao had come to the belief that it would be the peasants, rather than the workers whom Karl Marx championed, who would drive revolution in China, as he noted in 1939:

> The ruthless economic exploitation and political oppression of the Chinese peasants forced them into numerous uprisings against landlord rule . . . The scale of peasant uprisings and peasant wars in Chinese history has no parallel anywhere else. The class struggles of the peasants, the peasant uprisings and peasant wars constituted the real motive force of historical development in Chinese feudal society.[31]

Essential knowledge of ancient China

'Three Dynasties'

'Hua Xia' is a title accorded to the Chinese nation, whose 56 ethnic nationalities are often referred to as the Hua Xia nation. The Chinese people are also known as the 'sons and daughters of Hua Xia'. One explanation is that geographically 'Hua' and 'Xia' generally denoted the Central Plains area around the middle and lower reaches of the Yellow River in ancient times, and the people of the region were Han Chinese, the dominant nationality in China. According to another explanation, 'Hua' represented the more civilised Central Plains area and 'Xia' the more civilised nationalities, so a combination of 'Hua' and 'Xia' has come to denote China.

The name 'Zhongguo' or 'Middle Kingdom' emerged in ancient times as a designation of the Hua Xia area, synonymous with the Central Plains. At the time, the people of the area, predominantly of Han nationality (汉族), were surrounded by different ethnic nationalities, including Yi (夷), Di (狄), Rong (戎) and Man (蛮); thus the area was in that sense central and became known as the 'Middle Kingdom'. Because of their limited geographical knowledge, China's emperors perceived themselves as ruling a nation at the centre of the universe. This resulted in the complacency and conceit of later Chinese emperors, who adopted a closed-door and autarkic policy. When the Han later expanded from the Central Plains and dominated dynastic empires, the name was retained.

The first dynasty is called Xia (c. 2070–1600 BC). As the first embodiment of state power in Chinese history, it signifies the end of the era of primitive societies and the beginning of class societies, and is a milestone in Chinese civilisation. The Xia dynasty comprised 16 kings and lasted for about 500 years. Its emergence was an outcome of economic development and heralded the advent of Chinese political civilisation. When Xia was founded, economic civilisation reached a high level. The lunar calendar was developed then and is hence also called the 'Xia Calendar'. Agriculture played a dominant role in the Xia economy, and irrigation systems were well developed for farming purposes. Bronze was utilised to make farm tools, drinking vessels, carriages and weaponry.

The Shang dynasty (c. 1600–1046 BC), which replaced the Xia, further advanced material and spiritual civilisation. The period witnessed the most advanced bronze-working technology in the world at the time. Bronze smelting furnaces reached a significant scale, and some were as large as 10,000 square metres. Bronze wares were of great variety and featured fine artistic work, some being extremely large. It was during this period that China's ideographic writing system was developed. The system is also known as the 'oracle bone inscriptions' (甲骨文), as most characters or inscriptions were found written on flat cattle bones or tortoise shells. These inscriptions suggest that the writing system was already quite mature. 'The Shang writing system already evinced subject-verb-object syntax and methods of character formation by simple pictographs, abstract descriptive pictographs, and phono-pictographs that would remain basic in Chinese thereafter.'[32] Because of the development of the oracle bone inscriptions, the historical record of the Shang dynasty is more complete than that of the Xia.

A basic government structure was already in existence: there were six ministers dealing with policy-making and military affairs, 'civil officers' and 'officiants' handling agricultural and religious matters respectively, as well as officials in charge of husbandry, food, animals and carriages. However, because of the primitive nature of these positions, it is not clear how each was related to the others or who reported to whom. A form of taxation emerged, known as the 'tribute system', whereby farmers were required to pay to the government one tenth of the average of their production over a certain period of time.

Money emerged as a transaction medium in the Shang: cowry shells were used as currency, while animal bones, jade, pearls, dogs, horses and copper were utilised as commodity money, indicating the existence of market activities. The Shang system of government also grew in sophistication to deal with the sizeable state and the complexity of its activities, as Shang oracle bone inscriptions reveal that there were many titles associated with the central administration.[33] Since the Shang people made trading a significant activity, businesspeople or traders in China are generally still called *Shang ren* (商人) (the people of Shang) today.

After Shang came the West Zhou dynasty (1046–771 BC), a landmark era in Chinese history, to which the origins and principles of much Chinese civilisation are attributable. The Zhou dynasty witnessed not only the further development of bronze-working technology but also remarkable growth in the pottery industry. The production of glazed pottery became common, and its quality was close to that of porcelain. Tiles unearthed from the period proved to be the oldest ever found in China. Horse-drawn chariots are known to have existed, reflecting a certain level of coordination between different crafts and trades such as metalworking, hide processing and painting, which would have been necessary to make a chariot. Markets were quite developed and there were people charged with monitoring and maintaining order in market exchanges. Objects of exchange included jade, jewellery, weaponry, cattle, horses, silks and slaves.

The Zhou era may be described as one of centralised feudalism, similar to that of medieval Europe in form. The Duke of Zhou introduced five orders of nobility equivalent to duke, marquis, earl, viscount and baron, the holder of each being entitled to rule over a territory whose size was in proportion to his rank. At the beginning of the Zhou dynasty, there were a total of 1773 feudal states, their number being finally reduced to 7 as a result of civil wars among them.

It was during the Xia, Shang and West Zhou dynasties, which, with a total duration of 1300 years, are historically known as the 'Three Dynasties', that a slave-owning system was developed in China. This period has exerted a far-reaching influence on Chinese history. First, thanks to growing economic and military power, China's territorial borders were expanded and consolidated. This laid the foundation for the formation of a unified China with multiple nationalities, which was later fully realised under the Qin dynasty. Second, in the economic realm, production tools were gradually upgraded from bone, shell and stone implements to quality bronze ware. Agriculture was so much improved that great surpluses of grain and other crops were amassed. Market economies were significantly developed, centred on large cities as production bases and markets, while currencies were to some extent standardised. Third, in the political sphere, the system of autocratic monarchy was firmly established. There was a hierarchical political power structure incorporating kingdoms and dukedoms, which was predominantly a patriarchal clan system based on close and distant relationships. Slave masters at all levels held power from generation to generation on a hereditary basis in a hierarchical clan system which characterised ancient China for many centuries. The fourth area of enduring influence is ideological, as a theological system took a shape in which Heaven was seen to be in control of nature and society, so that the monarchs who exercised power on behalf of Heaven could not be challenged. Propriety rituals (or *li* in Chinese), derived from religious sacrificial rites, came increasingly to define people's ideology and behaviour, serving to protect the patriarchal clan system and having a great impact on the development of the ancient society.[34]

Pre-Qin and Qin dynasties

At the beginning of the Spring and Autumn period (770–476 BC) there were over 140 regional states, yet when the Warring States period (476–221 BC) began, fewer than 20 remained. There were seven main powerful states: Qin, Wei, Zhao, Han, Qi, Chu and Yan, commonly known as the 'Seven Powers of the Warring States'. It is perhaps surprising that, culturally, these periods were the most vibrant, prosperous, productive and resourceful times in Chinese history. Among the many great philosophers to emerge were Confucius, Mencius, Lao Zi, Guan Zi, Sun Zi, Han Feizi and Mo Zi, so this time is commonly known as the era of the 'Hundred Schools of Thought' (诸子百家). These Chinese philosophers were contemporaries of some of the world's great thinkers and teachers, such as the Buddha (c. 500 BC) in Nepal/India and Socrates (c. 470–399 BC), Plato (c. 427–347 BC) and Aristotle (384–321 BC) in Greece. The significance of these periods for China can be seen as equivalent to that of Classical Greece for Europe, with those seminal thinkers having laid the foundation for later Western civilisations.[35] Unsurprisingly, many classics of Chinese literature, psychology and strategic warfare can be traced back to this time.

It was at this time that the government's monopoly of the handicraft industry and commercial activities was dissolved, allowing private businesses to emerge. Different regional lords engaged in the production of military, luxury and ceremonial goods on an increasingly large scale. Metallurgical technology (iron and steel casting) began to be developed. In the early Warring States period, technology for the softening of cast iron was invented and malleable cast iron was produced. In the late Warring States period, galvanised iron, with lower brittleness and higher durability, started to roll out of factories. The technology for producing pig iron in ancient China is considered to have been ahead of the West by about 1900 years. The mining industry was also quite well developed as part of the supply chain of smelting operations.

These periods also witnessed active market exchanges. Following the dissolution of the state monopoly of trading activities, many markets and private traders of various sizes began rapidly to emerge. With the development of market activities, a monetary economy boomed. Previously, cowry shells, tools or bronze were used as monetary units, but in the late Spring and Autumn period, coins of cast metal, including gold and silver, began to replace these. Growth in commercial activity led to rapid urbanisation and the development of transport by land and water.

Through the implementation of Shang Yang's legalistic reforms, which greatly promoted productivity, the Qin state rapidly became stronger, both economically and militarily. Finally, in 221 BC, Qin conquered all other states and unified China under the Qin[36] dynasty (221–206 BC). Qin's ruler declared himself the 'First Emperor of Qin' (*Qin Shihuang*), with the intention of passing on his throne to his descendants as the 'Second Emperor', the 'Third Emperor' and so on. In order to control such a large empire, he became an autocratic monarch with absolute centralised power, signifying the beginning of imperialism in China.

Having rejected a recommendation by his officials to form a feudal structure of government, under which different parts of the country would be run by members of the nobility, the Emperor Qin divided the country into 36 prefectures, each of these being further subdivided into around 40 counties. Each county had its own local government, reporting to the central government and emperor. Thus there came into existence the first bureaucratic and centralised system of government in China. Qin put Han Fei's theories of legalism into practice with a degree of success. Although his dynasty was short-lived, history recognises Emperor Qin as having made great achievements relating to language, measurement and engineering.

First, he standardised China's language system. There were great differences in language from region to region during the Warring States period. Standardisation was made necessary partly by the need for communication between people in different regions and partly by the necessity to administer the unified country. Linguistic standardisation has been an important factor in the enduring nature of Chinese civilisation and culture, which could be passed on from generation to generation with great ease, allowing people in such a vast geographic area to maintain a shared identity.

Second, Qin unified the system of weights and measures and standardised the coinage. In particular, a uniform axle length for carriages facilitated transportation, while circular copper coins were struck with a square hole in the middle. All of these measures promoted the development of trade and economic activity.

Third, he was responsible for the completion of a number of large projects. The Great Wall in the north, which had been initiated under the West Zhou dynasty, was rebuilt on a grand scale, in a project taking ten years to complete, in order to defend against northern invaders, among which the Huns (Xiongnu) were the strongest and most threatening. Roads and irrigation canals were constructed throughout the country. Two magnificent projects realised by Emperor Qin were the building of a Royal Mausoleum and the creation of the spectacular Terracotta Army of 6000 pottery soldiers designed to 'protect' it.

In 219 BC, Xu Fu, a prominent sorcerer in the Qin court, told Emperor Qin that there were three divine mountains in the East Sea where all the immortals lived and that children should be sent to the immortals as sacrifices in exchange for the elixir of life. As a result, the emperor dispatched 3000 little boys and girls, together with hundreds of artisans, on just such a voyage, led by Xu Fu. However, knowing the impossibility of finding the elixir, Xu Fu planned not to return to the Qin Empire, in order to avoid execution. The travellers first reached the Tsushima Strait, then arrived in Kitakyushu, Japan, via Okinawa Island. Xu Fu brought with him to Japan relatively advanced ships, knowledge of oceangoing navigation and agricultural and metallurgical techniques. This led to a blending of Chinese culture with that of the Japanese islands which has endured to the present day.[37]

Han dynasty (206 BC – AD 220)

The Qin dynasty was replaced by the Han, which lasted for over 400 years and is normally divided into two periods: the West Han (206 BC – AD 25) and the East Han (AD 25–220). Thanks to the efforts of the first five emperors (206–141 BC), China entered a period of economic and cultural prosperity, with a great expansion of the empire's territory. During the period of the 'Martial Emperor' (140–87 BC), the empire became one of the strongest and most prosperous in the history of China. Because of the importance and influence of this period, the members of the ethnic majority of Chinese people are still called *Han Zu* ('People of the Han') and Chinese characters are also known as *Han Zi* (Han characters).

The Martial Emperor banned all schools of thought other than that of Confucius. From then on, Confucianism became the basis of the examination system for entry into the government bureaucracy and the dominant system of thought in China for over 2000 years. Although this policy was harmful to cultural development, it facilitated control over the nation by the autocratic monarchy. Social stability nurtured the development of the handicraft industry, commerce, science, literature and art during the Han period. This economic success enhanced the empire's political and cultural influence over Korea, Mongolia, Vietnam and the Central Asian countries.

During his reign (140–87 BC), the Martial Emperor twice dispatched Zhang Qian as his envoy to the Western regions, and the route Zhang pioneered became known later as the Silk Road, which runs today from Xian through Xinjiang and Central Asia to the east coast of the Mediterranean Sea. As silk trading increased between China and the West, Buddhism was introduced into China at the end of the West Han dynasty.[38] Many Chinese inventions, such as paper and gunpowder, were later exported to the West along the Silk Road.

The East Han Empire, historically known as the 'Guangwu Resurgence', witnessed a greater prosperity than the West Han Empire in terms of economy, culture and science. During this period, a technique for making fine paper was invented by an official named Cai Lun; this has been regarded as a seminal achievement in the history of civilisation. It first spread to Korea, Japan and Central Asia, then to Europe through the Arab countries.[39] Zhang Heng, a well-known astronomer, scientist and philosopher, as well as a minister in the emperor's court, invented the first seismoscope, a device for recording earthquakes, and constructed *Huntianyi*, a rotating celestial globe which was used to simulate cosmic events.

Traditional Chinese medicine (TCM) became established as a scientific field during this period. The *Huang Di Nei Jing* (*Yellow Emperor's Inner Classic*) is the earliest classic book written on TCM, laying its theoretical foundations and earning its author the epithet of 'father of traditional Chinese medicine'. Zhang Ji and Hua Tuo were best known for their skills and knowledge in pathological diagnosis and treatment; Zhang enjoys a reputation as the 'Medical Sage', while Hua is known for his pioneering surgery with the aid of anaesthesia.[40]

Sui dynasty (AD 581–618) and Tang dynasty (AD 618–907)

Despite lasting for only 37 years, the Sui dynasty has a special place in Chinese history, as it had a great impact on the subsequent powerful and prosperous

Tang dynasty in terms of governmental administrative systems. At the central government level, the Sui dynasty restored the centralised system created by previous dynasties, featuring the 'Three Departments and Six Ministries' which governed all state affairs. Within this structure, the function of decision-making was separated from that of evaluation and deliberation, and from implementation, each of these three being performed by different bodies, which enhanced the emperor's control of power. In local government areas, the existing three-tier form of government was reduced to a two-tier system, resulting in a more effective control of local affairs by the central government.

The Sui emperor abolished the system which had prevailed throughout the Jin and the Northern and Southern dynasties, whereby government officials were appointed on the basis of their family's nobility rather than on merit and ability. In addition, regular imperial civil examinations were held to select and appoint able people as civil servants, which promoted the effectiveness of government administration and played an important part in consolidating the centralised system. This imperial civil examination system was to endure for over 1300 years, until the last dynasty. Sui also promulgated a new legal system, which did not impose on the people as many harsh restrictions and punishments as those of the Northern and Southern dynasties.

From 605 to 610, Sui completed the Grand Canal, connecting five major Chinese rivers; with a total length of over 1553 miles, it is one of the greatest projects of its kind in the world. It consolidated the central control of local governments and became a major transportation artery between North and South China, continuing to play a key part in the Chinese economy to this day.

In the Sui dynasty, the textile, porcelain, shipbuilding and construction industries were well developed. Techniques for the production of porcelain, particularly the white-glazed type, reached an important stage. Shipbuilding technology advanced a great deal, allowing the construction of large vessels. Sui engineers were skilled in designing and building bridges, as epitomised by the work of Li Chun, who designed the Zhaozhou Bridge, China's earliest surviving stone arch bridge, which is 50.82 metres long, 9 metres wide and 7.23 metres high. Thanks to the application of structural mechanics, the design has many advantageous features which are still relevant today. Considering that the bridge was built over 1400 years ago, it is truly an outstanding piece of work.

The historical importance and enduring influence of the Tang dynasty cannot be overemphasised, as it is the most developed period in Chinese history, politically, economically and culturally. The Tang dynasty held power for 289 years, which may be divided into two periods. The first (618–755) was characterised by growth and prosperity and the second (756–907) by decline. The first period witnessed a number of economic, political and cultural zeniths such as those known as the 'Golden Years of Zhengguan' and the 'Heyday of Kaiyuan', marked by peace, prosperity, openness, and efficient and upright government.

> Under the Tang Dynasty, China combined prosperity, cultural grandeur, aristocratic sophistication, military power, and supremacy in foreign relations

to achieve an age of greatness unapproached since Han. The Tang capital at Chang-an became the world's largest and most brilliantly cosmopolitan city, a mecca to which traders, diplomats, and seekers after culture travelled from Japan, Korea, Central Asia, Vietnam, and the South China Sea, and where Arabs, Persians, Jews, and Christians from the Mediterranean basin were welcomed.[41]

Tang military prowess was matched by achievements in the fine arts and literature. Tang poetry became the model for later periods. The creative vigor of the Tang let it be a more open society . . . Buddhism had added an extra dimension to the Tang heritage from the Han. Younger states arising in East Asia modelled their institutions on the Tang.[42]

The empire significantly expanded its territory, occupying an even greater area than that of the Han dynasty. It established suzerainty in Central Asia, and a number of countries became Chinese protectorates. As a result of the expansion of the empire's borders and its development of international trade, foreign religions, particularly Buddhism, were introduced into China. Buddhism then went through a process of adaptation and became part of traditional Chinese culture. Chinese literature and art reached a peak of achievement in the Tang period, so that a number of its poets remain well known today, examples being Li Bai and Du Fu. Building on the basic penal code carried over from the Sui dynasty, Tang developed the first complete Chinese criminal code, elements of which still apply. Compared with the previous Sui version, the punitive severity of the Tang code was much alleviated.

Manufacture in the Tang period was further developed on the basis of Sui industry, including textiles, pottery, papermaking, iron smelting and casting. Silk products gained a great reputation for their high quality. Improvements were made in painting, dyeing and the technology used in the production of cotton goods. The white and green Tang porcelain was known for its unparalleled technical excellence and the tricolour porcelain pieces were widely recognised as superior works of art. Printing technology began to be developed and some Confucian classics were printed and published during the period. The emergence of printing greatly facilitated the retention, development and widening of culture and knowledge. Because of the worldwide influence of Tang China, overseas Chinese are often called *Tang Ren* ('Tang people') and the areas where they live or run their businesses are known as 'Tang Street'.

Song dynasty (AD 960–1279)

The Song dynasty is divided into two periods, beginning with the Northern Song from 960 to 1127, when the capital city was Dongjing (now called Kaifeng) in Henan Province. The second period, known as the Southern Song, ran from 1127 to 1279, when the capital was moved to present-day Hangzhou in Zhejiang Province. The dynasty lasted for 319 years, a little longer than the Tang, and is considered one of the most important periods in Chinese history, alongside the Tang and Han dynasties.

Although the influence of the Song dynasty was not as strong as that of the Tang, it saw a revival of the economy and great developments in culture and technology. In particular, achievements in art and literature reached new heights. As a result, the Song period is known as the 'Chinese Renaissance', comparable with the later European Renaissance. For instance, although Chinese classics began to be printed during the Tang dynasty, it was under the Song dynasty that the invention of movable type, by Bi Sheng in 1048, revolutionised printing technology. This milestone in the history of printing predated by four centuries the equivalent development in Germany, by Johann Gutenberg in 1450. The use of moveable type printing facilitated the production of paper money, which became official tender as a matter of government policy. Gunpowder was first used in warfare, as were the newly invented flamethrowers, catapult-projected bombs, cannons and firearms. Su Song, a multi-talented technologist and inventor, developed a water-driven astronomical clock tower. It was in the Song period that magnetic needles were used by diviners to indicate direction, for the purpose of judging *Feng Shui*.

The introduction of paper money became necessary partly because metal was then scarce in China and partly because copper coinage was too heavy to transport over long distances. The notes, which were called *Jiaozi*, carried a picture, a cipher code, a signature and a stamp. They could be traded or cashed and their use significantly promoted trading activity and market expansion.

The ancient literature reveals that during the Warring States period (475–221 BC), a wine seller used a flag to advertise his rice wine. In the Tang dynasty (AD 618–907), in the market district of the capital city, Chang-an (present Xian), there was a rule that all products were required to carry a signed trademark to identify the maker for the purposes of quality monitoring and product 'advertising'.

Yuan dynasty (AD 1279–1368)

The Yuan dynasty came into existence in 1271 and was overthrown in 1368, thus lasting 98 years. After 370 years of division and chaos, China was once more reunited under this great empire, built by the Mongols, which was the first time that the whole of China had been controlled by foreigners. The march into China of the Mongols was initiated by Genghis Khan, but it was his grandson Kublai Khan who founded the Yuan dynasty. The Mongols not only conquered China; their superior military capabilities also enabled them to expand into Western Asia, the Middle East (Iraq and Iran) and parts of Europe (Russia, Ukraine, Poland and Hungary).

The Yuan Empire, which was then the largest and richest in the world, more or less defined China's permanent territorial boundaries. Western diplomatic envoys, merchants, tourists and priests came to China in an endless stream. During the reign of Kublai Khan, Venetian trader Marco Polo travelled around major cities in China and took up an official local government position. In a book based on his travel experiences and entitled *Il Milione* (or *The Travels of*

Marco Polo), he describes the huge, prosperous and densely populated empire. The book was widely read in Europe, allegedly influencing many explorers such as Christopher Columbus, who was inspired to find a different route to the Indies. It also stimulated European interest in Chinese civilisation.

During this period, Chinese inventions such as the compass, paper and printing were introduced into Europe through the Arabs, while Arab astronomy, medicine and mathematics were transmitted to China. Christianity began to be known and to spread, while the practice of Islam and the building of mosques increased rapidly within China. Meanwhile, there was significant Chinese emigration to central, western and southern regions of Asia.

The extent of foreign trade reached new levels. Overland trade with Europe was carried out via Qibaq Ulus and the Crimean Peninsula, while that with the Arab countries passed through Il-Khanate. The Yuan also developed maritime trade eastwards with Japan and Korea and westwards with South Asia, Arabia and East Africa. The government imposed different levels of monopoly control over a number of major commodities such as salt, tea and wine, while domestic markets were largely controlled by the government, aristocrats and traders from tribes residing in the western region of China. Foreign trade was monopolised by the government.

Ming dynasty (AD 1368–1644)

In 1368, the Yuan dynasty was toppled by the Ming, which lasted for 276 years. Control of China was once more regained by the ethnic Han. The first Ming emperor chose Nanjing as the capital, and in 1421 the third emperor moved it to Beijing, where the Forbidden City was built as an imperial palace complex covering an area of 760,000 square metres. The first emperor abolished the existing government offices and set up the so-called Six Ministries, reporting to him directly: Personnel, Revenue, Rites, War, Justice and Public Works. This structure remained the foundation of government administration until the end of dynastic rule. The government spent 20 years drawing up laws and regulations including the Great Ming Code, one of the most important legal codes in Chinese history.

The Ming dynasty marked a period of great economic prosperity. The development of agriculture was very advanced compared with the previous dynastic period, leading to a boom in trade and industry. Blue and white Ming porcelain objects and Xuande burners (the first brass artefacts) have since become priceless works of art. The new economic prosperity led the government to expand its education and examination systems for the purpose of selecting competent bureaucrats. The numbers of schools and students then greatly exceeded even those under the Tang and Song dynasties. This nationwide enthusiasm for education promoted social stability and led to an increase in literacy and the proliferation of scholarly works. Three of the four Great Chinese Classics – *Journey to the West*, *Water Margins* and *Romance of the Three Kingdoms* – were written in the Ming period.

Around the 1500s, the Ming economy reached a new peak, exceeding that of the previous dynasty. High-quality farming tools made of iron were widely used, and agricultural technology was also improved a great deal, with a resultant increase in rural productivity. Iron smelting, iron casting and porcelain making witnessed great progress in terms of unit scale and number. In particular, as a result of technological advances in the textile industry, the productivity of silk weaving and cotton spinning made great strides forward, with a variety of colours and designs. Together, the growth in the craft industries and agriculture led to a rapid development of the banking sector and to flourishing commercial districts in town and city centres.

As a regional power, Ming China had a profound political, cultural and economic influence on Asian countries. Under the Ming government's policy of maintaining friendly relations with neighbouring countries, about 30 diplomatic envoys were dispatched to visit 12 nearby countries, while 17 states sent a total of 135 envoys to China. Trade with Asian countries, particularly Korea, Vietnam, Japan, Burma, Cambodia and India, became more frequent compared with the previous dynasty. However, the Ming government placed restrictions on trade missions from foreign countries, strictly limiting their duration and the numbers of people and ships. In addition, the government forbad private maritime trade without official permission. These measures hindered to some extent the development of trade with other Asian countries.

From 1405 to 1433, Zheng He, a eunuch also known as San Bao, led a grand fleet and made seven voyages overseas, which are regarded as highly significant in the history of ocean navigation. On his first voyage, the fleet comprised 63 ships, served by over 26,800 men, including officers, sailors, interpreters, technicians, soldiers, artisans, doctors and meteorologists. The largest ship in the fleet was 138 metres long and 56 wide, with nine masts bearing 12 large sails. The fleet carried large quantities of cargo, including copper utensils, silk goods, porcelain, gold and silverware. On the return journey, Zheng He brought back large quantities of pearls, precious stones, coral, ivory and rare and precious animals, such as giraffes and lions. The fleet sailed to East and Southeast Asia, Southern India, Ceylon, East Africa and the Persian Gulf, passing through over 30 countries and territories. These expeditions strengthened friendly relations between China and other countries in Asia and Africa, promoting cultural and economic exchange between them. Fairbank et al. (1998, p. 138) comment on these voyages: 'In the great age of sail that was just dawning around the globe, Ming China was potentially far in the lead but refused to go on. It took the Europeans almost another half century even to get started.'[43]

Qing dynasty (AD 1644–1911)

From 1644 to 1911, China was ruled by the Qing dynasty of the Manchu clan Aisin Gioro, based in present-day northeast China (Manchuria). The dynasty was founded in 1616 and known as the Late Jin. In 1636, its name was changed to Qing. It was the last dynastic empire of China and covered the largest territorial area in Chinese history, at 11.2 million square kilometres. Until the end of the eighteenth century, the Qing empire was the richest in the world.

During the first half of the dynastic period, many cities regained their previous prosperity and some advanced further. Beijing became China's commercial centre, and traders from all walks of life gathered there to sell and buy products in bulk. Foreign trade opened up further than it had under the previous dynasty. China now had close trade relationships with Russia, Korea, Vietnam and other Southeast Asian countries, as well as a number of European ones. Until the mid-Qing period, China's foreign trade was in surplus.

Around the end of the eighteenth century, a major diplomatic episode occurred when China was officially contacted by Britain to discuss diplomatic and commercial relations between the two countries. In 1685, after the Qing government took over Taiwan, restrictions on maritime trade had been eased and four trading ports opened up for foreign trade. However, in 1757, the emperor changed the policy and allowed only one port (Guangzhou) to be used for foreign trade. Soon afterwards, all kinds of stringent measures were taken to restrict and monitor foreign businesspeople, stipulating that they could conduct trade only through Chinese middlemen. At the time, Britain was China's largest Western trading partner.

At the end of the eighteenth century, Britain was a rising industrial power which greatly needed to open up more markets worldwide. Therefore, in 1793, King George III of England appointed Lord George McCartney to lead a diplomatic mission to China in order to gain commercial access to Chinese markets. The goal of the McCartney expedition was to persuade China to relax restrictions on trade between Britain and China, grant the establishment of a permanent British embassy in Beijing and allow the acquisition by Britain of a piece of land in South China where British traders could live and engage in commercial activity. However, the journey started on the pretext of commemorating the emperor's 83rd birthday.

The McCartney embassy arrived in China in June 1793. Feeling pleased at the arrival of the delegation, the emperor issued an edict that all measures be taken to care for the needs of the envoy. The office of the emperor's secretary put together a detailed programme, including an audience with the emperor at which a reward would be bestowed on the ambassador, who with his entourage would be invited to a banquet and regaled with entertainments and sightseeing. Despite the eagerness of the two parties to establish good relations, there occurred an unpleasant incident concerning a ceremonial issue. According to a stipulation of the Qing court, all foreign envoys should kneel and kowtow to the emperor when granted an audience with him. However, Lord McCartney believed that this would damage Britain's dignity, so maintained that he would kneel only on one knee, as he would do before his own monarch. The emperor was displeased at this and considered the members of the delegation arrogant. Eventually, all its requests were rejected by the emperor. However, this rejection was not a result of the ceremonial issue, but mainly because the emperor considered that the requests did not tally with the 'system of the Heavenly

Kingdom'. In essence, considering himself to be the centre of the universe, the emperor believed that China could produce all the best things in the world and would not need exotic products from a foreign land. The embassy was a failure for McCartney and Britain, but it was more so for the Qing dynasty, as it represented a missed opportunity to recognise the huge gap between China and the developed world in terms of science and technology and to begin to match the progress of the West in industrialisation. Among McCartney's rejected gifts were many scientific instruments and products that represented the most advanced technology of the time. Instead of being inspired by such modern products as drivers for industrialisation, the Qing emperor and his officials regarded them as worthless tributes by a 'vassal state'.

During the eighteenth century, Chinese tea, silk and porcelain were in high demand in Britain, where such imports were annually worth about £3 million, while British cotton cloth and woollen goods were less popular in China; these exports amounted to only about £1 million, creating a large trade deficit with China. All transactions were then settled in silver, so Britain had to buy silver from continental Europe for the Chinese trade, incurring further cost. British merchants saw the opium trade as a lucrative opportunity to put an end to the trade deficit. Although an illegal trade in opium had been conducted by British merchants for many years, it was in the early nineteenth century that the opium trade began to expand rapidly, causing the overall trade balance to shift in Britain's favour. The effects in China were disastrous: the excessive outflow of Chinese silver in exchange for opium caused silver prices to escalate rapidly, bringing severe inflation to the wider economy. An equally ruinous consequence of the opium trade was the degeneration of public morals and the damage to public health, with over two million opium addicts. This in turn had significant negative effects on the economy, including a sharp fall in tax revenues. The Chinese government was obliged to take action to combat the opium threat, so in June 1839, it confiscated 21,298 trunks of opium, mostly from British and American merchants, and publicly burnt it. In June 1840, the British government responded by sending a naval fleet to China, marking the outbreak of the so-called Opium Wars. There were two of these: the first took place from 1840 to 1843 and the second from 1856 to 1860. China was defeated in both wars and was forced to sign a number of unequal treaties, opening several ports to foreign trade and ceding Hong Kong to Britain for 99 years.

China's defeat in the Opium Wars was a reflection of the technological gap between Britain and China. However, ironically, one of the 'tributes' which the McCartney embassy had presented to the Qing court was a rifle, while the Qing officials were informed that in Europe the bow and arrow had long been replaced by firearms in war. Tragically, no one in China paid the slightest attention to this fundamental change in technology. Even after the Opium Wars, the majority of senior Qing officials remained indifferent to the technological gap. The Opium Wars were a turning point for the Qing dynasty, marking its approaching demise.

The People's Republic of China

Economic history: past, reforms and development

After the founding of the People's Republic of China on 1 October 1949, the new government took over control of numerous industrial goods manufacturers and large strategic businesses which were owned and operated by the previous government, such as mining, railways, shipping, the postal service, banking, wholesale and retail. At the end of 1949, large state-owned enterprises (SOEs) accounted for 40 per cent of total industrial output. At the beginning of 1952 there were three leading economic groups in China: (1) SOEs, which primarily controlled important industrial entities and accounted for 19.1 per cent of the national economy; (2) farmers, craftsmen and small retailers, who dominated the rural economy and were responsible for 71.8 per cent of economic activity; and (3) private industrial and commercial businesses, which operated mainly in manufacturing industries and distribution channels in urban areas and had a share of 6.9 per cent.[44]

In the early 1950s, China's development followed the centralised Soviet model, including the management systems of manufacturing, supply, transportation, labour force and remuneration, and capital construction; and the planning of supply, production and distribution.[45] Soviet experts then helped China to build 156 major projects, which played an important part in China's economic development. By 1956, a centrally planned economic system was established. The number of enterprises under the control of the central government reached 9300 in 1957, their output amounting to 50 per cent of the total state sector.[46] In 1953 the output of private-sector entities such as individually owned farming, handicraft enterprises and factories accounted for two-thirds of the total, but by 1957 it had fallen to less than 3 per cent, as most private businesses were reorganised into cooperatives.[47]

From the mid-1950s onwards, the government became overanxious for quick results. Two institutional reform measures were taken: (1) in the countryside, the extent of public ownership was increased by organising peasants into People's Communes, which covered about 99 per cent of the rural population; (2) in the urban areas, with decentralisation taking place, there was a transfer of decision-making powers on capital construction and planning, fiscal revenue and the supervision of SOEs from the central to regional governments (provincial, prefectural and municipal). For instance, the number of SOEs under direct central government authority decreased from 9300 in 1957 to 1200 in 1958, while its share of industrial output from these enterprises also declined from 40 to 14 per cent of the national total. Most decisions on capital construction were made by local authorities, and the central government's share of fiscal revenue was reduced from 75 to 50 per cent.

This decentralisation aggravated the negative outcome of the Great Leap Forward in 1958, as regional governments tried to impress the central government by actively and blindly pursuing capital construction and making false claims concerning economic performance. Both the People's Communes and the Great Leap Forward became sources of disastrous economic failures. Economic structure was severely unbalanced by unrealistic growth targets, exaggerated statistical reports and blind investment through administrative command. From 1958 to 1962, the net value of agricultural output decreased by 5.9 per cent, that of light industry fell by 2 per cent annually and national income by 3.1 per cent on average.[48]

In response, between 1961 and 1963, the Chinese government recentralised the decision-making powers delegated in 1958.[49] Then, in 1970, supervisory authority over large SOEs was once more relegated to regional governments; but the operations of large SOEs involved the nationwide coordination of supply, production and distribution, so this delegation of power caused disruption of the normal operational systems of the SOEs, as local administrators were unable to exercise national coordination. Once this became clear, supervision of SOEs was recentralised in 1973. Thus, the reform measures of the 1950s, '60s and '70s were locked into a cycle where centralisation led to rigidity, giving rise to complaints which were responded to by decentralisation; this then caused disorder, which led back to centralisation.

The essential characteristics of the economic system in the industrial sector prior to the economic reform are described as follows:

> It had no room for the laws of value and the market mechanism to play their roles and prevented the commodity economy from being fully developed. All enterprises ate 'from the big pot of the state' and all workers ate 'from the big pot of the enterprise', which greatly depressed the enthusiasm, initiatives and creativity of the enterprises and their workers, thus largely depriving the socialist economy, which should have been overflowing with vigour, of its vitality.[50]

The Third Plenum of the Eleventh Chinese Communist Party Congress, held in December 1978, inaugurated national economic reform. At the meeting, the Chinese Communist Party for the first time set its policy priority as economic development, marking the commencement of economic reforms with the goal of making a transition towards a market-driven economy. The late paramount leader Deng Xiaoping is regarded as the chief designer and helmsman of this initiative, which began with agricultural reform. The success of this reform greatly changed agricultural productivity and promoted reform in the industrial sector.[51]

The reform of SOEs began with the expansion of enterprise autonomy and profit retention, developing from a small-scale experiment in one region to a common practice nationwide. These reform measures enjoyed a certain level of success, but there were some serious problems: too much investment in the same area by different SOEs, non-conformance of state planning, excessive remuneration and uncoordinated reform measures. Therefore, in April 1981, the reform shifted its focus from the expansion of SOE autonomy to the implementation of an 'economic responsibility system', which was intended to achieve the combination of managerial autonomy with accountability and economic incentives. From the beginning of 1981 to the end of 1982, the policy was extended to over 80 per cent of SOEs. Although economic performance was improved somewhat as a result of this measure, it could not overcome some serious shortcomings such as equalitarianism in remuneration and unclear responsibilities; it was therefore short-lived.

From 1984 to 1993 economic reforms entered a new phase and significant strides were made. The great success in agricultural reform became a driver for the industrial sector. Two measures were taken: 'the two-tier plan/market system' (TTPS) and the 'contract responsibility system' (CRS). Under the TTPS, which came into force in 1985, the planning and market regulatory functions coexisted side by side. SOEs were given an output target for compulsory procurement and input quotas, with fixed planned prices. The part of input, production and output above the planned targets could be dealt with through markets, including output prices. Generally, market prices for output were significantly higher than planned. The TTPS acted as an effective mechanism for a transition from a planned economic system to market-orientated one, as it had the effect of 'growth out of the plan'.[52]

Under the CRS, the enterprise would sign a contract with its supervising government body (either central or local) on the production and profit quotas that the enterprise was to deliver. In essence, the system gave more autonomy and incentives (profit retention) to SOEs. By the end of 1987, the CRS had been extended to 8843 of the 11,402 medium-sized and large SOEs, accounting for 77.6 per cent of all SOEs. The CRS went some way to increasing the vitality and motivation of SOEs, and those which adopted it performed better than those which did not. However, the CRS remained limited, because it could neither separate government administrative functions from enterprise business ones nor resolve the ultimate predicament: how to provide motivation and drive for economic performance.

From 1981 to 1984, although reform measures made no substantial breakthrough, the non-state-owned economic sector was boosted. In urban areas, there were two major non-state-owned forces: collectively owned and private enterprises. In the early 1980s, there were over 20 million youngsters seeking employment, which exerted great pressure on all levels of government. Therefore, collectively owned enterprises and individuals were permitted and encouraged to develop or start up businesses. The year 1984 became a turning point for the development of non-state-owned enterprises. In urban areas, private enterprises were now permitted to employ more than eight people and experienced a consequent explosive growth. In rural areas the central government approved and encouraged the development of rural collective enterprises known as 'township and village enterprises', which became the cornerstone of the rural economy.

In December 1990, the Shanghai Stock Exchange was established, followed in April 1991 by the Shenzhen Stock Exchange. The 14th National Congress of the Communist Party of China, held in October 1992, was a landmark in China's economic reform, endorsing the establishment of a 'socialist market economy' as China's reform target. In November 1993, the *Decision on Issues Concerning the Establishment of a Socialist Market Economy*, a momentous document adopted by the Third Plenum of the 14th Party Congress, was a watershed in China's economic reform in terms of the transition towards a market-driven economy. A Company Law was passed in 1993 and took effect in 1994. From the beginning of 1994, important measures were taken by the government to implement reforms in the five key areas: fiscal and taxation, banking, foreign exchange control, enterprise and social security. In the meantime, the government initiated experimental reforms to establish a modern enterprise system based on the Company Law.[53]

The 15th National Party Congress, held in 1997, marked another significant step in China's economic reform with the abandonment, for the first time, of the traditional ideology that the state-owned sector should control a predominant proportion of a socialist economy. It was stipulated that while public ownership would remain as a mainstay of the economy, diverse forms of ownership should be allowed to develop as part of the basic economic system.[54] This economic reform brought about a fundamental structural change in China's market-driven economy: a mixed ownership pattern finally took shape, with a decline in the output of the state-owned and collectively owned sectors while that of all non-state-owned sectors increased significantly.

China's opening up to the world

The renewed diplomatic relationship between the USA and China marks a watershed in contemporary Chinese affairs, having had a major impact on China's international relations and standing.

> In a near-term sense, the restoration of Sino-American relations reversed China's international isolation and estrangement of the Cultural Revolution period. In a more long-term perspective, it ended two decades of diplomatic abnormality between the United States and China, and without it Peking's international emergence in the 1970s and 1980s would have been incalculably more difficult, and probably much less successful.[55]

The hostility between the USA and China became particularly acute mainly because of the Korean War, the Taiwan issue, the Vietnam War and ideological differences between the two governments during the 1950s and 1960s. However, the two sides then both found that reconciliation was in their interests, albeit as a result of somewhat different motivations. President Richard Nixon wanted to explore engagement with China for the purpose of reducing US military commitments in Asia. For its part, China saw the Soviet Union as the major threat to its national security at the time, because of the Soviet invasion of Czechoslovakia in 1968 and the border clash with China in 1969, which led it to seek to use the USA as a counterbalance or to 'play the American card' as the Chinese put it.[56] However, the process of rapprochement between the two countries did not come about as the result of a systematic grand design, but rather through political opportunism.

The first contact between the two countries took place through 'ping-pong diplomacy', whereby an American table tennis team made an officially sanctioned trip to China, followed by a secret visit in 1971 by Nixon's advisor Henry Kissinger. Subsequently, in February 1972, Nixon himself became the first American president to visit China, where he held a personal audience with Chairman Mao Zedong. President Nixon and Chinese Premier Zhou Enlai signed the Shanghai Communiqué, a landmark document signifying the beginning of the normalisation of relations between the two countries. In 1973, both sides agreed to open 'liaison offices'. The normalisation of diplomatic relations was consummated by American president Jimmy Carter and Chinese leader Deng Xiaoping in 1979. Since then, this new diplomatic relationship has been instrumental in encouraging China to shift towards a market-driven economy and away from the Soviet planning model.

In October 1978, General Motors, the largest firm in the world at the time, became the first foreign company to visit the People's Republic of China and explore business opportunities since the founding of the new regime. Its senior executives discussed with Chinese government officials numerous options for cooperation between Chinese and foreign companies. Deng Xiaoping then pinpointed a preference for the joint venture (JV) model as a way forward for such cooperation. During the discussions between GM's executives and Chinese officials on possible joint ventures, it was suggested that China should develop a 'joint venture law' by which both foreign and Chinese companies could abide. The suggestion was accepted by the Chinese government, and the Law of the People's Republic of China on Chinese-Foreign Equity Joint Ventures was promulgated in July 1979, followed by the Law of the People's Republic of China on Sino-Foreign Contractual Joint Ventures in April 1986 and the Law of the People's Republic of China on Wholly Foreign-Owned Enterprises in April 1988.[57] Since then, the Chinese government has adopted an open-door policy of developing foreign trade and attracting foreign direct investment (FDI), which may be considered the most important element of China's economic reforms. In a step of historic significance, China reversed its policy of inward-looking and autarkic economic development which had been followed since the Ming dynasty, the reward being strong growth in foreign trade and inward FDI. These in turn have brought in advanced technology, which has enabled China to undertake rapid industrialisation and modernisation.

China's opening up to the outside world has been a step-by-step process. In May 1980, it was decided that Guangdong and Fujian provinces would be the first allowed to adopt 'special policies' and take 'flexible measures' to deal with foreign trade and investment. In August 1980, four 'special economic zones' (SEZs) were set up in Shenzhen, Zhuhai, Shantou and Xiamen. The businesses established in SEZs were permitted to engage in export, manufacturing, agriculture, commerce, housing and tourism, with a high degree of autonomy in how they would attract investment. Goods imported into SEZs for export purposes were exempted from tariffs and from consolidated industrial and commercial tax.[58] The development of SEZs proved to be a successful experiment in the operation of a market-driven economy. In May 1984, the central government designated 14 'coastal open cities', designed to attract FDI with autonomies similar to those of the special economic zones. In 1992, more cities were granted coastal city status, including Shanghai (with even more autonomy), border towns and those along the Yangtze River.[59] At the end of 2000, the open up the West programme was launched, involving six provinces, five autonomous regions and one municipality. In 2006 came China's strategy for the Central and Western regions and Tianjin's Binhai New Area. As can be seen, the government strategic pathway to open up China is: the special economic zones – the coastal open cities – the coastal open regions – inland areas.[60]

These reform measures significantly promoted national and regional economic development as well as opening up the economy further. Following China's first joint venture, Beijing Air Food Catering Co., Ltd., between Beijing and Hong Kong in April 1980, Coca-Cola opened the first bottling plant in China, becoming the first company from the Global 500 list to enter China in 1981. By the end of 1990, FDI in the 14 coastal open cities exceeded $10 billion, with the setting up of over 2000 foreign-invested enterprises: Sino-foreign equity joint ventures, Sino-foreign contractual joint ventures and wholly foreign-owned enterprises. In 1990, the total export volume from 12 coastal provinces, autonomous regions and municipalities reached about $40 billion, accounting for about two-thirds of total national exports.[61]

On 1 January 1994, China reformed its foreign exchange system by abolishing the planned allocation of foreign exchange and merging the dual track system, in which an official rate and a market rate coexisted. Over the next seven years, China's foreign reserves rose from $21 billion to $200 billion, becoming the world's second largest after those of Japan. In November 2001, China joined the World Trade Organisation (WTO) and subsequently witnessed further growth of exports and FDI.

These reforms have thus gradually transformed a planned and closed economy into a market-based and open one; competition has intensified and China's seller's market has turned into a buyer's market. Since joining the WTO in 2001, China has increasingly been integrated into the global market. The Chinese market has witnessed a healthy increase in competition, while many Chinese companies have become global players, with the world at their feet.

The Korean War

Between 1950 and 1953, China was involved in the Korean War, which had a significant impact on the country's international relations and economic development. In the early morning of 25 June 1950, North Korean forces under Kim Il-Sung launched a surprise attack on South Korea, marking the outbreak of the Korean Civil War. The UN soon authorised the use of force by member nations to drive back the communist aggressors. The UN forces pushed the North Koreans back through the 38th parallel to the Yalu River, the border with China. On 19 October 1950, the Chinese People's Volunteer Army crossed the Yalu to the Korean battlefields, and on 25 October 1950, China's official engagement in the Korean War began. The war came to an end when the UN armies returned to the 38th parallel and a cease-fire agreement was signed on 27 July 1953.

In the short history of the People's Republic of China, the Korean War represents a significant event, having had a great impact on China politically, economically, militarily and spiritually. The country suffered great losses, as noted by a Chinese study:

> According to Chinese statistics, the CPV[62] had lost a total of 390,000 troops – 148,400 dead, 21,000 captured, 4,000 missing in action, and the remainder wounded. The CPV consumed approximately 5.6 million tons of war materials including 399 airplanes and 12,916 vehicles. The People's Republic spent more than 6.2 billion renminbi on the interventions.[63]

Chinese studies have tended to describe and illustrate most of the battles and military campaigns of the Korean War in a generally positive light, with political and military implications favouring the Chinese government. It is regarded as one of the most important incidents to have significantly boosted the morale of the Chinese people since the founding of the People's Republic of China. It has led them to believe that the outcome of warfare can be determined by people, not weaponry, given that the Chinese People's Volunteer Army, with its unsophisticated weaponry, proved a match for a UN force that was equipped with much more advanced military hardware. For six decades, the Korean War has been celebrated in China as a source of national pride and self-confidence. Internationally, some countries have begun to see China in a totally different light, with the realisation that the country has changed. Chinese leaders of the time believed that

> the intervention strengthened the security of a new China. 'We fought our way back to the 38th parallel and held firmly at the parallel.' Mao explained. 'If . . . [our] front lines had remained along the Yalu and Tammen rivers, it would have been impossible for the people in Shenyang, Anshan, and Fushun to carry on production free of worry.' Chinese leaders also believed that the CPV had so devastated American military strength that a general war between China and the US was delayed.[64]

No matter how the Korean War is evaluated politically and militarily, however, it has proven to be a humanitarian disaster.

> There was nothing good about the last Sino-American War, not even the 'peace' that resulted from it. The experience of this war, now nearly forgotten on both sides, should serve as a grim lesson for policy makers in both Washington and Beijing. The Korean War was anything but accidental, but

miscalculation and miscommunication both extended and broadened the war beyond its necessary boundaries.[65]

In addition to the huge loss of human life and resources by Korea, the USA and China, one outcome of the Korean War was that the relationship between the USA and China was seriously strained, with China becoming isolated from the international community, particularly the Western world, for over 20 years.

> The legacy of the war complicated China's international situation. In part because of the memory of Chinese intervention, but also in combination with China's domestic politics, the United States managed to keep the PRC isolated from the international system into the 1970s.[66]

Before the Korean War, there was not much hostility between the USA and China, and both sides were willing to explore the possibility of developing a diplomatic relationship. The US government had no intention of protecting or supporting the Taiwan government, wished to encourage Chinese 'Titoism' (which meant maintaining independence from the policy dictated by the Soviet Union) and even considered recognising the new Chinese government.[67] It was under Soviet pressure that China had engaged in the Korean War; thus she had no choice but to lean towards the Soviet Union. As a result, China was forced to adopt the Soviet central planning model of economic development and became isolated internationally for over two decades. Furthermore, an early opportunity had probably been missed for China to take back Taiwan.[68]

Evolution of marketing in China (1979–1990)

The Industrial Revolution in Western Europe and North America heralded the era of the modern market-based economy. As the market system grew, marketing thought, principles, and institutions gradually developed. It is over a hundred years since the first formation of marketing thought.[69]

The 'marketing concept' is the foundation of the Western marketing system; as such, it is the ideal starting point from which to scrutinise the development of marketing in China when the market system began to be developed. The marketing concept 'provides the philosophy for both the methodology and organisational structure of marketing'.[70]

When markets and market-related behaviour started to emerge in China, they can be, to some extent, comparable with that of the West in the past. Under the parallel market conditions, enterprises may behave similarly because of the forces of market discipline.

In the 1950s, 'marketing' as a working concept came to light, and a marketing title and new organisational unit – 'the marketing department' – in the company were created in America.[71] 'The '60s opened with a flurry of marketing reorganizations. . . . This is a continuation of the wave of marketing reorganization that swept over American business in 1959.'[72] Since then marketing has moved to a central position in many companies,[73] the marketing concept has been widely advocated and seen as an adaptive business philosophy[74] and it has been practised and generally regarded as a successful paradigm.[75]

Four ingredients of the marketing concept had been widely used by the end of the 1980s:[76]

> **Long-Term Profit Direction**: The kernel of the adoption of the marketing concept aims at the achievement of the organisational long-term goals, and usually of profit goals in commercial organisations.
>
> **Market Focus and Customer Orientation**: The company that adopts the marketing concept defines the boundaries of its markets and tailors a marketing plan for each target market; it defines customer needs and wants from the customer point of view in its marketing plan.
>
> **Integrated Marketing Efforts**: These comprise two points: (1) the various marketing functions within the company must be integrated; (2) the whole company must be tuned to the market with the integration of all its departments.
>
> **Business Philosophy**: The marketing concept has long been realised to be a business philosophy.[77] However, its connotations of the concept often seem to conceal or leave out this central characteristic.[78] It is this characteristic that may present a major difficulty in the practice of the deceptively simple concept.
>
> > A company philosophy comprises the guidelines that have become established as expected patterns of behaviour, either through trial and error or through leadership. Part of the foundation for a successful system of management is a philosophy that is consciously thought out, clearly spelled out, and consistently acted out in practice.[79]

Hong Liu (1991) identifies innovation as a key component of the marketing concept.[80] The positive relationship between marketing and innovation has been recognised by many early academics and practitioners.[81] King (1963) writes that the marketing concept involves 'Active company-wide managerial concern with innovation of products and services designed to solve selected consumer problems'.[82]

Innovation is a necessary condition of exercising the marketing concept, in that a market-orientated company must be innovative in the light of developing new products and services to satisfy customer needs better. However, an innovative company is not necessarily market-orientated.

Innovation is also logically aligned with the marketing concept. It ensures a continuous process to provide customers with new products or services matching their evolving needs and wants. Market orientation involves being better than or different from competitors, and this is largely achieved through innovation.

After the founding of the People's Republic of China, until the end of the 1970s when the economic reforms were initiated, the Chinese government adopted a planned economic system, based on the Russian model. Under the system, all economic decisions were made by government planners, while 'enterprises' were simply production units or factories. Factors of production were centrally allocated, production quotas were set by central or regional planners, and all consumer goods were purchased and sold through planning. All revenue, investment and expenditure were controlled by the government, while enterprises and individuals had no responsibility or accountability for economic outcomes. Large private businesses were simply nonexistent. Consumers had no say about what was needed or wanted. Consequently, there was no motivation or incentive for enterprises or individuals to study business management. There had been few publications on micro business management, except economics and macro management or 'industrial administration', dealing with issues about how industrial sectors should be planned and managed.

In China, since 1979, a series of reform measures have been undertaken to introduce the product market into the economic system. As a consequence, a nationwide survey in 1985 concluded that the market system had begun to play a significant role in the overall economic operating mechanisms.[83] In 1988, the output value of non-state-owned enterprises accounted for 35.6 per cent of the industrial total, increased by 15.9 per cent in comparison with 1978. The total profit margin of manufacturing industry decreased from 13.8 per cent in 1981 to 11.9 per cent in 1985 as a result of an increase in competitive intensity.[84]

The economic reform has regenerated and invigorated the market mechanism in China's economic system, in which markets have begun to play a significant role since the early 1980s.[85] Thus, education, training and research in business management have gradually become accepted practice in Chinese universities. In 1983, about 59,000 students in China majored in a subject associated with economics and management.[86] The Chinese University Association of Teaching and Research in Marketing was founded in 1984, and joint management education programmes in business studies were undertaken with Western organisational bodies. For instance, the State University of New York at Buffalo and the Dalian University of Technology jointly delivered China's first MBA programme in 1984. Meanwhile, the China Europe Management Institute (CEMI) was launched under the sponsorship of the European Commission and the China Enterprise Management Association. China's indigenous MBA programmes were officially launched in 1991, with nine MBA programmes in existence. Today the number of MBA programmes in China has reached 236.

In practice, many new types of enterprises characterised by market-driven behaviour have developed due to the disintegration of the past unitary and centrally controlled enterprise structure. The degree to which state-owned enterprises have been controlled by state bodies has varied considerably from sector to sector, from region to region and from enterprise to enterprise. Production-orientated, selling-orientated, as well as customer-orientated behaviour have been found among the different types of enterprise. A survey in 1988 concluded that the business concept of manufacturing enterprises has changed from production to production-market orientation.[87]

These significant changes in enterprise behaviour, market structure and enterprise control have been recognised by Western academics.[88] A nationwide survey of marketing practices in China carried out in 1989 examined the relationships among market impact, government control, market orientation and performance.[89] Although a number of Western academics carried out theoretical and interview-based studies on marketing in China since the economic reform, by the end of 1980s, little quantitative research had been undertaken concerning marketing-related activities in China. The following are the results and implications of the 1989 survey.

The practice of market orientation involved innovation in terms of new product development with a market focus and customer orientation. Integrated marketing efforts, pursuit of marketing research, marketing planning and (marketing) cost analysis were the major marketing activities associated with the practice of market orientation in China. A market-orientated enterprise tended to have better financial performance.

Impeding market orientation is direct government control, which was primarily motivated by the ideology and adverse economic situation in the earlier days, and subsequently solidified by various interested parties, that is government agencies at different levels, in the control system. Unsurprisingly, the reduction of governmental control leads to an increase in market impact. Consumer goods enterprises met less control and more market pressures than industrial goods enterprises, but showed no difference in marketing behaviour. Price control was so prevalent to the extent that there was no difference in the level of control between state-owned and non-state-owned enterprises. All other functional controls in state-owned enterprises were stronger than those in non-state-owned enterprises. There were significant differences in market impact and government control between the regions due to the varying processes of reform and different levels of economic development. Investment decisions were jointly made by enterprises and the government, with the weight of each being subject to individual projects.

The survey showed some obvious market-marketing relationships: the more impact market enterprises were subject to, the more market orientated these enterprises were. However, production-orientated enterprises remained dominant in China at the time, and the number of enterprises reporting a 'market orientation' was only 15 per cent, particularly considering that the sample was somewhat biased towards enterprises in the more developed regions. The majority of Chinese managing directors of enterprise had 'engineering' and 'manufacturing' backgrounds, which could constrain the exercise of marketing.

Enterprise size was positively correlated with government control – that is the larger the enterprise was, the stronger government control it was subject to – and negatively with market impact. Both large and medium-sized enterprises were more market orientated, and performed better, than small enterprises.

There were fewer differences in marketing-related activities between large and medium-sized enterprises. It appears that lower marketing knowledge and fewer technological and financial resources of small enterprises were mainly responsible for their lower market orientation and poorer performance.[90] The level of marketing knowledge was positively associated with the exercise of market orientation. All non-state-owned enterprises were more innovative than state-owned enterprises in terms of product development and improvement.

A certain proportion of enterprises were authorised to deal with businesses internationally. Within state-owned industries, the authorised enterprises appeared to be substantially more responsive to markets than the unauthorised enterprises. However, it was revealed that they still experienced relatively strong governmental control, and suffered from the lack of international business information.

Concluding remarks

In China, since antiquity, history has been taken seriously by imperial courts, politicians, military personnel and businesspeople as well as the populace. Therefore, China probably has the best-recorded history of any culture. Not only does history make Chinese people remember their identity, ancestry, glory and indignity, but also, more importantly, accumulated wisdom and knowledge, leading to the continued development of Chinese civilisation. From Chinese history, one may see through the personality of the Chinese people, such as diligent, persevering, hospitable, tenacious, intelligent, suspicious and corruptible.[91] These characteristics, together with other social factors, have made China the only civilisation that has survived in the world, lasting for over five millennia.

Most seasoned Chinese politicians, military personnel and businesspeople would be knowledgeable about Chinese history, because it contains a wealth of wisdom and knowledge about politics and military affairs. Those who are versed in Chinese history would be likened to engaging in political, military or business 'chess games' with the adequate knowledge of triumphant chess books.

As far as foreign businesspeople are concerned, knowledge of Chinese history may help them forge a close relationship with their Chinese business partners, avoiding possible cultural mistakes that may take place. Learning particular aspects of Chinese history enables one to appreciate Chinese wisdom. The larger the business involved in China, the more important the knowledge of Chinese history. Some key points of Chinese history are summarised as follows:

- From the beginning of the Qin, the dynastic empire that first unified China, to the end of the Qing, the last dynastic empire, was a period of 2133 years, during which China was ruled by 564 emperors. The longest individual reign lasted 61 years and the shortest 27 days.
- The government structure of the major Chinese dynasties was incomparably greater in scope and power than those of Japan, India or Persia. In modern Europe, there had been emperors of France, Russia, Austria-Hungary,

Germany and the British Empire (as well as many powerful popes in Rome), but monarchs ruled their kingdoms simultaneously. In contrast, most Chinese empires were ruled by only one emperor at any one time.[92]

- In pre-modern times, China enjoyed superiority in Eurasia in science and technology, agricultural productivity and military power. Until the fourteenth century, China was the clear world leader in technological areas such as metallurgy, gunpowder, the compass, silk and porcelain manufacture, paper and its use as currency, block printing and mechanical clocks.[93] However, many of the major technological applications were made by Europeans rather than by the Chinese.
- China attained a high degree of commercialisation and urbanisation, enjoying favourable conditions for commerce such as the application of paper money and the development of credit facilities, much earlier than Europe.[94] China's technological, cultural and economic development culminated in the Song period.[95] The Mongol invasion of Song China may thus be seen as a turning point, leading ultimately to China's economic downfall.[96]
- A form of money was first used for transaction purposes around the Shang period (1600–1046 BC). The objects used as monetary units went through an evolutionary process from cowry shells via knife-shaped bronze coins, silks and iron to paper. There were countless types of coinage in terms of material, shape, design, value and size before the Qin dynasty (221–206 BC), after which all were unified into a standard coinage: *ban liang qian* ('half liang money'). The *liang* was a unit of weight used at the time. The coins were round in shape with a square hole in the middle, reflecting the popular view that the round sky covered the square earth. This design continued to be used until the end of the Qing dynasty in 1911; however, these coins could be minted freely by the populace in different sizes and weights. During the Han dynasty the government centralised the mintage and standardised the size and weight to the *wu zhu* (5 zhu).[97] This coinage remained in circulation until the Tang dynasty. The paper money known as *jiaozi* was first introduced during the Song dynasty (960–1279). In contrast, the first banknote in the West was issued in Stockholm in 1660.
- It is commonly held that people in southern China are more business-minded and astute than those in northern China. Notably, most traditional Chinese emigrants to Southeast Asia, North America and Europe come from southern China, particularly from Guangdong, Fujian, Zhejiang and Shanghai. A review of Chinese history suggests that this pattern has historical roots. Historically, particularly about 1000 years ago, northern China suffered many attacks and invasions by northern nomads, especially Khitans and Turks, while southern China enjoyed the luxury of longer periods of peace, allowing its citizens to concentrate on production and commerce.
- The evolution of Chinese history shows that the rise and fall of imperial powers depend on their rulers' competence, integrity and personality, which tend to follow a cyclical pattern. When a new dynasty replaced the previous one, the new monarch was mostly capable and morally upright,

sparing no effort in governing the country well. As the throne was passed on to later generations, however, rulers eventually became inept, dissipated and despotic, leading to the demise of the dynasty. As the rise of each new empire was accompanied by mass destruction, this cycle prevented the economy from enjoying the accumulation of wealth necessary for major innovation and industrialisation.

But the dynastic cycle was an important element in the traditional Chinese view of history, which seemed to be an inexorable progression from strength to weakness, from centralisation to decentralisation, from order to chaos, from unity to fragmentation, over and over. That some dynasties nevertheless endured for three centuries and more testifies to the remarkable success the Chinese achieved in constructing stable social and governmental systems.[98]

- There appears to have been a common view among most Chinese emperors that China was the 'Middle Kingdom' at the centre of the universe, which resulted in a self-importance and complacency in the dynastic era. However, this self-centred view of a nation in the world was not unique, being held by most nations in ancient times, mainly because of limited knowledge of world geography. It was when Vasco da Gama led a Portuguese oceangoing expedition to South India in 1498 and Christopher Columbus took his three ships to San Salvador in 1492[99] that Western nations changed their views and their national policies, with resultant economic, political, cultural and military outcomes. In contrast, China persisted in its parochial illusion until its doors were forced open by Western powers in the nineteenth century.

- The founding of the People's Republic of China represents a new era in Chinese history. It was Mao Zedong who made China independent again, giving birth to the new country, without any past burdens and restrictions from foreign colonial powers. It was Deng Xiaoping who initiated economic reforms that have brought about China's transformation from a planned and backward economy into a dynamic and an invigorated one, making significant contributions to global economic growth and stability.

- The end of the 1970s is the watershed from which China's economic and social locomotive started to embark on the new journey of marketisation. The market mechanism began to function in the Chinese economic system, while the planning apparatus became increasingly weakened. Western market-based management and marketing theories and practices were being introduced into the Chinese educational and industrial systems. The rapprochement between the USA and China signifies a significant step in the implementation of China's open–door policy, with China witnessing the rapid introduction of foreign direct investment, leading to fundamental changes in Chinese business and society, such as management concepts and practices as well as social values and consumptions. If we see China as a nation from a product-life-cycle point of view, the period of Mao Zedong's rule (1949–1976) may be seen as the 'introduction' stage, the period of Deng Xiaoping – Jiang Zemin – Hu Jintao (1978–2013) as the 'early growth' stage and the current leadership of Xi Jinping (2013–present) as the 'late growth approaching maturity' stage. There may be two possible directions: (1) China is regenerated to start off another round of growth stage, as many companies or products have done, and (2) China is continuing at the stage of growth–maturity, consolidating its economic and technological strengths and capability and improving and enhancing its (social, environmental and economic) sustainability.

Notes

1 Hayley, U.C.V. and Hayley, G.T. (2006), "The Logic of Chinese Business Strategy: East vs. West: Part I," *The Journal of Business Strategy*, 27 (1), 35–42.
2 Javidan, M. and Lynton, N. (2005, December), "The Changing Face of the Chinese Executive," *Harvard Business Review*, 83 (12), 28–30.
3 Deng, K.G. (2000), "A Critical Survey of Recent Research in Chinese Economic History," *Economic History Review*, LIII (I), 1–28.
4 Kennedy, P. (1988), *The Rise and Fall of the Great Powers*, London: Fontana Press, p. 189.
5 Liu, S.H. (1974), "Time and Temporality: The Chinese Perspective," *Philosophy East and West*, 24 (2), 145–153.
6 Nixon, R. (1980), *The Real War*, New York: Warner Books Inc., p. 128.
7 Kissinger, H.A. (2011), *On China*, New York: Penguin Press, p. 2.
8 These are the remarks made to his ministers when Emperor Taizong of Tang was moved by the death of Wei Zheng (580–643), a trusted advisor to the emperor. On many occasions, Wei's cautionary advice prevented Taizong from making grave mistakes, a rare quality in a man in ancient China.
9 The New Encyclopaedia Britannica (2003), *The New Encyclopaedia Britannica, Micropaedia*, 11, The New Encyclopaedia Britannica, Inc.
10 The first unified China is called the Ch'in dynasty in Wade Giles and Qin Chao in the current Chinese phonetic transcription. Before 1949, all Chinese characters were transcribed using the Wade Giles system.
11 Lu, T. (1999), *Chinese Civilisation: History of Prior to the Qin Dynasty* (in Chinese). Shijiazhuang, China: Hebei Education Publishing House, pp. 461–462.
12 Leader of the Communist Party of China (1935–1976) and a great military strategist, who never suffered defeat in any battle, military campaign or war.
13 Lu, Z.D. (2009), *Mao Zedong Ping Guoxue (Mao Zedong's Comments on Chinese Classics)*, Beijing: New World Press. Sheng, X.C. and Li, Z.C. (2011), *Mao Zedong PinPing SiDa MingZhu (Mao Zedong's Commentaries on the Four Classics)*, Beijing: Central Compilation & Translation Press.
14 Snow, E. (1968), *Red Star Over China*, London: Gollancz, p. 133.
15 Schram, S. (1967), *Political Leaders of the Twentieth Century: Mao Tse-tung*, London: Penguin Books, p. 21.
16 Lieberthal, K. (1995), *Governing China: From Revolution to Reform*, New York: W.W. Norton & Co., p. 60.
17 Lu, Z.D. (2009), *Mao Zedong Ping Guoxue (Mao Zedong's Comments on Chinese Classics)*, Beijing: New World Press, p. 57.
18 Schram, S. (1967), *Political Leaders of the Twentieth Century: Mao Tse-tung*, London: Penguin Books, p. 21.
19 These are the authoritative Confucian texts written before 300 BC. The Four Books are *Great Learning, Doctrine of the Mean, Analects* and *Mencius*; and the Five Classics are *Book of Poetry, Book of Documents, Book of Rites, I Ching* and *Spring and Autumn Annals*.

20 Lu, Z.D. (2009), *Mao Zedong Ping Guoxue (Mao Zedong's Comments on Chinese Classics)*, Beijing: New World Press.
21 Salisbury, H. (1985), *The Long March: The Untold Story*, New York: Palgrave Macmillan, p. 72.
22 Yue Fei (1103–1142) was a military general of the Han Chinese during the period of the Southern Song dynasty. He has been widely acclaimed as a patriot and national hero in China, because he led Southern Song forces in the wars against the Jurchen Jin dynasty in northern China in the twelfth century. He was put to death by a court politician, Qin Gui (1090–1155), who was pushing an appeasement policy towards the Jin. Yue Fei is regarded as a patriotic martyr in China, while Qin Gui is remembered as a traitor.
23 Lu, Z.D. (2009), *Mao Zedong Ping Guoxue (Mao Zedong's Comments on Chinese Classics)*, Beijing: New World Press. Sheng, X.C. and Li, Z.C. (2011), *Mao Zedong PinPing SiDa MingZhu (Mao Zedong's Commentaries on the Four Classics)*, Beijing: Central Compilation & Translation Press.
24 Zedong, M. (1937), "On Contradiction," in Committee for the Publication of the Selected Works of Mao Tse-tung, Central Committee of the Communist Party of China (eds.), *Selected Works of Mao Tse-tung: Volume I* (1965 edition), Peking: Foreign Languages Press, p. 340.
25 Zedong, M. (1942), "A Most Important Policy," in Committee for the Publication of the Selected Works of Mao Tse-tung, Central Committee of the Communist Party of China (eds.), *Selected Works of Mao Tse-tung: Volume III* (1965 edition), Peking: Foreign Languages Press, p. 101.
26 Schram, S. (1967), *Political Leaders of the Twentieth Century: Mao Tse-tung*, London: Penguin Books, pp. 43–44.
27 Zedong, M. (1937), "On Contradiction," in Committee for the Publication of the Selected Works of Mao Tse-tung, Central Committee of the Communist Party of China (eds.), *Selected Works of Mao Tse-tung: Volumes I* (1965 edition), Peking: Foreign Languages Press, p. 324.
28 Schram, S. (1967), *Political Leaders of the Twentieth Century: Mao Tse-tung*, London: Penguin Books, p. 159.
29 Salisbury, H. (1985), *The Long March: The Untold Story*, New York: Palgrave Macmillan, p. 73.
30 Snow, E. (1968), *Red Star Over China*, London: Victor Gollancz, p. 134.
31 Zedong, M. (1939), "Chinese Society," in Committee for the Publication of the Selected Works of Mao Tse-tung, Central Committee of the Communist Party of China (eds.), *Selected Works of Mao Tse-tung: Volume II* (1965 edition), Peking: Foreign Languages Press, p. 308.
32 Fairbank, J.K. and Goldman, M. (1998), *China: A New History*, Cambridge, MA, and London: The Belknap Press of Harvard University Press, p. 42.
33 Hucker, C.O. (1975), *China's Imperial Past: An Introduction to Chinese History and Culture*, London: Duckworth, p. 66.
34 Wei, Q.Y. (1988), *History of Chinese Political System* (in Chinese), Beijing: Renmin University of China Publishing House, p. 14.
35 Fairbank, J.K. and Goldman, M. (1998), *China: A New History*, Cambridge, MA, and London: The Belknap Press of Harvard University Press, p. 51.
36 It is called the Ch'in dynasty in the Wade Giles system.
37 Feng, G.C. (2005), *A General History of China* (in Chinese), Beijing: The Guangming Daily Publishing House, p. 100.
38 Jian, B.Z. (2006), *The Essential History of China* (in Chinese), Beijing: Peking University Publishing House, p. 146.
39 Ibid, p. 157.
40 Ibid, pp. 156–167.
41 Hucker, C.O. (1975), *China's Imperial Past: An Introduction to Chinese History and Culture*, London: Duckworth, p. 139.

42 Fairbank, J.K. and Goldman, M. (1998), *China: A New History*, Cambridge, MA, and London: The Belknap Press of Harvard University Press, p. 78.

43 Fairbank, J.K. and Goldman, M. (1998), *China: A New History*, Cambridge, MA, and London: The Belknap Press of Harvard University Press, p. 138.

44 The collectively owned economy accounted for 1.5% and joint private-state cooperatives for 0.7%. See also Ma, H. (1982), *Encyclopedia of Chinese Modern Economy* (in Chinese), Beijing: Chinese Social Science Publishing House, p. 67.

45 Zhou, T. (1984), *Contemporary Economic Reform in China* (in Chinese), Beijing: Chinese Social Sciences Press.

46 Qian, Y.Y. (2000), "The Process of China's Market Transition (1978–1998): The Evolutionary, Historical, and Comparative Perspectives," *Journal of Institutional and Theoretical Economics*, 156, 151–171.

47 Twitchett, D. and Fairbank, J.K. (1987), *The Cambridge History of China: Volume 14, The People's Republic, Part I: The Emergence of Revolutionary China 1949–1965*, Cambridge: Cambridge University Press, pp. 156–157.

48 Qian, Y.Y. (2000), "The Process of China's Market Transition (1978–1998): The Evolutionary, Historical, and Comparative Perspectives," *Journal of Institutional and Theoretical Economics*, 156, 151–171.

49 Wu, J.L. (2005), *Understanding and Interpreting Chinese Economic Reform*, Singapore: Thomson/South-Western, p. 143.

50 United Nations (1989), "China's Experience in Economic Development and Reforms," *United Nations' Development Paper No. 7*, Economic and Social Commission for Asia and the Pacific, Bangkok, United Nations.

51 Qian, Y.Y. (2000), "The Process of China's Market Transition (1978–1998): The Evolutionary, Historical, and Comparative Perspectives," *Journal of Institutional and Theoretical Economics*, 156, 151–171.

52 Byrd, W.A. (1988), "The Impact of the Two Tier Plan/Market System in Chinese Industry," in R.L. Reynolds (ed.), *Chinese Economic Reform*, London: Academic Press, p. 9.

53 Qian, Y.Y. (2000), "The Process of China's Market Transition (1978–1998): The Evolutionary, Historical, and Comparative Perspectives," *Journal of Institutional and Theoretical Economics*, 156, 151–171. Wu, J.L. (2005), *Understanding and Interpreting Chinese Economic Reform*, Singapore: Thomson/South-Western, pp. 82–83.

54 Wu, J.L. (2005), *Understanding and Interpreting Chinese Economic Reform*, Singapore: Thomson/South-Western, p. 86.

55 Twitchett, D. and Fairbank, J.K. (1987), *The Cambridge History of China: Volume 14, The People's Republic, Part I: The Emergence of Revolutionary China 1949–1965*, Cambridge: Cambridge University Press, p. 402.

56 Fenby, J. (2008), *The Penguin History of Modern China: The Fall and Rise of a Great Power, 1850–2008*, London: Allen Lane, pp. 496–497.

57 Zhang, X.J. (2008), *Zhouxiang shijie shichang (Enter the Global Market)*, Beijing: China Development Press, p. 69.

58 Wu, J.L. (2005), *Understanding and Interpreting Chinese Economic Reform*, Singapore: Thomson/South-Western, p. 296.

59 Qian, Y.Y. (2000), "The Process of China's Market Transition (1978–1998): The Evolutionary, Historical, and Comparative Perspectives," *Journal of Institutional and Theoretical Economics*, 156, 151–171.

60 Zhang, X.J. (2008), *Zhouxiang shijie shichang (Enter the Global Market)*, Beijing: China Development Press, p. 137.

61 Wu, J.L. (2005), *Understanding and Interpreting Chinese Economic Reform*, Singapore: Thomson/South-Western, p. 296.

62 Chinese People's Volunteers

63 Zhang, S.G. (1995), *Mao's Military Romanticism: China and the Korean War, 1950–1953*, Lawrence: University Press of Kansas, p. 247.

64   Zhang, S.G. (1995), *Mao's Military Romanticism: China and the Korean War, 1950–1953*, Lawrence: University Press of Kansas, p. 248.

65   Farley, R. (2014), "Deadly Lessons: The Last Time China and America Went to War," *The National Interest*, 24 October 2014, http://nationalinterest.org/feature/deadly-lessons-the-last-time-china-america-went-war-11558

66   Ibid.

67   Twitchett, D. and Fairbank, J.K. (1987), *The Cambridge History of China: Volume 14, The People's Republic, Part I: The Emergence of Revolutionary China 1949–1965*, Cambridge: Cambridge University Press, p. 271.

68   Simmons, R. (1975), *The Strained Alliance: Peking, Pyongyang, Moscow and the Politics of the Korean Civil War*, New York: The Free Press, pp. 102–168. Twitchett, D. and Fairbank, J.K. (1987), *The Cambridge History of China: Volume 14, The People's Republic, Part I: The Emergence of Revolutionary China 1949–1965*, Cambridge: Cambridge University Press, pp. 276–277.

69   Schwartz, G. (1970), "Development of Marketing Thought: A Brief History," in B. Robert (ed.), *Marketing Theory and Matatheory*, Homewood, IL: Richard D. Irwin, Inc., pp. 29–57. Bartels, R. (1976), *The History of Marketing Thought*, Columbus, OH: Grid Inc.

70   Kaldor, A.G. (1971), "Imbricative Marketing," *Journal of Marketing*, 35 (April), 19–25.

71   Hahn, A.R. (1957), "The 'Marketing Concept': A Major Change in Management Thinking?" *Sales Management*, 10 November, 64–75. Viebranz, A.C. (1967), "Marketing's Role in Company Growth," *MSU Business Topics*, 15 (Autumn), 45–49.

72   Printers' Ink (1960), "Pursuit of Profit: How the Marketing Concept Builds New Balance of Power," *Printers' Ink*, 19 February.

73   Lynn, R.H. (1969), *Marketing: Principles and Market Action*, New York: McGraw-Hill, Inc.

74   Borch, F.J. (1957), "The Marketing Philosophy as a Way of Business Life," in E. Marting and A. Newgaden (eds.), *The Marketing Concept: Its Meaning to Management*, New York: American Management Association, Marketing Series, No. 99, 1–6. McKitterick, J.B. (1957), "What Is the Marketing Management Concept?" in F.M. Bass (ed.), *The Frontiers of Marketing Thought and Science*, New York: American Marketing Association, No. 71, 71–82. Keith, R.J. (1960), "The Marketing Revolution," *Journal of Marketing*, 24 (January), 35–38. Levitt, T. (1960), "Marketing Myopia," *Harvard Business Review*, 38 (July–August), 45–56. Levitt, T. (1962), *Innovation in Marketing*, New York: McGraw-Hill.

75   Hahn, A.R. (1957), "The 'Marketing Concept': A Major Change in Management Thinking?" *Sales Management*, 10 November, 64–75. Jewell, J.H. (1958), "New Marketing Concept at Westinghouse: Decentralize and Study the Consumer," *Printers' Ink*, 24 January. Lazo, H. and Corbin, A. (1961), *Management in Marketing*, New York: McGraw-Hill. Hise, R.T. (1965), "Have Manufacturing Firms Adopted the Marketing Concept?" *Journal of Marketing*, 29 (July), 9–12. Rothe, J.T. and Benson, L. (1974), "Intelligent Consumption: An Attractive Alternative to the Marketing Concept," *MSU Business Topics*, Winter, 29–34. Peters, T.J. and Waterman, R.H. (1982), *In Search of Excellence*, New York: Harper and Row.

76   Borch, F.J. (1957), "The Marketing Philosophy as a Way of Business Life," in E. Marting and A. Newgaden (eds.), *The Marketing Concept: Its Meaning to Management, American*, Management Association, Marketing Series, No. 99, 1–6. McKitterick, J.B. (1957), "What Is the Marketing Management Concept?" in F.M. Bass (ed.), *The Frontiers of Marketing Thought and Science*, New York: American Marketing Association, No. 71, 71–82. Felton, A.P. (1959), "Making the Marketing Concept Work," *Harvard Business Review*, July–August, 55–65. King, R.L. (1963), "An Interpretation of the Marketing Concept," in S.J. Shaw and C.M. Gittinger (ed.), *Marketing in Business Management*. London and New York: The Macmillan Company, Collier-Macmillan Limited. Kotler, P. and Zaltman, G. (1971), "Social Marketing: An Approach to Planned Social Change," *Journal of Marketing*, 35 (July), 3–12. Bell, M.L. and Emory, C.W. (1971), "The Faltering Marketing Concept," *Journal of Marketing*, 35 (October), 37–42. Stampfl, R.W. (1978), "Structural Constraints, Consumerism, and the Marketing Concept," *MSU Business Topics*, 26 (Spring), 5–16. McCarthy, E.J. and Perreault, W. (1984), *Basic Marketing*, Homewood,

IL: Richard D. Irwin, Inc. Kotler, P. (1980, 1988), *Marketing Management*, Upper Saddle River, NJ: Prentice-Hall, Inc. McGee, L.W. and Spiro, R.L. (1988), "The Marketing Concept in Perspective," *Business Horizon*, 31 (3), 40–45.

77 McKitterick, J.B. (1957), "What Is the Marketing Management Concept?" in F.M. Bass (ed.), *The Frontiers of Marketing Thought and Science*, New York: American Marketing Association, No. 71, 71–82. Felton, A.P. (1959), "Making the Marketing Concept Work," *Harvard Business Review* (July–August), 55–65. Levitt, T. (1962), *Innovation in Marketing*, New York: McGraw-Hill. Roberts, C.S. (1960), "A Changing World Requires New Marketing Concepts," in S.J. Shaw and C.M. Gittinger (ed.), *Marketing in Business Management*, London and New York: The Macmillan Company. King, R.L. (1963), "An Interpretation of the Marketing Concept," in S.J. Shaw and C.M. Gittinger (ed.), *Marketing in Business Management*. London and New York: The Macmillan Company, Collier-Macmillan Limited. Kotler, P. (1965), "Diagnosing the Marketing Takeover," *Harvard Business Review*, 43 (November–December), 70–72.

78 Kotler, P. and Zaltman, G. (1971), "Social Marketing: An Approach to Planned Social Change," *Journal of Marketing*, 35 (July), 3–12. Kotler, P. (1980), *Marketing Management*, Upper Saddle River, NJ: Prentice-Hall, Inc., p. 22. McCarthy, E.J. and Perreault, W. (1984), *Basic Marketing*, Homewood, IL: Richard D. Irwin, Inc., p. 35.

79 Bower, M. (1966), "A New Look at the Company Philosophy," *Management Review*, 55 (5), 4–14.

80 Liu, H. (1991), *Market, Marketing and Marketing Behaviour: An Empirical Examination in China and Britain*, unpublished doctoral dissertation, University of Warwick. Liu, H. (1995), "Market Orientation and Firm Size: An Empirical Examination in UK Firms," *European Journal of Marketing*, 29 (1), 57–71.

81 Drucker, P.F. (1954), *The Practice of Management*, New York: Harper & Row Publishers, Inc. McKitterick, J.B. (1957), "What Is the Marketing Management Concept?" in F.M. Bass (ed.), *The Frontiers of Marketing Thought and Science*, New York: American Marketing Association, No. 71, 71–82. Levitt, T. (1962), *Innovation in Marketing*, New York: McGraw-Hill. Alderson, W. (1965), "Marketing Innovations and the Problem Solver," in F.E. Webster (ed.), *New Directions in Marketing*, Homewood, IL: Richard D. Irwin, Inc., pp. 53–61. Zaltman, G. (1965), *Marketing: Contributions From the Behavioural Sciences*, New York: Harcourt, Brace & World, Inc.

82 King, R.L. (1963), "An Interpretation of the Marketing Concept," in S.J. Shaw and C.M. Gittinger (ed.), *Marketing in Business Management*. London and New York: The Macmillan Company, Collier-Macmillan Limited.

83 Reynolds, B.L. (1987), *Reform in China: Challenges and Choices*, New York: M.E. Sharpe Inc., p. 4.

84 Zhang, S. (1987), *Weiguan gaige zhong de chichang jiegou he qiye zhidu (Market Structure and Enterprise System in Economic Reform)*, Beijing: Zhongguo sehui kexue (Chinese Social Sciences Press), p. 4.

85 Reynolds, B.L. (1987), *Reform in China: Challenges and Choices*, New York: M.E. Sharpe Inc., p. 4.

86 Deng, S.L. and Wang, S.L. (1992), "Management Education in China: Past, Present and Future," *World Development*, 20 (6), 873–880.

87 Lu, Y.L., Zhang, F. and Yan, Y. (1988), "Xieng jie duang zhongguo gongye qiye de chichang yingxiao xingwei (Marketing Behaviour of Chinese Industrial Enterprise at Current Stage)," in Weiguan gaige zhong de chichang jiegou he qiye zhidu *(Market Structure and Enterprise System in Economic Reform)*, Chengdu, China: Sichang People's Publishing House.

88 Thorelli, H.B. (1983), "Concepts of Marketing: A Review, Preview and Paradigm," in P. Varadarajan (ed.), *The Marketing Concept: Perspectives and Viewpoints*, Proceedings of Workshop, Marketing Department, College Station: Texas A&M University, pp. 2–37. Holton, R.H. (1985), "Marketing and the Modernization of China," *California Management Review*, 27 (4) (Summer), 33–45. Vernon-Wortzel, H. and Wortzel, L.H. (1987), "The Emergence of Free Market Retailing in the People's Republic of China: Promises and

Consequences," *California Management Review*, 29 (3), 59–76. Child, J. (1987), "Enterprise Reform in China – Progress and Problems," in M. Warner (ed.), *Management Reforms in China*, London: Frances Pinter Limited, pp. 24–52.

89 Liu, H. (1991), *Market, Marketing and Marketing Behaviour: An Empirical Examination in China and Britain*, unpublished doctoral dissertation, University of Warwick.

90 Liu, H. (1995), "Market Orientation and Firm Size: An Empirical Examination in UK Firms," *European Journal of Marketing*, 29 (1), 57–71.

91 One might be surprised to know that corruption has been rampant since antiquity.

92 Fairbank, J.K. and Goldman, M. (1998), *China: A New History*, Cambridge, MA, and London: The Belknap Press of Harvard University Press, p. 46.

93 Deng, K.G. (2000), "A Critical Survey of Recent Research in Chinese Economic History," *Economic History Review*, LIII (I), 1–28.

94 Ibid.

95 Elvin, M. (1973), *The Pattern of the Chinese Past*, Stanford, CA: Stanford University Press, p. 313. Skinner, G.W. (1985), "The Structure of Chinese History," *Journal of Asian Studies*, 2, 217–292.

96 Jones, E.L. (1990), "The Real Question About China: Why Was the Song Economic Achievement Not Repeated?" *Australian Economic History Review*, 30, 5–22.

97 The zhu is a unit of weight; a liang = 12 zhu.

98 Hucker, C.O. (1975), *China's Imperial Past: An Introduction to Chinese History and Culture*, London: Duckworth, p. 71.

99 World History (2006), *World History With Atlas*, New Lanark, Scotland: Geddes & Grosset, pp. 101–103.

3 Chinese philosophical systems and business implications

Letting a hundred flowers blossom and a hundred schools of thought contend is the policy for promoting progress in the arts and the sciences and a flourishing socialist culture in our land.

– Mao Zedong

It is not the strongest of the species that survives, nor the most intelligent, but the one most responsive to change.

– Charles Darwin

The most incomprehensible thing about the world is that it is at all comprehensible.

– Albert Einstein

The *I Ching*[1]: the foundation of Chinese philosophical systems

Research indicates that management and organisational theories may be culture-bound.[2] The predominant components of national culture consist of philosophy, history, literature and language, among others, with philosophy at its heart. As explained in Chapter Two, during the Spring and Autumn period (770–476 BC) and the Warring States period (476–221 BC), many great Chinese philosophers emerged, including Confucius, Lao Zi, Mencius, Guan Zi, Xun Zi, Sun Zi, Han Feizi and Mo Zi, and they were contemporaries of some of the world's great thinkers and teachers, such as Siddhartha Gautama (c. 563–483) (or the Buddha) from India/Nepal[3] and Socrates (c. 470–399 BC), Plato (c. 427–347 BC) and Aristotle (384–321 BC) as well as the Pythagoreans and the Orphics from Greece.[4] It has been noted that Indian thinkers focus on the relationship between God and soul, and Greek philosophers on the nature of the material world, while Chinese philosophers concentrate on the humanities, predominantly on ethical, moral, social and political issues.[5] Such differences in cultural roots inevitably result in diversity in social behaviour and organisation.

Noticeable consequences of these differences are that the West has excelled at science and technology, with an emphasis on the understanding and conquering of the natural world, while the Chinese philosophical system has inherited and accumulated ancient heritage and tradition, stressing the unity of man with nature:

> Chinese culture has been essentially a culture of the humanities, while modern Western culture has been predominantly occupied with the development of science. In scientific studies there is an emphasis upon recent developments. A dictum for the scientist is, 'the more up-to-date the more acceptable' . . . But in the humanities the corresponding dictum, 'the more recent the more acceptable', can no longer hold.[6]

Although there have been a number of Chinese classics that have shaped Chinese history and culture, the most influential include *Yijing* or the *I Ching* in Chinese, commonly known as the *Book of Changes* in English translation, along with the classic texts of Confucianism, Taoism and Buddhism. These works are interrelated and complementary, each looking at the world from a different perspective.

The *I Ching* is considered the oldest and the foremost of all the Chinese classics. For instance, during the Zhou dynasty (1046–771 BC), there were six classics: the *I Ching*, *The Book of History*, *The Book of Rites*, *The Book of Poetry*, *The Classic of Music* and *The Spring and Autumn Annals*. The *I Ching* is also regarded as the source of all Chinese classics and culture. The book

> contains the roots of Chinese culture, including Confucianism, Taoism, and the School of Mo Tzu. Throughout all the dynasties up to the modern era, the *Book of Changes* and *The Ten Wings* have been the subject of extensive interpretation, not only in the school of Confucianism but also in [those] of Taoism and Buddhism.[7]

> [The *I Ching*] is unquestionably one of the most important books in the world's literature. Its origin goes back to mythical antiquity, and it has occupied the attention of the most eminent scholars of China down to the present day. Nearly all that is greatest and most significant in the three thousand years of Chinese cultural history has either taken its inspiration from this book, or has exerted an influence on the interpretation of its text . . . not only the philosophy of China but its science and statecraft as well have never ceased to draw from the spring of wisdom in the *I Ching*.[8]

The book first reached the West in the eighteenth century, and perceptions of it 'have varied greatly, from the highly reverential to the baffled, utterly sceptical, or dismissive'.[9] Many have articulated frustration and difficulty in the understanding of this book:

> In 1728, French Jesuit Claude de Visdelou . . . dictated the following words . . . : 'It [the *I Ching*] is not strictly speaking a book at all, or anything like it. It is a most obscure enigma, a hundred times more difficult to explain than that of the Sphinx.' . . . The British sinologist Herbert Giles referred to 'the apparent gibberish of the *Book of Changes*'. Bernhard Karlgren, the Swedish philologist, called it a 'barely intelligible rigmarole.' 'It

would have been wiser,' wrote a frustrated Joseph Needham in 1956, 'to tie a millstone about the neck of the *I Ching* and cast it into the sea.'[10]

Since the book is somewhat esoteric, its dissemination and understanding in the West have been limited. Having integrated the views of various authoritative scholars, Manford quotes Richard Lynn to suggest how the book should be read:

> [The reader should] allow the work to address the primary issues with which it is concerned: the interrelatedness of personal character and destiny; how position defines scope of action; how position and circumstances define appropriate modes of behaviour; how the individual is always tied to others in a web of interconnected causes and effects; how one set of circumstances inevitably changes into another; and how change itself is the great constant – and flexible response to it the only key to happiness and success. There is a core of insights here concerning the structure of human relationships and individual behaviour that can, I believe, speak to this and any other age – if we but allow it to do so.[11]

From a business viewpoint, at an initial stage, it may suffice for readers to understand the principles and rationalities of the *I Ching*, in order to have a basic appreciation of Chinese culture or social phenomena.

The principles set out in the *Book* have been widely used in various areas such as politics, economics, the military, astronomy, geography, philosophy, science and sociology in China for over two millennia. The *Book* is generally considered to derive from three sources.

(1) Fu Xi, one of the earliest mythological rulers in ancient China, is credited with having devised the eight trigrams, of which *yin* and *yang* are the basic elements and where the universe is regarded as constituted of these two components. Figure 3.1 depicts the eight trigrams.

The Great Treatise (*Dazhuan*), which is considered one of the most important commentaries on the Trigrams, explains their origin thus:

> Of old, when Fu Xi ruled the world,
> He gazed upward and observed
> Images in the Heavens;
> He gazed about him and observed
> Patterns upon the Earth,
> He observed markings on birds and beasts,
> How they were adapted to different regions.
> Close at hand, he drew inspiration from within his own person;
> Further afield, he drew inspiration from the outside world.
> Thus he created the Eight Trigrams,
> He made Connection with the Power of Spirit Light,
> He distinguished the Myriad Things according to their Essential Nature.[12]

Figure 3.1 An image for the eight trigrams

Richard Wilhelm provides further explanation:

> These eight trigrams were conceived as images of all that happens in heaven
> and on earth. At the same time, they were held to be in a state of continual
> transition, one changing into another, just as transition from one phenom-
> enon to another is continually taking place in the physical world. Here we
> have the fundamental concept of the Book of Changes. The eight trigrams
> are symbols standing for changing transitional states; they are images that
> are constantly undergoing change.[13]

(2) King Wen (1171–1122 BC) and the Duke of Zhou (c. 1094 BC) developed
the '64 hexagrams' during the Zhou dynasty, providing projections and expla-
nations of human lives and events in the universe.

> In order to achieve a still greater multiplicity, these eight images were
> combined with one another at a very early date, whereby a total of sixty-
> four signs was obtained. Each of these sixty-four signs consists of six lines,
> either positive or negative. Each line is thought of as capable of change, and

whenever a line changes, there is a change also of the situation represented by the given hexagram.[14]

(3) Confucian disciples compiled *The Ten Wings* to elaborate the 64 hexagrams, and by 'fitting' *The Ten Wings* to the classic form, they hoped that the *I Ching* would take flight, enabling it to unravel the universe and provide harmony to mankind. It is generally held that the *I Ching* is a product of a continuous process of composition extended over the centuries and contributed to by more than the number of known sagacious writers.[15]

The Ten Wings elaborates the *I Ching* in the following way:

> Therefore in the system of Change there is the Great Ultimate [tai ji]. It generates the Two Modes (yin and yang). The Two Modes generate the Four Forms (the major and minor yin and yang). The Four Forms generate the Eight Trigrams. The Eight Trigrams determine good and evil fortunes. The good and evil fortunes produce the great business [of life].[16]

A Chinese philosopher of the Song dynasty (1017–1073), Zhou Dunyi, explains further:

> The Supreme Polarity[17] [tai ji] in activity generates yang; yet at the limit of activity it is still. In stillness it generates yin; yet at the limit of stillness it is also active. Activity and stillness alternate; each is the basis of the other. In distinguishing yin and yang, the Two Modes are thereby established. The alternation and combination of yang and yin generate water, fire, wood, metal, and earth . . . The Five Phases are simply yin and yang; yin and yang are simply the Supreme Polarity; the Supreme Polarity is fundamentally Non-polar.[18]

The *I Ching* suggests that everything begins from the *tai ji* (太极) [derived from *wu ji* (无极), meaning emptiness or nothing], which gives rise to *yin* and *yang*, which give birth in turn to everything else in the universe. The *tai ji* is composed of two Chinese characters, '太' and '极', meaning the origin of all things, for example the cradle of life and the source of civilisation. The first character '太' also consists of two parts: '大' denoting 'big' or 'large' and a point (under the '大') with a meaning of 'leading to'. The second character '极' indicates limit or maximum. Therefore *tai ji* implies movement towards the limit: 'on one side, the things that are infinitely small and on the other, the things that are so large that they are boundless'. Figure 3.2 is the legendary *tai ji* (*yin-yang*) symbol which appositely describes potential interplays and changes in the eternal contradictory pair.

The outer shape of the symbol is circular, with the following connotations:

(1) It covers everything in the universe.
(2) It constantly changes, with no beginning and no ending.
(3) It signifies that the change is smooth and has a regular pattern.

Figure 3.2 The *tai ji* (*yin-yang*) symbol

Inside the circle, the inverted *S* curve that divides *yang* (represented by the white half) and *yin* (symbolised by the dark half) denotes the potential conversion between *yin* and *yang* in flux, with the following implications: (1) everything contains two sides (*yin* and *yang*) which change together; (2) the two sides correlate inversely: increasing or strengthening one side results in a reduction or weakening in the other and vice versa; (3) the change or conversion takes place in a gradual manner, from triviality to significance to transformation; (4) existence or change on one side depends on the other side; (5) the conversion between the two sides takes place continually. There is no borderline between *yin* and *yang*, with a dot of *yin* 'residing' in the *yang* side as a seed for growth and vice versa, forming a perpetually contradictory and changing unity.

A story popular in China illustrates how *yin-yang* thinking may make Chinese people react, adapt or behave differently from their Western counterparts. The story goes that Bill Clinton, the 42nd president of the United States, Mikhail Gorbachev, the last leader of the Soviet Union and Deng Xiaoping, then the de facto leader of the Chinese government, were once travelling in their limousines when they came to a fork in the road with two signposts, reading 'Socialism' and 'Capitalism'. They had to decide which road to take. Without hesitation, Clinton chose 'Capitalism' and Gorbachev 'Socialism'. Deng Xiaoping, having reflected for a while, had the two signposts swapped over, then set off firmly down the road signposted 'Socialism'. This reflects his pragmatic *yin-yang* thinking.

The smallest particles identified by physicists to date are known as quarks, which combine to form hadrons such as protons and neutrons, the components of atomic nuclei. Notably, this follows the pattern whereby the *tai ji* (quarks) generates *yin* and *yang* (protons and neutrons), which give rise to everything else. On the other hand, it should be noted that '*tai ji*' denotes the smallest particles that have been found to date at any given time, including a future where something more fundamental than quarks may have been discovered. However, in the field of physics, the question remains whether it is ever possible to identify the smallest things in the universe.

The first Chinese character of the *I Ching* (易经), the '*I*' (易), has been afforded a threefold connotation since the Han dynasty (206 BC):[19] 'simple and easy,' 'changing' and 'constant'.[20] The second character, '*Ching*' (经) means 'classic'. Thus, the title of the *I Ching*, in addition to the meaning of 'Book of Changes', has another level of interpretation: it is the classic that gives birth to 'classics' in an ever-changing manner. The initial (ancient) form of the Chinese character '易' (*I*) is 𖤚 a combination of the Sun (*yang*) on the top and the Moon (*yin*) at the bottom, representing the *tai ji* (*yin-yang*) symbol, with all of the implications for *yin-yang* principles.

The *I Ching* has the connotation of being 'simple and easy' because any changes in nature and society, and any laws of nature and humanities, can be understood and explained by the 64 hexagrams and 384 lines.

At the very beginning, in antiquity, the *I Ching* was a collection of linear signs for divination, which was widely practised. The oldest form of practice was associated with the answers yes and no, forming the basis of the classic. "Yes" was denoted by a simple unbroken line (_____) and "No" by a broken line (__ __). When it came to a time when greater differentiation was required to deal with more situations, the single lines were permutated in pairs (see Figure 3.3).

For the same reason, a third line was further added to each of these combinations, giving birth to the eight trigrams, as shown in Figure 3.1.

> These eight trigrams were conceived as images of all that happens in heaven and on earth. At the same time, they were held to be in a state of continual transition, one changing into another, just as transition from one phenomenon to another is continually taking place in the physical world. . . . The eight trigrams are symbols standing for changing transitional states; they are images that are constantly undergoing change.[21]

With the further understanding of the natural world, to accommodate the greater explainability, these 8 trigrams were further combined to form a total of 64 signs by ancient sages. "Each of these sixty-four signs consists of six lines, either positive or negative. Each line is thought of as capable of change also of the situation represented by the given hexagram."[22] In Figure 3.4 you will find

Figure 3.3 Single lines permutated in pairs

Figure 3.4 The 64 hexagrams of the *I Ching*

41	42	43	44
Sun: Decrease	Yi: Increase	Guai: Break-through	Gou: Encounter
45	46	47	48
Cui: Gathering Together	Sheng: Ascent	Kun: Confinement	Jing: The Well
49	50	51	52
Ge: Revolution	Ding: The Cauldron	Zhen: Quake	Gen: Mountain
53	54	55	56
Jian: Gradual Progress	Gui Mei: The Marrying Maiden	Feng: Canopy/Abundance	Lu: The Wanderer
57	58	59	60
Xun: Wind/The Gentle	Dui: Lake/Joy	Huan: Dispersion	Jie: The Chaste/Limitation
61	62	63	64
Zhong Fu: The Discreet	Xiao Guo: Slight Excess	Ji Ji: Complete/Completion	Wei Ji: Hope/Incomplete

Figure 3.4 (Continued)

the 64 hexagrams and the permutations and combinations of 384 lines, including their symbols, names and attributes.

Taking for example the hexagram Kun, Earth, The Receptive:

Kun: Earth/The Receptive

It symbolises the nature of the earth, being strong in devotion; among the four seasons, it denotes late autumn, when all forces of life lie dormant. If the bottom line changes, it turns into the hexagram Fu, Return:

The latter stands for thunder, signifying the movement that stimulates anew in the earth at the time of dormancy, heralding the return of light.[23] A series of situations are symbolically expressed by lines; through the alternation of these lines, the situations can change from one into another.

The 64 hexagrams and their 384 lines represent all situations in the planet, involving the law of change and the images of the states of change. In addition to these changes, one has to consider the course of action appropriate to each situation. 'In every situation, there is a right and a wrong course of action. Obviously, the right course brings good fortune and the wrong course brings misfortune.'[24]

> The sixty-four hexagrams and their 384 lines constitute the entire structure of the universe, the complete list of daos. The structure has a normative value, so that if the combinations of lines or hexagrams are followed, we are obeying the structure of the world and will have good fortune. If we obey the lines, we are doing what is right; if we disobey them, we are pursuing immorality.[25]

Box 3.1 provides an example about how the *I Ching* can be applied to a business scenario, including changes of situation and appropriate (corresponding) courses of action.

Box 3.1   Inspirations of the *I Ching* for one's career development

The *I Ching* may be seen as an encyclopaedia for all things in the universe, providing interpretations and wisdom for all fields such as politics, the military, commerce, diplomacy and lifestyle. The following example shows how the *I Ching* may afford inspiration for one's career development. All yang or unbroken lines are known as 'nine', and yin or broken lines as 'six'. All lines are counted from the bottom up, namely, the lowest is taken as the first.

The first hexagram is known as 'Qian', which is a shorthand for heaven, symbolising yang energy and creativity. It consists of six unbroken lines (yang), standing for Beginning, Supreme Fortune, Profitable and Steadfast: The image[26]:

The movement of heaven is full of power.
Thus the superior man makes himself strong and untiring.[27]

This image suggests that a person should act and work like heaven, and 'must make himself strong in every way, by consciously casting out all that is inferior and degrading. Thus he attains that tirelessness which depends upon consciously limiting the fields of his activity.'[28]

The hexagram has six lines, and each has its unique interpretations and implications. In the following, the hexagram is applied to the strategic considerations for the process of one's career development:

The Lines

Nine at the beginning

Dragon lies hidden. Do not act.

'In China, the dragon has a meaning altogether different from that given it in the Western world. The dragon is a symbol of the electrically charged, dynamic, arousing force that manifests itself in the thunderstorm. In winter this energy withdraws into the earth; in the early summer it becomes active again, appearing in the sky as thunder and lightning. As a result, the creative forces on earth begin to stir again.'[29] At the beginning of one's career development, yang energy occupies a lowly place, so one should abide in that place, lying low, as one's time has not yet come. One should avoid being drawn into ill-conceived action. Thus, like a hidden dragon, 'Do not act.' Here is an example where such wisdom has been utilised to the letter:

A computer scientist with a doctorate from a US university applied for a job with a well-known IT company, declaring his impressive qualifications in his application, but the company considered him overqualified for the starting position available. On reflection, he decided to declare only his bachelor's degree when applying for work. This tactic quickly landed him a job, and he began to work as a computer programmer. Thanks to his outstanding performance, he was soon promoted to the position of departmental head. Not long after this, he led an R&D team which achieved a technological breakthrough, and he was subsequently appointed director of software development, making key decisions on behalf of the company. His success in this post led to further promotion to the rank of vice president, with stock options, as a result of which he became one of the company's key shareholders. Only then did he present his doctoral certificate to the founder. It had taken about two years for him to advance from programmer to one of the top positions in the company.[30]

Nine in the second place

Dragon is seen in the fields, it profits to see a Great Man

'With this Yang Line in Second Place . . . Dragon Energy becomes manifest; it begins to be openly deployed. Just as in the natural world plants grow and bear fruit, so this Line represents an emergence into the open.'[31] After a hidden period, one has accumulated energy and power, and thus should show one's strength at a suitable time with a plan to take a stride forward in one's career. However, one needs to take care to avoid stepping on others' toes or being seen as a threat to others, as one is in the 'fields', not yet high in the sky. It is helpful to seek assistance from someone influential or in a higher position.

Nine in the third place

> The True Gentleman is vigilant all day long. His mind is still beset with care at nightfall. Danger. No harm.

At this stage, armed with Tao and talent, one starts to exert some influence on one's environment. However, one should remain alert to danger at all times, avoiding complacency. Many great business leaders are well prepared for danger in times of peace.

Nine in the fourth place

> He leaps into the deep. No harm.

The deep is the Dragon's natural place of repose. 'Leaping into the deep at an opportune moment, the Dragon finds rest. In similar fashion, the Sage always stirs (into action) at an opportune moment. He calculates before advancing; he judges the moment, and thereby avoids Harm . . . Dragon bides his time. He may descend, but he may also leap upward toward heaven.'[32] One should identify any opportunity that emerges and grasp it, but remain prepared to retreat from any course of action that turns out to be inopportune.

Nine in the fifth place

> The Dragon flies in Heaven. It profits to see a Great Man.

After a period of preparation and accumulation from the previous steps, one is transformed and takes off. 'The soaring flight is free progress, effortless and unhampered. Steadfastness has become spontaneity. One day it just happens. The transition to sagehood is like the passage from Apprentice to Master, for aspiring musician, painter, or calligrapher. All the toil of practice is suddenly transformed into an astonishing facility.'[33] However, at this moment, the most important thing is to identify someone who is in a (high) position to help or support one.

Nine at the top

> The Dragon overreaches himself. There is regret.

'The previous Place (the Flying Dragon) is the highest point in the Hexagram. It is the most opportune moment . . . To overstep that moment is to go too far, to overreach oneself, with conse-quent regret.'[34] One should know one's limits and understand when to advance or retreat, what to gain or lose and what result to seek in life and death. In China, it is particularly important for one to avoid being seen as arrogant when one appears to be successful. In most cases, one should attribute one's success to the leadership of the organisation and to the support of one's colleagues, in order to pros-per in the organisation.

When all the lines are nines, it denotes:

> There appears a host of dragons without heads. This is auspicious.

When there are no heads among the Dragons, 'there is a democratic relationship between the Leader and the members of the group. The situ-ation is close to the Taoist concept of ruling with Non-action.'[35] Upon reaching a top position in an organisation, one should act in such a way that others do not feel one's existence, a situation known as 'no head among a host of dragons', signifying a practice that is in line with Taoist thinking.

Those who can go through the six steps smoothly can be said to have a perfect career cycle or path.

The development of computer programming, for instance, is in line with the ideas in the *I Ching*, which can be considered to have inspired the use of 0 and 1 (*yin* and *yang*) as the (simple) basis of computer language, giving rise to unlimited applications. A study has even found countries that have embraced *I Ching* tradition tend to have better innovation performance.[36]

As the *yin-yang* symbol in Figure 3.2 shows, *yin* always evolves into *yang* in a curvilinear manner, rather than linearly, as explained by the Chinese expecta-tion that

> the universe is in a state of flux and that objects, events, and states of being in the world are forever alternating between two extremes or opposites ... As a result, East Asians, in comparison with their Western counterparts, are more likely to expect phenomena to undergo a change from the status quo.[37]

The ancient Chinese sages who wrote the *I Ching* noted that amidst the chang-ing phenomena, there are those which remain constant, such as the fact that the sun always rises in the east and sets in the west, or the ordered succession of the four seasons, inspiring them to crystallise the constant principles or unchanging rules into the *I Ching*.

All Chinese philosophies share the same root, 'Dao' (in the West generally known as 'Tao'), which literally means 'way' ('of the world', or 'of life'), 'route' or 'path' and sometimes also denotes 'doctrine' or 'principle'; this applies, for instance, to Taoism, Confucianism and neo-Confucianism,[38] but each has its own outlook and emphasis.

Tao is a Chinese concept and a unique category of thinking, which deals with the very essence and nature of an issue or phenomenon. It has convoluted, intangible or ineffable implications. Tao is described by Lao Tzu as: 'Perfect action. True virtue. Supreme power. This is how Tao is revealed through those who follow it completely. . . . Tao gives all things life. Te[39] gives them fulfilment. Nature is what shapes them. Living is what brings them to completion.'[40]

As the law of nature, Tao is the source and foundation of all living things on the planet and thus the mother of success. This concept is shared by all ancient Chinese philosophies and thinkers.

> Confucians and Taoists alike recognized an ultimate, undefinable, universal reality that supported, contained, and unified all things that people observed and the events that they experienced.[41]
>
> . . . This was the Tao – the Way of the universe, the universal principle of all things, nature's essential order, or moral law.[42]

At the core of Tao is the notion that all things consist of contradictions or are a unity of opposites, such as large and small, beauty and ugliness, long and short, light and dark, strong and weak, victory and defeat. The term *yang*, literally meaning 'sunshine', generally denotes those elements that are active, hot, bright, masculine, dry, hard and so on, while *yin* refers to the opposite of sunshine and indicates those that are passive, cold, dark, feminine, wet, soft and so forth. Lao Tzu says:

> Tao gives life to the one. The one gives life to the two. The two give life to the three. The three give life to ten thousand things. All beings support yin and embrace yang and the interplay of these two forces fills the universe.[43]

The *yin* and *yang* form a contradictory but interrelated pair and work in tandem to produce all things in the universe. However, these contradictory pairs can potentially turn into their opposites; within the *yin*, there is the seed of the *yang*, while within the *yang*, there is the seed of the *yin*; and the *yin* reaching its apex tends to evolve into the *yang*, while the *yang* will likewise tend to evolve into the *yin*, forming the principal pattern of motion in the universe. Mott and Kim (2006) explain:

> Continuous change within Tao occurred in changeless patterns that revealed individual Tao to people who recognized them and directed their

actions and thoughts toward, into, and within the patterns. The ruler's Tao was ruling, inspiring, and indulgent benevolence. The people's Tao was following, loyalty, and filial piety. If the ruler ruled through Tao, people would obey through Tao.[44]

The nature of Tao dictates that it is associated with Chinese cosmology, ontology and other general worldviews, and thus can have an effect, directly and indirectly, on everything. This section discusses a few core ideas.

Firstly, Tao is concerned with the nature of a matter, phenomenon or issue. Those who understand it and follow it will become successful in achieving their objectives. As Tao is something that is both Named and Nameless or ineffable,[45] it requires wisdom for one to comprehend it, and the closer one gets to it, the better. For instance, to achieve the effectiveness of 'management', a business leader must understand its 'nature' in a particular situation or cultural context. Ultimately, management is to get a group of (other) people to do things in order to attain the organisational objectives. In the West, since analytical cognition dominates, viewing time as linear, performance is measured, evaluated and rewarded/penalised through individual-based, task-orientated, quantitative and financial indicators, so that by comparing with benchmarks, people are driven to attain their organisational goals. In contrast, in China, holism is the predominant cognitive mode, seeing time as circular; to get things done in an organisation, the key to realise organisational objectives is 'people management' whereby relationship or *guanxi* management, qualitative performance measurement, group-orientation and welfare concerns are utilised altogether to generate a more effective organisational result, although quantitative performance indicators are also used by most companies. For instance, in 2008, the global financial crisis led Alibaba's share to plummet, witnessing a downfall of two-thirds of its IPO price. David Wei, CEO of Alibaba.com, while expecting a great deal of pressure from Jack Ma, told others: 'Jack never picked up the phone or came to see me about the share price. Never once. He never talked about profit growth.'[46]

Secondly, Tao is associated with 'greatness'. Lao Tzu writes:

> From Tao comes all greatness – It makes Heaven great. It makes Earth great. It makes man great. Mankind depends on the laws of Earth. Earth depends on the laws of Heaven. Heaven depends on the laws of Tao. But Tao depends on itself alone. Supremely free, self-so, it rests on its own nature.[47]

The scope of one's vision determines the extent of one's potential achievements: a narrow vision makes one mediocre and a great vision is the prerequisite of achieving greatness. For instance, in his late 20s, Mao Zedong expressed his vision as being 'the transformation of China and the world'; thereafter, he worked tirelessly towards the realisation of this vision and in doing so transformed both himself and China, with a significant influence on the world.[48]

Jack Ma, the founder of Alibaba, one of the world's largest Internet companies, at the start-up of his business in 1999, articulated his ambition: 'We don't want to be number one in China. We want to be number one in the world.'[49] Having laid out his vision, which might be considered as having been 'delusional' at the time:

> Jack's ambition then, as it remains today, was breathtaking. He talked of building an Internet company that would last eighty years – a typical span of a human life. A few years later, he extended Alibaba's life expectancy to 'a hundred and two' years, so that the company would span three centuries from 1999. From the very beginning, he vowed to take on and topple the giants of Silicon Valley.[50]

Thirdly, Tao is that at which Chinese philosophy aims and which the philosophers of China hold to be the highest of all attributes of life: 'sageness within and kingliness without'. It is the highest moral standard commanded by a sage, and by attaining it, the sage plays a kingly role in society. Fung (1962) writes:

> His [the sage's] character is described as one of sageness in its essence and kingliness in its manifestation. That is to say that in his inner sageness he accomplishes spiritual cultivation, in his outward kingliness he functions in society. It is not necessary that a sage should be the actual head of the government in his society . . . Therefore, what philosophy discusses is what the philosophers of China describe as the Tao (Way) of 'sageness within and kingliness without.'[51]

This Tao is embraced by all Chinese philosophy, whatever the school of thought.[52] Tao (or Dao) and Te (or De), the latter of which means ethics, conscience or morality, are the two central concepts in Lao Tzu's *Tao Te Ching*.[53] 'Te' originates from Tao, follows Tao and exerts Tao's influences on human behaviour by setting moral standards. Confucianism shares the Taoist concepts of Tao and Te, and Confucian ethics also include the Five Constant Virtues (Ethics): human-heartedness, righteousness, the ritual-observing disposition, wisdom and reliability (trustworthiness),[54] which have modelled people's thinking and behaviour. Since Te is dictated and controlled by Tao, anything that goes against proper Te (ethical) standards is bound to be unviable and to founder. Lao Tzu writes:

> To give without seeking reward. To help without thinking it is virtuous – therein lies great virtue. To keep account of your actions. To help with the hope of gaining merit – therein lies no virtue. The highest virtue is to act without a sense of self. The highest kindness is to give without condition. The highest justice is to see without preference.[55]

Chinese wisdom has it that small victory depends on strength; medium victory on intelligence; great victory on Te; and complete victory on Tao, which is the combination of strength, intelligence and Te.

In a nutshell, 'The central *I Ching* concepts, Yin and Yang, the Tao, Good Faith, and Self-Cultivation, have preoccupied almost every Chinese thinker until the twentieth century.'[56] 'Indeed, not only the philosophy of China but its science and statecraft as well have never ceased to draw from the spring of wisdom in the *I Ching*.'[57]

Box 3.2 presents an example in which the strategic actions of Huawei have followed Tao, providing the company with great momentum with outstanding performance.

Box 3.2 The adoption of Tao in Huawei

Huawei, a latecomer to telecommunications, began with a modest technological base and resources but became a top player in the industry. Huawei's success is, to a great extent, attributable to the fact that its founder had a clear vision at the very beginning of the venture: 'Mr Ren's mission is to help China develop its own telecoms technology (Huawei means both "China can" and "splendid act").'[58]

Huawei, founded in 1987, made its ambitious vision known in 1994: 'In ten years the telecommunication equipment market will be divided into thirds, among Siemens, Alcatel and Huawei.'[59] In 1997 the company restated its vision: to become 'the world's first-class telecom enterprise'. In 2010, Huawei was the first Chinese private company to be ranked in the Global 500 list, in 397th place, climbing to 129th in 2016.

In the West, any company reaching a size or scale comparable to that of Huawei would generate numerous millionaires and billionaires. In particular, the founder would generally be in the world's richest list. It may come as a surprise to many Westerners to know that Ren Zhengfei, the founder of Huawei, holds only 1.42 per cent of Huawei shares, while the remaining 98.58 per cent are owned by about 70,000 Huawei employees. This is a uniquely Chinese phenomenon, unprecedented in world business history. Ren Zhengfei explains his decision thus:

> I did everything initially in Huawei, but why should I divide the shares among the other employees? Huawei is a high-tech company, which needs more talented and ambitious people to join, to work together for better or for worse. We in the older generation of pioneers and senior managers should think of sacrifice and dilute our share in order to encourage and inspire more people to join Huawei.[60]

This action reflects Ren's Tao: sacrifice, enthusiasm, self-discipline, unselfishness and endurance. By adopting this shareholding structure, Ren intended to inspire a spirit of assiduousness, teamwork and zeal within Huawei. This reflects the Confucian doctrine of leading by benevolence (as a role model).

Huawei has followed Tao, with an understanding of what determines the success or failure of firms in high-tech industry. In the early 2000s, Huawei's technology was not as advanced as that of its competitors such as Cisco and Alcatel-Lucent. However, it mastered the fundamentals of competitiveness in the industry, leading to its winning strategy. In high-tech industries, those with a command of the core technology can be said to be qualified to compete in the market, whereas the ability to remain in the market in the long term depends on a firm's stamina or sustainability, which is not dependent entirely on the level of advance in core technology, but on a combination of (optimal or good enough) core technology and (low) cost. Huawei has outdone many of its strong competitors in international markets because of its advantage in this combination; in other words, in stamina.[61]

Confucianism and Chinese culture

Contributors to Confucianism

Confucius

Confucius (孔子) was born in the city of Qufu in Shandong Province (then the state of Lu) during the Spring and Autumn period, in 551 BC; he died in 479 BC at the age of 72. Regarded as a great Chinese philosopher, educationist and thinker, he is known as the Sage and model teacher for all ages in China. He was actually named Kong Qiu (孔丘), but respectfully referred to as Kong Zi (孔子), meaning 'Master Kong', or Kong Fuzi (*Fuzi* meant 'teacher' in ancient China). 'Confucius' is a Latinised form of 'Kong Fuzi'. Although there had been a number of private schools before he established his college in China, it was he who was responsible for the great flowering of private education. He devoted most of his adult life to education and to the collection and collation of cultural classics. As the most highly regarded professional teacher, he had over 3000 disciples, among whom 72 were considered highly accomplished wise men.[62] At the age of 63, Confucius, who was hardworking, optimistic, kind and modest, travelled with his disciples around eight states to promote his ideas to their rulers.[63]

Before and during the Spring and Autumn period, the Chinese term '*ru*' (儒) was used to denote a profession whose members 'helped with expert advice on the rituals and regularly gave teaching on them. They had a practical knowledge of these matters, including the forms of the traditional music, as dealt with in certain accepted handbooks.'[64] Therefore, Confucianism can be interpreted as having founded a school of *ru* philosophy which is based on the teachings of Confucius and his followers. Confucius said: 'I transmit but do not innovate; I am truthful in what I say and devoted to antiquity.'[65] 'This is what the ordinary ju [ru] had all along been doing, but Confucius in speaking thus really meant that by transmitting he created. Because he created by transmitting, he was not merely an ordinary Ju, but the creator of a Ju philosophy.'[66] Confucianism is not a religion, but a set of political, social, philosophical and moral doctrines. It consists of the teachings and writings of Confucius, Mencius and a number of other followers. To honour the great teacher, his disciples compiled his teachings into a highly influential book, *The Analects of Confucius.*

> This book does not provide carefully organized or argued philosophical discourses, and the sayings seem to have been haphazardly arranged. Yet this short text became a sacred book, memorized by beginning students and known to all educated people. As such it influenced the values and habits of thought of the Chinese for centuries.[67]
>
> If we were to characterize in one word the Chinese way of life for the last two thousand years, the word would be 'Confucian'. No other individual in Chinese history has so deeply influenced the life and thought of his people, as a transmitter, teacher, and creative interpreter of the ancient culture and literature, and as a molder of the Chinese mind and character.[68]

Confucianism is thus a dominant element of Chinese culture. Confucius 'exerted a profound influence on the development of Chinese culture through his teachings.'[69] His impact has been felt on almost every facet of life in Chinese society, whether political, commercial, educational, religious or social, as well as spreading to other Asian countries, particularly Japan, Korea and Vietnam.[70] The East Asian mind-set is still dominated by Confucian paradigms.[71]

Confucianism has been one of the key factors in the uninterrupted survival of Chinese civilisation over the past 2000 years. The Qin dynasty first unified China under the influence of Confucianism but later adopted an anti-Confucian policy, prosecuting Confucian scholars and burning their books, which resulted in the premature demise of this great empire. From the Han dynasty onwards, Confucianism was made the dominant social and political thinking in China; knowledge of Confucian classics became compulsory for entry to the imperial bureaucracy and thus a unifying influence on thinking and behaviour, particularly among the Chinese literati. The nature of Confucianism, promoting social harmony, modesty, self-discipline, strong family ties and non-aggression, helped China to refrain from aggressive overseas expansion and to maintain a stable society.

Other interpreters of Confucianism

One of the major interpreters and followers of Confucianism, whose actual name was Meng Ke (孟轲), was given the respectful name of Meng Zi (孟子), Latinised as Mencius. Because of his major contribution to Confucianism, he earned the appellation of 'The Lesser or Second Sage' (after Confucius). He lived from 372 to 289 BC and is the author of one of the Four Books, *The Mencius* (孟子), the other three being *The Great Learning* (大学), *The Doctrine of the Mean* (中庸) and *The Analects of Confucius* (论语). These Four Books and the Five Classics comprise the kernel of orthodox Confucianism and were at the core of the official curriculum for imperial examinations in later dynasties. 'While Confucius laid the solid groundwork for Confucianism, Mencius clearly defined the principles, penetrated into their meanings more profoundly, and built a more comprehensive system.'[72] Notably, he is the only Chinese historical figure other than Confucius whose name was Latinised.

The fact that Confucianism has stood out against all other schools of thought and become the dominant thinking in Chinese history is inextricably associated with Dong Zhongshu, a thinker and philosopher, who brought Confucianism to the distinct position that it has occupied in China for over two millennia. 'Credit for the political success of Confucianism belongs in large part to thinkers like Dong Zhongshu (ca. 179–104 BC) who developed Confucianism in ways that legitimated the new imperial state and elevated the role of emperor.'[73] It was Dong who persuaded Emperor Wu of Han to pay supreme tribute to Confucianism while banning all other schools of thought.

> He [Dong] joined Confucian ideas of human virtual and social order to notions of the workings of the cosmos in terms of *Yin* and *Yang* and the Five Agents (wood, metal, fire, water, and earth). Man still has a very major role in his cosmic scheme, and the ruler has a unique position because he can link the realms of Heaven, earth, and man through his actions.[74]

Dong Zhongshu also developed the theory that man is an integral part of nature. He put forward the notion that Heaven has given rise to everything on earth, using this to provide strong support for national unity. The emperor was the Son of Heaven, assigned by Heaven to govern the nation. Society and human thought should therefore be unified under the emperor as intermediary with Heaven. Dong believed that it would be difficult for the populace to understand the notion of Heaven, but that Confucianism would enable its followers to understand and express what Heaven meant. His thought was conveyed in one of his most important books, entitled *Luxuriant Dew of the Spring and Autumn Annals*, which suggested that Confucius understood the interaction between Heaven and man, and was thus in a position to interpret portents and omens from Heaven.[75]

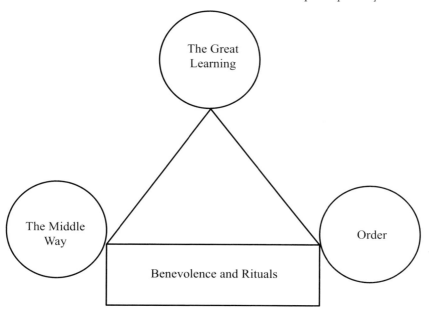

Figure 3.5 Core components of Confucianism

The core components of Confucianism

Figure 3.5 displays the structure of Confucian core components, whereby *ren* and *li* are the cornerstones of Confucianism, while the Middle Way, the Great Learning and Confucian hierarchical relationships are the core components. These are explained as follows.

Ren *and* Li: *cornerstones of Confucianism*

The widespread and profound influence of Confucianism in China and elsewhere is derived from its social, ethical and political aspects, which consist of a number of interrelated concepts and doctrines, such as *ren* and *li*. *Ren* (仁), literally meaning 'benevolence', 'goodness' or 'humanity', lies at the heart of Confucianism and is concerned with the development of an individual's moral standards. The attainment of *ren* is the ultimate goal of the ideals and ambitions of worthy individuals. When asked what *ren* meant, Confucius replied: 'Love your fellow man.'[76] To Confucians, societal stability and development depend on the morality of individuals. 'Benevolence is more vital to the common people than even fire and water.'[77] Thus, every individual should strive to be a benevolent person.

How can one become benevolent? Confucius believed that the root of benevolence was to be good as a son and obedient as a young man. Five qualities are associated with benevolence: 'respectfulness, tolerance, trustworthiness in word, quickness and generosity'.[78] In addition, 'Unbending strength, resoluteness, simplicity and reticence are close to benevolence.'[79] For Confucius, the golden rule is: 'Do not do to others what you would not wish to be done to yourself.'[80]

Confucius was the first to extend the concept of *ren* to government and put forward the political idea of 'benevolent government' (仁政), which is one of the pillars of Confucianism. Confucians believe that a ruler should exercise government by means of his virtue; Confucius explains: 'The rule of virtue can be compared to the Pole Star which commands the homage of the multitude of stars without leaving its place.'[81] When the ruler applies such a benevolent approach to government, the common people will follow him and society will be in order and harmony. Confucians believe that the fundamental aim of a benevolent government is to make people affluent. Only by doing so can the ruler win support and maintain power.

The measures for pursuing benevolent government stress exemplification and education, rather than the use of law and force. It was a Confucian belief that the people would follow and emulate an exemplary ruler but would disobey the laws if the ruler was himself not benevolent or principled. Confucius said:

> Guide them by edicts, keep them in line with punishments, and the common people will stay out of trouble but will have no sense of shame. Guide them by virtue, keep them in line with the rites, and they will, besides having a sense of shame, reform themselves.[82]

Confucius repeatedly emphasised the role of exemplification in benevolent government:

> To govern is to correct. If you set an example by being correct, who would dare to remain incorrect?[83] . . . If a man is correct in his own person, then there will be obedience without orders being given; but if he is not correct in his own person, there will not be obedience even though orders are given.[84]

Thus, to exercise benevolent government, those with virtues should be recruited. A ruler should cultivate himself, pacify the people and set an example by his own conduct.

The concept of *li* (礼), meaning 'rites of propriety' or 'proper conduct', is another pillar of Confucian political, ethical and social thought. Ritual systems in the previous Zhou dynasty had played a special part in educating the people, regulating their words and deeds and consolidating and maintaining social order and stability. Having seen the abuse and breakdown of the rules of propriety in his time, Confucius endeavoured to revive the Zhou ritual systems. The Confucian *li* is not only the rites and ceremonies of social life but also a political and legal system and a set of moral norms. Confucius said: 'If a man is able to govern a state by observing rites and showing deference, what difficulties will he have in public life? If he is unable to govern a state by observing ritual and showing deference, what good are the rites to him?'[85] As can be seen, to Confucius, a fundamental role of *li* is concerned with government. It was an ethical rule (*li*), rather than law, that maintained and enforced the standards of morality and human behaviour in ancient China.[86] *Li* demonstrated and defined each person's hierarchical position and proper conduct through proper rites and ceremonies, thus reflecting an unequal and hierarchical social structure. It was a means to maintain social control. Thus, people should be educated to be benevolent and ethical, and the Confucian *li* should be used to regulate people's behaviour, as Confucius proposed:

> To return to the observance of the rites through overcoming the self constitutes benevolence. If for a single day a man could return to the observance of the rites through overcoming himself, then the whole Empire would consider benevolence to be his . . . Do not look unless it is in accordance with the rites; do not listen unless it is in accordance with the rites; do not speak unless it is in accordance with the rites; do not move unless it is in accordance with the rites.[87]

These words suggest that *li* affects or constrains people's vision, speech and actions. One should do something only if it conforms to *li*. Confucius said: 'Unless a man has the spirit of the rites, in being respectful he will wear himself out, in being careful he will become timid, in having courage he will become unruly, and in being forthright he will become intolerant.'[88] Therefore, without the constraint of *li* on their behaviour, people might be perceived as impolite, immoral or uncivilised, and societal harmony would be damaged.

The Confucian notions of *ren* and *li* are inextricably interrelated. *Ren* is the internal moral basis for the performance of *li*, whilst *li* is the external manifestation of *ren*. Without *li*, *ren* would be empty verbiage. In other words, to be benevolent or loving towards others, one must follow *li*, which is not a universal love or benevolence but a hierarchical phenomenon, with differences of priority, of favour and disfavour and of class. For instance, love for immediate family members and men of eminence should come before love for those of lowly origin or social status and for more distant blood relations. If one loved the latter group in the same way and with the same passion as the former, it would not fit with *li* and it would not be *ren*. A person with *ren* would always follow *li*, doing what is right for his social role, and so become *junzi* (son of a ruler), by which Confucius meant a person of moral worth, an ideal gentlemen or a superior man. All people should be exhorted to become *junzi* and avoid its opposite, '*xiaoren*', meaning 'small/petty person' or 'inferior man'. Confucius said: 'The gentleman understands what is moral. The small man understands what is prof-itable.'[89] He believed that profit was a source of temptation to do wrong.

> The pursuit of profit did not coincide, but more often directly conflicted with the dictates of virtue; it was the concern only of the small and unen-lightened mind. The gentleman, mindless of comfort and safety, must fix his attention upon higher things.[90]

These Confucian ethical and political precepts have exerted a great influence on Chinese society – ethically, socially, culturally, politically and economically – and played a central part in maintaining societal harmony and stability since the West Han dynasty (206 BC – AD 25). They have moulded the thought of the Chinese people, for instance, to be benevolent, pious towards their parents and loyal to the country, as a Chinese Confucian motto exhorts: 'Everyone has responsibility for the rise and fall of his/her country.'

The pursuit of virtuous individual morality and benevolent government is at the hub of Confucianism. Confucians have emphasised benevolent government by practising virtues, regulating behaviour through *li* and relying on relation-ships to secure trust, while downplaying legal functions or law enforcement. Therefore, for over two millennia China has been under the rule of man, rather than the rule of law, while its rulers have used law mainly as a tool of power, instead of governing to maintain fairness, equity and justice, with the social consequence that the legal consciousness of the Chinese people has been rather weak.

In China, management by example is important, and the selection and pro-motion of both government officials and enterprise managers tend to empha-sise 'morality', mostly manifested by uprightness, sincerity, unselfishness and loyalty, among other factors. This tends to encourage managers to pay attention to their moral behaviour. In management, harsh, strict and penal approaches are de-emphasised, while lenient, empathic and gentle methods are preferred. A person's loyalty to his or her superiors, for instance, is often more important in deciding matters of promotion than his or her capability.

Order

The Chinese character structure of *ren* (仁) consists of two elements: 'man' plus two, suggesting the relationship between people, with the meaning of benevo-lence, humanity or goodness. The earliest form of the character was written as | 二, denoting *yin yang*: the vertical line represents *yang*, symbolising man, sun and odd numbers and the two horizontal lines *yin*, standing for female, moon and even numbers. Therefore, 仁 implies that it is the seed and root of everything.

Confucius believed that human beings are innately humane; in any society there are five cardinal relationships: father-son, ruler-subject, brother-brother, husband-wife and friend-friend. These relationships are bound by certain moral

Table 3.1 The five basic relationships and corresponding virtues of Confucianism

Five Basic Relationships	Appropriate Virtues
Father–son	Filial piety
Ruler–subject	Loyalty
Brother–brother	Brotherliness
Husband–wife	Love and obedience
Friend–friend	Faithfulness

standards or virtues, listed in Table 3.1. These relationships are by nature of a superior-subordinate, hierarchical type, and family relationships account for a great deal in Confucianism. The concept of *li* underlies the five relationships.

> *Li* are necessary for the maintenance of roles and statuses within the Confucian hierarchical order. They dictate right behavior and decorum within relationships and guide relationships such as the ones between children and parents, subject and ruler, and prince and minister. *Li* serve to mark out differentiated roles; they support and uphold these hierarchies: actions were considered appropriate or inappropriate according to one's status in a particular relationship.[91]

To Confucius, social harmony and stability are built on a structured society, whereby the ruler is benevolent and the subjects are loyal; a father loves his son and his son is reverent to his father; a husband is kind to his wife and his wife is obedient; an elder brother is gentle to his younger ones and the younger are respectful of their elder brother; and two friends are careful for and respectful of each other. These relationships dictate that each individual should recognise his or her social role and act appropriately according to the prescribed propriety and 'music'; as Confucius puts it: 'Let the ruler be a ruler and the subject a subject. Let the father be a father and the son a son.'[92] If everyone performs his or her duties, then society will be in complete order and harmony. It is notable that these relationships are reciprocal; that is, not only has the son an obligation to the father and the subject to the ruler, but the father is also obligated to be a proper father and the ruler a proper ruler.[93]

The Middle Way

A *YANG* PERSPECTIVE: THE GOLD STANDARD OF BEHAVIOUR

Zhong yong (中庸), meaning 'the Doctrine of the Mean' or 'the Middle Way', represents the third generation of the Confucian School.[94] It is an important concept and method in Confucianism, occupying a pivotal place in Chinese culture. If the Confucian *ren* is content and *li* is form, then the Middle Way is the method of achieving the unity of content and form, making it a crucial component of Confucianism. Zi Si, Confucius's grandson and follower, compiled a book, *Zhong Yong (The Middle Way* or *The Doctrine of the Mean)*, which has become one of the four Confucian classics and has had a far-reaching influence on the Chinese people since the Song dynasty. Confucius said: 'Supreme indeed is the mean as a moral virtue. It has been rare among the common people for quite a long time.'[95] Thus, the Middle Way is held to be the highest standard of moral virtue and therefore difficult to reach.

The term *zhong yong* comprises two Chinese characters, *zhong* (中), meaning 'middle' or 'centrality', and *yong* (庸), which denotes 'utilisation' or 'commonplace'; together, they suggest the fundamental Confucian ideas of balance, moderation and appropriateness, or simply the middle way. To Confucians, going too far is as bad as not going far enough. The Middle Way is the yardstick of behaviour in social and political life and an effective means of balancing conflicting social relationships. In essence, it advises people that there is a proper 'degree' in social behaviour and affairs, and that one should avoid the extremes of either deficiency or excess. The ancient emperors considered the Middle Way the best way to rule the country and to maintain the balance and harmony of society.

Confucius offers the following views on how to be a man of the Middle Way: 'A gentleman agrees with others without being an echo. The small man echoes without being in agreement.'[96] That is, all worthy men pursue harmony by allowing differences to exist, while small-minded people always want conformity without harmony. 'The gentleman is at ease without being arrogant; the small man is arrogant without being at ease.'[97] 'The gentleman is conscious of his own superiority without being contentious, and comes together with other gentlemen without forming cliques.'[98] He is 'devoted to principle but not inflexible in small matters'.[99] Finally, the worthy man is 'generous without its costing him anything, works others hard without their complaining, has desires without being greedy, is casual without being arrogant, and is awe-inspiring without appearing fierce.'[100] All of these maxims express the ideas of harmony, balance and appropriateness or the proper degree. The adoption of the Middle Way in dealing with social and political life is intended to avoid or reduce tension and conflict; it often combines firmness with flexibility, justice with mercy and leniency with severity. It can never be overstated that the Chinese way of life, whether social, political or personal, has been profoundly influenced by this mentality for over two millennia.

Historically, it is the Confucian *ren* and the concept of the Middle Way which have restrained China from engaging in aggressive wars against other countries. *Ren* requires people to be benevolent and righteous towards others, doing everything with justification or for the right reason; as a Chinese saying warns: 'Those who commit unrighteous acts bring ruin on themselves.' The Middle Way thinking means avoiding trouble wherever possible and adopting the general principle that one will not attack unless attacked. This has prevented China from being mired in prolonged warfare and has preserved her from ruin over the past two millennia.

Wu Qingyuan (1914–2014), also known as Go Seigen in Japan, was a Chinese-born Japanese grandmaster of the board game of *wei qi* or Go. He dominated the professional game for over 25 years, gaining a reputation as the greatest Go player of the twentieth century. His supreme skill and performance in Go are attributable to his 'Middle Way' philosophy. In his biography, entitled *The Spirit of the Middle Target*, he elucidates his guiding philosophy: *liuhe* or the Unity of Six Dimensions (East, South, West, North, Heaven and Earth), which he claims to be the '*wei qi* of the twenty-first century'. He believed that the *wei qi* board represents the universe and that its centre, *tianyuan* in Chinese, corresponds to *tai ji* in the *I Ching*. From the empty universe (the board), the one (one piece) gives birth to two; the two give birth to the three, which give rise to everything. The *yin-yang* balance is the ultimate goal; therefore the ultimate aim of competition or combat in any game should be the achievement of the Middle Target, balancing forces in all directions.[101] It was by applying this philosophy that Wu Qingyuan remained the world's best *wei qi* player for 25 years.

The Chinese multinational company Huawei has attained steady and rapid growth by embracing the Middle Way in its strategic actions, as discussed in Box 3.3.

Box 3.3   Huawei: embracing the Middle Way

In the West, the pursuit of innovation is often a matter of policy, being greatly encouraged and advocated within blue-chip companies. Huawei's founder, Ren Zhengfei, has adopted a Middle Way approach to innovation, as he explains:

> Some Western telecom companies generate the world's most rapid innovation; they can do so because they 'have beef'. Since Huawei 'eats grass', it cannot catch up with these Western innovators. However, some Western companies are too aggressive and run so fast that they exceed the bounds of safety and therefore cannot help but fall off the cliff. Because Huawei does not run so fast, when one of its 'legs' is about to trip, it is able to regain its balance and pull itself back.[102]

Research by Huawei has shown that companies which over-innovate and run too far ahead of what the market will accept suffer as much as those that are not innovative enough. Two cases in point are the Japanese companies Fujitsu and NEC. During the period of the analogue phone, their technological supremacy granted them an absolute advantage over their competitors, but when the digital phone began to dominate, they slowed down in their innovation and were surpassed by Lucent, Siemens and Alcatel. To turn the situation around, Fujitsu and NEC launched a model that was technically far in advance of most other digital phones on the market. However, because their technology was too far ahead of what customers then wanted, they were forced to exit the market altogether. Therefore, Huawei's innovation strategy has been that it strives to be just 'half a step' better than its competitors.[103]

In the West, firms generally have an explicit written strategy that establishes direction and objectives, as well as specifying the means to achieve these objectives. A company with strong technological capabilities such as Google or Apple can sail ahead like a great ocean liner that follows a clear direction set by the captain. By contrast, Huawei, which Ren sees as a medium-sized ship, sails under a different guidance system from that in the West, based on the founder's 'greyscale theory' (or simply the Middle Way principle). In his view, the business environment changes so fast that it is difficult to discern the ideal future direction for the company. Therefore, he explains:

> the best way to go forward would be that internally, we strive for unity and externally, we seek cooperation, so that together we will identify the future direction . . . Twenty years ago, we turned many of our friends into enemies; twenty years later, we want to turn our enemies into friends.[104]

In Ren's view, based on the *yin-yang* principles, the rise and fall of an organisation originate from the same source with reciprocal causation. In the information society, on one side, there is the 'boundless unknown'; on the other is the 'changing boundless unknown'. Business leaders should confront the challenging situation, explore and analyse the unknown, then approach the 'truth' (the direction), in an endlessly repeating process.[105]

Ren Zhengfei believes that the personalities of human beings are greyscale by nature, so viewing them as either white or black is misleading. Leading people to a correct direction requires the adoption of the greyscale perspective, with compromise and forgiving. Chinese people tend to go to extremes, whether in public or private organisations. It is easy to go to either white or black, but it is very difficult to blend the two. Based on the greyscale principle, Huawei respects individuals but emphasises teamwork; it never goes to extremes in its management or organisation.[106]

When Ren Zhengfei was asked what had made Huawei successful, he responded with a three-point summary: 'openness', 'compromise' and 'greyscale'. These have led to the development of Huawei from nothing into existence, from the small to the large and from the weak to the strong. 'Openness' means that Huawei strives to learn from other companies and upgrade its goals continuously. An important quality of a leader is the setting of direction and pace for organisational development, while the achievement of balance between direction and the pace of growth is the art of leadership, and the key to the proper balance is to learn to attain compromise and greyscale. The process of realising harmony is known as 'compromise' and the outcome of harmony is 'greyscale.' For instance, young employees of Huawei tend to work arduously, approaching tasks with aggressiveness and full energy, but do not understand how to compromise, often resulting in the opposite to the desired effect.[107]

Ren Zhengfei firmly believes that the company's success is ultimately attributable to the practice of 'the Middle Way'.[108]

The Middle Way, however, like other aspects of Confucian thought, is a double-edged sword in terms of its impact on contemporary Chinese society and economy, as it can be difficult to manage or attain. Having brought a great deal of good and harmony to society, the Middle Way, which has probably deviated from what Confucians intended, has also given rise to undesirable consequences, just as any good medicine tends to have some side effects. On the positive side, when the late paramount leader, Deng Xiaoping, launched economic reform and implemented a policy of common prosperity ('let everybody get rich') in the 1980s, it was a reflection of the Middle Way. The policy of the previous Chinese government, led by President Hu Jintao, was 'the creation of a harmonious society', an expression of the same ethos. The present economic system in China, a mixture of the invisible and visible hands (the market and state), is an attempt to balance the advantages and disadvantages of both mechanisms, a middle way between them.

In the business field, a confrontational approach or direct competition between firms would normally be avoided; a Chinese saying indicates that 'amiability begets riches'. This is why in negotiations, when the Chinese party disagrees with a foreign partner's proposal, he or she hardly ever says 'no'. Instead, the Chinese party would say, for instance, 'Let us think about it,' 'Let us go back and have a discussion about it' or simply 'Let us study it further.' In addition, within organisational management, emphasis is placed on a spirit of teamwork, while an approach based on individual brilliance is normally discouraged. The maximisation of profit, which is a common goal for most Western businesses, would not be widely embraced by Chinese enterprises. A certain degree of profitability would generally satisfy most Chinese business managers, following the Chinese maxim: 'Leave while the going's good.'

The Middle Way, in discouraging the extremes of deficiency and excess, is reminiscent of the normal (Gaussian) distribution in statistics, where the behaviour of the majority falls into the middle range, while small numbers are distributed at the two ends of the scale. Therefore, it tends at a cultural level to clash strongly with those who are aggressive, innovative, heroic or oriented towards winning (on the excess side), and this tends to result in a negative Confucian effect. Some of these ideas have been expressed and recorded in the form of sayings and fables in Chinese literature and dictionaries. Examples include: 'The outstanding usually bear the brunt of an attack'; 'Fame portends trouble for men just as fattening does for pigs'; 'A tall tree catches the wind'; 'The rafter that juts out rots first'; and 'Contentment is happiness.' Competitive or innovative people may be criticised for 'careerism' or 'showing off'. Becoming a winner, a hero or an innovator can often provoke a response of malevolence and resentment.

Historically, the Middle Way has been largely responsible for the conservative nature of Chinese culture and government policies. Until the early period of the Ming dynasty, China had remained well ahead of the rest of the world in terms of government administration and economic and technological development, particularly in iron and steel making, printing, gunpowder, the magnetic compass, irrigation, canals and shipbuilding. At that time, Chinese junks were comparable to later Spanish galleons, and the fleet led by Zheng He was unparalleled in the world. However, in 1433, the government issued an imperial edict banning maritime trade and the construction of seagoing ships, so that existing large ships were left to rot. One of the major reasons for this decline was

> the sheer conservatism of the Confucian bureaucracy – a conservatism heightened in the Ming period by resentment at the changes earlier forced upon them by the Mongols. In this 'restoration' atmosphere, the all-important officialdom was concerned to preserve and recapture the past, not to create a brighter future based upon overseas expansion and commerce.[109]

The Great Learning: a model of Chinese management

Representing the second generation of the Confucian School,[110] *The Great Learning*, one of the Confucian Four Books, was compiled by an accomplished disciple of Confucius, Zeng Shen (505 BC – 432 BC), also a philosopher honorifically known as Zeng Zi or 'Master Zeng', around 2500 years ago. Initially, it was Chapter 42 of the *Book of the Rites*, one of the Five Classics, and was first extracted from the classic by Neo-Confucianists Cheng Hao and Cheng Yi to become a separate treatise during the Northern Song period (960–1126). It was Zhu Xi, another Neo-Confucian scholar during the Southern Song period, who made it one of the Four Books. With its insightful, inspirational and practical guidelines, it has exerted profound influence on Chinese society and behaviour, providing a framework for people to pursue or plan their career paths, with implications for the government of enterprise and state, as well as the understanding and interpretation of Chinese political, administrative and organisational structures.

The book was originally intended to be a guidebook for princes, nobles and officials to pursue 'sageness within and kingliness without', the highest moral standard or ideology in antiquity, providing a systematic methodology and procedures to achieve it. One and a half millennia later, its principles and procedures made it possible for lower-class people to change their lives and become members of a higher class or elite by following the path laid out in the book.

As a 'bible' for nobles and princes to pursue their political careers in antiquity, it outlines the path for one to become an 'ethical' or 'perfect' person, leading to one's success in government or society. The core ideas or ethical goals include 'manifesting the lucid virtue', 'becoming close to the people' and 'abiding in the highest good'. To achieve these, one should carry out research on the nature of the humanities, attaining perfect knowledge. With perfect knowledge, one is able to realise sincerity. With sincerity, one is able to put right one's mind, to become an ethical or moral person and thus to apply self-cultivation. Once one is cultivated, the family becomes harmonious. With the family in harmony, the state can be governed appropriately. If all of these goals are accomplished, peace will come about on earth.

Based on the principles and procedures laid out in *The Great Learning*, the starting point is self-cultivation, which is required to be pursued by everyone, including the ruler and the entire populace. If everybody is cultivated with a proper ethical mind, social order and harmony can be brought into families and then the state, resulting in peace and prosperity on earth. In China, the governance of a state is seen as similar to the governance of a family; in Chinese, the state is known as a 'state family'. With a superior moral mind, one can take an objective view of another person without bias or prejudice. For instance, within a family, parental love may blind the parents to the faults of their children, making them overindulgent. Similarly, if one dislikes someone, one may not (be willing to) see the merits that the person may have, while if one likes someone, one may overlook or fail to recognise that person's weaknesses or shortcomings. Thus, only with properly cultivated minds can families be harmonious and the state operate smoothly, with resultant peace under heaven.

A key question arises: How can individuals cultivate themselves? Based on what criteria should they do it? The 'bible' for self-cultivation is the *Analects* of Confucius. The prime minister of Northern Song, Zhao Pu, once famously made a comment on the *Analects*: 'One can govern all under Heaven with just one half of the *Analects*.'[111] This classic contains the essence of Confucianism, with teachings on how to learn to behave and do things, achieving the Tao of attaining to the sublime and performing the common task. With the knowledge of the *Analects*, can one understand 'benevolence', 'righteousness', 'propriety', 'wisdom' and 'sincerity' as the fundamental values of Chinese tradition, becoming a truly 'self-cultivated' person.

Implicitly or explicitly, relationships from individual self-cultivation to family harmony, the effective governance of the state and peace on earth have become a model of practice in China. However, this is a notably idealistic model, in that few individuals really achieve a high moral standard, while most simply follow mechanically the chain of individual – family – friends – state. As a result, Chinese organisations are seen to be run by (different levels or groups of) individuals (top and middle managers), while middle managers or employees tend to be loyal to individuals, rather than to organisations. If a senior executive or manager leaves a company, those who are loyal to him or her may leave with him or her.

Behind most successful Chinese businesses, there is generally a 'ruler' (a strong leader) who makes all the strategic decisions or acts with absolute authority within the organisation. Those who are able to sustain their development tend to be those whose leaders are visionary, insightful, open-minded and decisive. To name a few, each of the following successful Chinese companies has one person as the founder or leader behind its success: Haier – Zhang Ruimin, Huawei – Ren Zhengfei, Alibaba – Ma Yun, Tencent – Ma Huateng, JD.com – Liu Qiangdong, TCL – Li Dongsheng, Wanxiang Group Corporation – Lu Guanqiu, Mengniu – Niu Gensheng, Galanz – Liang Qingde and Lenovo – Liu Chuanzhi.

This model has the following managerial implications:

(1) The model reflects a philosophy that has a market/customer orientation. The goals of 'becoming close to the people' and 'achieving a high standard of goodness' are in line with a market-oriented philosophy. If the key individual (founder or CEO) embraces the philosophy of 'becoming close and kind to customers', the organisation will have a solid grounding for the attainment of market orientation. For instance, two Chinese multinational companies, Haier and Huawei, have developed rapidly and joined the Global 500 within a short period of time. At early stages of their development, neither company had adequate resources or technological capabilities, but they fully committed themselves to the pursuit of market or customer orientation, working closely with customers and meeting their needs and requirements with fast responses. They have been able to successfully implement this orientation because the key individuals embraced the market/customer philosophy. The 2014 China Innovation Survey carried out by PwC indicates that 'responsiveness to *customers* has become embedded in Chinese firms' capabilities.'[112] McKinsey Global Institute also finds that Chinese companies perform better in consumer-focused innovation than engineering- and science-based innovation.[113]

Many Western companies have adopted a market orientation because their senior executives have become aware of this philosophy, which was crystallised in the West in the 1950s, through their education or exposure to publications or the media. Various consulting firms have been available to help companies to make a transition towards a market orientation. However, companies in the West tend to have a more rigid or bureaucratic structure, pursuing management by objective (MBO) or by result (MBR), making them more efficient but less flexible. In contrast, Chinese companies are character-ised by 'management by (the key) individual'. Although Chinese organisa-tions are also departmentalised, the structure is quite flexible. If the founder or CEO has accepted a market-oriented philosophy, the organisation will be more responsive to market changes. For instance, in the case of Haier, once a special requirement for refrigerators for the US market had been recognised and raised at a board meeting, a prototype was developed to respond to this requirement within 24 hours.[114] Such a case in a Western company would take much longer before any kind of response occurred, involving a proposal, approvals by heads of different levels and an allocation of resources to develop a prototype.

On the other hand, since the structure of Chinese companies is more flex-ible, it would be likely to involve waste of resources, inefficiency and even corruption (because of poor financial control). Porter Erisman, a former vice president of Alibaba, expressed his view on this point: 'In a Chinese company, I'd learned, the informal structure was just as important as the organizational chart. And before you could focus on strategy, it was impor-tant to get to know your teammates.'[115] When he was asked to draw an organisational chart for Alibaba two years after its founding, this proved to be a formidable task:

> In any other company this would have been a simple and straightforward task, but in the case of Alibaba it was daunting. Alibaba was almost two years old and had never had an organizational chart. I didn't particularly relish the task of trying to make sense out of the amorphous blob that was our structure.[116]

The harmoniousness of one's family has a direct or indirect effect on one's abil-ity to lead or manage an organisation effectively. Family harmony will influence one's judgement, fairness or how one is seen as a role model.

(2) In China, key individuals, in terms of their capability and moral standards, have more influence on the success or failure of their organisations than do organisational factors such as structure and collective decisions, compared with organisations in the West.

Given the crucial role of key individuals in Chinese organisations, their required capabilities are different from those in the West. In addition to their technological or managerial competences, they must be skilful in dealing with personal relationships or *guanxi* (long-term reciprocal and mutually beneficial relationships) with adequate emotional intelligence, which particularly involves a knowledge of Chinese tradition, the ability to sense others' unarticulated needs and desires, and the embracing of the Middle Way. There are numerous cases in which graduates from top US or European universities with consider-able working experience in multinationals have failed to survive or develop within Chinese companies because of their inability to understand or cope with *guanxi*, resulting in losses for both individuals and companies.

Effective management in Chinese organisations requires senior executives to manage the expectations, satisfaction and loyalty of middle managers and employees. If they are satisfied and loyal, they will be willing to sacrifice themselves for the company, taking more initiative and working long hours or on weekends. Chinese culture dictates that subordinates should listen and obey, without challenging or being critical of company policy, their superiors or the status quo. Thus, it falls to senior managers to soften the effects of this mentality so that workers feel able to speak out without fear. Leading Chinese high-tech companies Baidu and Vimicro have specific policies to address employees' concerns, encouraging them to innovate and take responsibility without needing to worry about potential negative consequences. The former Alibaba.com CEO once made a comment on Jack Ma's priority and capability: 'Jack understands people more than any business. He knows business well, but if you ask me the three skills Jack has amongst people, business, or IT, IT is the worst. Business second. First is people.'[117]

Relationship-focused organisational management (vs. rule-based management) tends to generate internal strife, that is substantial internal arguments back and forth, a time-consuming process which results in inefficiency. It is easy for people to argue over who should be doing what and to shirk responsibility when things do not go well. Furthermore, the execution of a firm's strategic plan by middle managers often deviates from its original form. Within Chinese organisations, strategy formation tends to be informal and plans are often passed on as verbal instructions to lower management. With inflated self-confidence, many middle managers often 'adjust' corporate strategic plans by following their own strategic thinking, resulting in the deviation of outcomes from the original strategy. A famous historical story may throw light on this point. During the period of the Three Kingdoms (AD 220–280), in one of the life-and-death battles between the Shu and Wei kingdoms, a Shu general was given a specific order to defend a crucial town which had a strategically advantageous position over attacking forces. However, the general, believing himself to be versed in strategy, ignored the order and deployed the army according to his own strategic thinking. The battle was lost, the general was executed, and the Shu were defeated by the Wei. If the general had simply followed the defence plan given to him, this part of Chinese history might have had to be written differently.

Confucianism: the other side of the coin

The influence of Confucian ethical and political thought, with an emphasis on *ren* and the five cardinal relationships, is a double-edged sword: on one hand, it has succeeded in helping to build harmonious societies through hierarchy;[118]

on the other hand, it gives people little sense of equality and individual personality, which can be seen, particularly from a Western perspective, as a negative effect.

> What is deemed of primary importance in the Confucian ethical scheme is not procedural justice or individual rights but becoming a person of *jen* (*ren*). The society Confucians aim to build is not one that is an aggregate of self-interested claimers but one composed of virtuous individuals who live in harmonious relationships with other members of the community. Thus, Confucians emphasize the primacy of virtues over rights, the primacy of substantial justice over procedural justice and the primacy of common good over self-interest.[119]

In Western societies, liberty and equality are defined and supported by constitutional documents and by Christianity. America's Declaration of Independence, for instance, states that 'all men are created equal.' The concept of equality in the West has three major elements: equality before God, equality before the law and equal access to opportunity. The Confucian value system, in fact, has brought about a paradoxical phenomenon. That is, the promotion of *ren* is at the heart of the system, emphasising the espousal of benevolence, humanism or good-heartedness among people. However, this concept is implemented primarily through the five hierarchical relationships and the rites of propriety or *li*, giving rise to an unequal social structure and the acceptance of submissiveness in Chinese culture. The consequent absence of equality has been one of the key factors leading to the dearth of universal love and fraternity or *ren* among unrelated Chinese people. This largely explains why historically there have been so few philanthropists and charity organisations in China.

In addition, under the framework of the five Confucian relationships, people tend to lose their individuality and even their dignity, while most people are generally not at ease in dealing with officials, often showing excessive reverence and caution. If improper words or deeds accidentally occur to break the code of *li*, some serious consequences may befall the person. For instance, a careless remark may unintentionally offend a superior, who will subsequently make the person's life difficult or even remove him or her from a managerial position.

In a person's lifespan, as a teenager he or she will be subject to restrictions applied by parents and older brothers at home and by teachers at school under the *li* or obligations of the Confucian frame of mind. This has resulted in a cultural phenomenon whereby children never challenge parents and students never question teachers. In adulthood, one is constrained by one's obligations to older colleagues and superiors. All too often, when someone becomes a leader, the frustrations arising from the constraints of his or her past are then visited

upon his or her underlings. A relationship of true mutual respect between superiors and subordinators is virtually impossible in Chinese culture. Confucianism

> requires the individual to obey the superior so that a streamlined social
> order can be established. The group is primary in this respect. Within the
> group, network and hierarchy play an important role. In a Chinese network,
> the person who makes a decision at the top of a hierarchy is never held
> responsible in that capacity. Other people bear the responsibility for his
> decision and its implementation. Nevertheless, he will seldom fire a subor-
> dinate who does not perform optimally. . . . 'In the West, people are born
> with individual rights, in China people are born with social obligations.'[120]

Confucians went to great lengths to educate people in the importance of rulers and to minimise the rights of the individual.[121] Paradoxically, in pursuing
the aim of maintaining a harmonious society, Confucian thought has also sown
the seeds of social instability. It gives rise to a mentality of respect for absolute power or dictatorship, which has a tendency to lead an organisation or
a country astray; as Lord Acton stated: "Power tends to corrupt, and absolute
power corrupts absolutely." The Confucian 'Three Cardinal Guides' (the ruler
guides his subjects, the father his sons and the husband his wife) and the Five
Constant Virtues – *ren* (benevolence), *yi* (righteousness), *li* (rite), *zhi* (wisdom)
and *xin* (faith) – have modelled people's thinking and behaviour. A major social
consequence of Confucian influence, among other things, is that it has made
the Chinese people accept dictatorial rule willingly and readily. Thus, it became
possible for one man (the emperor) to rule over millions of people for such a
long period of time. Nor is this a distant historical truth; the influence or control over the masses of a single individual has remained a cultural phenomenon
to this day.

Under a culture which so easily accepts absolute authority, if the ruler happens to be upright, intelligent, sensible and knowledgeable, the organisation or
country will benefit from a great momentum in its development and prosperity.
For instance, Deng Xiaoping, who masterminded the economic reform initiated in 1978, was effectively in the national driving seat until his death in 1997,
despite for many years having no official title as leader of the nation.

Many a dictator, however, will eventually turn out to be arrogant, unrealistic
and despotic, with disastrous consequences. Examples are innumerable in the
cyclical evolution of Chinese dynastic empires and in the rise and fall of many
private businesses. Under the influence of Confucianism, the ruler has supreme
power, so gradually becomes immune to any opposing views, let alone criticisms. Even when it is apparent that a particular policy or directive is likely to
lead to disaster, it will rarely be rectified, as no one dares to offend the leader
by challenging it. If someone tries, it is more than likely to be in vain and to
bring severe consequences. In the Confucian culture, if a ruler is challenged or
criticised, this does not conform with *li* or with the five cardinal relationships,
whereby subjects should obey and revere their ruler, and the ruler will see

opposing views or criticisms as a loss of face or of the 'power of Heaven'. Two negative consequences tend to follow. First, the ruler may act wilfully without seeing potential dangers ahead, which is likely to give rise to a catastrophe. Second, it is common for a ruler to accept too easily ill-intentioned remarks against others or flattery from those with a personal agenda, at the expense of the public interest. Chinese history is littered with cases in which rulers have acted errantly or were misled, where the outcome has been disastrous.

- During the period of the Three Kingdoms, when the great Shu strategist Zhu Geliang was about to conquer one of his major enemies, the Wei Kingdom, which would have given him the opportunity to unify China, the king believed a false charge against him and issued an edict to call off the battle. Consequently, it was the Wei that soon subjugated the Shu, following Zhu Geliang's death. Thus, the course of Chinese history was changed.
- When the Manchu expanded into China from the north in the 1640s, their advance was initially halted by a capable general named Yuan Chonghuan. As a desperate measure, the Manchu used a plot to let the Chinese emperor believe that General Yuan was working with them. Even though many ministers saw through the plot, no one dared to draw the emperor's attention to its falsity. As a result, the emperor had General Yuan executed. Having removed the last barrier to entering China, Manchurian armies soon marched into its capital, Beijing, without serious resistance.

There are many firms which have attained initial success because of their leaders' vision and courage but have later been ruined by the same leaders, because their fatal mistakes could not be contained or prevented, due to their absolute power and management style of arbitrary decisions and peremptory action. The following is an example:

In the early 1990s, a Chinese medical researcher, Mr X, successfully developed a health care product and founded a company which grew exponentially. In less than three years, its turnover reached CNY 1000 million (about $120 million) and its profit CNY 200 million (about $24 million). As a result, Mr X received some national awards, such as the Chinese Reformist and the National Distinguished Young Entrepreneur. In 1995, the company was approved to be listed on the Hong Kong Stock Exchange. However, Mr X unilaterally decided that the company should withdraw from the opportunity to be listed because he found out during the due diligence process that the company's management left much to be desired.[122] Soon after this disastrous decision, he undertook an inspection tour of the company's 22 subsidiaries nationwide. He unexpectedly discovered that the management system was totally disorganised, then decided, once again without consultation, to announce publicly that the company was going into a process of restructuring, sending a confusing signal to wholesalers, retailers and consumers. Following this announcement, the company's sales fell dramatically.

In retrospect, it is clear that Mr X tried to run his business on a peremptory basis. Given absolute power over decision-making, he made no attempt to seek or introduce necessary professional management inputs or to adopt a scientific management approach. In a Confucian culture, top managers can readily fall into such a trap, as it is easy for them to demand obedience and behave as if they were absolute rulers in their business empires. With an authoritative management style, if decisions are right and proper the business may grow and prosper, while wrongful decisions can quickly result in disastrous consequences.

A comparative study of successful and unsuccessful Chinese privately owned enterprises has found that both groups share some common characteristics such as having strong aspirations for success and ambitions, enjoying challenges, actively pursuing innovation, excelling at sensing and grasping business opportunities, possessing charisma with a mass of followers, devoting themselves to social community services, with passion for contributions to charities and donations. However, they are distinct from each other on a major point: the failures tend to expand their businesses aggressively without the consciousness of risk control. For instance, one company entered 6 unrelated industries and acquired over 20 pharmaceutical companies within half a year; another made inroads into multimedia, mobile phone, logistics and so forth in less than two years and built 27 software parks nationwide within four years. Although some successful companies also involved active diversifications, they differed from the failures in that the successful companies tended to be 'conservative' venturists with a sense of risk containment, while the failures were 'aggressive' venturists with limited risk consciousness. The aggressiveness of unsuccessful companies was further rooted in three causes:

(1)   Over self-confidence with absence of rational thinking. These entrepreneurs are characterised by an overestimation of their own capability, judgement and control ability, resulting in a low level of the rationality quotient (RQ).[123] Consequently, they make misjudgements and take risky strategic actions.

(2)   Overreliance on the government-company relationship. Indeed, companies' relationships with government agencies are important for doing business in China, but these enterprises see these relationships as their core competence, without spending sufficient resources to develop technological and organisational capabilities.

(3)   The imperial complex. Seeing themselves as the 'emperors' of the enterprise kingdom, they like to do things by following their own interests, preferences and desires, without paying enough attention to companies' capabilities, environmental constraints or long-term interests. On the other hand, subordinates like to cater to these tendencies, rather than challenge

or propose counter-opinions.[124] In other words, there are no any mechanisms within the organisation to contain the potential wrong decisions. It is notable that the Chinese people have a fascination with history and empire. Since the early 1990s, Chinese historical dramas and films, based on the stories of emperors from various dynasties, particularly the Han, Tang, Ming and Qing, have proved to be among the most popular entertainments, not only in mainland China but also in Hong Kong, Taiwan and Singapore.

In Box 3.4, a comparison of the backgrounds of Mao Zedong and Zhou Enlai, two great Chinese leaders in the twentieth century, shows distinctively how Confucian thought has shaped their personalities and to a great extent defined their positions in Chinese history.

Box 3.4   Mao Zedong versus Zhou Enlai

Mao Zedong was the paramount leader of the Communist Party of China (CPC) from 1935 to 1976, while Zhou Enlai was China's prime minister from 1949 to 1976. Both were major contributors to the development of the People's Republic of China. Notably, unlike many other Chinese leaders, Mao was not constrained or inhibited by Confucianism and its emphasis on obedience to authority, because he disliked or indeed hated Confucius from the age of eight. Mao was therefore rebellious against his father and teachers at a young age and later became a foremost revolutionist. The seed of rebellion was sown in his youth, and circumstances gradually moulded him into a decisive, courageous and fearless man. This is in marked contrast to the background of Zhou Enlai, who is described as a 'Confucian gentleman'.[125] Richard Nixon (1982) writes:

> His [Zhou Enlai's] family had been rooted in the ways and manners of old China, its members maintaining their social position for centuries by training their children in the Chinese classics and placing them in positions in the imperial bureaucracy . . . he could never rid himself of their cultural imprint, nor did he wish to. He always retained a certain respect for China's past – for those elements of the 'old society' that deserved preservation.[126]

From 1931 to 1934, Zhou was Mao's superior, but after the Zunyi meeting of the CPC in early 1935, Mao's leadership position in the CPC was gradually established.[127] 'Zunyi was over. The Long March continued. Mao was in charge. China's course had been set for at least half a century to come.'[128] Richard Nixon, 37th president of the United States (1969–1974), spoke highly of Zhou Enlai and regarded him as one of the world's great leaders and statesmen. Nixon believed that Zhou lived in the shadow of a giant, Mao Zedong, and 'discreetly let the limelight shine on Mao'.[129] As a Confucian, once a pecking order was established between him and Mao in the mid- and late 1930s, Zhou became a Mao loyalist and remained so until the last minute of his life, making no attempt to stand against him, even when some of Mao's policies were apparently inappropriate. Harrison Salisbury writes:

> Now Zhou threw his full support to Mao. Never to the end of their lives, in the fateful year of 1976, would Zhou challenge Mao's leader-ship. The complex factors that underlay Zhou's decision cannot be fully explored. Not enough is known of his inner feelings. But from Zunyi forward, whatever his title, he would, in fact, act as chief of staff for Mao Zedong. It was a partnership that had little precedent in Chinese politics.[130]

However, Mao and Zhou needed and supported each other during the Chinese Revolution and China's socialist development. 'Without Mao the Chinese Revolution would never have caught fire. Without Zhou it would have burned out and only the ashes would remain.'[131]

Confucian effect: guanxi

A salient characteristic of Chinese culture has been the extensive role of 'inter-personal relationships' or *guanxi* in business, politics and society in general. *Guanxi* involves interpersonal connections that facilitate exchanges of favours between people with implications for long-term reciprocally beneficial rela-tions, mutual commitment, loyalty and obligation.[132] Traditionally, *guanxi* has been vital for doing business, attaining an official or senior managerial position and even judging right or wrong and guilt or innocence.

Guanxi finds its roots in kinship associations, specifically under Confucian-ism those concerning the five cardinal relationships, between sovereign and subject, parents and children, brothers, husband and wife, and friends. Weber (1951) notes:

> The retention of personalism is especially evident in its effect on social eth-ics. Hitherto in China no sense of obligation has existed toward impersonal communities, be they of political, ideological, or any other nature. All social ethics in China merely transferred the organic relations of piety to other relations considered similar to them. Within the five natural social relations

the duties to master, father, husband, older brother (including the teacher), and friend comprised the sum total of the ethically binding.[133]

A *guanxi* relationship can be used as an effective marketing tool, having a significant and positive effect on business and marketing performance.[134] With the rising influence of the Chinese economy in the world and the sheer volume of business between Chinese and Western firms, it is believed that marketing practices by Western firms are moving towards a *guanxi* style of business dealings. The increasing interest in 'relationship marketing' and 'virtual integration supply chain management' in the West can be seen as signs of this trend.[135]

The influence of Confucian values extends to other Asian countries, some of which have become known as Confucian societies, including Japan, South Korea, Singapore, Vietnam and Hong Kong, where *guanxi*-based relationships are widely practised.[136] In mainland China, interpersonal relationships are seen as important as a 'second currency',[137] and given their reciprocal nature they can even be compared with written agreements.[138]

The very basis of marketing lies in the need for exchange. Any enterprise wishing to exchange effectively in a market-based competitive environment must be sensibly and rationally market-orientated, in order for its products to be acceptable in the marketplace. Generally, a legal system is a necessity to maintain compliance with the agreed transactional conditions of the two parties. However, in a relationship-based context, a legal system cannot develop and work properly; consequently, enterprises cannot be constrained to behave according to economic rationality.

The extensive influence of the Confucian *li* and hierarchical relationships is manifested in Chinese management behaviour and culture. *Li*, which played an important role in ancient China, remains prevalent in modern Chinese social and commercial contexts. China has been known as the land of ceremony and propriety for over two millennia. The practice of *li* is meant to create harmony: 'Of the things brought about by the rites, harmony is the most valuable.'[139] In modern China, *li* reflects the level of civilisation, morality and virtues such as filial piety towards parents and respect for teachers and senior citizens, but also a set of hierarchical relationships between the parties involved. When Confucius upheld this set of relationships, his intention was to create social harmony and maintain societal stability.

Some of these values would, however, be perceived as less desirable in today's society. For instance, ordinary people tend to treat senior government officials or business leaders with excessive reverence and prudence (in case something they say or do is inappropriate in terms of *li*), being extremely reluctant to voice different views, compared with their counterparts in Western countries. On social occasions, people in senior positions always keep themselves apart from those of lower rank. Junior people hardly ever express views opposing those of their superiors. Students at schools and universities are only there to be taught, not to question or challenge. From the standpoint of traditional Chinese values, all of these tendencies are considered virtuous and desirable, but from the viewpoint of current internationally shared values, they are likely to be seen as obsolete and undesirable, lacking equality and inimical to learning, development and good management.

The importance of the Confucian five cardinal relationships has given rise to the characteristics of Chinese management that place great emphasis on a relationship-orientated management philosophy. Decisions to select or promote management staff are often based on relational closeness rather than on merit. There is a Chinese saying describing this: 'When a man gets to the top, all his friends and relations get there with him.' In seeking trading or business partners, priority would traditionally be given to related parties because of implicit mutual obligations embedded in these relationships. This has given a special place in Chinese business culture to *guanxi*, which includes the following major elements: (1) connections through family, hometown, school, workplace or simply friendship; (2) obligations at appropriate times and places; (3) a reciprocal relationship whereby obligations are mutual; and (4) the importance of long-term relationships. Since the mid-1990s, considerable attention has been paid to the meaning, role and implications of *guanxi* in the development of business in China.[140] *Guanxi* has long been considered a key to success in doing business there.[141]

With the development of China's Internet Plus economy, as strongly promoted by the Chinese government, the role of *guanxi* will be increasingly reduced. *Guanxi* is inversely related to the degree of Internet penetration in society, Alibaba's Jack Ma claims: 'In Alibaba, I fiercely object to making all sorts of complicated, curious guanxi.'[142] Box 3.5 presents an analysis of the role of *guanxi* in China.

Box 3.5   Role of *guanxi* in China

In contemporary China, *guanxi* has continued to play an important part in business,[143] but its role seems to be diminishing.[144] The strategic rationale and relevance of taking a *guanxi* approach to business are mainly associated with two factors: market demand and industry regulation. *Guanxi* is more important in a seller's market than a buyer's market. In the former, the buyer needs *guanxi* to secure supply, while the seller relies on it to find a buyer. In a regulated industry, a firm's operations will be subject to regulation and influenced by the regulators. Considering a combination of the two dimensions, there are four types of situation in terms of the strategic role of *guanxi*, as shown in Figure 3.6.

In Figure 3.6, Cell 1 represents a situation in which a firm faces a seller's market for its supply and an industry that is regulated, in which case *guanxi* is extremely important. This was the case for many Chinese enterprises before the economic reforms of the early 1990s. In Cells 2 and 3,

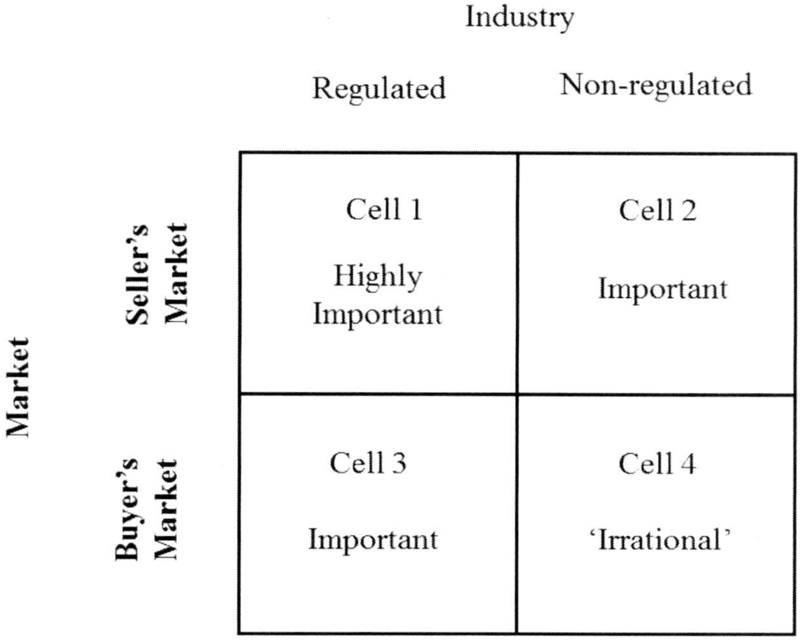

Industry

	Regulated	Non-regulated
Seller's Market	Cell 1 Highly Important	Cell 2 Important
Buyer's Market	Cell 3 Important	Cell 4 'Irrational'

Market

Figure 3.6 Rationality of *guanxi* application

a single factor – either the type of market or regulation – plays a part in determining the importance of *guanxi*. Notably, in a developed economy only special products such as unique talents, researchers or senior executives in certain fields or industries would fall into Cell 2. In Cell 4, where the prerequisites of market and industry do not apply, if a firm pursues a *guanxi* business approach, this is not rational and would be determined by non-economic factors. For instance, if the firm does not buy products from a seller who is a *guanxi* partner, the seller would be bankrupted, so the firm proceeds with the purchase, although the product quality and price are not the best in the market. This tends to happen in a long-term supply chain network. Notably, it can often be seen in Japanese *keiretsu* business networks as well as in many overseas Chinese business networks. Another typical case is where the buyer receives generous commission from a seller whose products are not the most competitive in the market.

Since the *guanxi* phenomenon is so widespread in China, its effect on business is worth further discussion. In Western countries, although

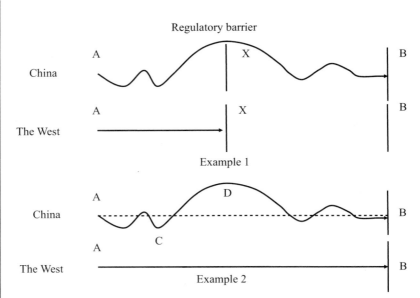

Figure 3.7 Role of *guanxi* – a comparative view

it is possible to find examples of a relationship-based business approach, whereby a firm acquires a large project through personal networks, the nature and scale are by no means comparable to those of Chinese *guanxi*. If government policy or regulations, for instance, put restrictions on a business partnership, trade or transaction in an industry, it is more than likely that no firms will pass through the policy or regulatory barrier. However, in China, the picture is different. If a firm has 'hard' *guanxi*, meaning connections with top central government officials, any legal and regulatory hurdles can be surmounted, with appropriate official justifica-tion. It appears that in a controlled business context, a *guanxi* approach can be effective, as shown in Example 1 of Figure 3.7. Some multinational CEOs learned this quickly and used *guanxi* to set up joint ventures in Chinese regulated industries in the early 1990s.

However, in China there are also many cases where things could be done immediately but firms have to go through *guanxi*, with a resultant dissipation of time and resources. For instance, a problem could be easily resolved between A and B, but because of *guanxi*, A would go to C and D first, then to B, as seen in Example 2 of Figure 3.7. It can be said that a *guanxi* business approach is inefficient but in some cases effective in China.

Taoism and Chinese culture

Contributors

Lao Zi, who lived around 570 to 500 BC, was the founder of Taoism (or Dao-ism) and the author of *Daodejing* (*Tao Te Ching*) or *Lao Zi* (The Classic of the Way and of Virtue), which has had a profound impact on the thinking of Chi-nese people for over two millennia. 'Lao Zi' literally means 'Old Master', and his actual name was Li Er, alias Bo Yang (伯阳). He worked as an archivist in the Imperial Library of the West Zhou dynasty. His book has been translated into over 20 major languages and in number of copies printed is second only to the Bible; it has become increasingly influential worldwide, particularly in East Asia.

Taoism consists mainly of the teachings, concepts and ideas of Lao Zi and Zhuang Zi, who was the leading contributor to *Zhuang Zi* (or *Chuang Tzu*). Zhuang Zi (literally meaning 'Master Zhuang') was an influential Chinese thinker, philosopher and man of letters who lived around the Warring States period (c. 369–286 BC). Zhuang Zi, whose given name was Zhou (周) and whose alias was Zixiu, came from the town of Meng in the state of Song (pres-ently Shangqiu, Henan).

Joseph Needham, a renowned British historian and sinologist, claims that Taoism plays a vital role in shaping the thoughts of all Chinese people: 'A Chi-nese thought without Taoism is like a tree without roots.' It has been described as a 'guide to the art of rulership'.[145] Taoist influence in China has also been noted and emphasised by Chinese philosophers.[146] *Daodejing* consists of 81 chapters. Chapters 1–37 are known as '*Tao* Classic' and Chapter 38–81 as '*Te* Classic'. Some major teachings of Taoism are summarised in the following subsections.

Governance by non-interference (wu wei)

As explained earlier, Tao, meaning 'Way' or 'Path' in the sense of the natural order or condition of the universe, is the core concept of Taoism. Tao, which cannot be seen, heard or described, underlies all existence, dictates all change and governs all life. Lao Tzu writes at the beginning of *Tao Te Ching*: 'A way that can be walked is not The Way. A name that can be named is not The Name. *Tao* is both Named and Nameless. As Nameless, it is the origin of all things. As Named, it is the mother of all things.'[147] In other words, the universe has its own natural law, which human beings should follow steadfastly. Taoism holds that people should live a life based on Tao, practising humility, calm and effortless-ness or *wu wei* (non-action or non-interference).

Taoism was also concerned with the application of the Tao to the nature of government, actively encouraging a *wu wei* approach to state affairs. Lao Zi writes: 'Tao does not act, yet it is the root of all action. Tao does not move, yet it is the source of all creation. If princes and kings could hold it, everyone under them would naturally turn within.'[148] 'I do nothing and the people are reformed of themselves. I love quietude and the people are righteous of themselves. I deal in no business and the people grow rich by themselves. I have no desires and the people are simple and honest by themselves.'[149] This principle can be extended to the case of business management, if one embraces Taoism.

While most Chinese dynastic governments chose Confucianism rather than Taoism as the state philosophy, the Taoist liberal idea of government has been identified by Western scholars and adopted by many political and economic leaders. 'In the mid-18th century, the French physician and economic thinker Francois Quesnay translated Lao Zi's idea of wu wei into a concept of laissez-faire, which greatly inspired Adam Smith, who later established the principles of modern free-market economics.'[150] Two renowned economists, Rothbard[151] and Boaz,[152] recognised Lao Zi as the world's first libertarian, and in particular, Rothbard identified Lao Zi with the theory of spontaneous order of F.A. Hayek, a Nobel Prize-winning economist, in his defence of capitalism.[153]

The *wu wei* approach to business has been preached and practised by many successful Chinese businesspeople. Under this management philosophy, top management should only set up strategies and organisational structure, leaving management operations to those who are assigned to do the jobs with minimum interference, thus letting the organisation run itself. In addition, Taoism implies that a firm's leaders should follow Tao as manifested in the laws of market mechanism. To do this, the firm should undertake market research to establish what the market wants and should then deliver product offerings accordingly. Furthermore, a Taoist management philosophy will entail respect for the value of each employee and his or her initiative. Improper interference is both bad management practice and an indication of distrust and disrespect to the individual. Box 3.6 presents a case in point.

Box 3.6   'Doing nothing' to win

An increasing number of entrepreneurs in China's mainland, Hong Kong, Macao and Taiwan attribute their success directly to the application of the Taoist 'do nothing'. Shih Wing Chin, for example, is an outspoken proponent of Lao Zi's *wu wei*. As chairman of the Centaline Property Agency, he has led his firm's rapid growth since its establishment in 1978. It later became Hong Kong's leading real-estate agency, with more than 2600 employees, 180 branch offices and annual property transactions amounting to tens of billions of HK dollars. According to Shih, the 'do nothing' theory of management creates an environment in which employees feel they are valued as integral elements of the company, free to contribute their talents and realise their full potential, not only as workers but also as human beings. Managers on the mainland, by contrast, tend to ask the average worker to act as a cog in a machine. This means that employees have no choice but to follow what is predetermined by management, without fully contributing their own unique talents. 'This is not good for them, and Hong Kong shares the same problem,' says Shih. 'What I want to give employees is much more freedom to make decisions and reduce intervention by management.'

Another advocate of Lao Zi's management philosophy is Wu Yijian. With only 50 yuan (US$6) in his pocket in the early 1990s, Wu started an estate agency in the Hainan Special Economic Zone in Haikou, Hainan Province. By the end of 1997, Wu's company, the Ginwa Group, had become a leading business giant, with fixed assets amounting to 6.8 billion yuan (US$819 million). Wu's company motto is taken directly from Lao Zi: 'Value the character of water.' 'A drop of water looks not as powerful as metal,' says Wu, 'but a flood can devour a vast amount of land. So we should be flexible in harsh competition and become a powerful force by uniting every individual's power into one.' 'As a Chinese businessman, . . . I want to reintroduce the glorious Chinese culture to our group.'

Extracted and adapted from *China Daily* (North American ed.), 6 March 2002

Dialectical thinking: the unity and transformation of opposites

The teachings of Taoism represent a major source of the differences in logical thinking and thus in communication and behaviour between Chinese and Western people. In Western countries, logical thinking is based on the laws of non-contradiction and the excluded middle. An example of the former is that one cannot be both wearing gloves and not wearing gloves at the same time, in the same place and in the same way; more simply, something cannot be both *this* and *that*. The law of the excluded middle states that something is either 'A' or 'not A'; this is either a glove or not a glove. This is commonly referred to as 'either/or' logic. When one of the two laws is broken, it is known as a contradiction and normally considered unacceptable or wrong.

> Because a single truth is thought to exist, Westerners seek to reconcile apparent contradictions. Using formal logic to evaluate propositions, Westerners tend to examine both sides of an opposing argument and reject the least, in favor of the most, plausible proposition, even to the point of polarizing their initial preferences for one proposition over another . . . The end result of this reasoning process is synthesis and the resolution of seeming contradiction.[154]

In contrast, reflecting the earlier traditional Chinese thinking of '*yin* and *yang*', Lao Tzu has crystallised the dialectical logical thinking that incorporates contradictions or a unity of opposites:

> Tao gives life to the one; the one gives life to the two; the two give life to the three; the three give life to ten thousand things. All beings support *yin* and embrace *yang* and the interplay of these two forces fills the universe.

Yet only at the still-point, between the breathing in and the breathing out, can one capture these two in perfect harmony.[155]

According to Lao Tzu, all things in the world consist of two opposite sides, such as large–small, long–short, alive–dead, strong–weak, beautiful–ugly and hard–soft, which are contradictory but interrelated. Each has the potential to produce the other. Such seemingly paradoxical forces comprise the foundation of the entire universe. It is the tendency to adopt this pattern of thought which often gives rise to the characteristic behaviour of the Chinese people that seems to be indecisive and baffling.[156]

Taoist dialectic 'uses contradiction to understand relations among objects or events, to transcend or integrate apparent oppositions, or even to embrace clashing but instructive viewpoints . . . It is the Middle Way that is the goal of reasoning.'[157] It thus differs from the Hegelian dialectic, 'in which thesis is followed by antithesis, which is resolved by synthesis, and which is "aggressive" in the sense that the ultimate goal of reasoning is to resolve contradiction'.[158] Taoist dialectic is well embraced in the language. For instance, the Chinese word 矛盾 ('contradiction' or 'conflict') consists of two characters: 矛 (*mao*) meaning 'spear' and 盾 (*dun*) denoting 'shield'; and the word 里外 ('everywhere') is composed of two characters: 里 (*li*) indicating 'inside' and 外 (*wai*) connoting 'outside'. The word for 'crisis' in Chinese consists of two characters: danger (危) and opportunity (机), representing the dialectical view that dangers come with opportunities. A crisis, if managed properly, may turn into a profitable opportunity. For example, in a five-star hotel, a valuable customer was badly offended by unexpectedly poor customer service and complained angrily to the hotel management. Facing the crisis, the hotel management took the timely step of addressing the customer's grievance by sending him an apologetic letter with a complimentary bottle of champagne. As a result of the hotel's proper handling of the complaint, the customer was happy and remained loyal. On the other hand, if a successful company has become too complacent, it can easily turn in the opposite direction. In Western countries, the positive potential of crisis has also been recognised and can often become an agent to initiate necessary organisational changes.[159]

Lao Tzu writes:

He who is to be made to dwindle (in power) must first be caused to expand.
He who is to be weakened must first be made strong.
He who is to be laid low must first be exalted to power.
He who is to be taken away from must first be given.
This is the Subtle Light.
Gentleness overcomes strength:
Fish should be left in the deep pool,
And sharp weapons of the state should be left where none can see them.[160]

The soft overcomes the hard and the weak the strong. The dialectical perspective on change in the universe is reflected in some Chinese sayings: 'Things turn into their opposites when they reach the extreme' and 'The higher the climb, the harder the fall.' When one becomes overjoyed, it is easy to fall into sadness. It is precisely when a nation or empire becomes too powerful that it is at most risk of becoming weakened, as was true of the Roman Empire (which once dominated most of Europe, parts of the Middle East and Asia Minor), the Ottoman Empire (covering much of Southeast Europe, the Middle East and North Africa) and the Napoleonic Empire (which controlled much of continental Europe). 'Bad fortune, yes – it rests upon good fortune. Good fortune, yes – it hides within bad fortune.'[161] In a text of the *Huainanzi*, there is a tale that illustrates dialectic relationships between misfortune and good fortune. It goes as follows:

Once upon a time, a beautiful white mare owned by an old man ran away, and he was saddened by this loss. Neighbours came to extend their sympathies, but the old man responded by saying: 'It may not be a bad thing for me.' A few days later, the mare returned and brought with her another horse, a beautiful wild mare. Now the old man's neighbours came to congratulate him on the new acquisition. However, he refrained from becoming excited, saying: 'It may not be a good thing for me.' Next day, the old man's only son fell from the wild mare when trying to tame it and broke his leg. A year later, war broke out in the area; all strong male adults were recruited for the fight and nine out of ten people in the region were killed. It was only because of their lameness that the father and son were left at home to protect each other.[162] Therefore, as the book concludes:

Good fortune becoming calamity,
Calamity becoming good fortune,
Their transformations are limitless,
So profound they cannot be fathomed.[163]

Lao Tzu gives a further explanation: 'Nothing in the world is softer than water; yet nothing is better than water at overcoming the hard and strong.'[164] Despite its appearance of softness, water has a remarkable corrosive power, as a Chinese saying recognises: 'Dripping water wears holes in stone.' Lao Tzu writes:

When man is born, he is tender and weak; at death, he is hard and stiff. When plants are alive, they are soft and supple; when they are dead, they are brittle and dry. Therefore, hardness and stiffness are the companions of death, while softness and gentleness are the companions of life. Therefore, when an army is headstrong, it will lose in battle. When a tree is hard, it will be cut down. The hard and strong belong underneath. The gentle and weak belong at the top.[165]

Most successful companies start small and weak, and step-by-step, through hard work and intelligence, eventually become large and strong. Li Ka-shing, Hong

Kong's richest tycoon, for instance, arrived from Guangdong as a refugee when he was ten. He started his first job as a waiter at a teahouse at the age of 14. After that, he worked as a salesman, then a manager in a factory, before launching his first company and developing his business empire. Most present leading brands in the Chinese consumer goods market, including Haier, Huawei, Alibaba, Galanz, TCL, Gome, Chery, Wahaha and many more, have evolved from a small and weak base to their current dominant positions. From a Taoist point of view, business leaders should put themselves in a 'soft' and 'weak' position, avoiding complacency and overconfidence; as Lao Tzu puts it: 'Therefore when two equally matched armies meet, it is the man of sorrow who wins.'[166] Companies should think of danger in times of prosperity and plan for further developments assuming the worst case.

Select teachings relevant to management

Taoism casts light on how a company should establish its mission and gain longevity. Lao Zi writes: 'The universe is everlasting. The reason the universe is everlasting is that it does not live for Self. Therefore it can long endure.'[167] As far as a company is concerned, if it wants to survive and develop on a long-term basis, it must devise its mission independently of its own interests. This line of thinking coincides with the practices of some of the most successful companies. For instance, eBay's mission statement is: 'We help people trade practically anything on earth. We will continue to enhance the online trading experience of all – collectors, dealers, small businesses, unique item seekers, bargain hunters, opportunity sellers, and browsers.'[168] Since the 1950s, the marketing concept, a management philosophy that emphasises the importance of customers and the meeting of customer needs and wants, has been the foundation of modern marketing management. The implementation of the marketing concept is known as 'market orientation'.[169] These fundamental business concepts and ideas are quintessentially similar to those of Lao Zi.

   Lao Tzu says: 'One who knows others is intelligent. One who knows himself is enlightened. One who conquers others is strong. One who conquers himself is all-powerful. One who approaches life with force surely gets something. One who remains content with where he is surely gets everything.'[170] Good leaders know how to judge and use people to serve their causes, and this quality is often the key to success; as Andrew Carnegie once famously declared: 'Take away my people, but leave my factories, and soon grass will grow on the factory floors. Take away my factories, but leave my people, and soon we will have a new and better factory.' From Lao Tzu's point of view, self-realisation (of strengths and limitations) is an even higher realm of cognisance. A popular Chinese historical anecdote recorded in the *Shi Ji* by Sima Qian is illustrative. Emperor Gao of Han led a rebellion to overthrow the repressive and decadent Qin dynasty. Despite being illiterate, he once proudly explained why he could be successful:

   With regard to devising strategies in a command tent and ensuring victory on the battlefront from a thousand *li*[171] away, I am not as good as Zhang

Liang. With regard to defending the nation, pacifying the populace, supplying soldiers' provisions and pay, and ensuring food distribution, I am not as good as Xiao He. With regard to leading millions of soldiers to fight invincible battles, I am not as good as Han Xin. They are among those of exceptional ability. I can utilise them, and this is why I can take over the country!

However, it is difficult to know others and even harder to know oneself; thus, a Chinese saying tell us that a man's virtue lies in taking a proper measure of himself. Therefore, one should endeavour to understand one's own strengths and weaknesses to become enlightened. As well as knowing and overcoming others, one can also conquer oneself and one's weaknesses to become mighty. When one is enlightened and mighty, one has commanded the quintessence of the Tao. By following the Tao, one becomes content with what one has; by definition, one is thus both rich and happy. In China, many good Chinese leaders are seen to possess such qualities, realising their own limitations and taking advantage of others.

In contradistinction to a conventional Western mentality where people are encouraged to strive for the top position in any field such as sport or management, or in rankings of size, performance or excellence, Taoism teaches the value of avoiding the pinnacle, where one would stand out conspicuously against others. Lao Tzu writes:

I have Three Treasures;
Guard them and keep them:
The first is Love.
The second is, Never too much.
The third is, Never be the first in the world.
Through Love, one has no fear;
Through not doing too much, one has amplitude (of reserve power);
Through not presuming to be the first in the world,
One can develop one's talent and let it mature.[172]

This cultural trait is reflected in Chinese business by the fact that organisations tend to embrace a follower's strategy, just as in long-distance races, where most runners tend to prefer to follow the leader for most of the early stages. This seemingly uncompetitive or unaggressive stance, however, is a foundation for taking up the leading position at a later stage. For example, Huawei, a Chinese multinational, was officially recognised as the largest telecommunication equipment maker in the world in 2012, having overtaken Ericsson.[173] In fact, it had already been larger than Ericsson before the official announcement, but deliberately permitted itself to be seen as the second largest player in the industry, until it had to stand out. Notably, when Huawei first joined the Global 500, the overall reaction of its top managers was not one of elation but of concern and apprehension.[174]

Concluding remarks

Chinese philosophical systems put great emphasis on humanity, on pragmatism and on social and ethical dimensions, but less on natural science, espousing the unity of human beings with nature, thereby de-emphasising the value of studying nature in order to dominate it. Thus, traditionally there has been little pure scientific research activity in China. In contrast, Western philosophy has embraced just such a relationship between humankind and nature, whereby the former endeavours to understand and conquer the latter, resulting in the proliferation of great scientists and scientific theories.

Chinese philosophy is an important part of Chinese culture, having a great impact on the behaviour of Chinese people. As the oldest and earliest Chinese classic, the *I Ching* is a foundation of other Chinese philosophies including Confucianism and Taoism. One cannot really understand Chinese culture and philosophy without knowledge of the *I Ching*. At the heart of the *I Ching* and other Chinese philosophies is the concept of *yin* and *yang*, denoting two primal and opposing but complementary forces that exist in all things in the universe. The two opposites are interdependent and mutually supportive, so neither can exist without the other. Each has a seed of the other within it and can transform into the other. The changing relationship between the two opposites leads to the constant flux of the universe. In other words, a good command of the *I Ching* enables one to get closer to an understanding of the laws of nature or course of nature.

Confucianism and Taoism are the two schools of thought that have had the most profound impact on Chinese culture over the past two millennia, but it is the former which has been especially closely associated with the prosperity and adversity that have characterised Chinese history since the Han dynasty. In particular, Confucianism, as the orthodox system of thought, has crystallised the core values of the Chinese people. It is mainly concerned with social relations, behaviour and human society, while Taoism more closely addresses the behaviour of each individual in terms of his or her relationship with nature.

In essence, Confucianism is concerned with governing the world, leading to the creation of harmony in society, and Taoism with allowing things to follow their own course, so that a harmonious society will come about. With regard to the means of accomplishing the aim of harmony, Confucianism places emphasis on education and inspiration, and Taoism on guidance by nature, which has its own underlying laws of movement. Confucianism is consistent with a culture of striving and initiative, and Taoism with observance of the laws of nature. The Confucian characteristics of a moral person include benevolence, righteousness, propriety, wisdom and fidelity, while Taoism promotes enlightenment, abiding by the laws of nature, non-action and leading a simple life. Confucianism could be described as a this-worldly philosophy that educates and inspires people to strive to become benevolent and reach the highest realm of life, whereas Taoism is an other-worldly philosophy that encourages people to live a simple life and purify their minds in the absence of all material and physical temptations.

In many ways, the two schools of thought are opposed, yet they are also to some extent complementary. An individual can be a Confucian on official duty and a Taoist at leisure or in retirement, seeking harmony with nature. In ancient times, it was often said that Confucianism should be used to govern the country and Taoism the heart.

Notes

1 Also known as the *Book of Changes* in the West.
2 Hofstede, G. (1993), "Cultural Constraints in Management Theories," *Academy of Management Executive*, 7, 81–94.
3 He is believed to have been born in a small kingdom on the Indian-Nepalese border but lived and taught mostly in ancient India.
4 Puett, M. and Gross-Loh, C. (2016), *The Path: A New Way to Think About Everything*, London: Viking, pp. 17–18.
5 Xu, Z.Y. (2014), *Zhongxi wenming de duizhao (A Contrast Between Chinese and Western Civilisations)*, Hangzhou, China: Zhenjiang People's Publishing House, pp. 73–74.
6 Wu, J. (1972), "Western Philosophy and the Search for Chinese Wisdom," in A. Naess and A. Hannay (eds.), *Invitation to Chinese Philosophy*, Oslo: Universitetsforlaget, p. 5.
7 Wong, W.C. (2006), "Understanding Dialectical Thinking From a Cultural-Historical Perspective," *Philosophical Psychology*, 19 (2), 239–260.
8 Wilhelm, R. (2003), *I Ching or Book of Changes*, translated by R. Wilhelm with a forward by C.G. Jung, London: Penguin Books, p. xlvii.
9 Minford, J. (2015), *I Ching (Yijing): The Book of Changes*, translated with an introduction and commentary by John Minford, New York: Penguin Books, p. xxi.
10 Minford, J. (2015), *I Ching (Yijing): The Book of Changes*, translated with an introduction and commentary by John Minford, New York: Penguin Books, p. xxi.
11 Ibid, p. xxiii.
12 Ibid, p. xiii.
13 Wilhelm, R. (2003), *I Ching or Book of Changes*, translated by R. Wilhelm with a forward by C.G. Jung, London: Penguin Books, p. l.
14 Ibid, p. li.
15 Fung, Y.L. (1962), *The Spirit of Chinese Philosophy*, translated by E.R. Hughes, London: Routledge, p. 82.
16 Chan, W.T. (1963), *A Source Book in Chinese Philosophy*, translated and compiled by W.T. Chan, Princeton, NJ: Princeton University Press, p. 267.
17 The Great Ultimate and the Supreme Polarity are alternative translations of *tai ji*.
18 Adler, J.A. (1999), "Zhou Dunyi: The Metaphysics and Practice of Sagehood," in W.T. De Bary and I. Bloom (eds.), *Sources of Chinese Tradition* (2nd ed.), New York: Columbia University Press, 669–678.
19 Wong, W.C. (2006), "Understanding Dialectical Thinking From a Cultural-Historical Perspective," *Philosophical Psychology*, 19 (2), 239–260.
20 Fung, Y.L. (1962), *The Spirit of Chinese Philosophy*, translated by E.R. Hughes, London: Routledge, p. 89.
21 Wilhelm, R. (2003), *I Ching or Book of Changes*, translated by Richard Wilhelm with a forward by C.G. Jung, London: Penguin Books, pp. xlix–l.
22 Ibid, p. li.
23 Ibid.
24 Ibid, p. liii.
25 Leaman, O. (1999), *Key Concepts in Eastern Philosophy*, London and New York: Routledge, pp. 30–31.

26 'Image', an important term in the *I Ching*, is a method to understand the universe, and often used for classification and analysis in antiquity. A 'large image' is associated with a hexagram, while a 'small image' with a line. Readers can visualise an image, such as heaven, wind, storm, water, dragon, fire etc.

27 Ibid, p. 6.

28 Ibid, p. 7.

29 Ibid.

30 Chen, B. (2013), *Gen Yijing Xue Biantong (From the* I Ching *to Learn Adaptation)*, Changchun, China: Jilin Publishing Group Limited, p. 9.

31 Minford, J. (2015), *I Ching (Yijing): The Book of Changes*, translated with an introduction and commentary by John Minford, New York: Penguin Books, p. 18.

32 Ibid, p. 20.

33 Ibid, p. 22.

34 Ibid, p. 23.

35 Ibid, p. 24.

36 Lu, Y.D. and Qian, Y. (2011), "Implications of I Ching on Innovation Management," *Chinese Management Studies*, 5 (4), 394–402.

37 Spencer-Rodgers, J., Williams, M.J. and Peng, K. (2010), "Cultural Differences in Expectations of Change and Tolerance for Contradiction: A Decade of Empirical Research," *Personality and Social Psychology Review*, 14 (3), 296–312.

38 Shaughnessy, E.L. (2010), *Chinese Wisdom: Philosophical Insights From Confucius, Mencius, Laozi, Zhuangzi and Other Masters*, London: Duncan Baird, p. 9.

39 *Te* means moral principles or character.

40 Tzu, L. (2003), *Tao Te Ching*, translated and compiled by J. Star, New York: Penguin Books, p. 64.

41 Mott, W.H. and Kim, J.C. (2006), *The Philosophy of Chinese Military Culture*, New York: Palgrave Macmillan, p. 16.

42 Ibid, p. 17.

43 Tzu, L. (2003), *Tao Te Ching*, translated and compiled by J. Star, New York: Penguin Books, p. 55.

44 Mott, W.H. and Kim, J.C. (2006), *The Philosophy of Chinese Military Culture*, New York: Palgrave Macmillan, p. 17.

45 Tzu, L. (2003), *Tao Te Ching*, translated and compiled by J. Star, New York: Penguin Books, p. 14.

46 Clark, D. (2016), *Alibaba: The House That Jack Ma Built*, New York: HarperCollins Publishers, p. 110.

47 Tzu, L. (2003), *Tao Te Ching*, translated and compiled by J. Star, New York: Penguin Books, p. 38.

48 Ren, Z.G. (2013), *Wei Shen Mo Shi Mao Zedong? (Why Is Mao Zedong?)*, Beijing: Guang Ming Daily Publisher, p. 3.

49 Clark, D. (2016), *Alibaba: The House That Jack Ma Built*, New York: HarperCollins Publishers, p. 212.

50 Ibid., p. xiv.

51 Fung, Y.L. (1962), *The Spirit of Chinese Philosophy*, translated and compiled by E.R. Hughes, London: Routledge, p. 4.

52 Ibid.

53 *Tao Te Ching* consists of two sections: Section One comprising Chapters 1–37 is known as the 'Tao *Classic*' and Section Two comprising Chapters 38–81 is termed the 'Te *Classic*'.

54 Fung, Y.L. (1962), *The Spirit of Chinese Philosophy*, translated by E.R. Hughes, London: Routledge, p. 11.

55 Tzu, L. (2003), *Tao Te Ching*, translated and compiled by J. Star, New York: Penguin Books, p. 51.

56 Minford, J. (2015), *I Ching (Yijing): The Book of Changes*, translated with an introduction and commentary by John Minford, New York: Penguin Books, p. xiii.

57 Wilhelm, R. (2003), *I Ching or Book of Changes*, translated by Richard Wilhelm with a forward by C.G. Jung, London: Penguin Books, p. xlvii.
58 The Economist (2011), "The Long March of the Invisible Mr Ren," *The Economist*, 2 June 2011.
59 Yang, S.L. (2013), *Huawei Kao Shenme (What Huawei Relies On)*, Beijing: China CITIC Press, p. 20.
60 Tian, T. and Wu, C.B. (2012), *Xia yige dao xia de hui bu hui shi Huawei? (Is Huawei the next one to fall?)*, Beijing: China CITIC Press, pp. 46–48. Author's translation.
61 Yang, S.L. (2013), *Huawei Kao Shenme (What Huawei Relies On)*, Beijing: China CITIC Press, pp. 42–43.
62 Lu, T. (1999), *Chinese Civilisation: History of Prior the Qin Dynasty* (in Chinese), Shiji-azhuang, China: Hebei Education Publishing House, p. 379.
63 Ibid, p. 381.
64 Fung, Y.L. (1947), *The Spirit of Chinese Philosophy*, translated by E.R. Hughes, London: Routledge, p. 10.
65 Lau, D.C. (1979), *Confucius: The Analects*, translated with an introduction by D.C. Lau, London: Penguin Books, p. 86
66 Fung, Y.L. (1947), *The Spirit of Chinese Philosophy*, translated by E.R. Hughes, London: Routledge, p. 10.
67 Ebrey, P.B. (1993), *Chinese Civilization: A Sourcebook*, New York: The Free Press, p. 17.
68 Bary, W.T., Wing-Tsit Chan, and B. Watson (1960), *Sources of Chinese Tradition*, New York: Columbia University Press, p. 15.
69 Ebrey, P.B. (1993), *Chinese Civilization: A Sourcebook*, New York: The Free Press, p. 17.
70 Shenkar, O. and Ronen, S. (1987), "The Cultural Context of Negotiations: The Implications of Chinese Interpersonal Norms," *The Journal of Applied Behavioral Science*, 23 (2), 263–275. Robertson, C.J. (2000), "The Global Dispersion of Chinese Values: A Three-Country Study of Confucian Dynamism," *Management International Review*, 40 (3), 253–268. Hasegawa, H. and Noronha, C. (2014), *Asian Business and Management: Theory, Practice and Perspectives*, New York: Palgrave Macmillan.
71 Asiaweek (2001), "Enterprise: Cover Story: The Next Revolution," *Asiaweek*, 5 October, 1.
72 Chang, C. (1959), "The Significance of Mencius," *Philosophy East and West*, 8 (1/2), 37–42.
73 Ebrey, P.B. (1993), *Chinese Civilization: A Sourcebook*, New York: The Free Press, p. 57.
74 Ibid.
75 Tang, Y.J., Zhang, Y.N. and Fang, M. (2001), *A Grand Exposition of Chinese Culture: Chinese Confucianism* (in Chinese), Beijing: Peking University Press, p. 27.
76 Lau, D.C. (1979), *Confucius: The Analects*, translated with an introduction by D.C. Lau, London: Penguin Books, p. 116.
77 Ibid, pp. 136–137.
78 Ibid, p. 144.
79 Ibid, p. 123.
80 Ibid, p. 135.
81 Ibid, p. 63.
82 Ibid.
83 Ibid, p. 115.
84 Ibid, p. 119.
85 Lau, D.C. (1979), *Confucius: The Analects*, translated with an introduction by D.C. Lau, London: Penguin Books, p. 74.
86 Michael, F. (1962), "The Role of Law in Traditional, Nationalist and Communist China," *The China Quarterly*, 9 (January–March), 124–148.
87 Lau, D.C. (1979), *Confucius: The Analects*, translated with an introduction by D.C. Lau, London: Penguin Books, p. 112.
88 Ibid, p. 92.

89 Ibid, p. 74.
90 De Bary, W.T., Chan, W.-T. and Watson, B. (1960), *Sources of Chinese Tradition*, New York: Columbia University Press, pp. 16–17.
91 Lai, K.L. (1995), "Confucian Moral Thinking," *Philosophy East and West*, 45 (2), 249–272.
92 Lau, D.C. (1979), *Confucius: The Analects*, translated with an introduction by D.C. Lau, London: Penguin Books, p. 114.
93 Hucker, C.O. (1975), *China's Imperial Past: An Introduction to Chinese History and Culture*, London: Duckworth, pp. 84–85.
94 Chan, W.T. (1988), "Exploring the Confucian Tradition," *Philosophy East and West*, 38 (3), 234–250.
95 Lau, D.C. (1979), *Confucius: The Analects*, translated with an introduction by D.C. Lau, London: Penguin Books, p. 85.
96 Ibid, p. 122.
97 Ibid, p. 123.
98 Ibid, p. 135.
99 Ibid, p. 137.
100 Ibid, p. 159.
101 Wu, Q.Y. (2015), *Wu Qingyu zhizhuan: Zhongdi jingshen (Biography of Wu Qingyuan: The Spirit of the Middle Target)*, Beijing: China CITIC Press, pp. 196–197.
102 Yang, S.L. (2013), *Huawei Kao Shenme (What Huawei Relies On)*, Beijing: China CITIC Press, p. 39. Author's translation.
103 Ibid, pp. 38–39.
104 Tian, T. and Wu, C.B. (2012), *Xia yige dao xia de hui bu hui shi Huawei? (Is Huawei the Next One to Fall?)*, Beijing: China CITIC Press, pp. 124–125.
105 Ibid, p. 125.
106 Wu, C.B. (2014), *Huawei meiyou mimi (Huawei Has No Secrets)*, Beijing: China CITIC Press, p. 27.
107 Tian, T. and Wu, C.B. (2012), *Xia yige dao xia de hui bu hui shi Huawei? (Is Huawei the Next One to Fall?)*, Beijing: China CITIC Press, p. 126.
108 Ibid, p. 102. Author's translations.
109 Kennedy, P. (1988), *The Rise and Fall of the Great Power*, London: Fontana Press, p. 8.
110 Chan, W.T. (1988), "Exploring the Confucian Tradition," *Philosophy East and West*, 38 (3), 234–250.
111 Shen, V. and Shun, K.L. (2008), *Confucian Ethics in Retrospect and Prospect*, Washington: The Council for Research on Values and Philosophy, p. 42.
112 Yip, G.S. and McKern, B. (2016), *China's Next Strategic Advantage: From Imitation to Innovation*, Cambridge, MA: MIT Press, p. 71.
113 Woetzel, J., Chen, Y., Manyika, J., Roth, E., Seong, J. and Lee, J. (2015), *The China Effect on Global Innovation*, Seattle: McKinsey Global Institute, McKinsey & Company, http://www.mckinseychina.com/wp-content/uploads/2015/07/mckinsey-china-effect-on-global-innovation-2015.pdf
114 Liu, H. and Li, K.Q. (2002), "Strategic Implications of Emerging Chinese Multinationals: The Haier Case Study," *European Management Journal*, 20 (6), 699–706.
115 Erisman, P. (2015), *Alibaba's World*, New York: Palgrave Macmillan, p. 28.
116 Ibid., p. 55.
117 Clark, D. (2016), *Alibaba: The House That Jack Ma Built*, New York: HarperCollins Publishers, p. 210.
118 Hofstede, G. and Bond, M.H. (1988), "The Confucius Connection: From Cultural Roots to Economic Growth," *Organizational Dynamics*, 16 (4), 4–22.
119 Lee, S.H. (1996), "Liberal Rights or/and Confucian Virtues?" *Philosophy East and West*, 46 (3), 367–379.
120 Jagersma, P.K. and Gorp, D.M. (2003), "Still Searching for the Pot of Gold: Doing Business in Today's China," *Journal of Business Strategy*, 24 (5), 27–35.
121 Pye, L.W. (1991), "The State and the Individual: An Overview Interpretation," *The China Quarterly*, 127, 443–466.

122 This decision was considered a strategic mistake, as the company had already spent several hundred million RMB and management improvement could have been undertaken after listing.

123 Stanovich, K.E., West, R.F. and Toplak, M.E. (2016), *The Rationality Quotient: Toward a Test of Rational Thinking*, Cambridge, MA: MIT Press.

124 He, J.X., Leng, Y.H. and Ye, K.T. (2015), *Sanshinian Xinshuai (Thirty Years of Rise and Fall)*, Beijing: China CITIC Press, pp. 13–20.

125 Nixon, R.M. (1982), *Leaders*, New York: Simon & Schuster, p. 226.

126 Ibid, pp. 226–227.

127 Although Mao had been in control of the CPC since 1934, it was in 1943 that he was officially elected as 'Chairman Mao' by the CPC Politburo.

128 Salisbury, H. (1985), *The Long March: The Untold Story*, New York: Palgrave Macmillan, p. 126.

129 Ibid, p. 3.

130 Salisbury, H. (1985), *The Long March: The Untold Story*, New York: Palgrave Macmillan, p. 132.

131 Nixon, R.M. (1983), *Leaders*, New York: Simon & Schuster, p. 248.

132 Chen, X.P. and Chen, C.C. (2004), "On the Intricacies of the Chinese *Guanxi*: A Process Model of *Guanxi* Development," *Asia Pacific Journal of Management*, 21, 305–324. Dunning, J.H. and Kim, C. (2007), "The Cultural Roots of *Guanxi*: An Exploratory Study," *The World Economy*, 30 (2), 329–341.

133 Weber, M. (1951), *The Religion of China*, translated from German and edited by H.H. Gerth, New York: The Free Press, p. 209.

134 Luo, Y. and Chen, M. (1997), "Does *Guanxi* Influence Firm Performance?" *Asia Pacific Journal of Management*, 14 (1), 1–17.

135 Lovett, S., Simmons, L.C. and Kali, R. (1999), "*Guanxi* Versus the Market: Ethics and Efficiency," *Journal of International Business Studies*, 30, 231–241.

136 Alston, J.P. (1989), "Wa, Guanxi and Inhwa: Managerial Principles in Japan, China and Korea," *Business Horizons*, March–April, 26–31. Yeung, I.Y.M. and Tung, R.L. (1996), "Achieving Business Success in Confucian Societies: The Importance of *Guanxi* (Connections)," *Organization Dynamics*, 25 (2), Autumn, 54–65. Vanhonacker, W.R. (2004), "When Good *Guanxi* Turns Bad," *Harvard Business Review*, 82 (4), 18–20. Hasegawa, H. and Noronha, C. (2014), *Asian Business and Management: Theory, Practice and Perspectives*, New York: Palgrave Macmillan.

137 Wall, J.A. (1990), "Managers in the People's Republic of China," *Academy of Management Executive*, 4 (2), 19–32.

138 Jacobs, L., Guopei, G. and Herbig, P. (1995), "Confucian Roots in China: A Force for Today's Business," *Management Decisions*, 33 (10), 29–34. Yau, O.H.M., Lee, J.S.Y., Chow, R.P.M., Sin, L.Y.M. and Tse, A.C.B. (2000), "Relationship Marketing the Chinese Way," *Business Horizons*, 43 (1), January–February, 16–24.

139 Lau, D.C. (1979), *Confucius: The Analects*, translated with an introduction by D.C. Lau, London: Penguin Books, p. 61.

140 Yeung, I.Y.M. and Tung, R.L. (1996), "Achieving Business Success in Confucian Societies: The Importance of *Guanxi* (Connections)," *Organization Dynamics*, 25 (2), Autumn, 54–65. Luo, Y. (1997), "Guanxi and Performance of Foreign-Invested Enterprises in China: An Empirical Inquiry," *Management International Review*, 37 (1), 51–70. Lee, D.Y. and Dawes, P.L. (2005), "*Guanxi*, Trust, and Long-Term Orientation in Chinese Business Markets," *Journal of International Marketing*, 13 (2), 28–56.

141 Xin, K.R. and Pearce, J.L. (1996), "*Guanxi*: Connections as Substitutes for Formal Institutional Support," *Academy of Management Executive*, 39, 1641–1658. Yeung, I.Y.M. and Tung, R.L. (1996), "Achieving Business Success in Confucian Societies: The Importance of *Guanxi* (Connections)," *Organization Dynamics*, 25 (2), Autumn, 54–65. Luo, Y. and Chen, M. (1997), "Does *Guanxi* Influence Firm Performance?" *Asia Pacific Journal of Management*, 14 (1), 1–17. Tsang, E.W.K. (1998), "Can *Guanxi* be a Source of Sustained Competitive Advantage for Doing Business in China?" *Academy of Management*

Executive, 12 (2), 64–73. Abramson, N.R. and Ai, J.X. (1999), "Canadian Companies Doing Business in China: Key Success Factors," *Management International Review*, 39 (1), 7–35. Pearce, J. and Robinson, R. (2000), "Cultivating *Guanxi* as a Foreign Investor Strategy," *Business Horizons*, January–February, 31–38.

142 The Economist (2015), "Alibaba: Love on the Rocks," *The Economist*, 17 February 2015.

143 Luo, Y. (2007), *Guanxi and Business* (2nd ed.), Singapore: World Scientific Publishing.

144 Fock, H.K.Y. and Woo, K. (1998), "The China Market: Strategic Implications of *Guanxi*," *Business Strategy Review*, 9 (3), 33–43.

145 Graham, A.C. (1989), *Disputers of the Tao: Philosophical Argument in Ancient China*, La Salle, IL: Open Court, p. 170.

146 Peng, K., Spencer-Rogers, J. and Nian, Z. (2006), "Naïve Dialecticism and the Tao of Chinese Thought," in U. Kim, K. Yang and K. Hwang (eds.), *Indigenous and Cultural Psychology: Understanding People in Context*, New York: Springer, pp. 247–262.

147 Star, J. (2003), *Lao Tzu: Tao Te Ching*, translated and compiled by J. Star, London: Penguin Books, p. 14.

148 Ibid, p. 50.

149 Lin, Y.T. (1976), *The Wisdom of Taotse* (A translation of *Tao Te Ching*, edited and with an Introduction by Lin Yutang), New York: The Modern Library, pp. 265–266.

150 Wang, H. and Nash, P. (2002), "'Doing Nothing' to Win," *The China Daily* (North American Edition), 6 March, 9.

151 Rothbard, M.N. (1990), "Concepts of the Role of Intellectuals in Social Change Toward Laissez Faire," *The Journal of Libertarian Studies*, IX (2), Fall, 44–67.

152 Boaz, D. (1997), *Libertarianism: A Primer*, New York: Free Press, p. 27.

153 Rothbard, M.N. (1990), "Concepts of the Role of Intellectuals in Social Change Toward Laissez Faire," *The Journal of Libertarian Studies*, IX (2), Fall, 44–67.

154 Spencer-Rodgers, J., Williams, M.J. and Peng, K. (2010), "Cultural Differences in Expectations of Change and Tolerance for Contradiction: A Decade of Empirical Research," *Personality and Social Psychology Review*, 14 (3), 296–312.

155 Star, J. (2003), *Lao Tzu: Tao Te Ching*, translated and compiled by J. Star, London: Penguin Books, p. 55.

156 Chen, M.J. (2001), *Inside Chinese Business: A Guide for Managers Worldwide*, Boston: Harvard Business School Press, p. 97.

157 Nisbett, R.E. (2003), *The Geography of Thought: How Asians and Westerners Think Differently . . . and Why*, New York: Free Press, p. 27.

158 Ibid.

159 Martin, C.I. (2005), "Blending Services and Crises: A Few Questions and Observations," *Journal of Service Marketing*, 19 (5), 346–350.

160 Lin, Y.T. (1976), *The Wisdom of Taotse* (A translation of *Tao Te Ching*, edited and with an Introduction by Lin Yutang), New York: The Modern Library, p. 191.

161 Star, J. (2003), *Lao Tzu: Tao Te Ching*, translated and compiled by J. Star, London: Penguin Books, p. 71.

162 Liu, A. (2009), *Huai Nan Zi (The Huainanzi)*, translated and edited by J.Y. Jai and A.P. Xi, Guilin, China: Guanxi Normal University Press, pp. 1306–1307.

163 Liu, A. (2010), *The Huainanzi*, translated and edited by J.S. Major, S.A. Queen, A.S. Meyer and H.D. Roth, New York: Columbia University Press, p. 729.

164 Star, J. (2003), *Lao Tzu: Tao Te Ching*, translated and compiled by J. Star, London: Penguin Books, p. 91.

165 Lin, Y.T. (1976), *The Wisdom of Taotse* (A translation of *Tao Te Ching*, edited and with an Introduction by Lin Yutang), New York: The Modern Library, p. 305.

166 Ibid, pp. 293–294.

167 Ibid, p. 73.

168 Kotler, P. (2003), *Marketing Management*, London: Pearson Education International, p. 92.

169 Kohli, A.K. and Jaworski, B.J. (1990), "Market Orientation: The Construct, Research Propositions, and Managerial Implications," *Journal of Marketing*, 54, April, 1–18.

170 Star, J. (2003), *Lao Tzu: Tao Te Ching*, translated and compiled by J. Star, London: Penguin Books, p. 46.
171 A Chinese distance measurement: 1 *li* = 0.31 mile. However, here *li* is only a metaphorical description.
172 Lin, Y.T. (1976), *The Wisdom of Taotse* (A translation of *Tao Te Ching*, edited and with an Introduction by Lin Yutang), New York: The Modern Library, p. 291.
173 De Cremer, D. and Zhang, J. (2014), "Huawei to the Future," *Business Strategy Review*, 25 (1), 26–29.
174 Tian, T. and Wu, C.B. (2012), *Xia yi ge dao xia de hui bu hui shi Huawei? (Is Huawei the Next to Fall?)*, Beijing: China CITIC Press, p. 73.

4 Ancient military classics and Chinese business

When you point a finger at the moon to indicate the moon, instead of looking at the moon, the stupid ones look at your finger.

– Mao Zedong

When it is obvious that the goals cannot be reached, don't adjust the goals, adjust the action steps.

– Confucius

The history of the failure of war can almost be summed up in two words: too late.

– Douglas MacArthur

Chinese stratagem culture

Many readers may wonder what Chinese military classics have to do with business in China. A short answer is that military classics have long been part of Chinese culture and the crystallisation of Chinese political, philosophical, ethical and military thinking, reflecting to a considerable extent the cultural characteristics of Chinese people in the realm of resolving disagreements and conflicts. For instance, benevolent, holistic and dialectical thinking is prevalent in Chinese military writings. It is because of the application of dialectical thought that many weak but 'righteous' forces have found the strength to triumph over 'sinful' powers. Nor do the military classics apply only to battles and wars; they are also invaluable in diplomacy, politics, commerce, sport and education. It is said that the marketplace is a battlefield and business competition is a bloodless war, so it is clear that military strategy can be effectively applied to business as well as other fields.[1]

It can be said that China is characterised by a culture favouring the use of stratagems, because of its long and war-torn history. Carl von Clausewitz, one of the greatest thinkers on warfare in the West, has described the nature of 'stratagem':

Stratagem implies a concealed intention, and therefore is opposed to straightforward dealing, in the same way as wit is the opposite of direct proof. It has therefore nothing in common with means of persuasion, of self-interest, of force, but a great deal to do with deceit, because that likewise conceals its object. It is itself a deceit as well when it is done, but still it differs from what is commonly called deceit, in this respect that there is no direct breach of word.[2]

According to the *Shiji-Wudi* (*Records of the Grand Historian – the Five Mythical Emperors*), a historical and literary masterpiece covering the period from prehistory in 3000 BC to the early Western Han dynasty (206 BC – AD 25), Huang Di (2697–2598 BC) won a number of crucial battles against Yan Di and Chi You, leading to the unification of various tribes in the Central Plain. His victories were mainly attributable to his application of smart stratagems. For instance, he lured his enemies in deep and lay in ambush, leading to battles of annihilation. 'I have examined the art of war as practiced from the Yellow Emperor [prior to 2070 BC] on down. First be orthodox, and afterward unorthodox; first be benevolent and righteous, and afterward employ the balance of power [*ch'uan*] and craftiness.'[3]

A widespread adoption of stratagem in China is rooted in antiquity. Two conditions have driven Chinese stratagem thinking and writings: a high rate of warfare, and great thinkers and writers who are able to crystallise successful strategic ideas from warfare experiences. Considerable warfare created a fertile soil for stratagem thinking. From 215 BC to AD 1684, there were 1109 major military conflicts between the Chinese and northern nomads and from 210 BC to AD 1900, there were 225,887 recorded armed rebellions.[4] Another study identified as many as 3790 wars, including those with foreign invaders and domestic rebellions, from 1100 BC to AD 1911.[5] It is noted that 'virtually every year witnessed a major battle somewhere in China, significant conflicts erupted nearly every decade, and the nation was consumed by inescapable warfare at least once a century.'[6]

China's substantial warfare created a fertile ground that generated numerous eminent military and philosophical thinkers, many of whom left their mark on Chinese history, just a few of the most prominent being Lu Shang (1156–1017 BC), Sun Wu or Sun Tzu (544–496 BC), Wu Qi or Wu Tzu (440–381 BC), Bai Qi (332–257 BC), Han Xin (231–196 BC), Ban Chao (AD 32–102), Zhuge Liang (181–234), Liu Yu (363–422), Li Shimin (598–649), Yue Fei (1103–1142), Genghis Khan (1162–1227), Liu Bowen (1311–1375) and Yuan Chonghuan (1584–1630).[7] Meanwhile, the Spring and Autumn (770–476 BC) and Warring States periods (476–221 BC) witnessed many sagacious philosophical thinkers such as Confucius, Mencius, Lao Tzu, Guan Tzu and Mo Tzu, and thus this time is commonly known as the era of the 'Hundred Schools of Thought'. These thinkers have also contributed to military thinking and writings.

Chinese philosophers during the periods were keenly involved in discourse on military issues for two reasons. First, during these periods, conflicts between states mainly took the form of warfare; as all Chinese philosophies had a focus on rulers' Tao or strategies for societal harmony and peace, they could not avoid a discussion about the military. Politics and military and economic development were all interwoven and inseparable. Second, battles and wars themselves embraced rich dialectic phenomena, which could often be used to make philosophical points.[8] For instance, Lao Tzu's *Tao Te Ching* contains substantial military wisdom. Research shows that over 10 chapters of the classic directly discourse about military issues, while over 20 chapters have indirect military implications.[9] Lao Tzu's military teachings differ from or complement those of Sun Tzu.[10] These thinkers have contributed to Chinese military thinking and writings. From subsequent dynastic periods, military writings and practices have generated the accumulated and enhanced knowledge by which organisations or individuals could effectively achieve their intended (strategic) objectives. Such knowledge and belief have been passed on from generation to generation till the present day.

Wars and military thinkers gave rise to a sizeable body of ancient Chinese literature on military strategies and tactics, and the earliest writings date back over two millennia. The *Zuo Zhuan or Tso Chuan* (左传), the earliest Chinese work of narrative history as well as a literary masterpiece, covering the period from 722 BC to 468 BC, indicated that there were texts in the West Zhou dynasty (1046–771 BC) such as the *Military Annals* (军志) and the *Military Administration* (军政) which were lost during subsequent chaotic dynastic transitions.[11] In antiquity, a total of 3380 books with 23,503 recorded volumes were written on various aspects of military strategy, tactics and organisation in ancient China.[12] From this huge volume of military literature, two emperors of the Song dynasty (960–1279) dictated that seven of them were designated as standard military textbooks, known as *Wu Jing Qi Shu* or *The Seven Military Classics of Ancient China*. The seven works are *Sun Tzu's Art of War, Tai Gong's Six Secret Teachings, Wu Tzu, The Methods of the Sima, Wei Liao Tzu, Three Strategies of Huang Shigong* and *Questions and Replies between Tang Taizong and Li Weigong*. These became compulsory texts at military academies and the standard knowledge required to qualify for senior military positions in ancient China. Of all the classics, Sun Tzu's work has been most influential, but other thinkers and classics have also contributed to China's military literature. In the Introduction to *Liu An's Art of War*, part of an ancient Chinese classic, *Huainanzi*, Andrew Meyer writes:

> The Sunzi, however, is only the most outstanding extant product of a very voluminous corpus. The Wuzi, Weiliaozi, Sima fa, Taigong liutao, and Huangshigong lüe are other surviving military texts from the era, and other composite texts such as the Lüshi chunqiu and Guanzi contain examples of the genre. Beyond these, the bibliographical treatises of the imperial histories list many military writings that have since been lost.[13]

From the periods of the Xia, Shang and Zhou dynasties (2070–771 BC) onwards, stratagems have widely been used in politics, commerce, warfare, diplomacy and in cultural and social activities. Different major schools of thought in the Spring and Autumn and Warring States periods, such as Confucianism, Taoism, the

Political Strategists, the Military Strategists and the Legalists, all embraced the idea of the stratagem as a key component. Lu Shang, also honorifically known as Tai Gong (or T'ai Kung), has been regarded as the father of the stratagem, as Sima Qian declares in the *Shi Ji*: 'If all under Heaven were divided into thirds, two-thirds had [already] given their allegiance to the Chou.[14] The Tai Gong's plan and schemes occupied the major part.'[15] The importance of stratagems in the Spring and Autumn period (770–476 BC) was noted by Confucius, as indicated in *The Analects*:

> Tzu-lu [a disciple of Confucius] said: 'If you were leading the Three Armies, whom would you take with you?' The Master [Confucius] said: 'I would not take with me anyone who would try to fight a tiger with his bare hands or to walk across the Rivers and die in the process without regrets. If I took anyone it would have to be a man who, when faced with a task, was fearful of failure and who, while fond of making plans, was capable of successful execution.'[16]

To Confucius, having the ability to utilise stratagems to win victories was more important than valour in order to be qualified as a commander-in-chief. As the basis of the school of Military Strategists, Sun Tzu's thought strongly advocates winning through stratagems without fighting. 'Strategy' (战略) in Chinese comprises two characters: *zhan* (战), meaning 'war', 'warfare' or 'combat' and *lue* (略), meaning 'stratagem', 'astuteness' and 'resourcefulness'; the compound thus literally connotes the pursuit of warfare with stratagems.

A sizeable number of strategic thoughts and wise sayings have been influential by their inclusion in many popular readings, novels, dramas and fairy tales as well as the historical, literary and philosophical classics with which the Chinese people are familiar. The *Zuo Chronicle*, the first Chinese work of narrative history, for instance, recorded in detail battles and wars between different states with the vivid descriptions of people and events involving intrigues, treachery and heroism in the period from 722 to 468 BC.[17] As it recounts a large number of the successful stratagems used by states to conquer their enemies, it was appreciated by many generals in the later dynastic periods as a book on military strategy and tactics. A historical literary allusion is 'Sleep on Firewood and Taste Gall', a household tale recorded in the *Zuo Chronicle* and *Shi Ji*, relating a historical event in which a deceptive stratagem was applied perfectly. During the Spring and Autumn period, the Wu army defeated the Yue and captured their king, Goujian. In order to gain an opportunity to stage a comeback, Goujian pretended to bow his head to acknowledge his allegiance and acted as a servant to the king of Wu, Fucai. Goujian went as far as tasting Fucai's stools when he was sick (as a way of assessing the degree of sickness based on the taste) to delude him. Having convinced Fucai that he was loyal and obedient, Goujian was freed to return to his territory (the state of Yue). From then on, Goujian slept on firewood and tasted gall every night in order to remind himself of the revenge he pledged to take for the national humiliation. After 10 years of working assiduously, he managed to build up a strong army and eventually conquered the state of Wu, whereupon Fucai committed suicide.[18] A Chinese literary classic, the *Romance of the Three Kingdoms*, is full of stratagems and plots which are demonstrated to be the key to winning battles, wars and power struggles. It is considered to deserve the title of the most complete work of political and military plotting and scheming. A culture of stratagems started to emerge in the Spring and Autumn period (770–476 BC) or even earlier, as Confucius said:

> The Master said, 'The ancients had three weaknesses, which moderns are not even capable of. The eccentricity of the ancients was carefree, whereas modern eccentricity is licentious. The pride of the ancients was blunt, whereas modern pride is cantankerous. The naivety of the ancients was straight, whereas modern naivety is crafty.'[19]

Liu (2015) has analysed the nature of Chinese stratagem culture and the factors that have shaped its formation and its strategic implications for business, politics and international relations.[20] In a society with a culture of stratagems, people tend to be ready to take any opportunity to outwit their rivals to gain advantage and intuitively on guard against the plots and deceptions of others, whether politically, commercially, militarily or even socially. For instance, when Jack Ma, the founder of Alibaba, launched Taobao to compete with the existing incumbent, eBay, it was done in an extremely secretive manner. 'In taking on eBay, Jack wanted to preserve the element of surprise.'[21] Another 'stratagem' utilised by Alibaba was that just when eBay's China arm, EachNet, ran into declining performance, Alibaba indirectly exposed the information in *Forbes* magazine, exerting pressures on eBay's strategy through its investors.[22] 'He [Jack Ma] plays business like a game of chess.'[23] There is a Chinese saying which reflects this tendency: 'One should never intend to harm others; nor should one forget to guard against their evil intentions.'

As part of stratagem culture, Chinese companies tend to act swiftly and flexibly and respond to any emerging opportunity promptly. Chinese individual-led organisational structure, compared with Western bureaucracy-based hierarchical organisational structure, allows Chinese companies to take action rapidly. This idiosyncrasy has been noted by Harvard academics.[24]

In a society with a culture of stratagems, people tend to be constantly on alert and think holistically about the consequences of each event in order to counterbalance any potential negative impact. The great Chinese philosopher Chuang Tzu (or Zhuang Zi), one of the founders of Taoism (c. 396–286 BC), saw through this cultural attribute and rejected repeated offers of public office, in order to avoid excessive stratagem-related politics. An offer came from Lord Wei of Chu for him to be prime minister, but even at the price of a thousand pieces of gold, he was not at all tempted. Despite having lived in poverty all his life, he was content with his spiritual freedom, living according to Tao and remaining true to himself.

In earlier centuries, Chinese culture had a strong influence on other Asian countries, into which Sun Tzu's *Art of War* was introduced. As a result, these countries have also embraced a culture of stratagems. In those (Asian) societies in which such a culture plays a part, the people are known to have a low level of trust of others and a strongly suspicious attitude. Research shows that 'The overall level of trust among business partners in China and between employers and employees within Chinese organizations is much lower compared with the United States, Germany, and Japan.'[25] Business transactions are mainly carried out on the basis of cash on delivery, as a Chinese saying suggests: 'One would not release the hawk without seeing the hare.' The borrowing and lending of money takes place largely between family members and long-term trusted friends or partners. In addition, social research in Asian societies proves to be much more difficult in terms of collecting empirical data, particularly from face-to-face-interviews, compared with Western societies.

This cultural phenomenon affects Chinese business and public organisations, whose middle managers often go to a great length to fathom what their superiors have in mind, both professionally and socially. Those who are capable of working out the intentions of their superiors (and catering to them) can often do well in their career development. This ability is considered implicitly a part of the skill portfolio of those working in Chinese business and public organisations.

In addition, a unique cultural trait derived from the impact of the historical importance of stratagems is that it is generally difficult for Chinese people to work together in teams, because they have little trust in each other. Without a strong leader, corporate culture, family or other special ties[26] to pull people together, most teamwork within an organisation tends to lack strong bonds, with difficulty in achieving synergy. Most business partnerships are more than likely to fall apart once they have become sizeable and grown strong. Among the companies that have a history of over two hundred years, 3146 were Japanese, 837 German, 222 Dutch and 196 French, but none Chinese. Some key factors attributed to the absence of the longevity of Chinese companies include a lack of trust between the founders (normally the fathers), descendants and professional managers and internal struggles or 'cats and dogs' between family members.[27] A comparison of American and Chinese management styles can be expressed metaphorically: the Americans play bridge while the Chinese play mah-jong. To play bridge well, the two partners need to cooperate closely and form an alliance based on agreed conventions. Playing mah-jong is an individual activity where the player considers only his or her own interests. To win the game, the player has to beware of the preceding player and guard against the next player.

Huawei's founder, Ren Zhengfei, has made a comment on the impact of lacking organisational capability, as a result of their obsession with stratagem, on society in Chinese culture:

> Because Chinese people are too clever, they have lived a poor life for five
> millennia. Japanese and German people are not so clever, but they have

been richer than Chinese for innumerable times. If Chinese people do not contain their cleverness, they will outsmart themselves in the future.[28]

Sun Tzu's *Art of War* (孙子兵法)

Sun Tzu and his influences

Bin Fa or *The Art of War* was written by Sun Wu (孙武), alias Chang Qing (长卿), honorifically known as Sun Tzu (孙子). He was born in the state of Qi (present-day Shandong Province) in the Spring and Autumn period and was a contemporary of Confucius. Sun Tzu's ancestors were Qi nobles and generals, and he was naturally influenced by what he saw and heard. In his time, there were frequent wars between states as well as 'a hundred schools of thought' such as Confucianism, Taoism and Moism, all of which contributed to the foundations of his strategic thinking. To avoid the complicated politics in the state of Qi, Sun Tzu moved to the state of Wu, where he completed the writing of *The Art of War*. He also personally commanded and won victories in a number of crucial battles against the state of Chu and helped Wu to become one of the major powers of the day. Sun Tzu is revered as a great Chinese strategist, as well as a world-renowned military thinker.

One of Sun Tzu's descendants, Sun Bin (孙膑), a contemporary of Mencius, was also a great strategist and wrote *Sun Bin's Art of War*. Sun Bin studied military strategy and tactics under Gui Guzi (鬼谷子), a historically renowned strategist, with a person named Pang Juan, who later became a general in the state of Wei. Pang Juan tricked Sun Bin into serving the king of Wei, only to punish him by having his kneecaps removed, as he was jealous of his former fellow student and afraid that his superior strategic knowledge might allow Sun Bin to overshadow him in the state of Wei someday. Sun Bin's second name was derived from this penalty, *bin* meaning 'kneecapping' (removing someone's kneecaps for the purpose of punishment) in ancient China. His original name remains unknown. Pang Juan kept Sun Bin alive and imprisoned because he wanted him to recite Sun Tzu's *Art of War*, the original of which was burnt by Sun Bin deliberately (thus no one else could have the same knowledge). However, a Qi diplomatic envoy managed to extricate Sun Bin from Wei and so saved his life. Subsequently, Sun Bin helped the state of Qi to beat the Wei, having Pang Juan killed in an ambush. Sun Bin is also renowned as a historic Chinese strategist.[29]

Chinese philosophy is characterised by thinking about and interpreting things in a simple manner. Notably, the all-inclusive strategic teachings of Sun Tzu's *Art of War* are expounded with just over 6000 Chinese characters. Since it was written, Sun Tzu's *Art of War* has been held in high esteem and studied thoroughly by Chinese generals, officials and some monarchs. Those who were influenced by Sun Tzu historically include Sun Bin, Zhang Liang and Han Xin, great strategists from the Han dynasty; Zhuge Liang and Cao Cao, generals and prime ministers as well as strategists in the period of the Three Kingdoms; Li Shimin, general and emperor in the Tang dynasty; and Yue Fei, general in the

Southern Song dynasty. It is particularly notable that the first Chinese emperor, Qin Shihuang, studied Sun Tzu's *Art of War* and united China for the first time around 200 BC, while Mao Zedong used Sun Tzu's strategies to defeat Chiang Kai-shek's Nationalists in 1949, again leading to the unification of China.[30] *The Art of War* is known as the 'Father of Oriental Military Studies'. John Collins, former director of Military Strategy Studies of the National War College in the USA, has written:

> The first great mind to shape strategic thought in that setting belonged to Sun Tzu, who produced the earliest known treatise on *The Art of War* sometime between 400 and 320 B.C. His thirteen little essays rank with the best of all time, including those of Clausewitz, who wrote twenty-two centuries later. No one today has a firmer feel for strategic interrelationships, considerations, and constraints. Most of his ideas make just as much sense in our environment as they did in his.[31]

The influence of Sun Tzu's treatise on other Asian countries has been noted:

> For the past two thousand years it remained the most important military treatise in Asia, where even the common people knew it by name. Chinese, Japanese, and Korean military theorists and professional soldiers have all studied it, and many of the strategies have played a significant role in Japan's storied military history, commencing about the eighth century A.D.[32]

The Art of War was introduced into Japan around 760 AD and was absorbed by Japanese generals; it helped the samurai to transform Japan from a collection of fragmented feudal states into a unified nation.[33] Together with two other Chinese classics, *Romance of the Three Kingdoms* and *Journey to the West*, it is among the highly recommended readings for Japanese CEOs. Many Japanese firms have adopted a military-strategic approach to entering and conquering world markets, owing much to Sun Tzu's war strategies.[34] The book has been translated into more than ten languages and first reached Europe in 1772 after a Jesuit priest translated it into French. The book *1999: Victory Without War*, by the former American president Richard Nixon (1988), directly applies Sun Tzu's fundamental concept of 'winning all without fighting'.[35] The great British general of the Second World War, Bernard Law Montgomery, has recommended *The Art of War* as compulsory reading at all military academies in the world. Harvard professor Michael Porter was known to have quoted Sun Tzu's strategies when giving lectures to National Football League owners, and *The Art of War* was made required reading for a course in entrepreneurship at Columbia University.[36]

Sun Tzu's approach to strategy

Sun Tzu takes a holistic view of strategy development. *The Art of War* has thirteen chapters which constitute a system of strategy formulation and implementation. Sun Tzu suggests that five factors be analysed thoroughly and systematically before a war is pursued. Sun Bin once successfully applied a holistic approach to horse racing, which was very popular in the state of Qi at the time and involved a great deal of gambling money. The king of Qi often competed with his general Tian Ji and always beat him. The rules of racing were such that each side chose three horses of different qualities to compete in separate races; the side which won two of the three races would be the overall winner. Normally, the two sides would set equivalent horses to compete with each other: the best against the best, the next best against the opposing intermediate horse and the weakest against the weakest. Since the king had first choice of horses within the kingdom, his horse in each grade was somewhat better than General Tian's. In one of the major competitions, General Tian therefore deployed a different approach, based on Sun Tzu's advice. As Figure 4.1 shows, General Tian first used his weakest horse (A3) to compete against the king's best (B1), thus losing the first race. This allowed him then to employ his best and second best horses (A1 and A2) respectively against the king's second best and weakest horses (B2 and B3), and he won both of these races. Thus, General Tian was the overall winner. In business, Asian companies have often used their first-class products to compete in second-class segments (the best quality and normal market price, for instance) in order to become leaders or major players in those segments. When Japanese car and motorcycle companies first entered European and North American markets, they used this strategy, which many Korean companies still employ heavily.

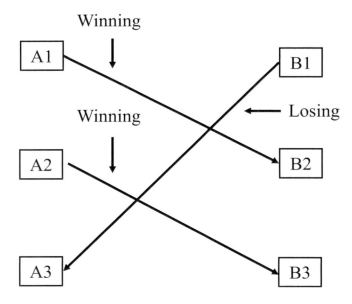

Figure 4.1 Sun Tzu's strategy application

Sun Tzu's strategic approach is characterised by dialectics, adaptability and flexibility. His treatise explains that the weakness of small armies is relative and that they can overcome stronger and larger ones by adopting appropriate strategems. For instance, a small army can concentrate on attacking an enemy's weak point, making itself a strong force in that particular area. Sun Tzu wrote: 'I can concentrate [my forces] while the enemy is fragmented. If we are concentrated into a single force while he is fragmented into ten, then we attack him with ten times his strength. Thus we are many and the enemy is few.'[37] In addition, in Sun Tzu's view, speed can compensate for limited resources both by reducing the consumption of food, logistics, ammunition and the maintenance of vehicles and weapons, and by repeatedly using the same force to attack multiple targets.

Sun Tzu's teachings 1: winning without having to fight

The logic of Sun Tzu's *Art of War* is that warfare, a matter of life and death, is the most important business of the state and so should be thoroughly investigated and analysed. The purpose of waging war is always to achieve political objectives through victory, and as warfare is only a means to an end, the best strategy must be one which allows these objectives to be attained without engaging in warfare. If warfare is unavoidable, it should be undertaken through stratagems, with swift moves to overcome the enemy in order to minimise casualties. Sun Tzu said: 'Subjugating the enemy's army without fighting is the true pinnacle of excellence.'[38] 'Thus the army values being victorious; it does not value prolonged warfare.'[39]

Sun Tzu put emphasis on deception (stratagems): 'Warfare is the Way of deception. Thus although [you are] capable, display incapability to them. When committed to employing your forces, feign inactivity. When your objective is near, make it appear as if distant; when far away, create the illusion of being nearby.'[40] Those stratagems which can lead to the defeat of the enemy without fighting are the best and most highly desirable. Fighting is often a necessary and unavoidable evil, in which case it should be done through deception-based stratagems to keep casualties to the minimum. The utilisation of stratagems in warfare is therefore at the heart of Sun Tzu's *Art of War*.

An important business implication of 'winning without fighting' is that companies should endeavour to achieve market dominance, through developing and implementing strategies, without destroying the profitability of their industries.[41] The US airline industry, for instance, witnessed price-cutting competition because of deregulation in the late 1980s. Between 1989 and 1993, 120 airlines became bankrupt, with a loss to the industry of $12 billion.[42] Many companies are susceptible to head-to-head competition. In the 1980s, for instance, there were several hundred television-manufacturing companies in China. From the late 1980s to the 1990s, RMB 28 billion were invested in the industry and accumulated profits of RMB 450 billion were generated. All of the manufacturers enjoyed good profits. However, starting in the mid-1990s, price wars broke out and the industry underwent a shakedown, which only about 70 companies survived. In 2000, average profitability in the industry was only 2 per cent, and many companies operated at a loss.

How can firms win without fighting in the business context? There are a number of ways of achieving this strategic outcome.

(1) A firm can find a non-confrontational strategy or use an indirect competitive approach.[43] For instance, in the early 1990s, a Chinese retail company selling high-end toys at premium prices opened an outlet (A) on a busy street. In the first few months, although many people visited the shop, few made purchases. Not long after this, another company opened a shop (B) on the opposite side of the street, selling similar products at slightly lower prices. Soon, many people started to buy from Shop B, as they saw that it offered good value compared with Shop A. It appeared that Shop A was performing poorly while Shop B prospered. However, Shop A was kept open to boost Shop B's sales, because both belonged to the same owner, who, by opening two shops under different names with slightly different prices, had given customers a sense of obtaining value for money. In this way, everyone was a winner.

(2) The firm can also proceed in a dramatically different way from what its competitors expect or in a way that is difficult for competitors to respond to.[44] Sun Tzu said: 'In general, in battle one engages with the orthodox and gains victory though the unorthodox.'[45] By the unorthodox Sun Tzu means the unusual, the unexpected and the surprising. In particular, the marketing concept tallies with Sun Tzu's idea of winning without fighting. 'The marketing concept holds that the key to achieving organisational goals consists of being more effective than competitors in creating, delivering, and communicating superior customer value to . . . chosen target markets.'[46] A company pursuing a market-driven strategy avoids head-to-head competition with competitors and tries to serve customers better than or differently from its competitors. The Japanese car manufacturer Toyota, for instance, like many other high-performing companies, puts great emphasis on the provision of excellent service to its customers. In preparation for its entry into the US family car market, unlike many companies which rely on survey research conducted in shopping malls, Toyota went so far as to send its researchers to live with American families in order to get to know its potential customers better. The researchers were instructed to keep records of family members' sleeping and eating habits, their favourite food and drink, leisure activities and even TV programmes. Such data are carefully studied by marketing experts and used as the basis of the company's product designs for the US market. In addition, the company offers study tours of production lines run by professional guides, who explain to visitors every step in the production process and the steps taken to ensure product quality and performance; the visitors are even provided with free accommodation. All these processes are intended to help visitors to understand the company's products and services, allowing them to form deep

impressions which it is hoped will have an impact on marketing in the future.

(3) It is also possible for a firm to make an early move into the market with a new product or into a new segment with an existing product.[47] For instance, Hewlett-Packard took out numerous patents in inkjet printers, successfully blocking Japanese competitors.[48] General Electric was the first large US company to enter emerging markets such as China, India and Mexico, and its CEO, John Welch, believed that GE's earlier move into these markets would deter its competitors from following.[49] In the late 1980s, when most international car makers had doubts about the Chinese passenger car market, Volkswagen (VW), whose top management was admirably insightful and audacious, entered the market with one of its mature models, the Santana, setting up a joint venture with the Shanghai Automotive Industry Corporation. Soon after VW's entry, the joint venture achieved a near monopoly of the car market, recuperating its initial investment within a short period of time.

Sun Tzu's teachings 2: five fundamental factors in winning wars

(1) **The Tao:** 'The Tao causes the people to be fully in accord with the ruler. Thus, they will die with him; they will live with him and not fear danger.'[50] By this Sun Tzu means that if the ruler or leader is united with his solders and has the same shared beliefs, or if the war to be fought is for a righteous cause, the soldiers will be willing to sacrifice their lives for him and will thus become a formidable fighting force. This is derived from the same idea in the *I Ching*, Taoism and Confucianism as discussed in Chapter Three. In modern business terms, it is of paramount importance that organisational leadership has the right policy and a shared culture with its employees in order for them to work hard for the organisation. During the period of economic recession, for instance, most companies fired their employees as a way to survive the difficult times. However, Matsushita Konosuke, the Japanese founder of Matsushita Electric, which owned the well-known electronics brand Panasonic, was a business leader with a long-term vision. Although the company also suffered from financial losses arising from the overstocking of goods, Konosuke resisted pressure from the board of directors to fire employees, deciding that production volume would be halved but not a single employee would be made redundant. His sincerity and loyalty to the employees earned their redoubled efforts and boosted the company's social reputation. As a result, within half a year, all product inventories were sold out. Not only did all the production lines return to normal but the company also expanded its production lines during the recession. With the right Tao, the company later became one of the Global 500 and a world leader in the semiconductor industry.

(2) **Heaven:** 'Heaven encompasses yin and yang, cold and heat, and the constraints of the seasons.'[51] In terms of business, this is equivalent to the

environment. A company must understand its business climate – political, social, cultural, technological and economic – and be sensitive to environmental changes. Although this strategic requirement, which is essential from Sun Tzu's point of view, is clearly understood by informed business-people, it may not be appreciated to such an extent by many companies. There have been indications that many CEOs in Western companies, for example, have little faith in market research.

> In the face of increasing competition and financial pressures to perform, marketing executives for the most part continue to rely on a seditious combination of outdated beliefs and convictions – what we call marketing mythology. This includes instinct and observations about competitors to make mission-critical, multimillion-dollar decisions in a hurry.[52]

In China, sensitivity and adaptability to the business environment are even more important, because it differs greatly from that in the West and is susceptible to substantial changes. An analysis of such changes also requires great insight and learned judgement. For instance, Mary Kay and other American direct-sales companies such as Avon Products, Nu Skin and Amway entered the Chinese market with get-rich-quick direct-sales schemes at the end of the 1980s. Within a short period of time, these companies experienced a rapid growth of turnover and profit. However, in April 1998, the Chinese political environment suddenly changed and the State Council announced these practices to be illegal, constituting a threat to social stability. The companies were ordered to terminate such activities and began to experience sharp falls in sales and profits. By that time, Mary Kay, Avon and Amway had an estimated investment of $200 million in China, with substantial turnover and profits. In 1997, for instance, Avon had revenues of $75 million, but then witnessed losses in the next three years. However, these American firms soon found ways of adapting to the environmental changes and saw their profits recover. They simply abandoned the system by which individuals acted as 'sales agents' (buying and selling merchandise) and changed them into 'sales promoters' (working on a commission basis). To the Chinese authorities, these individuals had become employees in the retail business, while to consumers nothing had really changed, reflecting a Chinese saying: 'old wine in a new bottle'.[53]

(3) The Earth: 'Earth encompasses far or near, difficult or easy, expansive or confined, fatal or tenable terrain.'[54] This indicates the battlefield, represented by the marketplace in business. Sun Bin led armies to victory in a number of battles, before which he always thoroughly studied the battlefields personally. In the early 1990s, Japanese television sets almost completely dominated the Chinese market, based primarily on solid market research and product adaptation. For instance, the Japanese manufacturers understood that China used a different voltage system from that in Japan, that Chinese consumers were concerned to minimise consumption of electricity and wanted a louder sound system, a warranty and after-sale service, that they mostly lived in apartments with confined space, which limited TV size, and importantly that the market would bear a premium price because of the limited competition.

Whether a company can understand the marketplace correctly or not can often determine whether it becomes a loser or a winner. When Volkswagen and Peugeot entered the Chinese market by setting up joint ventures at approximately the same time in the mid-1980s, the two companies experienced quite different performance outcomes. From the beginning of its operation, VW underwent rapid growth, with sales of over $2 billion by 1995. With a capacity of 300,000 cars, it produced around 200,000 units per year, taking more than a 50% share of the passenger car market until the early 2000s. In contrast, having the capacity to make 90,000 cars, Peugeot sold only 2000 in 1996 and suffered heavy losses in subsequent years. Interestingly, it was located in a more favourable region, that is Guangzhou, with a more open government policy and greater wealth, while VW's venture was established in Shanghai, a conservative area more tightly controlled by the government. However, Peugeot made a fatal mistake in wrongly projecting that market growth would be driven by consumer wealth and demand, while in fact over 70 per cent of cars in China were then purchased by commercial organisations.[55]

(4) The General: 'The general encompasses wisdom, credibility, benevolence, courage, and strictness.'[56] These are the qualities that Sun Tzu believes a general should have to lead armies, and that are also applicable to business leaders. In particular, a general is seen by Sun Tzu to play a vital role in warfare and the nation's security, as he emphasises repeatedly in his treatise:

> Therefore, a general who understands warfare is Master of Fate for the people, ruler of the state's security or endangerment.[57]

> The general is the supporting pillar of the state. If his talents are all-encompassing, the state will invariably be strong. If the supporting pillar is marked by fissures, the state will invariably grow weak.[58]

Similarly, a company's 'fate' is also determined by its top management or CEO, who must have the right qualities and abilities. In addition, the leader should command the art of leadership, which requires first the selection of the right people.

Sun Tzu said:

> Thus one who excels at warfare seeks victory through the strategic configuration of power, not from reliance on men. Thus he is able to select men and employ strategic power . . . One who employs strategic power commands men in battle as if he were rolling logs and stones. The nature of wood and stone is to be quiet when stable but to move when on precipitous ground.[59]

In Sun Tzu's view, the outcome of warfare depends on the overall strategic power,[60] not on individuals. However, it is important that the right people are chosen to take advantage of strategic power. One kind of strategic power, for instance, arises at the opportune time and on advantageous terrain from popular support (i.e. when Heaven, Earth and human factors all work in harmony).

Who then are the right people? Sun Tzu said:

> He does not understand the Three Armies' military affairs but directs them in the same way as his civil administration. Then the officers will become confused. He does not understand the Three Armies' tactical balance of power but undertakes responsibility for command. Then the officers will be doubtful. When the Three Armies are already confused and doubtful, the danger of the feudal lords arises. This is referred to as 'a disordered army drawing another on to victory'.[61]

In business organisations, this means that managerial jobs must be done by the people who know how to manage (with proper managerial training) and who understand the businesses that the organisation is in. In many research-based organisations or universities, for instance, when people have proved to be highly competent in research (with significant high-quality research outcomes), they are often promoted to managerial positions. Since research competence and managerial capabilities are two different things, managerial confusion and disorder can often occur in such organisations.

Sun Tzu said: 'When the general regards his troops as young children, they will advance into the deepest valleys with him. When he regards the troops as his beloved children, they will be willing to die with him.'[62] This was quite an effective way of directing and leading armies in ancient China. Leading through love is also quite common in many successful Asian business organisations. Senior managers in these organisations often forge close relationships with their employees and pay great attention to their career development, family issues and cultural life. Many Japanese companies have a life-long employment policy and treat their employees as family members. Senior managers will attend their birthday parties and wedding ceremonies.

(5) **The Laws (for military organisation and discipline):** 'The laws encompass organisation and regulations, the Tao of command, and the management of logistics.'[63] In terms of business, these correspond to a firm's organisational design, division of labour and responsibility, reward and discipline, logistics and value chain management, all of which are fundamental to carrying out the company's mission and strategy. The importance of organisation and discipline is best illustrated by the example of McDonald's, the global leader in fast-food retail, with one of the world's most valuable brands. Its success is built on a scientific management process and organisation combined with its global brand. Globally, over 30,000 franchised McDonald's restaurants all operate on the basis of the same

philosophical formula: QSC&V, standing for quality, service, cleanliness and value. As a result, they do not require highly educated staff or the most talented managers, yet the parent company maintains a strong and sustainable developmental momentum.

Sun Tzu's teachings 3: intelligence and strategic deduction

Sun Tzu wrote:

> Before the engagement, one who determines in the ancestral temple that he will be victorious has found that a majority of factors are in his favour. Before the engagement one who determines in the ancestral temple that he will not be victorious has found that few factors are in his favour.[64]

By this Sun Tzu suggests that before the real war breaks out, the general should carry out a plan that analyses and predicts the final outcome, namely a war on paper. If the analytical outcome shows a victory, the army stands a strong chance of winning. However, in order to undertake such a realistic and meaningful analytical exercise, intelligence must be generated and gathered. Sun Tzu said: 'Thus it is said if you know them [enemies/competitors] and know yourself, your victory will not be imperilled. If you know Heaven and know Earth, your victory can be complete.'[65]

A Chinese blue-chip company, Galanz, began in business with a single farmer manufacturing eiderdown in a small Chinese town in 1978. It has expanded step-by-step based on sound market intelligence and analyses and has now grown into a leading home appliance manufacturer in China and the global leader in the microwave market. After its initial success, the company first diversified into advertising, property and trade. There were two watersheds that transformed the company. In 1991, the founder spent a year studying the microwave market in China and found that it was dominated by imports, while domestic manufacturers were rather weak. In particular, the market potential was enormous. The ownership of microwaves in the USA was then about 80 per 100 households, in Japan and Korea 50–60 and in Western Europe 40–50, while in China only 3–4 per cent of homes had one. The market appeared to be poised for rapid growth. As a result, in 1992 the company introduced a production line from Toshiba with the most advanced microwave technology of the time. In 1993, 10,000 ovens rolled off the production line, and in 1994, 100,000 were sold. In 1995 the company's turnover reached 200,000 and Galanz became the best-known Chinese microwave brand, with a market share of 25 per cent.

Galanz's rapid growth attracted the attention of international competitors such as Panasonic, Sharp, Samsung and LG, which adopted two strategies to contain Galanz's development. From a position of financial strength, they took an approach of strategic loss by lowering prices and increasing their market shares. On the other hand, they started to acquire other Chinese competitors to expand their market territories. It was evident that a 'microwave war' was pending between the foreign companies and Galanz. A marketing expert offered two strategic options to the Galanz president: (1) giving up the microwave business and selling out to the competitors at a high price or (2) mustering all available resources and fighting to the bitter end. The president chose the second option. This was implicitly based on Sun Tzu's strategic principles. Sun Tzu said: 'On fatal terrain you must do battle.'[66] 'Cast them into hopeless situations and they will be preserved; have them penetrate fatal terrain and they will live. Only after the masses have penetrated dangerous terrain will they be able to craft victory out of defeat.'[67] To be fully prepared for the coming war, Galanz reluctantly sold all its other profitable businesses at prices far lower than full market value because of the time pressure. In 1996, having made everything ready, Galanz staked everything on a single throw by launching an all-out price war. It lowered its prices at the high end of the product range (competing against foreign brands) by 40 per cent and threw the competition into chaos. By the end of 1998, Galanz's market share was over 35 per cent and it had become the market leader in China. This action and outcome followed Sun Tzu's strategies to the letter. Sun Tzu said:

> Thus if I determine the enemy's disposition of forces while I have no perceptible form, I can concentrate my forces while the enemy is fragmented. If we are concentrated into a single force while he is fragmented into ten, then we attack him with ten times his strength. Thus we are many and the enemy is few.[68] . . . Attack where they are unprepared. Go forth where they will not expect it.[69]

Galanz gathered all its resources to seize the territory of foreign brands – the premium segments – and managed to catch the enemy unprepared.

Tai Gong's *Six Secret Teachings* (六韬)

The author and his historical significance

Six Secret Teachings was written by Jiang Tai Gong (姜太公) or the Duke of Zhou, named Lu Shang (吕尚) and also known as Jiang Ziya (姜子牙).[70] As a legendary figure known throughout Chinese history, Jiang Tai Gong is regarded as a great statesman and strategist, the father of strategic studies. He is often described as wisdom incarnate, and his military theory holds an important position in the history of Chinese military studies. Having acted as the advisor to King Wen and his son King Wu, he helped the latter to defeat the strong armies of the Shang dynasty, taking personal command of the crucial battle leading to the downfall of the Shang dynasty. Regarded as a major contributor to the rise of the Zhou dynasty, Jiang Tai Gong was granted the dukedom of Qi. At the time, the kingdom, as well as the Zhou dynasty, was seriously threatened by rebels from the old dynasty and ethnic minorities. Jiang Tai Gong successfully devised various strategies and foiled the rebel threats. His personal command of various battles accorded him first-hand experience of military strategy and enabled him to write the first treatise on strategy, *Tai Gong's Six Strategic Teachings* (or *Tai Gong's Liu Tao* in Chinese), which has been a major source of strategic wisdoms for centuries. Jiang Tai Gong was also appointed prime minister in the early period of the Zhou dynasty, and his classic work, *The Rites of Zhou*, had a strong influence on later Chinese culture and society.

Six Secret Teachings takes the form of dialogues between Jiang Tai Gong and Kings Wen and Wu. It consists of six chapters, and is concerned with politics, economics and culture as well as military strategy and tactics. The first three chapters, namely Wentao (文韬) (Civil Secret Teaching), Wutao (武韬) (Martial Secret Teaching) and Longtao (龙韬) (Dragon Secret Teaching), mainly focus on strategic and organisational issues, while the other three, Hutao (虎韬) (Tiger Secret Teaching) Baotao (豹韬) (Leopard Secret Teaching) and Quantao (犬韬) (Canine Secret Teaching) largely deal with tactical concerns.

Key point 1: importance of political considerations and strategies

In his *Art of War*, Sun Tzu places Tao (rightful or righteous political strategy) as the most important of the five key success factors, while in the *Six Secret Teachings*, a chapter is devoted to a discussion of political strategy and emphasis is placed on the fundamental role of political considerations in warfare. A major difference between the treatises of Sun Tzu and Tai Gong is the scope of discussion, the latter covering much broader issues and putting particular emphasis on political strategy. In essence, this chapter is about how 'Tao' should be put into practice.

Tai Gong writes:

> All under Heaven is not one man's domain. All under Heaven means just that, all under Heaven. Anyone who shares profit with all the people under Heaven will gain the world. Anyone who monopolises its profits will lose the world. Heaven has its seasons, Earth its resources. Being capable of sharing these in common with the people is true humanity. Wherever there is true humanity, All under Heaven will give their allegiance.[71]

Tai Gong believed that a monarch having absolute power should do things for the people, not for himself, and should share the benefits of power with the people in order to retain it. In terms of military affairs, wars fought to share profits with others are just, while those waged to monopolise profits are unjust. Just wars will be won eventually. Historically, those empires that have tried to take over others have all ended in failure, such as the Egyptians, Romans, Byzantines and Ottomans. In business, a firm should share profits with its stakeholders, business partners, suppliers, distributors and even competitors (allowing competitors to exist) if it is to survive and prosper. The richest person in Hong Kong, Li Ka-shing, has shared his secret of success: when he forms partnerships, he always makes a concession to let his partners get more than they are

entitled to get. One of his widely quoted remarks is that 'It doesn't matter how strong or capable you are; if you don't have a big heart, you will not succeed.'
    Tai Gong writes:

> Sharing worries, pleasures, likes and dislikes with the people constitutes righteousness. Where there is righteousness the people will go. . . . In general, people hate death and take pleasure in life. They love and incline to profit. The ability to produce profit accords with the Tao. Where the Tao resides, All under Heaven will give their allegiance.[72]

Only by doing righteous things can one win hearts and minds of employees, partners and opponents, whether in politics, military affairs or business. Tai Gong viewed 'loving the people' as the foundation for prolonged political stability, peace and social tranquillity. He said:

> Thus one who excels at administering a state governs the people as parents govern their beloved children or as an older brother acts towards his beloved younger brother. When they see their hunger and cold, they are troubled for them. When they see their labours and suffering, they grieve for them . . . Rewards and punishments should be implemented as if being imposed upon yourself. Taxes should be imposed as if taking from yourself. This is the Way to love the people.[73]

Although Tai Gong refers to statesmanship and the effective ways of governing a state and maintaining national stability, his words are also applicable to business organisations. That is, business leaders should love their employees as recommended by Tai Gong. It is known that most successful Chinese and Japanese companies protect and look after their employees well. For instance, Haier is one of the most successful Chinese companies, with an international reputation. In its pioneering days, when the general manager took up his post, the first thing he did was to purchase a large bus to provide shuttle services for his employees.[74] At the time, several thousand employees all had lunch in the company's canteen, which was not large enough to serve everyone at the same time. The general manager decided that frontline workers would be served first and managers last. Haier's management also made great efforts to improve working conditions for employees in all workshops. In Japan, top management endeavours to make the employees feel at home and create a relaxed and even entertaining working environment. While there are strict rules within the company, their employees are well taken care of. Japanese companies generally mark employees' birthdays, weddings and funerals; as a result, the employees demonstrate enormous loyalty to the companies.

Key point 2: attaining victories without fighting

In line with Sun Tzu's core military thinking, Tai Gong not only strongly echoes the strategic outcome of winning without fighting but also details 12 strategies to attain such an outcome.[75] 'If you can attain complete victory without fighting, without the great army suffering any losses, you will have penetrated even the realm of ghosts and spirits.'[76]

> Thus who excels in warfare does not await the deployment of forces. One who excels at eliminating the misfortunes of the people manages them before they appear. Conquering the enemy means being victorious over the formless. The superior fighter does not engage in battle.[77]

It can be seen that Tai Gong strongly advocates attaining complete victory without fighting as the best strategic outcome, but implies that it would be an ideal and extreme result. He expounds 12 strategies for achieving the outcome of winning without fighting. Although most of these are obsolete by today's standards, they express two basic principles: using stratagems to cause the enemy to collapse and relying on the Tao – blocking the enemy's access to resources and key personnel.

During an early period of the Tang dynasty (618–907), the second Tang emperor, Li Shimin, also known as Taizong, succeeded to the throne in 626. He was regarded as one of the greatest emperors as well as strategists in Chinese history. When he was just enthroned, Eastern Tujue leaders were about to launch a military campaign with hundreds of thousands of troops ready to be marching into the central plains, to take advantage of a potentially chaotic state. The danger was imminent to the new regime.

As an experienced commander, Taizong first dispatched one of his most capable generals to engage in a preemptive heavy blow on the enemy's advance detachment, with an effect of striking terror in the invaders' heart. Becoming nonplussed, the Tujue leader sent an emissary to meet Taizong, with an intention to ascertain the circumstances. To continue his preemptive tactic, the emperor kept the emissary in-house and deployed a grand military arrangement in front of the invading force, making the opponents feel somewhat frightened. However, instead of launching a strike, Taizong made his own army retreat to a great distance, while he remained standing there to talk to the Tujue's leader. Taizong explained to his ministers that the Tujue army dared to invade because they knew that the Tang had a new emperor who was not in firm control yet; if his forces took a defensive stance and showed their weaknesses, he would be more than likely to be defeated. However, if Taizong approached the Tujue alone, without taking them seriously, while his army appeared to be ready to stake everything on a single throw, he would be in control, either fighting or talking. As Taizong anticipated, the Tujue leader soon sent a representative to beseech peace negotiations. This episode has become a classic case of winning without fighting.

An example illustrates the stratagem of 'blocking the enemy's access':

> Another tactic for utilizing a strategic position is to capture a key decision-maker in the buying process. Federal Express does this by earning the loyalty of corporate secretaries through a periodical called 'Via FedEx.'

The free magazine has over one million readers and is focused on helping secretaries improve their job performance. Corporate secretaries are a strategic customer set to capture, since they are often the ones who determine when a package should be sent overnight and which carrier to use.[78]

By circulating its magazine, FedEx has managed to control the important corporate 'gatekeepers' for packages and block its competitors from access to these companies, thus winning a battle without fighting.

Key point 3: the vital role of generals

In the *Six Secret Teachings*, Tai Gong goes to great lengths to emphasise and discuss the importance of generals in deciding military outcomes. For example, 'If one obtains a Worthy man to lead it, the army will be strong and the state will prosper. If one does not obtain a Worthy general, the army will be weak and the state will perish.'[79] In his view, a country's fate depends on the qualities of its generals. Tai Gong discusses five critical talents for a good general: courage, wisdom, benevolence, trustworthiness and loyalty. 'If he is courageous he cannot be overwhelmed. If he is wise he cannot be forced into turmoil. If he is benevolent he will love his men. If he is trustworthy he will not be deceitful. If he is loyal he will not be of two minds.'[80] Echoing the Confucian view of benevolent government, Tai Gong emphasises leadership by example:

> If in winter the general does not wear a fur robe, in summer does not carry a fan, and in the rain does not set up a canopy, he is called a 'general of proper form.' Unless the general himself submits to these observances, he will not have the means to know the cold and warmth of the officers and soldiers . . . If, when they advance into ravines and obstacles or encounter muddy terrain, the general always takes the first steps, he is termed a 'general of strength.' If the general does not personally exert his strength, he has no means to know the labours and hardships of the officers and soldiers.[81]

These are considered by Tai Gong as techniques for attaining victory. A good general should lead from the front and share both happiness and suffering with his soldiers. In this way, his soldiers will devote their lives to fight with him. In terms of business implications, a business leader should lead by example and work closely with employees in order to understand their working conditions and environment as well as their personal and family needs. Huawei's founder, Ren Zhengfei, has well embraced such a leadership philosophy. At the stage of business start-up, to develop a kind of central-office digital automatic switch needed by a customer, Huawei concentrated all the company's funds and personnel, with over 50 R&D staff, to fight a 'life and death' battle. Ren worked with his staff day and night consecutively for a number of months, eating and sleeping in a rented office building, many without a bed but simply on polystyrene foam boards. Finally they succeeded and delivered the product as required by the contract.

If employees have encountered unexpected difficulties, companies should provide the necessary support, both moral and financial. This is known as human-based corporation culture. One of Haier's key success factors is its emphasis on leadership by example, and all managers in Haier must work with great motivation and drive. With stringent criteria for management evaluation, their performance is closely monitored. Underperforming managers are criticised and fined to varying degrees, often being exposed in the company's newspaper, *Haier People*. Haier's management philosophy is that the quality of managers is the determinant of company performance and that there are no incompetent workers, but bad managers. As a result, the company has created a corporation culture with great cohesiveness. Some of its middle managers have rejected job offers from other companies with much more attractive financial packages, because they feel extremely proud of working for Haier.

Tai Gong stresses the independence of military affairs from interference by the ruler and flexibility in warfare. He writes:

> Military matters are not determined by the ruler's commands; they all proceed from the commanding general. When the commanding general approaches an enemy and decides to engage in battle, he is not of two minds.[82] . . . In general, as for the Tao of the military, nothing surpasses unity. The unified can come alone, can depart alone.[83]

These principles are still fully applicable to today's business domain and consistent with contemporary organisational theories. Nevertheless, in many organisations, particularly public institutions, these principles are often ignored. The degree of interference often depends on the personality of the leader: some like to meddle, while others adopt a Taoist approach, letting things follow their own courses without interference.

Tai Gong teaches that it is important for a general to create prestige and awe in order to establish effective leadership.

> The general creates awesomeness by executing the great, and becomes enlightened by rewarding the small . . . When rewards extend down to the cowherds, grooms, and stablemen, these are rewards penetrating downward to the lowest. When punishments reach the pinnacle and rewards penetrate to the lowest, then your awesomeness has been effected.[84]

These may be seen as special and effective parts of the reward and punishment policy. In a business sense, if a senior manager, particularly one who has made major contributions to a company's development, has made a serious mistake, a severe punishment, rather than a soft-hearted and merciful response, will bring about a strong awe-inspiring effect. Similarly, if junior members of staff have made contributions to the organisation, rewarding them will have a strong effect on their colleagues. Thus, one of the key success factors for Haier has been its clear policy of applying a graded set of appropriate rewards and punishments.

The methods of the Ssu-ma (Sima)[85] (司马法)

The author and significance of the treatise

The Methods of the Ssu-ma (Sima), also known as *Ssu-ma Jang-chu (Sima Rang Ju) Bing Fa* or *The Military Methods of the Sima Rang Ju*, is generally considered to have been written and compiled by *Sima Rang Ju*. It will be referred to below by the abbreviated title of *Sima Fa*. 'Sima' is an ancient military title, meaning the officer in charge of horses, and because of the horse's vital importance to the military in antiquities, it eventually came to designate military matters in general. 'As an official title it apparently first appeared in the earliest dynasties of the Sage Emperors, and by the Chou (Zhou) dynasty it had been elevated to Ta Ssu-ma – "Great" Ssu-ma, or Minister of War.'[86]

According to the *Shiji*, Sima Rang Ju was a military leader and an official in the state of Qi during the Spring and Autumn period (770–476 BC). Having been highly knowledgeable about military strategies and tactics, Rang Ju was recommended by King Wei's advisor Yan Ying to serve the king as a general. Having repulsed enemy invasions and recovered lost territory, he was appointed by King Wei as Great Sima or minister of war. Rang Ju was subsequently entrusted by King Wei to collate and compile earlier writings by holders of his post, to which he added his own ideas; therefore, the book acquired the title of *Military Methods of Sima Rang Ju*. Since the new book was based upon earlier versions that were primarily written by Great Simas or ministers of war, it included and represented strategic wisdom from before the Spring and Autumn period. The original had 155 chapters, but only 5 survived the Han dynasty. The book has been regarded as a major source for treatises on military strategy and tactics in later times. It was introduced into Japan around the fifteenth century and was published in a French translation in 1772.

The book places great emphasis on administration, organisation and discipline, rather than military strategy and tactics. *The History of the Former Han Dynasty* by Pan Ku (Ban Gu), a well-known historian from the Eastern Han dynasty, classified it under the category of *li* or rites.[87] In ancient China, *li* included not only social ceremonies and proprieties but also, more importantly, state political and military systems, regulations and laws, as there was no distinction between rites and laws in those days. The military 'rites or laws' covered in the book exerted a great influence on later dynasties.

Key point 1: aggression leads to demise

The *Sima Fa* states: 'Thus, even though a state may be vast, those who love warfare will inevitably perish. Even though calm may prevail under Heaven, those who forget warfare will certainly be endangered.'[88] If the rulers of many great ancient civilisations, such as the Egyptian, Roman, Byzantine and Ottoman empires, had had a chance to listen to and embrace this piece of advice, they might have survived as long as China. Overindulgence in warfare not only wastes limited national resources, natural and financial, but also diminishes its human potential by sacrificing the talented and youthful. On the other hand, many Chinese emperors were overindulgent, lascivious and decadent, paying too little attention to warfare, which resulted in the demise of their empires. This is particularly true of the last dynasty during the nineteenth century, when ill-prepared imperial armies encountered those of the Western industrial powers, suffering heavy defeats and humiliation and bringing about a decline in China's fortunes which has lasted for over two centuries.

In terms of the application of this analogy to business, if a large firm is wantonly pursuing unrelated mergers and acquisitions to conquer many other businesses or expanding into too many other unrelated sectors through greenfield development, sooner or later it will collapse. The financial and human resources of even the largest firm are limited, so that if it spreads them too thinly, it will be unable to manage its business portfolio effectively. On the other hand, if a large and successful firm is complacent, it is likely to fail to take proactive strategic approaches to development, running the risk of facing a decline. Following the same logic, a successful firm should seek expansion through innovation and the introduction of new products at a steady pace.

Key point 2: laws and disciplines are fundamental for victory

In the governance and administration of armies, benevolence is the foundation, but rites or laws should be used as organisational assurance. In the pursuit of benevolent government, war must be used against rebels (feudal lords); in the administration of an army, moral education should be at the core, but those who disobey orders should be executed; enemies should be allowed to surrender and be treated with humanity, while those who resist should be annihilated without mercy. In terms of the implications for business management, a firm should combine organisational humanity and compassion with discipline. Successful Asian organisations, including Chinese and Japanese, exemplify this line of thinking by treating employees as if they were family members, while also requiring them to follow company rules.

As in other military classics, *Sima Fa* takes a holistic view of successful warfare by pointing out the five key factors: the overall macro-environment, resources, people, the battlefield and weapons. 'Accord with Heaven; make material resources abundant; bring joy to the people; take advantage of the resources of Earth; and value military weapons.'[89] It also stresses the vital role in warfare of the people, generals and soldiers. 'The first is termed men; the second, uprightness; the third, language; the fourth, skill; the fifth, fire; the sixth, water; the seventh, weapons. They are referred to as the Seven Administrative Affairs.'[90] Notably, people come first and weapons last among the major administrative considerations.

While sharing many points with other military classics, the *Sima Fa* puts forward a number of distinctive general principles on the formation of organisational rules or laws.

> All human qualities must be sought among the masses. Test and evaluate them in terms of name and action to see if they cohere, for they must excel at implementation. If they are to perform some action but do not, then you yourself should lead them. If they are to perform some action and do so, then ensure that they do not forget it. If you test them three times successfully then make their talents evident. What is appropriate to human life is termed the law.[91]

This means that the wording of laws and their application must be consistent and appropriate in terms of their acceptability by the people, so any rules must be tested and evaluated before being officially enforced. In addition, laws should have the following characteristics: 'The Tao for establishing the laws consists of first, acceptance (by the people); second, the law (constraining); the third, establishment (the documents for enforcement); fourth, urgency [in administration]; fifth, distinguishing them with insignia; sixth, ordering the colours; seventh, no nonstandard uniforms among the officers.'[92][93] Furthermore, laws should emphasise moral education, constraint and the minimisation of punishment, but should have awe-inspiring effects: 'When those below the ruler all fear the law, it is termed "law".'[94] Most of these principles are applicable to today's businesses. To summarise, the formulation of organisational rules and disciplinary codes should be tested and evaluated carefully before being put into practice. They should be acceptable to the majority of the organisation's members, clearly laid out and swiftly implemented.

Wu Tzu

Wu Tzu and historical position

Wu Tzu or *Wu Tzu Bing Fa* (*Wu Tzu's Art of War*) was written by Wu Qi, respectfully known as Wu Tzu. He was a military leader and politician in the state of Wei (today's Dingtao County in Shandong Province) during the Warring States period. Historically, *Wu Tzu's Art of War* has been seen as equal in importance to that of Sun Tzu, so that the two treatises have often been jointly referred to as *Sun Wu's Art of War*. 'According to the Shih chi, whenever people discussed military theory Sun and Wu were invariably mentioned together, and Ssu-ma Ch'ien's famous biographical chapter permanently canonised that bond.'[95] *Wu Tzu* exerted a profound influence on later military strategic thinking and warfare, the book being circulated overseas in English, French, Japanese and Russian versions.

It is generally believed that Wu Tzu lived in the period of 440–381 BC. As a young man, he was ambitious and went to study Confucianism under Zeng

Shen, the son of one of Confucius's favourite disciples, in the hope of becoming an official in the state of Lu. When his mother died, he failed to attend her funeral, so Zeng Shen refused to continue having him as a student because of his violation of Confucian filial ethics. Wu Qi then turned to military studies, with outstanding results. When the state of Qi attacked the state of Lu, Wu Qi was appointed as general to defend against invasion. As the head of a relatively small and weak Lu army, he defeated a much stronger Qi force, demonstrating his military talents and potential. As a result, he was the victim of jealous plots by other officials and had to go into exile in the state of Wei. Having won the favour of King Wen of Wei, Wu Qi was made a general and mayor of Xihe County, going on to victory in more than 60 battles against other states. After the death of King Wen, his successor, King Wu, dismissed Wu Qi, who then left for the state of Chu, where he was appointed prime minister by King Dao of Chu. Feeling a debt of gratitude to Dao for his appreciation and recognition of his talents, he endeavoured to undertake all-round reform and made the state of Chu a strong power in the Warring States period. Following the death of King Dao, Wu Qi was killed by those who opposed his reforms.

Although both Sun Tzu and Wu Tzu are of great importance in Chinese military affairs, it should be noted that they lived in different periods, a century apart. Sun Tzu's style emphasises the principles of winning without fighting and applying stratagems and deceptions. Sun Tzu's *Art of War* is more comprehensive and theoretical, describing military strategies and principles in a highly abstract manner with few concrete examples. Since Wu Tzu was himself a military leader with abundant practical experience gained in numerous victorious battles, his *Art of War* has more practical illustrations of military principles than expositions of strategic theory. Wu Tzu was influenced by Confucianism because of his earlier education under Zeng Shen, so that his military thinking embraces more Confucian benevolence, righteousness and codes of behaviour, emphasising victory combined with benevolence. When Wu Tzu was a general during the Warring States period, his actions followed Confucian teachings: 'He took the same food and wore the same clothes as the lowliest of his troops. On his bed there was no mat; on the march he did not mount his horse; he himself carried his reserve rations. He shared exhaustion and bitter toil with his troops.'[96] A particular story highlights the effectiveness of his Confucian-based leadership:

> One of his soldiers was suffering from an abscess, and Wu Ch'i [Tzu] himself sucked out the virus. The soldier's mother, hearing this, began wailing and lamenting. Somebody asked her, saying: 'why do you cry? Your son is only a common soldier, and yet the commander-in-chief himself has sucked the poison from his sore.' The woman replied: 'Many years ago, Lord Wu [Wu Tzu] performed a similar service for my husband, who never left him afterwards, and finally met his death at the hands of the enemy. And now that he has done the same for my son, he too will fall fighting I know not where.'[97]

According to *The History of the Former Han Dynasty*[98] by Pan Ku (Ban Gu), the original *Wu Tzu* had 48 chapters, of which only 6 have survived, these being Planning for the State, Evaluating the Enemy, Controlling the Army, The Tao of the General, Responding to Change and Stimulating the Officers. The following are some of the most important ideas.

Key point 1: the factors determining competitiveness

Wu Tzu's strategic thinking was that in order to develop its competitiveness, a nation should develop internal coherence, culture and integrity in parallel with external competitive capability. Based on historical lessons, Wu Tzu believed that if one of the elements were missing, the nation would be doomed:

> In antiquity the ruler of the Ch'eng Sang clan cultivated Virtue but neglected military affairs, thereby leading to the extinction of his state. The ruler of the Yu Hu clan relied on his masses and loved courage and thus lost his ancestral altars. The enlightened ruler, observing this, will certainly nourish culture and Virtue within the domestic sphere while, in response to external situations, putting his military preparations in order.[99]

The most important thing for a ruler to govern effectively is to win the affection of the common people. Wu Tzu put forward four factors: the Way (Tao), righteousness, plans and the essence. 'The Way' here means the natural law or pattern, 'righteousness' the system and culture by which the people are motivated, 'plans' the measures by which threats are avoided and opportunities are taken, and 'the essence' the methods by which the momentum of victory is maintained. Wu Tzu writes: 'Now if behaviour does not accord with the Way [Tao], and actions do not accord with righteousness, but instead one dwells in magnificence and enjoys nobility, disaster will inevitably befall him.'[100] Wu Tzu suggests four Virtues: 'For this reason the Sage rests the people in the Way [Tao], orders them with righteousness, moves them with the forms of propriety [*li*], and consoles them with benevolence. Cultivate these four virtues and you will flourish. Neglect them and you will decline.'[101]

In terms of the external outlook, Wu Tzu places emphasis on being well prepared for possible warfare and thinking of danger in times of peace: 'In general, first being cautious is the true treasure in the Way [Tao] for ensuring the security of the state. As you have now awakened to the trouble, disaster can be kept away.'[102] A sense of uncertainty on the part of organisational leaders can make them alert so that they think about strategic issues constantly. Huawei and Haier are among the Chinese companies that have embraced this idea. For instance, the top management of the Haier Group believes that business competition has no limits, while constant dangers and threats beset the company, so that the sense of crisis is a major driver for innovation and development. The greatest challenge facing the company comes from the internal (a lack of self-consciousness of the company's vulnerability), not the external (its competitors), and Haier's success depends on innovation and its ability to break free from complacency. To the company's decision-makers, crisis is the driver for survival and development.[103]

Ren Zhengfei, the founder of Huawei, is a follower of Mao Zedong in terms of sharing his ethos and taking history as a mirror for guidance. After the Communist Party won the victory over the Kuomintang-led Nationalist government in China, Mao decided to include the following words in the Chinese national anthem: 'The Chinese nation has reached a point where its very existence is at stake.' The same idea has been frequently utilised by Ren to warn his executive members of an imminent crisis upon Huawei. In 2000, Huawei's sales reached a new higher level, well ahead of its competitors as the industry leader. However, instead of seeing this as a symbol of success, Ren published an article in 2001 entitled 'Huawei's Winter', shocking the industry with such an unexpectedly austere-sounding piece, followed by another paper, 'Huawei's Winter (II)', in 2002 to caution his management team about 'imminent' crisis and beseech the avoidance of complacency.

In the field of management, Wu Tzu's wisdom has been echoed by Western publications on the important role played by corporate culture in business development. However, Wu Tzu's thought goes further in stressing the importance of combining the promotion of organisational culture and coherence with competitive capability.

Key point 2: winning through control

Believing that the outcome of warfare depends on the combat capability of soldiers, which does not lie in their number but how they are controlled, Wu Tzu writes:

> What is meant by control is that when stationary [in camp] they observe the forms of propriety [*li*] and when in action they are awesome. When they advance they cannot be withstood; when they withdraw they cannot be pursued. Their advancing and withdrawing are measured; the left and right flanks respond to the signal flags. Even if broken off from the main order they preserve their formations; even if scattered they will reform lines. They will hold together in peace; they will hold together in danger. Their number can be assembled together, but cannot be forced apart. They can be employed, but they cannot be exhausted. No matter where you can dispatch them, no one under Heaven will be able to withstand them.[104]

To cultivate an army with discipline, solidarity, coherence and thus strong combat capability, education is first and foremost. Wu Tzu advises that 'to govern the state and order the army, you must instruct them with forms of propriety [*li*], stimulate them with righteousness, and cause them to have a sense of shame. For when men have the sense of shame, in the greatest degree it will be sufficient to wage war, while in the least degree it will suffice to preserve the state.'[105]

Second, a capable and benevolent general should be appointed. The qualified general should 'combine both military and civilian abilities', 'uniting both hardness and softness', with not only courage but also wisdom.[106] However, 'his awesomeness, Virtue [*te*], benevolence, and courage must be sufficient to lead his subordinates and settle the masses. Furthermore, he must frighten the enemy and resolve doubts. When he issues orders, no one will dare disobey them.'[107] The general must attend to five critical matters: regulation, preparation, commitment, caution and simplification.

> Regulation is governing the masses just as one controls a few. Preparation is going out of the city gate as if seeing the enemy. Commitment means entering combat without any concern for life. Caution means that even after conquering, one maintains the same control and attitude as if just entering a battle. Simplification means that the laws and orders are kept to a minimum and are not abrasive.[108]

Third, soldiers should undergo necessary training in combat skills and the use of weapons, as unprepared and unskilled armies are destined to be defeated. 'Now men constantly perish from their inabilities and are defeated by the unfamiliar. Thus among the methods for using the military, training and causing them to be alert are first.'[109]

Fourth, a clear policy of reward and punishment is important. Wu Tzu states that 'for advancing there should be generous rewards; for retreating heavy penalties; and they should both be properly implemented so that they will be believed in.'[110] Without such a policy, the army would not have discipline, and become chaotic: 'If the laws and orders are not clear, rewards and punishments not trusted, when sounding the gongs will not cause them to halt or beating the drum to advance, then even if you had one million men, of what use would they be?'[111] Soldiers should be treated with benevolence, while the relationship between the commander and his soldiers should be like that of a father with his sons, so that they will be motivated to fight with bravery. Thus,

> when you issue commands and promulgate orders the people take pleasure in hearing them; when you raise the army and mobilise the masses the people take pleasure in battle; and when the weapons clash and blades cross the people take pleasure in death, then these three are what a ruler of men can rely on.[112]

From Wu Tzu's point of view, how an organisation is controlled is a decisive factor in its performance.

Wei Liao Tzu (尉缭子)

The author and background

As one of the *Seven Military Classics*, *Wei Liao Tzu* has been influential in Chinese history, in particular as what is considered the earliest treatise to discuss the relationship of military affairs with politics and economics. However, there has been substantial controversy about its authorship, because historical sources record two different accounts. An important source is *Shiji: The Biography of Qin Shihuang*, by Grand Historian Sima Qian, according to which, Wei Liao was a native of Ta-liang, an advisor to the king of Ch'in (Qin). Later he was appointed by the king as a commander, and his plans and strategies were utilised.[113]

Another source is *The Book of Han*, by Ban Gu, in which there are two treatises by Wei Liao: one is the *Wei Liao 29 Chapters* under the 'miscellaneous' category and the other *Wei Liao 31 Chapters* under the heading of 'military terrains' during the Six Kingdoms period. It may be inferred from an analysis of the content of the two treatises that there were two men called Wei Liao. The first, who had the surname of Wei and the personal name of Liao, wrote the *Wei Liao 29 Chapters*, corresponding to the first ten chapters plus 'Army Orders I' and 'Army Orders II' in the current version of *Wei Liao Tzu*. The second, from Ta-liang (Daliang) in the kingdom of Wei (today's Kaifeng, Henan Province) had the official title 'Wei'[114] and the given name of Liao. He served Emperor Ch'in (Qin) in the tenth year of his reign. His *Wei Liao 31 Chapters* is homologous with the last ten chapters of the present version. However, during the Song dynasty, when the *Seven Military Classics* were compiled, only incomplete texts were found for the two treatises, which were thus merged into one, namely the current *Wei Liao Tzu*.

Main points and implications

Wei Liao Tzu contends that military victories can be won through three measures: the *Tao*, awesomeness and strength. Victory is attained through the *Tao* by careful planning, thoroughly studying and evaluating the enemy force and subjugating the enemy without causing destruction. Building a well-organised and motivated army with fully committed soldiers and formidable fighting capability is to seek victory through awesomeness, while destroying the enemy's armies, overwhelming the populace and occupying territory amount to gaining victory through strength. According to *Wei Liao Tzu*, 'Being victorious in battle externally and preparations being controlled internally, victory and preparations are mutually employed, like the halves of a tally exactly matching each other.'[115] By this the author means that external victory goes hand in hand with internal preparations. Formulating sensible strategies, selecting a capable general to lead the army and organising the army with clear laws, disciplinary codes and policies of reward and punishment are some of the necessary internal preparations. 'When one is victorious without exposing one's armour, it is the ruler's victory; when victory comes after deploying [the army], it is the general's victory.'[116]

Wei Liao, like Sun Tzu and Tai Gong, places emphasis on victory through the *Tao* (without fighting) and the use of stratagems:

> The tactical balance of power [*quan*] lies in the extremities of the Tao. If you have something, pretend not to have it; if you lack something, appear to have it.[117]

... In general, whenever about to mobilise the army, you must first investigate the strategic balance of power [*quan*] both within and without borders in order to calculate whether to mount a campaign. [You must know] whether the army is well prepared or suffers from inadequacies, whether there is a surplus or shortage of foodstuffs. You must determine the routes for advancing and returning. Only thereafter can you mobilise the army to attack the chaotic and be certain of being able to enter the state.[118]

According to *Wei Liao Tzu*, before engaging in warfare, one must be well prepared by knowing the strengths and weaknesses of the enemy and of oneself.

Chapter summary

Because of China's long history and a high incidence of warfare, there exists a wealth of Chinese military literature. Military thinking has not only had a tremendous impact on warfare, commerce and politics but has also become part of Chinese culture, affecting the thinking and behaviour of ordinary people. A major consequential cultural attribute derived from military influence is a proneness to thinking and behaving in terms of stratagems: maximum surprising and rapid action, a low level of trust, a high alertness of guard, ineptness of partnership and cooperation, an indirect and tacit approach to communication, an obsession with chance-based activities and a propensity to compete through detour or ruse. This stratagem culture, together with Confucian and Taoist thought and the political and economic systems, has shaped some major characteristics of the Chinese business environment.

The remarkable body of Chinese military literature has been represented here by the *Seven Military Classics*, which contain innumerable strategic insights developed by ingenious Chinese strategists with rich first-hand field experience as military generals and commanders, and are part of a treasure house of knowledge that should be shared with the world. These classics of warfare have a high degree of consensus on some critical perspectives, but each has its own emphases. Some of the main commonalities and differences may be summarised as follows:

- All schools of Chinese military thought put emphasis on the role of Tao in warfare, which is regarded as the cornerstone of military triumph. The best strategy is the one that attains victories without having to engage in fighting. If warfare is unavoidable, stratagems should be deployed to win in order to minimise casualties and destruction. This view is propounded by Sun Tzu, Tai Gong and Wei Liao Tzu, each having his own degree of emphasis. In a business context, firms should circumvent head-to-head competition or price wars, pursue differentiation strategies and innovation, and act swiftly without leaving competitors time to formulate a reaction.
- To maximise the chance of winning battles, a leader must consider a number of related factors from a holistic perspective, including politics, the

business environment, the marketplace, organisation, senior and middle management, logistics, capabilities and resources. Only when all these factors appear on paper to be favourable can the organisation pursue its battles with a clear prospect of victory.

- The quality of the business leader is regarded as one of the determinants of organisational performance, even to the extent of deciding the survival of the organisation. The leader should be free of interference in his or her leadership, leading by example and sharing happiness and bitterness with employees. It is important to establish prestige and awe. The general qualities of a leader should include wisdom, credibility, benevolence, courage and strictness.
- Organisation is seen as a decisive factor in determining success or failure. In particular, an organisation should have a culture that brings discipline, solidarity, coherence and capabilities. The combination of organisational care and love for the employees on one hand and discipline on the other can be a powerful motivator of employees' commitment to the organisation and their willingness to be innovative and to show initiative.
- The considerable body of literature on military strategy has been one of the major contributions that Chinese civilisation has made to the world and has crystallised all major schools of thought in Chinese history. By studying the Chinese military classics, one can not only apprehend ancient Chinese strategic wisdom but also gain a deeper knowledge of how traditional Chinese schools of thought such as Confucianism, Taoism and Legalism can be seen to work in the military field. Chinese military thinking puts more emphasis on stratagems and less on the role of weapons, in contrast to Western military literature, which heavily stresses weaponry or power as well as grand strategy.

The intention of the preceding chapters has been to help readers to understand Chinese culture in terms of history, philosophical thought and military classics, as knowledge of these domains is fundamental to an understanding of the thinking and behaviour of Chinese executives and consumers. However,

> no generalisation about a nation and its typical attitudes can be true of all its people. Especially in the case of the Chinese, typical attitudes may be eroded and changed by long residence in other countries and prolonged contact with foreign cultures. But the central concept of Chinese society is functionality.[119]

It would be erroneous to assume that Chinese people in all walks of life and in different regions behave alike, or are influenced by the cultural factors that have been discussed. Notably, Chinese elites, particularly those in political and commercial spheres, tend to be affected by these factors more or less. For instance, there is a common misperception of Chinese by Western people that most of the Chinese populace know how to practise martial arts. A good command of martial arts involves the knowledge of Chinese philosophy as well as physical stamina and flexibility. There are many professional and amateur practitioners in China from the eyes of a Westerner, but they account only for a very small proportion of Chinese population. Most Chinese urban dwellers know what martial arts are, and may imitate a few simple movements or punches that would have been seen from Chinese movies or TV programmes. Notably, many Chinese companies often use the practitioners of martial arts to promote their products on TV. However, the average Chinese citizen would not do much better than a normal layman.

Notes

1 Santamaria, J.A., Martino, V. and Clemons, E.K. (2004), *The Marine Corps Way: Using Maneuverer Warfare to Lead a Winning Organization*. New York: McGraw-Hill. Cawood, D. (1984), "Managing Innovation: Military Strategy in Business," *Business Horizons*, 27 (6), 62–66. McNeilly, M.R. (2011), *Sun Tzu and the Art of Business Six Strategic Principles for Managers*, Oxford: Oxford University Press. Bungay, S. (2011), "How to Make the Most of Your Company's Strategy," *Harvard Business Review*, January–February, 132–142.
2 Graham, J.J. (1997), *Carl von Clausewitz: On War*, translated by J.J. Graham, London: Wordsworth Editions Limited, p. 173.
3 Sawyer, R.D. (1993), *The Seven Military Classics of Ancient China*, Oxford: Westview Press, Inc., p. 322.
4 Deng, K.G. (2000), "A Critical Survey of Recent Research in Chinese Economic History," *Economic History Review*, LIII (I), 1–28.
5 Zhang, S.G. (1999), "China: Traditional and Revolutionary Heritage," in K. Booth and R. Trood (eds.), *Strategic Culture in the Asia-Pacific Region*, New York: Palgrave Macmillan, p. 1.
6 Sawyer has made the comment in the Introduction to Liu Bowen's treatise: Liu, B.W. (1996), *One Hundred Unorthodox Strategies: Battle and Tactics of Chinese Warfare*, translated by R.D. Sawyer, Oxford: Westview Press, Inc, p. 1.
7 In ancient China, several hundred Chinese generals have been recorded by history for their excellent military performance and strategic wisdom.
8 Lu, T. (1999), *Zhonghua wenming xianqin shi (Chinese Civilisation: History of Pre-Qin Period)*, Shijiazhuang, China: Hebei Education Publishing House, p. 120.
9 Yao, J.M. (2012), *Laozi zhihui (Lao Tzu's Wisdom)*, Jinan, China: Shandong People's Publishing House, p. 171.
10 Ibid, p. 174.
11 In Chapter 7 of Sun Tzu's *Art of War*, a reference is made to 'Military Administration': Griffith, S.B. (1963), *Sun Tzu: The Art of War, Translated and With an Introduction by Samuel B. Griffith and Forward by B.H. Liddell Hart*, Oxford: Oxford University Press, p. 161. Lu, T. (1999), *Zhonghua wenming xianqin shi (Chinese Civilisation: History of Pre-Qin Period)*, Shijiazhuang, China: Hebei Education Publishing House, p. 118.
12 Xu, B.L. (2002), *Zhong guo bing shu tong lan (An Overview of Chinese Military Books)*, Beijing: PLA Publishing House, pp. 20–21.
13 Liu, A. (2012), *The Dao of the Military, Liu An's Art of War*, translated with an introduction by A.S. Meyer, New York: Columbia University Press, p. 2.
14 Around the period of 1046 BC–771 BC.
15 Sawyer, R.D. (1993), *The Seven Military Classics of Ancient China*, Oxford: Westview Press, Inc., p. 29.

16 Confucius (1979), *The Analects*, translated and introduction by D.C. Lau, London: Penguin Books, p. 87.
17 Ebrey, P.B. (1993), *Chinese Civilization: A Sourcebook*, New York: The Free Press, p. 14.
18 The allusion is used to describe those who painstakingly strive to become stronger and make determined efforts to better themselves.
19 Confucius (1979), *The Analects*, translated and introduction by D.C. Lau, London: Penguin Books, p. 146.
20 Liu, H. (2015), *The Chinese Strategic Mind*, Northampton, MA: Edward Elgar Publishing.
21 Clark, D. (2016), *Alibaba: The House That Jack Ma Built*, New York: HarperCollins Publishers, pp. 156–157.
22 Erisman, P. (2015), *Alibaba's World*, New York: Palgrave Macmillan, pp. 110–111.
23 Ibid., p. 116.
24 Hout, T. and Michael, D. (2014), "A Chinese Approach to Management," *Harvard Business Review*, 92 (2), 103–107.
25 Liang, X.Y., Marier, J.H. and Cui, Z.Y. (2012), "Strategic Human Resource Management in China: East Meets West," *Academy of Management Perspectives*, May, 55–70.
26 Other special ties may include life-and-death friendships, whereby two people have forged a friendship through sharing a life-or-death experience and holding common beliefs, such as both being convinced that Business A will be a 'category killer' in the future.
27 Zhou, X.B. (2014), *Zhongguo jiazhu qiye weishenme jiaobuliaoban? (Why Chinese Family Enterprises Cannot Pass on Their Businesses to Their Next Generations?)*, Beijing: The Eastern Publisher.
28 Yang, S.L. (2013), *Huawei Kao Shenme (On What Huawei Relies)*, Beijing: China CITIC Press, p. 103. Author's own translation.
29 Sun Bin won many battles against Pang Juan's more powerful armies mainly because he skilfully applied and adapted Sun Tzu's *Art of War*, although he also wrote his own *Art of War*. He is often confused with Sun Tzu or Sun Wu.
30 McNeilly, M.R. (1996), *Sun Tzu and the Art of Business*, Oxford: Oxford University Press, pp. 3–4.
31 Collins, J.M. (1973), *Grand Strategy: Principles and Practices*, Annapolis, MD: Naval Institute Press, p. xx.
32 Sawyer, R.D. (1993), *The Seven Military Classics of Ancient China*, Oxford: Westview Press, Inc., p. 149.
33 McNeilly, M.R. (1996), *Sun Tzu and the Art of Business*, Oxford: Oxford University Press, p. 4.
34 Wee, C.H., Lee, K.S. and Bambang, W.H. (1991), *Sun Tzu: War & Management*, Singapore: Addison-Wesley Publishing Company, pp. 4–5.
35 Nixon, R. (1988), *1999: Victory Without War*, New York: Simon & Schuster.
36 Michaelson, G.A. (2001), *Sun Tzu: The Art of War for Managers*, Avon, MA: Adams Media Corporation, p. xviii.
37 Sawyer, R.D. (1993), *The Seven Military Classics of Ancient China*, Oxford: Westview Press, Inc., p. 167.
38 Ibid, p. 161.
39 Ibid, p. 160.
40 Ibid, p. 158.
41 McNeilly, M.R. (1996), *Sun Tzu and the Art of Business*, Oxford: Oxford University Press, p. 13.
42 Ibid, p. 14.
43 Michaelson, G.A. (2001), *Sun Tzu: The Art of War for Managers*, Avon, MA: Adams Media Corporation, p. 23.
44 McNeilly, M.R. (1996), *Sun Tzu and the Art of Business*, Oxford: Oxford University Press, p. 18.

45 Sawyer, R.D. (1993), *The Seven Military Classics of Ancient China*, Oxford: Westview Press, Inc., p. 165.

46 Kotler, P. (2003), *Marketing Management*, London: Pearson Education International, p. 19.

47 Wee, C.H., Lee, K.S. and Bambang, W.H. (1991), *Sun Tzu: War & Management*, Singapore: Addison-Wesley Publishing Company, p. 44.

48 McNeilly, M.R. (1996), *Sun Tzu and the Art of Business*, Oxford: Oxford University Press, p. 101.

49 Ibid, p. 31.

50 Sawyer, R.D. (1993), *The Seven Military Classics of Ancient China*, Oxford: Westview Press, Inc., p. 157.

51 Ibid.

52 Clancy, K.J. and Krieg, P.C. (2001), "Surviving Death Wish Research," *Marketing Research*, 13 (4), 8, 5.

53 Lo, A. (2001), "Selling Dreams: The Mary Kay Way," *Asianweek.com*, 29 June.

54 Sawyer, R.D. (1993), *The Seven Military Classics of Ancient China*, Oxford: Westview Press, Inc., p. 157.

55 Yan, R. (2004), "Short-Term Results: The Litmus Test for Success in China," in Kenneth G. Lieberthal (ed.), *Harvard Business Review on Doing Business in China*, Boston: Harvard Business School Publishing Corporation, pp. 95–96.

56 Sawyer, R.D. (1993), *The Seven Military Classics of Ancient China*, Oxford: Westview Press, Inc., p. 157.

57 Ibid, p. 160.

58 Ibid, p. 161.

59 Ibid, p. 166.

60 This is a unique concept also known as *shi* in Chinese culture, and will be explained further in Chapter Five.

61 Sawyer, R.D. (1993), *The Seven Military Classics of Ancient China*, Oxford: Westview Press, Inc., p. 162.

62 Ibid, p. 177.

63 Ibid, p. 157.

64 Ibid, p. 159.

65 Ibid, p. 177.

66 Ibid, p. 171.

67 Ibid, p. 182.

68 Ibid, p. 167.

69 Ibid, p. 158.

70 In China, there has been some debate about whether the book was genuinely written by the Duke of Zhou. On the whole, the balance of evidence is on the positive side.

71 Sawyer, R.D. (1993), *The Seven Military Classics of Ancient China*, Oxford: Westview Press, Inc., p. 41.

72 Ibid, pp. 41–42.

73 Ibid, p. 44.

74 In the 1980s, public transport was inconvenient, and with limited financial resources, the outlay for a large bus was a significant item within the company's total budget.

75 Chronologically, his ideas precede those of Sun Tzu.

76 Sawyer, R.D. (1993), *The Seven Military Classics of Ancient China*, Oxford: Westview Press, Inc., p. 53.

77 Ibid, pp. 68–69.

78 McNeilly, M.R. (1996), *Sun Tzu and the Art of Business*, Oxford: Oxford University Press, pp. 101–102.

79 Sawyer, R.D. (1993), *The Seven Military Classics of Ancient China*, Oxford: Westview Press, Inc., p. 72.

80 Ibid, p. 62.

81 Ibid, p. 66.

82 Ibid, p. 65.

83 Ibid, p. 51.

84 Ibid, pp. 65–66.

85 Ssu-ma is the Wade-Giles system for Chinese language, while Sima is the current phonetic alphabet system. Since readers tend to have more exposures to current Chinese phonetic alphabets, in this book, they are mainly used; but the old Wade alphabets are also introduced whenever necessary. Two exceptions are Sun Tzu and Lao Tzu, in which 'Tzu' is the Wade alphabet while the new system is 'Zi'. However, the two Sages have been known in Western countries for much longer, many people are familiar with the Wade system, and thus this form is kept in the book.

86 Sawyer, R.D. (1993), *The Seven Military Classics of Ancient China*, Oxford: Westview Press, Inc., p. 111.

87 Ibid, p. 115.

88 Ibid, p. 126.

89 Ibid, p. 133.

90 Ibid, p. 136.

91 Ibid, p. 137.

92 The last three points are associated with the standardisation of dress codes, which has been a common practice by most medium-sized and large corporations.

93 Sawyer, R.D. (1993), *The Seven Military Classics of Ancient China*, Oxford: Westview Press, Inc., p. 137.

94 Ibid, p. 137.

95 Ibid, p. 191.

96 Griffith, S.B. (1963), *Sun Tzu: The Art of War*, translated and with an introduction by S.B. Griffith and Forward by B.H. Liddell Hart, London: Watkins Publishing, p. 203.

97 Giles, L. (2013), *Sun Tzu on Art of War*, translated and with an introduction by Lionel Giles, New York: Routledge, p. 110.

98 It is often translated as the *Book of Former Han*.

99 Sawyer, R.D. (1993), *The Seven Military Classics of Ancient China*, Oxford: Westview Press, Inc., p. 206.

100 Ibid, p. 207.

101 Ibid.

102 Ibid, p. 210.

103 Yan, J.J. and Hu, Y. (2000), *Haier: Zhong Guo Zao (Haier: Made in China)*, Haikou, China: Hainan Publisher, p. 112.

104 Sawyer, R.D. (1993), *The Seven Military Classics of Ancient China*, Oxford: Westview Press, Inc., pp. 214–215.

105 Ibid, p. 208.

106 Ibid, p. 217.

107 Ibid, p. 218.

108 Ibid, p. 217.

109 Ibid, p. 215.

110 Ibid, p. 214.

111 Ibid.

112 Ibid, p. 223.

113 Ibid, p. 231.

114 This was equivalent to 'Imperial Minister of Military Affairs'.

115 Sawyer, R.D. (1993), *The Seven Military Classics of Ancient China*, Oxford: Westview Press, Inc., p. 243.

116 Ibid.

117 Ibid, p. 262.

118 Ibid, p. 272.

119 Bonavia, D. (1989), *The Chinese*, London: Penguin Books, p. 57.

5   Strategy and marketing in China

A business that makes nothing but money is a poor business.

– Henry Ford

Strategy is the art of making war upon the map, and comprehends the whole theatre of operations.

– Antoine-Henri Jomini

The theory of marketing is solid but the practice of marketing leaves much to be desired.

– Philip Kotler

The nature and context of strategy

Western views of strategy

'Strategy' is understood differently by people of different cultures. Hong Liu (2015) points out that there have been substantial differences in the ways of thinking of and formulating strategies between the Chinese and those who follow the Western tradition.[1] There are a number of key points about strategy in the West that readers should understand in order to have a better view of strategy in the context of China.

(1) Strategy as a discipline and an academic course in business administration emerged at Harvard Business School in the 1950s,[2] and was relabelled 'strategic management' in 1979,[3] signifying the maturity of the academic field.[4] There have been many definitions of strategy, and no unanimity has to date been attained regarding the concept. Although there has been substantial research in this field, a universal theory of strategy has yet to be developed.

> The 'theory of strategy' remains as elusive as ever. Powerful statistical techniques are mobilized to squeeze the 'essence of strategy' out of empirical data, and sophisticated game theory is marshalled to achieve,

by deduction, the same goal. Yet one cannot avoid the feeling that, in fact, in many respects these efforts and the ensuing literature fail to advance our understanding of the universe of strategy in substantive ways.[5]

(2) Eleven representative definitions of strategy have been identified,[6] each with a different focus. Typically, in the context of business, a strategy involves one or more of the following areas: business policy,[7] organisational performance,[8] the external environment,[9] internal resources[10] and strategy implementation.[11] Strategic management generally involves 'those subjects of primary concerns to senior management, or to anyone seeking reasons for success and failure among organisations.'[12]

> Strategic management acts as an intellectual brokering entity, which thrives by enabling the simultaneous pursuit of multiple research orientations by members who hail from a wide variety of disciplinary and philosophical regimes. At the same time, however, these diverse community members seem to be linked by a fundamental implicit consensus that helps the field to cohere and maintain its identity.[13]

The following are three exemplary definitions:

> The determination of the basic long-term goals and objectives of the enterprise and the adoption of courses of action and the allocation of resources necessary for carrying out these goals.[14]
>
> The pattern of major objectives, purposes, or goals and essential policies and plans for achieving those goals, stated in such a way as to define what business the company is in or is to be in and the kind of company it is or is to be. In a changing world it is a way of expressing a persistent concept of the business so as to exclude some possible new activities and suggest entry into others.[15]
>
> Strategic management entails the analysis of internal and external environments of firms to maximize the utilization of resources in relation to objectives.[16]

(3) In the area of military studies, there has been a recognition that existing definitions or models of strategy based on the Western tradition have a number of limitations. These may also be applicable to strategic management in the field of business studies.

In strategy development and implementation, the process is such that an ideal form is set as the goal, and then a course of action is subsequently taken to make it happen. This tends to create a problematic dichotomy: a gap between the (theoretical or ideal) goal and reality. This problem is derived from Western scientific thinking whereby warfare or business reality is often quantified through mathematised models, 'With a unilateral point of view that failed to take variability into account and was exclusively concerned with material factors, such theorization was incapable of "dominating real life".[17] In addition, in current strategic models, efforts mainly focus on 'material factors', such as investment, capital, resources and technology, while in business activities, spiritual and moral forces play an important part in performance outcomes. Furthermore, the action of only one of the opponents is taken into consideration in strategic analysis, while business activities often involve dynamic reciprocal actions. A hypothetical example may be illustrative.

A large university has set itself the objective of becoming one of the world's top 20 research-driven universities within ten years. It has taken measures to implement this strategy by increasing internal seed research funds to encourage staff to develop research proposals for external funding, by trying to recruit more academics who are able to publish in top journals and by putting more pressure on existing staff to increase their output. It appears that the university has done everything it should have to achieve the objective. However, in this strategic process, there are some potential barriers to the materialisation of the objective.

University departments are run by academics who have not been trained as professional managers, and departmental heads have limited knowledge about leadership and management. As this hypothetical university is fairly large, organisational issues tend to be more complicated than in small and medium-sized universities; thus, inadequate leadership within some departments has led to a situation where the morale of many members of staff has not been as high as would be desired. Consequently, the number of competent researchers who have newly been recruited has almost been matched by those who have left the university, while the morale of some remaining members of staff has been low enough to inhibit a concentration on research. Furthermore, many competing universities have performed as well or better in some respects. Therefore, unless the university can take radical measures to address these issues, it appears to be heading for a failure to achieve its strategic objective.

As a result of the lack of consensus on the concept of strategy, the teaching of strategic management as a discipline in business schools has many different structures, but each usually has a well-formed strategic system. The following elements are generally included:

- Corporate vision, mission and objectives;
- Strategic content, context and process;
- Intended, emergent and realised strategies;
- Industrial and competitive analysis;
- Evaluation of external and internal environments;
- Different levels of strategy: corporate, business and function;
- SWOT (strengths, weaknesses, opportunities and threats) analysis;
- Company resources and competitive capabilities;
- Resource-based theory (view);
- Generic strategies: cost leadership, differentiation and focus;
- Competitive advantage;

- Strategies for globalisation or internationalisation;
- Strategies for the Internet economy;
- Mergers and acquisitions;
- Assessment of organisational performance;
- Corporate ethics and social responsibility;
- Board of directors; and
- Strategy execution/implementation.

Chinese ways of doing strategy

Since the initiation of economic reforms in China in the late 1970s, the Western concept of strategy has been introduced and taught in China. However, few Chinese senior executives have fully applied such concepts in reality, mainly because in Chinese companies, strategic decisions tend to be made by the leader, that is the founder or CEO. Personal experience, knowledge, insights, inspirations and backgrounds tend to be dominant; sometimes, consulting companies are used to provide strategic analysis and recommendations, but these rarely supplant the leader's own strategic ideas. However, in the areas of management, such as new product development and human resource management, some major Chinese companies have successfully adopted Western tools and techniques.

Chinese approaches to developing strategy may be seen as incremental, quite unlike those in the West. Rather than some concrete goals, many Chinese companies tend to have some kind of long-term 'vision'.[18] This establishes the broad direction in which the firm wants to go and identifies a few steps on the way, but without a detailed path or concrete courses of action to implement the vision. Goals generally involve quantified and definite steps, with the signposts pointing in a specific direction that the firm should take. For instance, Huawei was founded in 1987 and its founder, Ren Zhengfei, stated his vision in 1994, despite the firm still being at an early stage of its development: 'In ten years the telecommunication equipment market will be divided into thirds, among Siemens, Alcatel and Huawei.'[19] In 2010, the company realised its vision, establishing itself as the world's second largest supplier, then in 2012, it became the world's largest telecommunications company. Although most Western firms have a vision statement, emphasis tends to be placed more on goals, as they can be measured and assessed for the purpose of performance evaluation.

A major Chinese way of contemplating strategy involves the term '*shi*', which is generally translated as 'situation', 'potential', 'power' or 'energy' and is an important part of Chinese strategic thinking.[20] Sun Tzu says: 'A skilled commander seeks victory from the situation and does not demand it of his subordinates.'[21] In other words, an advantageous situation (*shi*) to be created or utilised by a commander is more important than the role of his soldiers in battle. In Sun Tzu's *Art of War*, the term has three dimensions of connotation: 'circumstances' or 'conditions'; 'physical disposition' in relation to the deployment of military forces; and the occupation of a superior position and access to the potential advantages which it accords. Ames provides a summary of these dimensions: 'The word [*shi*] can refer either collectively or individually to the superior position, the advantage inherent in the position, and the manipulation of this advantage.'[22] François Jullien describes it as 'the kind of potential that originates not in human initiative but instead results from the very disposition of things.'[23]

Shi is viewed as a situation-based strategic advantage, but Lau and Ames warn Western readers against simply assigning it to one side in a given conflict, because it:

> refers to all of the factors on both sides of the conflict (numbers, terrain, logistics, morale, weaponry and so on) as they converge on the battlefield to give one side the advantage over the other. It is the tension generated in the contest between surplus and deficiency that becomes the 'force of circumstances'.[24]

Different generals may utilise the potential differently, resulting in different outcomes. A consummate commander is able to adapt to the situation expediently and take appropriate action to achieve victory. A situation may be so created that it has a deterrent effect on the enemy and determines both the willingness of its army to wage battle and the display and enforcement of power. Sun Tzu explains:

> When torrential water tosses boulders, it is because of its momentum.[25] . . . He who relies on the situation uses his men in fighting as one rolls logs or stones. Now the nature of logs and stones is that . . . if round, they roll. . . . Thus, the potential of troops skilfully commanded in battle may be compared to that of round boulders which roll down from mountain heights.[26]

When Jack Ma, the founder of Alibaba, was asked how the company survived great hardship in its earlier years, his response was, 'We didn't have any money, we didn't have any technology and we didn't have a plan.'[27] A Goldman Sachs consultant went to Hangzhou to assess Alibaba's potential for investment, with the impression: 'The whole place stank. Jack's ideas were not entirely original – they had been tried in other countries. But he was completely dedicated to making them work in China.'[28] The company's success has been attributable to three factors: e-commerce, logistics and finance, known as the 'iron triangle'.[29] In a speech at Harvard, he confessed to the audience that he did not have a clear idea about what Alibaba's business model was.[30] By e-commerce I mean that he has identified and ridden the Internet *shi*, doing the right things at the right times with the right people. When Jack Ma embarked on his e-commerce journey, the Chinese Internet market was described thusly:

> With only two million Internet users in China, less than 1 percent of the country's population was online. And of that 1 percent, even fewer would

consider purchasing something online. The barriers were simply too great. Consumer purchasing power was too low. Credit card penetration was negligible. Logistics infrastructure was primitive. It was unclear whether the government would embrace or reject the Internet.[31]

Notwithstanding the 'inauspicious' environment for e-commerce, Jack Ma sensed or simply happened to sit on the Internet '*shi*', taking Alibaba into a treasure island. Lei Jun, the founder of Xiaomi, a successful Chinese smartphone company, once used a memorable metaphor to underline the importance of *shi* in driving the take-off of his company: 'Even a pig can fly if it is in the middle of a whirlwind'. The Economist (2015), "Back to Business," September 12th 2015, p. 6.

The Wanxiang Group is a Chinese conglomerate involved in businesses such as real estate, finance and automotive component manufacturing. It was founded by Lu Guanqiu, who was born into a farming family and did not even finish high school, yet who managed to turn the company into not only the largest auto parts maker in China but also a multinational with operations in developed countries. In the 1990s, Lu Guanqiu, through reading media reports, discerned *shi* (or a 'tide') whereby China would soon develop its automotive industry on a grand scale. At the time there had been no official sign or government policy on China's auto industry, but the founder decided to enter the auto component industry. Based on an assessment of the company's resources, competence and industrial potential, it was decided to begin by producing universal joints, which could be widely used by most auto manufacturers, leading to the successful development of a mega-multinational business.

Notably, CCTV's News Broadcast has become one of the most popular TV programmes for Chinese entrepreneurs and business leaders who wish to emulate Lu Guanqiu by spotting forthcoming business or political *shi*. Apart from business opportunities, viewers may also get some clues about changes, for instance, in financial or environmental policies, which would have vital implications for business leaders.

In the current knowledge society, one powerful type of *shi* is the concept of 'Internet Plus', representing the integration of Internet technologies with traditional industries and/or business functions, which may be explored, ridden or borrowed:

(1) **Channels – Web traffic:** Those retailers and e-business firms which can find ways to generate heavier Web traffic will attain an advantageous position.
(2) **Marketing – social networking:** Internet connections have shortened distances between individuals both domestically and globally. A well-established or widely connected social network can effectively promote brand image and deliver marketing messages with a greater chance of success.
(3) **Product – innovation:** Although innovation has always been vital, it is even more important in the current turbulent business environment for companies to undertake innovation in order to survive and prosper.

(4) **Organisation – tapping into all brains:** To fully utilise their human resources, companies may rely on three types of innovation: incremental (70%), platform (20%) and disruptive (10%).[32]

Without the ability to identify, create or utilise '*shi*', many Chinese companies simply follow their competitors, in terms of their strategic and marketing approaches, including products and services, with necessary modifications. The adoption of a competitor orientation is considered part of Chinese strategic thinking.[33] Few Western executives would doubt that Chinese companies are among the best imitators in the world. Behind many successful Chinese companies, one may find Western counterparts, for instance, eBay versus Alibaba's Taobao, Hertz versus eHi, Uber versus Didi Chuxing, Amazon versus JD.com and Dangdang.com, Vipshop.com versus VP (Vente-Privee) and Google versus Baidu, to name just a few. 'Although most of its services originated in the United States, such as eBay and Amazon, Alibaba's ability to implement the many, often idiosyncratic adaptations needed for China has allowed it to defeat its Western rivals in China. Alibaba is the champion of 'Sinaptation' – that is, adaptation of foreign products and services, such as Amazon and eBay, to China.'[34] A recent study identifies three successive phases of Chinese innovation: 'from copying to fit for purpose', 'from followers to world standard,' and 'from new resources to new knowledge.' The first phase involves a 'follower or competitor orientation', while the second and third are concerned with market or technology orientation. At the third phase 'Chinese companies are buying the market access, the brands, the technology, and the human expertise that will allow them to mount a formidable innovation challenge to the incumbent companies of the developed countries.'[35] These would include Chinese companies such as Lenovo and Fosun, whose strategies and behaviour have converged with Western companies. However, many Chinese companies, such as Huawei and Yangtze River Pharmaceutical Group, still embrace Chinese traditions with Chinese characteristics.

A comparative view

Both approaches have advantages and disadvantages. The Western way has worked for many decades, and many examples can be found of companies for which the approach has brought substantial rewards. As Dwight D. Eisenhower famously put it, 'Plans are nothing. Planning is everything.'[36] Rationally, the approach would give a company a direction of travel and provide impetus towards its goal. It is generally suitable for a stable business environment.[37] In a turbulent environment, by contrast, the hierarchical organisational structure of most Western multinationals makes them intrinsically incapable of responding to changes in a timely manner, because of organisational inertia or the high cost of timely response. Jack Ma of Alibaba has gone as far as saying: 'If you plan, you lose. If you don't plan, you win.'[38] Clearly, this is associated with the environment of Internet-based business, which is turbulent and unpredictable.

The Chinese business environment has tended to be dynamic or turbulent, involving unpredictability in government policies, consumer and competitor behaviour and business relationships, as well as regional variability and differences in sub-cultures and economic development; therefore, in order for businesses to survive and prosper in China, it is essential to be responsive, agile and culturally adaptable. A study published in the *Harvard Business Review* asserts that

> Chinese companies teach us management's current imperatives: responsiveness, improvisation, flexibility, and speed. These abilities give them a critical edge . . . Chinese companies have learned to manage differently over the past 30 years because they've had to cope with a turbulent environment.[39]

These phenomena have not only been observed by Western academics and practitioners; they are part of the natural behaviour of Chinese companies, not a conscious strategic move. In China, many founders/owners of successful Chinese privately owned companies have been intrigued by Western CEO/owner training programmes, immersing themselves in acquiring and applying Western strategy and management theories and models, with a sense of elevating themselves to a higher plane of knowledge. However, some of the owners have become bankrupt and others have witnessed deterioration in their firms' performance because they too eagerly applied what they had learned from the programmes. The bankruptcies occurred mainly because these owners/founders wanted to use their newly acquired knowledge as a shortcut to profitability, moving away from their core competence in manufacturing to playing the stock market, where they felt that it would be easy to make huge sums of money without having to labour or sweat. Those who rigidly applied Western strategic frameworks, models or practices found that they were unfitted to their industries or businesses in China.

Theoretically, Western firms may incorporate adaptability and flexibility into their strategic models, rapidly reacting to environmental changes as fast as Chinese firms. However, the flexibility and agility of Chinese firms is built into their culture and organisational structure. Under the long-established stratagem culture, Chinese people think and behave as if they were military personnel, leading to an emphatic competitor orientation. Sun Tzu says: 'Speed is the essence of war. Take advantage of the enemy's unpreparedness; travel by unexpected routes and strike him where he has taken no precautions.'[40] To outdo its competitors, a firm has to act faster than them; to be faster, it has to be more agile and responsive. 'Therefore at first be shy as a maiden. When the enemy gives you an opening be swift as a hare and he will be unable to withstand you.'[41] Furthermore, the structure of most Chinese organisations places a key individual or leader at the centre, steering and leading autocratically, without the organisational hierarchy on which their Western counterparts rely.

Although this structure can be seen as according Chinese companies a degree of flexibility and responsiveness, its looseness can sometimes lead to organisational inefficiency and waste of resources. In the eyes of many Western-trained scholars, it is hard to believe that the kind of success achieved by these Chinese companies is possible with such a 'chaotic' organisational structure. The founder of Huawei, Ren Zhengfei, specifically discourages the firm's top managers from studying Western strategy books, but the company has spent hundreds of millions of US dollars implementing an integrated product development (IPD) system from IBM and a human resource management system from the Hay Group. Ideally, a balance between Western and Chinese ways should be achieved, although this may be easier said than done. Huawei appears to have attained such a balance, but we have yet to see how the company performs in a post-Ren era, when the godfather of Huawei leaves the driving seat.

The major strategic difference between many Chinese and Western companies may be represented figuratively by the image of a Chinese company travelling downriver by canoe, being carried along by the power of the flowing water (*shi*), without having to choose a direction and without need of a motor or even having to paddle hard. Different industries may be seen as streams or rivers with diverse complexities, risks and destinations. In contrast, many Western companies may be compared to ships or – in the case of multinational corporations (MNCs) – ocean liners, whose captains have to identify a direction of travel with a compass or GPS to follow it, as well as a power source to propel the ship forward. The canoeists may be taking a risk in drifting without a clear idea of where they may end, but their voyage is much less costly. The seafarers, for their part, have a clearer direction, but a higher cost structure. Alibaba's Jack Ma has used an analogy to describe the nature of battle between eBay and Alibaba: 'eBay may be a shark in the ocean, but I am a crocodile in the Yangtze River. If we fight in the ocean, we lose, but if we fight in the river, we win.'[42]

Box 5.1   Strategic comparison: Lenovo versus Huawei

Lenovo and Huawei are among the strongest Chinese companies in the global business arena. They are chosen for comparison because their business ventures were launched at similar times and under similar conditions, and have been led by founders with a similar background. The main difference between them is that Lenovo's leadership has predominantly followed Western strategic and management philosophy and approaches, while Huawei has been strategically guided by Chinese tradition, with strong Chinese characteristics. This comparison may thus shed light on the essential differences between Western and Chinese strategic and managerial philosophies and approaches.

Company background

Lenovo, previously known as Legend, was founded on 1 November 1984 by a group of 11 like-minded scientists from the Computer Institute of

the Chinese Academy of Sciences, led by Liu Chuanzhi, with the registered name of New Technology Developer Inc. The group initially ran
their business from a receptionist's office, with a start-up loan of RMB
200,000 (about $25,000) from the Academy of Sciences. In 1986, the
company successfully developed the Legend Chinese Character Card,
making China a possible mass market for personal computers. In 1989,
it was renamed the Legend Computer Group, in reference to the game-
changing product. In 2004, it changed its name again, to Lenovo.

During its early development, the company survived by acting as a
distributor of foreign information technology products. AST Research, a
fairly strong brand at the time, provided it with everything it needed to
know about building PCs. The company decided to locate its production
and operational base in Hong Kong, and in April 1988, a joint venture
company, Legend Hong Kong, was formed with Legend Beijing as the
main shareholder. Soon afterwards, Legend Hong Kong acquired Quantum, a Hong Kong computer company, and the combined entity successfully developed four new products within six months. The year 1990 saw
the very first Legend PC successfully launched in the market, marking a
change of its role from mere agent for imported brands to producer and
vendor of its own brand. By the end of 1993, Legend had developed integrated international operations including R&D, production, distribution
and after-sales services.

Huawei was founded by Ren Zhengfei in 1987, with its headquarters located in Shenzhen, Guangdong. 'Huawei' is a transliteration of the
company's Chinese name, 华为, meaning 'both "China can" and "splendid act".'[43] At the time of its founding, with a registered capital of RMB
21,000 (about $5,680), Huawei relied on acting as an agent selling phone
switches from a Hong Kong company, then began manufacturing similar
products. It later expanded its business to focus on networking and telecommunications equipment manufacturing with operational and consulting services.

Founders' background

Born in 1944, Liu Chuanzhi graduated from the Xian Military Communication Engineering College, now known as Xidian University
(1961–1966), then served two years in a military establishment. In 1970,
he joined the Chinese Academy of Sciences as an engineer-administrator,
involving himself in the development of mainframe computers. In 1984,
he left the Academy to co-found Legend. His father was a renowned
senior executive in the Bank of China and Chairman of a technology
licensing company, with a close connection to the Communist Party of
China (CPC). This family background may have had some impact on
his business spirit and ethos. His notion of strategy development and

implementation includes a firm belief in the best Western management theories and practices, through which the firm should create and nurture a global brand.

Ren Zhengfei, also born in 1944, acquired a bachelor's degree in engineering from the Chongqing Institute of Civil Engineering and Architecture in 1963, then joined the civil engineering industry until 1974, when he was conscripted into the Engineering Corps of People's Liberation Army (PLA), later rising to a rank of deputy director. Seen as an outstanding performer in his work, he was elected as a representative of the National Science Conference in 1978 and the 12th National Congress of the CPC in 1982. After the Engineering Corps was disbanded in 1983, he worked briefly for the Shenzhen South Sea Oil Corporation, before setting up Huawei in 1987, with a 1.42 per cent shareholding in the company. Ren has fully embraced Chinese tradition and is a devoted follower of Mao Zedong's strategic ideas and thought. During his service in the PLA, he was regarded as a PLA role model for his knowledge of Mao's selected works. Indeed, Mao's works and actions can be seen to be reflected in Huawei's R&D strategy, to use the 'concentration of a superior force to destroy the enemy's forces one by one', and its marketing strategy, which echoes the 'encirclement of cities from the countryside'.[44]

Corporate performance

Lenovo is the world's largest PC maker, with 21 per cent of market share, and it ranked 202nd in the Global 500 in 2016, moving up from 286th in 2014 and 231st in 2015. However, its revenue and gross profit both fell slightly between 2015 and 2016, down 3 per cent and 1 per cent respectively, from $46 billion to $45 billion and from $6682 million to $6624 million.

Huawei is the world's largest telecommunications equipment maker and network service provider. In 2016, its revenue was $61 billion, an increase of 37 per cent over the previous year, while its net profit was $5.7 billion, up 33 per cent. In the past three years, its Global 500 ranking has improved markedly, from 285th in 2014 to 228th in 2015 to 129th in 2016.

A comparative view: strategy and performance

The two companies had comparable start-ups, at similar times and with a modest capital, but Lenovo had the slight advantage of the support, albeit limited, of the Chinese Academy of Sciences, which loaned the venture $25,000. In contrast, Huawei relied on Ren Zhengfei's personal savings.

To get off the ground, both businesses initially had to act as sales agents. However, Huawei is located in Shenzhen, where the business environment has been more open and conducive to start-ups than in Beijing, where Lenovo was initially based. Later, Lenovo managed to overcome this handicap by setting up a joint venture in Hong Kong, moving its production and operations there.

Lenovo has, to a great extent, followed a Western-style strategic expansion. In 1994, it was listed on the Hong Kong Stock Exchange, laying the financial foundation for its international expansion, and its PC business division was formally established. Bypassing the conventional Chinese incremental strategic approach, Lenovo became a global giant of the computer industry overnight through its acquisition in 2005 of IBM's Personal Computing Division (desktop and notebook computers), which made it the world's third largest personal computing company. Apart from the fact that Liu Chuanzhi, co-founder of Lenovo, has fully embraced Western management theories, the characteristics of the company oblige it to follow Western practices. Its board of directors has international representatives, operating on the basis of global management principles. Its top management committee comprises nine people from six different countries, who all have considerable international experience of the firm's products, markets and functions. Lenovo's strategic trajectory closely resembles that of General Electric, relying on mergers and acquisitions (M&As) for growth. In Japan, Lenovo acquired NEC's PC operations; in Germany, a controlling interest in PC manufacturer Medion and in Brazil, CCE, the leading domestic manufacturer of PCs and mobile devices.[45] In 2014, it acquired Motorola Mobility from Google and System X from IBM.

Huawei's contrasting strategy has been to expand its international business interests incrementally and organically, yet audaciously. At an early stage of its development, in order to meet customer requirements, it concentrated its funds and personnel on fighting a life-or-death battle, employing over 50 R&D staff and reaching a point of no return when it had no funds left; if the undertaking had failed, the company would have become bankrupt. Before 1995, the firm adopted Mao's 'encirclement' strategy, which proved successful; in 1996 it started to enter emerging markets and from 2004 onwards it made inroads into developed markets. Unlike his counterparts in Western multinationals, the founder has refused to list the company on the stock market and has upheld his shareholding at 1.42 per cent in order to motivate Huawei's employees and maintain its freedom of strategic management, free from shareholder pressure. In a sense, its international expansion has been steady and incremental, but successful. Today, its information and communications technology (ICT) solutions, products and services are used in over 170 countries. In 2012 it had become the world's largest telecommunication equipment manufacturer and in 2015, the third largest smartphone maker, after Samsung and Apple, with the potential to advance further.

Both companies have been generally successful, notwithstanding their different strategic philosophies. However, there appears to be an increasingly wide gap between them in terms of momentum, viability and performance. As noted above, Huawei has recently recorded a strong growth in sales and profits, while Lenovo's performance has declined. By its strategy of global expansion and brand building through M&As, Lenovo has achieved a degree of market success, but this strategy has constrained the development of its in-house innovative capability, as heavy financial resources have had to be channelled to M&As, while it is hard to secure breakthrough technology through acquisitions. On R&D spending, intensity and patent applications, Lenovo is far behind Huawei, which spent $6.5 billion, $8.1 billion and $9.5 billion on R&D from 2014 to 2016, while Lenovo's ten-year accumulative R&D spending has been only two-thirds of Huawei's one-year R&D outlay. Huawei has made the world's largest number of PCT applications over the past two years. Lenovo entered the smartphone business in 2002 and Huawei in 2003, and since then the former has acquired Motorola Mobility and achieved third ranking in 2014; but Google has retained the ownership of a majority of its patent portfolio and Lenovo lost its third place to Huawei in 2015. The latter also replaced Samsung to become the top smartphone vendor in China in the same year. Furthermore, on 19 October 2016, Huawei introduced the next-generation Kirin 960 chipset, providing the company's smartphone business with a distinct advantage over its competitors that bodes well for the future. It is notable that Huawei's strategy is guided by Chinese tradition.[46]

Strictly speaking, the absolute level of performance may not be compared between the two companies, as they operate in completely different industries, but the strategic influences on the performance may give us some insights. This comparison does not imply that a Western strategic approach is inferior to a Chinese one, but suggests that it may not be suitable for Chinese companies that have a different DNA from that in Western firms. For instance, it would be hard for Chinese companies to acquire breakthrough technology through M&As, compared with Western companies.

MNC strategies and context

As discussed above, strategy is conceived very differently between the West and China, so that when discussing the development and implementation of a particular strategy, one has to specify whether the organisation concerned is

Chinese or Western. In this section, we examine the context of China in which Western firms do business and how they should develop their strategies in alignment with that context.

The way in which the Chinese government defines industry has a major impact on strategic decision-making and approaches to doing business in China. A list of foreign investment projects is published in the *Catalogue for the Guidance of Foreign Investment Industries (Amended in 2015)*, enacted on 10 March 2015. The catalogue is divided into three sections:

(1) Encouraged Industries

> These are industries in which the Chinese government actively seeks foreign investment. Tax incentives, cheaper land and simplified approval procedures are sometimes granted to investors in these industries.

(2) Restricted Industries

> In this group, the government has imposed restrictions such as foreign shareholding ratios, special approval requirements and limits on the operation of companies.

(3) Prohibited Industries

> Foreign companies are not allowed to invest in these industries.

If a foreign party wishes to invest in a restricted industry, the Chinese partner(s) must account for the controlling or leading shareholding. The restricted industries and products are generally associated with China's industrial base, major revenue generation, social stability, public security and health. They often involve only certain specific products within an industry. Many restrictions have been officially phased out in some sectors as WTO rules take effect, but it will be a long before these become as open as other consumer goods industries, since the implementation of WTO rules can be complicated, and it can be expected that indirect restrictions will persist.

In restricted industries, the ownership structure tends to be determined by the setting of a maximum of 50 per cent foreign holdings, rather than by strategic choices, and thus foreign investors with an interest in these industries have no choice beyond that maximum level. The major Chinese partner has to account for, at least, half of the members of the board of directors. An example of a restricted industry is the manufacturing of automobiles, special vehicles and motorcycles.

As the majority shareholder, the Chinese partner often takes control of major business decisions, particularly in marketing matters such as pricing and distribution. In the Shanghai-General Motors (GM) 50–50 joint venture, the agreement between the parties was that GM would inject the technology and management skills to support a world-class car company, while the Chinese partner would have the exclusive rights to undertake marketing tasks, including decisions on distributorship, pricing, product lines and production quantities.

Another example is Shanghai GKN Huayu Driveline Systems, consisting of four partners: GKN (35.42%), GKN China Holdings (14.58%), BOCOM-Bank of Communications (Shanghai Branch) (5%) and Huayu Automotive Systems (45%). As the major foreign partner, GKN is responsible for providing world-class driveline technology and operations, while the leading Chinese partner delivers marketing.

In the encouraged industries, the shareholding structure is not subject to government regulation. When investing in these industries, foreign companies now usually choose to be the sole owners of the business venture, while many foreign partners of existing joint ventures have been transformed into wholly foreign-owned entities. In 1993, for instance, Henkel and KfW Bankengruppe (German Development Bank) formed a joint venture with the Tianjin Synthetic Detergent Factory, which had a total registered capital of $30 million. Tianjin initially held 70 per cent of equity shares in the form of land, plant and equipment, while the two foreign partners owned 30 per cent. As a result of three stages of shareholding restructuring, Henkel became the sole owner of this venture in August 2001. The majority of multinationals have chosen the form of wholly foreign-owned enterprise as their preferred mode of operations in China.

In 2006, about two-thirds of multinationals operated in the form of wholly foreign-owned enterprises as new entrants, while 23 per cent of all foreign invested enterprises in China were still in the joint venture mode.[47] Since 2010, however, according to a report by McKinsey,

> China's hot growth has boosted valuations and increased competition for outright acquisitions of Chinese companies that are often less interested in being acquired. That makes joint ventures a more appealing option, and so does a growing pool of healthier prospective Chinese partners. All this is prompting some multinationals to reconsider the joint-venture approach as an alternate avenue for getting a stake in the continuing strength of China's economy.[48]

It appears that the joint venture has reappeared on the radar screens of multinationals as a strategic entry mode in China. As there has been a huge body of literature on joint ventures, past results or conclusions are regarded as still valid. Some past lessons involve

> choosing partners that can make tangible business contributions, safeguarding intellectual property, ensuring operational control of the joint venture, and managing talent. Others are critical for joint ventures in all geographies, such as aligning strategic priorities, creating a structure that permits rapid responses to change, and preparing up front for eventual restructuring.[49]

Past experience also provides the following advice on successful joint ventures in China:[50]

(1) Defining the right strategic positioning.

- If you are in a restricted industry, you need to assume that the conditions for the core business activities will be there for good. If it is not an attractive model for you, you should not invest in the hope that it will change.
- Closely follow the evolution of government policy and communicate your commitment to China to the government.
- Be clear about your position: You are in China for business opportunities there, or you are there because it creates opportunities for the company elsewhere in the world. These will not result in the same presence in China.

(2) The objectives of Chinese joint venture partners are different from the past, going after foreign capital and technology, and now they mainly see foreign partners as accelerators of growth.

- Avoid the outdated mentality that 'this is our way of doing things'. Align your commitment in China to your Chinese partner's international expansion, which should be seen as part of the total China investment.
- From the outset, it should be clear who will interact with whom in the joint venture partnership and with relevant government officials. The committed executives should turn up at board meetings and the like.

(3) Place a senior executive in China with a commitment to have the person there for the long term.

There are a number of business areas that are generally *guanxi*-sensitive. In traditional equity and contractual joint ventures, as well as other forms of strategic alliance, an effective management of *guanxi* may be considered vital for successful operations. In joint ventures, targets for *guanxi*-building would involve regional government officials (or for large operations, central officials), key domestic suppliers, partners, customers and employees (internal customers).

Since the 1990s, the concept of relationship marketing has emerged and been advocated in the Western context.[51] Payne identifies six markets where relationship marketing may be effectively applied: customer markets, internal markets, supplier markets, recruitment markets, influence markets and referral markets.[52] In these areas or markets, *guanxi* plays a crucial part in business development in China. However, there are some major differences between relationship marketing in the West and *guanxi* marketing in China. In the West, for instance, relationship marketing is

> the ongoing process of identifying and creating new value with individual customers and then sharing the benefits from this over a life of association. It involves the understanding, focusing and management of ongoing collaboration between suppliers and selected customers for mutual

value creation and sharing through interdependence and organisational alignment.[53]

As can be seen, relationship marketing puts emphasis on a rational appeal, with value and benefits. The underlying model is one of equal transactions with customers by jointly creating and sharing value through interdependence. In contrast, a *guanxi*-based business approach stresses an emotional and ethical influence based on traditional Confucian values. Although benefits and value would also be considered, they are of secondary importance and do not necessarily arise from an equal transaction at a particular point in time. Payback value may be delivered at a later time, which is often represented as a 'credit' value in the partner's *guanxi* 'account'.

A strategic framework: linking strategy to context

Figure 5.1 depicts a strategic planning framework containing two strategic paradigms: *guanxi*-driven and market-driven. In the framework, the former is associated with the *guanxi*-sensitive context, while the market-driven paradigm relates to a competition–intensive context. The framework suggests that an alignment of the strategic paradigm with its context results in enhanced performance.

Guanxi-*driven strategies*

Guanxi can be seen as a resource for the firm[54] and even its 'chief asset',[55] but there can be formidable costs in terms of time and effort in acquiring, maintaining and cultivating the required contacts and networks.[56] This effort may well divert the attention of top management from areas where it is most needed, and strategic opportunities may be missed or resources inappropriately allocated. In some cases, defective adoption of the *guanxi* paradigm can result in liabilities,[57] deal-killing and an image that implies inadequate quality of offerings. In a nutshell, *guanxi*-based business approaches must be deployed in the right (*guanxi*-sensitive) context to have a positive impact on performance.

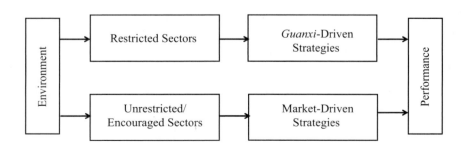

Figure 5.1 A strategic framework in China

The key elements of *guanxi* can be summarised as: (1) connections, (2) mutual obligations and trust, (3) reciprocation of favours and (4) a long-term orientation.[58] A study has noted two potential traps into which Western companies may fall: first, many have failed to realise that the Chinese business environment is changing. China's development is increasingly being integrated into the global economy, driving a greater alignment between Chinese business practices and what Western counterparts expect. China's regulatory and legal systems are also becoming more transparent and effective in resolving disputes. Many Chinese companies have started to de-emphasise *guanxi*, focusing instead on the value that Western businesses can bring. Second, many Western companies still see *guanxi*-building as an expression of social etiquette, friendship or family ties. Although the Chinese tend to blend personal relationship with business, too much emphasis on socialising or networking will often be counterproductive. An effective way of developing *guanxi* with Chinese companies is to build trust across cultural boundaries.[59]

The *guanxi*-driven paradigm is associated with the belief of a company's top management that business success depends on how well the company manages its *guanxi* with key stakeholders, which generally requires the full commitment of the company's top executives and resources. The *guanxi*-driven paradigm tends to work at two different levels: strategic and operational.

Central and municipal governments: strategies

Any foreign firm seeking a foothold in a restricted industry will normally require a licence, which because of the limited access may often be seen as granting the right to make profits. Although there are generally government criteria for qualification, a successful application will ultimately depend on the strength of *guanxi* with the authorities, represented by a number of key individuals or decision-makers at the central or municipal government levels. The CEOs of many multinationals which have successfully entered China's restricted industries have formed close relationships with Chinese national or municipal leaders such as the prime minister, senior ministers or mayors, who are the ultimate decision-makers for strategic industries. It is notable that GM achieved a massive and lucrative joint venture while Ford, which had worked on the same project for much longer and had expended far greater resources, failed to secure a deal. One of the key reasons was that GM had played the *guanxi* card better.[60] However, while a cordial government relationship is necessary, it is not a sufficient condition; the aspiring company has to work with all stakeholders in the project to ensure success.

The following are the key success factors at this level:

• Showing top management's commitment by building up a rapport with Chinese officials and potential partners and by visiting the central and municipal governments, as well as potential Chinese stakeholders, as frequently as appropriate.

A study of foreign businesses in China has rated the top management's commitment to Chinese business as the number one key success factor. Jack Welch of General Electric, Bill Gates of Microsoft and Bob Allen of AT&T, for instance, are known to have been personally involved in strategic visioning and relationship building in China, thus contributing significantly to their companies' success in the marketplace.[61] The American company AIG was the first insurer to be granted a licence to operate in China, in major part at least because its CEO developed a good relationship with the Chinese government.

- Recruiting a person, as either employee or agent, who has an appropriate background and the right connections.

The appointee should have the educational background and in-depth knowledge of Chinese culture needed to succeed in the characteristically indirect mode of communication in a high-context culture[62] and should be able to gain access to the relevant government bodies. For example, GM employed a key person who was fluent in Chinese, had strong connections with Chinese senior government officials and held the right educational qualifications.[63]

- Providing assistance to relevant organisations in China and presenting the firm as a friend of China.

For instance, AIG provided a great deal of assistance and 'free' services to Chinese insurance companies and authorities. Boeing enhanced its competitive position in China by helping to develop a modern air-traffic control network, donating flight simulators to local colleges and training Chinese mechanics and pilots in the USA.[64]

- Adopting a balanced perspective on technology policy.

Many foreign firms have been concerned about losing their technology to Chinese partners, and thus unwilling to use their most recent technology in China. This would put them at a disadvantage in applying for the necessary licence to enter the Chinese market; even if one were initially granted, late entrants would soon gain a competitive edge in the marketplace. *Guanxi* normally works only when the level of technology is equal and it is itself a *guanxi* tool. Introducing newer technology to China is seen as giving face to Chinese leaders, earning a major *guanxi* benefit. Kodak experienced rapid and significant growth when it entered the Chinese market, because, among other factors, the company assured the Chinese government that it would build the world's most advanced photosensitive materials industry in China.

Strategic decisions on the technology to be transferred to China should take a forward-looking perspective. In many cases, when a multinational appears to transfer the latest technology, more advanced technology has been developed in-house by the time the project is completed. Thus, the technology transferred actually becomes less advanced and may be considered just right to exploit the less developed Chinese market, without posing a serious threat to the firm's other markets. GM's success in China is partially attributable to its technology policy. Its promise to bring the best technology to China and help the country to build up a world-class automotive industry has been a powerful weapon, this advantage being further enhanced by establishing a sophisticated R&D centre in Shanghai and collaborative relationships with five leading Chinese universities.

Partners, suppliers/distributors, customers and employees: operations

At present, there are still a significant number of Sino-foreign equity and con-tractual joint ventures in China; in this context, the *guanxi*-driven paradigm remains influential, depending on the degree of interdependence between the partners, often indicated by the ratio of their shareholdings. Having good *guanxi* with the stakeholders in the Chinese business context is of paramount importance to ensure smooth and efficient operations in China. To achieve this demands cultural sensitivity and adaptation. There are many cases in which cul-tural insensitivity has offended joint venture partners and employees, resulting in the dissolution of the partnership. On the key question of how to develop and maintain good *guanxi*, the literature makes the following suggestions:

* Nurturing long-term and mutual benefits; cultivating personal relation-ships and trust.[65]
* Regularly auditing the firm's *guanxi* with its external stakeholders; identi-fying and repairing weak *guanxi* areas.[66]
* Learning Chinese to enhance expatriates' ability to establish *guanxi* in China.[67]

To play the relationship card well, the localisation of management is important and the profile of marketing personnel should emphasise relationship-building skills. It is notable that Volvo Trucks, the world's number two truck company after Daimler Trucks, has outperformed its rival in China, largely thanks to its superior localisation of management.

A study has found that a successful long-term cross-cultural relationship is built on trust. There are two crucial stages in building trust, the first of which is devel-oping the counterpart's trust in the company's capability. Since Chinese compa-nies now place great value on what a foreign company can bring, their trust in the company's deliverability becomes important. The second stage is building a per-sonal dimension of trust. This involves the development of affective trust, which in turn depends on acquiring an in-depth knowledge of Chinese culture.[68]

The market-driven paradigm

In the marketplace of the encouraged industries, the role of *guanxi* has lost ground at a strategic level in the marketplace to a set of different market-driven competitive rules which tend to determine winners and losers. Furthermore, the number of restricted industries in which *guanxi* still plays a dominant role has been reduced because of government deregulation and market development. Thus, it is the particular conditions that have precipitated the change, not any general diminution in the importance of *guanxi* in China.

As far as foreign companies in encouraged industries are concerned, they can play the game to very different rules. Since most foreign companies have dominant control of business ventures in China, they are able to make independent strategic choices, integrate their global strategies better, reduce conflicts with their partners and retain profits from their China operations.

The market-driven paradigm includes the following key elements:

- a high level of adaptation to local needs and requirements,
- management of local/Chinese competition,
- management of marketing dynamics and
- localisation of management.

High level of adaptation 1: standardisation versus adaptation

Although the standardisation/adaptation argument has been debated for about three decades, it remains inconclusive and under-researched.[69] However, it is suggested that the key to business success in China is organisational adaptability or flexibility.[70] Wall's ice cream, a Unilever brand which has been successful in the Chinese market, offers different flavours from region to region.[71] There are two fundamental conditions or assumptions for the global standardisation approach to work: (1) that there is a consumer base with homogeneous needs and wants and (2) that considerable economies of scale can be gained through restricting sources of supply.[72]

The needs and wants of Chinese consumers are far from homogeneous. The regions differ in level of economic development, in culture and thus in consumption patterns/preferences and buying behaviour, as well as in disposable income.[73] For instance, the people of Shanghai are significantly more fashion conscious than the northern Chinese. Even within the same region, consumer behaviour is hard to predict.

One of the major benefits of standardisation is cost reduction as a result of economies of scale. This is normally achieved by using a limited number of production bases to supply global markets, which would not be a likely strategy for a foreign firm, for a number of related reasons. Even within China, one base generally cannot meet demand from all national markets. There are major constraints on manufacturing supplies and distribution channels. Quality raw materials and components often cannot be supplied from within China, so have to be imported. Few national distribution/trading companies exist, and transportation systems (roads and railways) are still underdeveloped. There are often substantial trade barriers between regions and cities, as each tries to protect its own economy and employment. Therefore, it is often necessary for multinationals to develop multiple supply bases to surmount these barriers and to use different marketing approaches in different regions to adapt to local market needs and wants.

> The need for multiple ventures in China is unavoidable for most companies seeking to build a substantial presence. Setting up a string of alliances is the way to manage the fragmented nature of the Chinese market effectively. The far-reaching degree of decentralisation and the rapid changes that presently take place at the regional and national levels serve in this respect as the last move in the direction of starting up alliance strategies.[74]

Procter and Gamble's local organisation has evolved over the past decade, as it has learned to adapt. Initially, it had a three-tier organisational structure whereby the local level reported to the regional and the regional to the global. This was very bureaucratic, resulting in poor responsiveness to market changes. To address this problem, the company removed the regional layer and divided the globe into seven areas, each having a small number of business units, thus improving its market response, efficiency and innovation.

High level of adaptation 2: Chinese versus Western markets

Over a 30-year period, China has gone through a market development process which took Western countries about 200 years to complete. In the West, the norm is that business is undertaken in a relatively orderly manner, and there is a well-developed marketing infrastructure to help individuals or firms to do business professionally. Consumers are relatively responsive to market research, while markets are relatively predictable, in such aspects as consumer response to marketing stimuli and competitor reaction to company offers. The behaviour of firms is monitored and regulated to ensure that they conduct business in a responsible and accountable fashion vis-à-vis consumers and society. Laws and regulations monitor and control the behaviour of firms and protect consumers' interests.

Given the short period of market development in China, consumer behaviour is more fickle and unpredictable than in the West.[75] Although Western multinationals are equipped with sophisticated marketing skills and techniques, these tend to be seriously handicapped by inadequate marketing infrastructure and a lack of published market and industrial data.[76] Consumers are suspicious of market surveys because of the traditional Chinese stratagem culture, making them reluctant to cooperate with market research. Laws and regulations governing markets and company behaviour are yet to prove effective, so that counterfeit brands and products are often seen in the marketplace. It would therefore be difficult for Western multinationals to develop business in China if they followed homegrown marketing logic, strategies and operations. For example, Reckitt Benckiser has made significant adaptations across its whole product range to suit local market demand. McDonald's, together with its primary competitor KFC, has been known to make great efforts to adapt to the diversity of Chinese tastes. As a matter of policy, McDonald's has decided to standardise about 80 per cent of its menu in China, allowing 20 per cent to be different in order to reflect varying regional tastes, particularly addressing the nutrition and health concerns of Chinese consumers. Similarly, KFC has brought a number of Chinese foods into its menu and removed chips from set meals.

In some cases, the need to adapt is recognised but the transition is incomplete. Some core brands which have remained highly standardised have underperformed compared with those which have adapted more freely. In order to achieve the best combination of global standardisation and local adaptation, firms should concentrate research effort on understanding consumer reactions to existing core products by test marketing in different parts of China and by monitoring promotional campaigns, making adjustments where necessary.

Box 5.2   Know your Chinese customer

It is quite challenging to gauge correctly Chinese consumers' needs and values: price, product style, ease of use and so on. Simply asking Chinese consumers what they want will not lead to success. There is often misalignment between what consumers say they value and what research identifies as truly influencing their actual buying behaviour. For example, respondents cited trustworthiness, reliability and quality as the product attributes they considered most important in their purchase decisions in general. In practice, though, familiarity with a brand is actually the key consideration when looking across a broad range of product categories; it often trumps trustworthiness when it comes to a purchasing decision, while a brand's reliability is a far less important factor.

Measuring the alignment of a company's offerings and value proposition with the buyer values of intended customers will frequently yield unexpected results. One aspect of customer knowledge that marketers need to understand is the extent to which buyer behaviour in China is influenced by a brand's national origin. For instance, German and French brands had relatively low awareness but high levels of consideration, whereas Japanese brands were found to enjoy very high awareness in China without being able to translate this into high levels of consideration among buyers.

Therefore, aligning your value proposition with your Chinese prospects' buying values requires that you assess everything that is relevant to the customer about your company, including its global reputation, its nationality, the reputation of its products and the value inherent in the products themselves. In a sense, success in China's consumer sectors means going back to the basics of marketing.

Adapted from Lay Lim Teo, Susan A. Piotroski and Paul F. Nunes (2007), "Why Winning the Wallets of China's Consumers Is Harder Than You Think," *Outlook*, September.

Managing competition 1: different rules of the game

Many multinationals which have entered the consumer goods sector of the Chinese market have seen a sales surge at an early stage of entry, but they have often undergone a drastic decline in sales after a promising start. For instance, when Unilever launched the Wall's brand in China, sales initially grew explosively, even though the products were very expensive for most Chinese consumers. However, the early surge was soon halted by the entry of over 1000 domestic ice cream companies. Although Wall's remains the brand leader, the greatest threat has been posed by two indigenous companies, rather than multinational competitors.

A Korean market entrant made pies under special conditions that required maximum standards of hygiene, attained by heavy capital investment in advanced technology that few Chinese food companies could match. It duly moved into profit in its second year of operation, but was soon surprised to discover three indigenous products in the market, each similar in style or taste and at a much lower price. This has raised serious concerns about future market share.

Why is it that high-quality global brands often cannot sustain strong performance in the Chinese market? When a new foreign brand first appears in China, most consumers are curious to try it, so sales inevitably build. However, it is equally inevitable that Chinese competitors will soon launch products with similar features. Although the foreign brands tend to be of higher quality, with attendant higher prices, the manufacturers seldom have a technological monopoly, so that domestic firms will always be able, in one way or another, to acquire the technology to make similar products.

Although the quality of Chinese products may be inferior, the ratio of price to quality is often conspicuously more attractive. In other words, the price for an imitative product can be so low that on balance it offers better value for money. Competition from domestic manufacturers can often be irrational, in that they are not driven by profit maximisation but by market share or simple survival. Some secure low-cost loans to promote their products, with the support of local government, even when their standards and performance would be considered deplorable in the Western environment. Manufacturing capabilities have become a Chinese competitive advantage.

The Chinese home appliance market was one of the first industries to be opened to foreign investors, in the mid-1990s. Initially, foreign brands dominated the market, with their superior technology and management. During the early period of market entry, however, they were quickly exposed to such problems as poor after-sales service, high cost, and technology that was ill adapted to local demand. In the meantime, Chinese companies learned from their foreign competitors and rapidly improved their quality and technology, to the extent that foreign brands were almost driven out of the Chinese market. Multinationals such as Electrolux, Samsung and Siemens soon readjusted their China strategies to fight back with more focused and adaptive approaches, resulting in some restoration of their market shares in the early 2000s.

Managing competition 2: the fallacy of superior skills and knowledge

Multinationals appear to gain a competitive edge from their superior management knowledge, international experience and skills in marketing research, compared with most Chinese companies that have only recently been exposed to a market economy. This perceived superiority tends to make many of them underestimate the local competition.

Although conventional market research techniques are limited in China, because of its underdeveloped marketing infrastructure and the cultural aversion of Chinese consumers to 'scientific' market research, marketing decision-makers in Chinese companies are themselves typical consumers and often carry out their own marketing research by visiting or talking to consumers or clients. This dual role enables them to understand and respond to any emerging opportunities more quickly and effectively than their foreign competitors. For instance, the CEO of Haier, a leading Chinese home appliance manufacturer with operations in the USA and many developing countries, once received a report on the poor quality of a washing machine during the early years of its success. He personally visited customers in rural areas, finding that farmers were using it to wash melons and potatoes that were covered in mud and soil, blocking the drainage pipe. Having identified the problem, or rather a particular need, Haier developed a special machine with a wider drainage pipe, which could be used by rural buyers to wash both clothes and produce. Chinese-style market research thereby secured a large slice of market share for the company.

Managing competition 3: the fallacy of under-resourced Chinese companies

It can be misleading to assume that foreign multinationals are better resourced than Chinese companies and can thus succeed by outspending them. It has been noted that many multinationals have failed to pay adequate attention to Chinese competitors, mistakenly considering them uncompetitive or insufficiently sizeable.[77] eBay entered China by acquiring the Chinese company EachNet with a total outlay of $180 million in 2003, becoming the market leader with 90 per cent of market share in China and aspiring to navigate with China's e-commerce tidal wave. Embarking on the voyage with newly learned lessons from its recent failure in Japan, eBay was determined to succeed in China. In the same year, Alibaba launched its Taobao, a chief competitor with eBay in the local market. Although there had been a clear sign showing Alibaba's ambition and action in China's e-commerce market, eBay paid insufficient attention to this principal opponent. In 2004, when an eBay vice president was asked by *Business Week* about its rival in China, one name was mentioned: 1Pai.[78] Two years later, eBay was pushed out of China's competitive arena as a major player by Alibaba.[79] Because the Chinese market is so vast, well-run Chinese companies can grow significantly in a short period of time, thereby accumulating sufficient financial resources to compete effectively.

Managing marketing dynamics

In the Western world, business concepts have gone through a process of evolution from production through sales to market orientation, as the business environment has changed. Similarly, as the business environment in China becomes increasingly competitive, business concepts in many Chinese and foreign companies have also evolved. The adoption of an appropriate business orientation is crucial for corporate success in China. During the 1990s, many multinational firms went through an evolutionary process from an operational to a market orientation.

When foreign firms first entered Chinese markets through joint ventures or solely owned businesses, demand for their products was high and competition was relatively low. High-quality imports were too expensive for most Chinese consumers to afford and many domestic products were too poor quality to be attractive, whereas foreign products made in China were just right in terms of price, quality and availability. During this early period, the main tasks and concerns of early entrants' top management were to increase capacity, improve and control product quality, reduce costs and overcome distribution barriers to achieve as wide a distribution coverage as possible.

Intensifying competition has led joint ventures and wholly foreign-owned firms to be more responsive to market changes and consumer/customer requirements, becoming more market-driven. They have enhanced their marketing research and modified or adapted more products to cater to Chinese consumers' needs and wants. More companies have utilised focused marketing strategies, increased the budgets of their marketing departments and broadened their responsibilities. Marketing has begun to play a more important role in many companies.

Reckitt Benckiser entered a joint venture with a Chinese partner in 1996. Initially, its marketing functions mainly involved developing new products and building up brands from nothing. By placing emphasis on sales programmes to increase sales and market share, the company became one of the fastest-growing joint ventures in China. However, its success also led to such potential problems as a high advertising-to-sales ratio, plus heavy spending on trade and consumer promotions and overheads. The many and varied trade campaigns resulted in a chaotic and confusing pricing structure. Local competitors grasped the opportunity that this situation presented, a price war broke out in all markets and profitability declined rapidly. The company responded by downsizing its organisational structure and cutting overhead costs. It also made a strategic shift from a sales-driven strategy to a market-driven one. The responsibilities of the marketing department were broadened, while budgets for trade sales were reduced by 20 per cent and those for marketing increased by 25 per cent. The focus shifted to profits from volume and market share.

General Electric entered a joint venture with a Chinese partner in 1992, with the aim of securing more import licences. Marketing was not an issue, since supplies to the market were limited. After the licence system was abolished in

China in 1994, marketing problems became more evident. Until then, the company had made little effort to understand Chinese culture and markets. Management was disorganised and distribution ineffective. Following a major strategic restructuring, a four-point strategy was adopted: to improve product offers; to restructure the distribution network and strengthen distribution coverage; to localise management; and to make the Chinese operation a global player, using GE China as the global sourcing base. These strategic initiatives have enabled the company to remain one step ahead of its competitors, to improve its performance dramatically and to achieve an annual growth rate of 50 per cent in the Chinese market.

The Chinese market is now well integrated with the global economy, so any firm that operates in China should treat the market as if it were competing in a developed economy, with a market orientation or considerable adaptation or localisation.

Localisation of management

We have already seen that local management personnel have dual identities: in the company they are managers, while in the marketplace they are consumers who understand the market better than expatriates can. In addition, the cost of employing an expatriate at senior management level is typically many times that for a local person in the same position. The cost of 'local expatriates', who have local nationality but are educated and appointed in foreign countries, is also significantly lower than that of foreign expatriates. More often than not, they are an ideal means of bridging the gap between global strategic aspiration and local market orientation.

The relationship between global and local leadership has an impact on local management and thus on the stability and efficiency of local organisation. A global consumer goods company in China placed emphasis on global leadership in all but the sales area, where it had little choice but to use local senior managers. The fact that locals had little chance of career advancement in the other major business areas, such as marketing and finance, resulted in an unstable organisation with a high turnover of management staff. This disrupted continuity as they were replaced by new managers having little knowledge of local markets and thus little ability to respond to local needs. As a result of this structural problem, the company gradually lost its competitive edge in some of the markets where it had been the market leader.

Summary

Since China has emerged as an important part of the global economy, the success or failure of global firms there often has a significant impact on their business performance elsewhere in the world. To succeed in China, planners and strategists must first be aware of different 'rules' in different business sectors. In 'controlled' sectors and those areas that are *guanxi*-sensitive, they would be well advised to pay close attention to the *guanxi*-driven paradigm, by involving top management in *guanxi*-building and employing people with skills in developing human relationships and important connections. Because *guanxi* is an important resource in the Chinese context, incompetent application of its principles will result in missed strategic opportunities and increased operating costs.

In 'encouraged' sectors or competitive markets, competition is increasingly intense, and Chinese consumers and enterprises both behave quite differently from their counterparts in the West. Multinationals should build a flexible organisational structure and employ adaptive and responsive approaches to business. Marketing diligence with Chinese characteristics is vital for companies to succeed in China, so efforts should be made to understand what Chinese consumers say and what they really value; the two often do not go together. Localisation of marketing management can help to achieve two key objectives: being closer to the market and reducing operating costs. Strategic reviews should be performed to examine their local responsiveness and influencing factors, and then strategic plans should be constructed or modified accordingly.

In reality, to succeed in China, companies would be well advised to employ a combined *guanxi*- and market-driven approach to develop business in many sectors. Motorola is an excellent case in point: its earlier success had reflected the company's skills in applying both Western and Chinese logic to develop its strategies in China, combining general innovation, marketing, organisational and human resource strategies, similar to what the company did globally, but with commitment and close attention to the Chinese *guanxi* dimension.

MNC marketing strategies in China

Figure 5.2 presents a framework for MNC marketing strategies in China. The model suggests that China's environment (both internal and external) influences both the marketing strategy of the subsidiary firm and its corporate control (from the company's headquarters and its Asia/China centre), which affects marketing strategy of the subsidiary. Both corporate control and marketing strategy have an impact on the performance of the company's China operations, in terms of qualitative measurement (competitiveness and viability) and quantitative measurement (profitability). Various elements of the model are discussed below, beginning with the business environment.

China's business environment

The corporate control that multinationals exercise over their subsidiaries in China and the business strategies that they pursue are prone to the influence of environmental factors: both internal and external.

The internal environment

The internal environment generally embraces a firm's resources, organisational structure, leadership, and international experience, as well as the attitude of its management towards internationalisation. For instance, when a firm with little

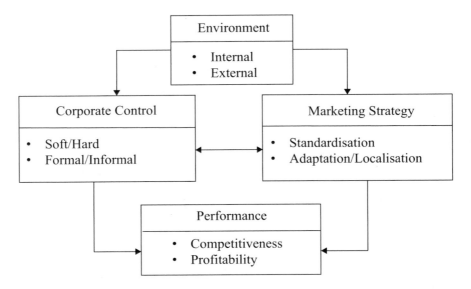

Figure 5.2 A model of MNC marketing strategy in China

international experience of operating in developing countries enters the Chinese market, it is very likely to be subject to a high degree of corporate influence and to adopt a strategy with a high degree of standardisation. Generally, those head offices led by managers with a Chinese background tend to have the view that the Chinese market has its unique characteristics which require the adoption of a highly adaptive approach (i.e. delegation of decision-making power). There has been a recognition that the headquarters of European and American multinationals have exhibited a disappointingly poor understanding of China and that an outdated perception of Chinese ways of life prevails. Furthermore, head office decision-makers are often slow to seize market opportunities.[80]

The external environment

The external environment includes government policies and regulations, marketing infrastructure, market structure, competition and other political, economic, technological, cultural and social factors that constrain the development of a firms' business strategy. A less politically stable environment, for instance, would result in weaker corporate commitment and management control, involving fewer strategic resources. The Chinese external environment is known to have the following characteristics, which are mostly derived from the legacy of the erstwhile planned economic system.

GREAT SIZE AND SHARP CONTRASTS

China has a population of 1.3 billion and the world's third largest physical area of all countries, at 9.6 million square kilometres. With the fastest economic growth in the world, China's market potential has become attractive to any multinational business targeting the global market. However, it is equally significant that this vast national market is fragmented into many regional ones, which are characterised by differences of sub-culture, education, income and resource endowment, as well as the protection of regional economy by the local government.

UNCERTAINTY

The environment has undergone constant change in terms of government organisations, regulations and policies, as well as consumer behaviour. For instance, in 2010, the People's Bank of China (PBOC) issued new rules governing China's third-party payment platforms on the Internet. However, these rules were unclear, and subject to multiple interpretations. Consequently, a serious dispute occurred on the legitimacy of Jack Ma's action between Alibaba's major shareholders and Jack Ma, because of different interpretations of relevant rules.[81] Meeting a reporter from the *Washington Post*, the former CEO of Yahoo has aired his frustration on China's legal system:

> To be doing business in China, or anywhere else in the world, we have to comply with local law.... We don't know what they want that information for, we're not told what they look for. If they give us the proper documentation and court orders, we give them things that satisfy both our privacy policy and the local rules.[82]

In 2015, a senior official from the Chinese government agency responsible for Chinese Internet firms, the State Administration for Industry and Commerce (SAIC), published a 'white paper' online and later deleted it, making some allegations about Alibaba's management and causing commotions among the firm's shareholders and stakeholders.[83] A 2015 survey carried out by the American Chamber of Commerce in China revealed that only 25 per cent of its members in the service sector were optimistic about China's regulatory environment.[84]

Despite great efforts by the Chinese government to regulate the domestic market, fake and pirated products can still be found in the marketplace. The infringement of intellectual property rights has remained a concern for multinationals.

DIVERSITY

There are great differences between regions, in terms of culture, economic development, fashion consciousness and government competence and policies.

For example, the Shanghai government is characterised by the adoption of a notable professionalism in its dealings with business affairs, particularly those involving foreign businesses, acting with significantly more competence, fairness and efficiency than the authorities in many other parts of the country.

Research by the Boston Consulting Group (BCG) has identified three trends in China: 'the rise of upper-middle-class and affluent households as the drivers of consumption growth; a new generation of freer-spending, sophisticated consumers; and the increasingly powerful role of e-commerce.'[85] According to the Credit Suisse 2015 Global Wealth Report, the middle-class population of China, defined by the income range of $50,000–$500,000, was 109 million, while the USA had 92 million and Japan 62 million. China expects an increase of 100 million in the number of middle-class households in the next decade, and over 50 per cent of urban households should become middle class by 2020, although the average household income will be $20,000–$40,000.

Chinese consumers, which account for over 30 per cent of global luxury spending,[86] are becoming more selective about where to purchase, shifting from products to services and from mass to premium segments. They are paying more attention to health, family and experiences, while their increasing loyalty to a few preferred premium brands makes launching and promoting new brands more difficult or less effective.[87]

China is the world's largest e-commerce market, whose transaction value of $672 billion in 2015 was equivalent to that of Europe and the United States combined, and consumers increasingly purchase online. However, physical stores in China continue to play an important part in consumption. Consumers engage with brands both online and offline, still gaining more satisfaction from physical stores than from online activity, but the gap is reducing, particularly as satisfaction with hypermarkets declines.[88]

> Through 2020, 81% of consumption growth will come from households whose annual income is more than $24,000. Furthermore, consumers 35 or younger will account for 65% of growth. E-commerce will become a far more important retail channel, driving 42% of total consumption growth, 90% of that growth coming from mobile e-commerce.[89]

Governmental policy remains an important force shaping China's economy. The government influences GDP growth and employment through investment in infrastructure and deregulation of the pricing of water, electricity, land and capital.

Many Chinese state-owned businesses are under increasing pressure on costs and earnings. Their margins have declined by a third in four years. Operating in what are now mature industries, they are experiencing a much slower growth.[90]

Chinese competitiveness

China has enjoyed the world's fastest GDP growth over past three decades; for instance, the annual growth rate was 9.2 per cent in 2009, 10.5 per cent in 2010, 9.3 per cent in 2011, 7.7 per cent in 2012, 7.7 per cent in 2013, 7.4 per cent in 2014 and 6.8 per cent in 2015.

Since 2010, China has become the world's largest manufacturer, the position which had been taken by the USA from 1895 to 2009. According to the IMF, in 2013, China's manufacturing accounted for 36.9 per cent of GDP, while US manufacturing accounted for 12.4 per cent. China is the world's largest producer in many industrial sectors, to name just a few as examples in Table 5.1.

China is also the world's top producer in many product categories, including electricity generation, textile, air conditioner, refrigerator, cotton, motorcycle, furniture, piano, fishery and meat. In addition, in numerous areas of construction, China has acquired the world's top position, such as highway, high-speed rail, subway, water transport, ports, tunnel, water conservancy construction, power grid and bridge. For instance, a website, highestbridges.com, lists the world's highest bridges; 8 out of the top 10 are located in China, and 85 out of the top 100 are situated in China. In August 2016, China opened the world's highest and longest glass-bottomed bridge.

China has been the world's largest exporter since 2009 and the second largest economy since 2010. Despite China's economic slowdown in 2015, the IMF reports that from 2014 to 2015, China's share of global GDP increased from 13.4 per cent to 15.4 per cent, while its share of exports rose from 12.9 per cent to 14.6 per cent. The eight next largest exporting nations in 2015 were the USA (8.96%), Germany (8.04%), Japan (4.24%), South Korea (3.42%), France (3.29%), the Netherlands (3.18%), Italy (2.84%) and the UK (2.64%).

China has seen the emergence of some of the world's largest and most innovative and successful e-commerce companies, such as Tencent, Alibaba and JD.com. One of the reasons for holding the 2016 meeting of the G20 in Hangzhou was that it is China's powerhouse and e-business hub, where the economic development is greatly facilitated by e-business or m-business; people

Table 5.1 Percentage of China's industry in the world in 2013

Industry / Product	Percentage of World's Total
Shipbuilding	41
Iron	59
Fertiliser	35
Construction machinery	43
Automobile	25
Flat glass	50
Television	49
Mobile phone	71
Electrolytic aluminium	65

there can do almost anything with a smartphone. Tencent's WeChat and Alibaba's Alipay provide third-party online payment platforms that allow users, for instance, to purchase goods, pay taxis and order takeaway without credit cards or cash and without transaction fees, indicating that in some respects, Chinese e-commerce companies have gained an edge over their Western counterparts, such as Facebook, Twitter and Amazon.

The Fortune Global 500 annual ranking is considered to indicate a nation's economic strength. The list published by *Fortune* magazine on 20 July 2016 shows that the number of Chinese companies increased from 106 in 2015 to 110 in 2016, when by comparison there were only 52 Japanese companies and a total of 83 French, German and British ones. In the past few years, the number of US, European and Japanese companies on the Fortune 500 list has declined as China's contribution has increased.

The China Enterprise Confederation also annually ranks the Chinese Top 500 (CT500) enterprises, representing the overall competitiveness of Chinese enterprises. In 2015, the total revenue of CT500 companies reached RMB 59.5 trillion, with total assets of RMB 197.5 trillion. Among the 500 enterprises, 293 (58.6%) are state-owned or controlled, and 207 (41.4%) are privately owned. According to the China Enterprise Confederation, the CT500 showed the following trends in 2015:

(1) For the first time, the sales of service enterprises surpassed those of manufacturing enterprises, accounting for 40.2 per cent of all CT500 sales.
(2) The number of enterprises in the high-tech manufacturing and service sectors increased, while there were fewer in the traditional (heavy) industrial sectors.
(3) R&D investment increased 7.4 per cent over 2014 and the number of invention patents rose 32.9 per cent. CT500 enterprises were involved in the development of over 1600 international standards, an increase of 12.4 per cent.
(4) Total sales of CT500 companies were equivalent to about 80 per cent of those of the US Fortune 500 companies, reducing the gap by 2.4 per cent compared with 2014.

China's challenges

According to the Chinese Bureau of Statistics, notwithstanding China being the world's second largest economy, its annual per capita income is about $8000, while in 2014, the average figure for the developed economies was $12,616. It is estimated that China will not achieve parity on this measure until about 2040, indicating just how far the country has to go before joining the 'developed club'.

China's labour productivity is only 7.4 per cent of that of the United States. This indicates both that the economy is at a relatively underdeveloped stage and that there is great potential for further development. Productivity will improve as China undergoes structural changes in industry, with more mechanisation, computerisation and intellectualisation, resulting in the enhancement of China's competitiveness. Meanwhile, the low level of mechanisation and labour productivity mean that the adverse economic impact of China's ageing population is not as acute as in the developed economies.

The availability of arable land per head in China is only 40 per cent of the world's average, while the ownership of land per household is one-400th of that in the USA, indicating the small scale of agricultural production. This poses great difficulties for the task of increasing agricultural productivity. On the other hand, about 54 to 60 per cent of China's population still lives in the countryside, and it is difficult to reallocate a rural labour force to non-agricultural sectors. However, many farmers are moving to urban areas, providing both the workforce needed in labour-intensive sectors and the demand required to boost economic development.

Although an increasing number of Chinese companies have joined the Fortune Global 500 over the years, do the current 110 members really reflect Chinese competitiveness? Comparing these Chinese companies with Fortune 500 companies in the USA may shed light on this question.

Notably, most Chinese Fortune 500 companies operate in the utilities sector (gas, electricity, water) or in finance, non-ferrous metals, iron and steel, automobiles or coal. These industries are mostly in a position of monopoly, quasi-monopoly or excessive supply. China also has the largest number of real estate companies on the Fortune 500 list, including Vanke, Wanda, and Hengda. In contrast, US and European Fortune 500 companies are spread among retail, Internet, high-tech manufacturing, electronics, medical, and other fields; in other words, they essentially fall into the market- and technology-driven sectors.

The US Fortune 500 companies have average annual sales of $63.2 billion, making $5.1 billion in profits. In contrast, 10 Chinese banks make a total profit of $181.6 billion, accounting for 55 per cent of all Chinese Fortune 500 profits, with $147 billion to be shared among 93 non-bank enterprises (an average of $1.6 billion each). There are 21 loss-making Chinese Fortune 500 companies.

Among the CT500, state-owned businesses still dominate, while two-thirds of the 110 Chinese Fortune 500 companies are state-controlled. Table 5.2 shows a comparison of state-owned and privately owned companies, in terms of 2015 performance indices.

As can be seen, among the CT500 or major Chinese business players, state-controlled enterprises continue to dominate. Between 2014 and 2015, for the first time, the CT500 suffered a decrease in sales growth, despite an increase in profit growth by 6.3 per cent; the number of loss-making enterprises and the value of losses also increased.

The fact that most US or non-Chinese Fortune 500 companies operate in market-driven sectors, whereas most CT500 companies are in resource-based, monopoly or quasi-monopoly sectors, means that multinationals with operations in China compete locally with mostly small and medium-sized Chinese companies. Metaphorically, this competition may be seen as warfare between

Table 5.2 A comparison of SOEs and privately owned CT500

	Sales	Assets	Profits	Tax	Employees
SOEs	78.3%	90.2%	81.1%	88.7%	81.0%
Private	21.7	9.8	18.9	11.3	19.0

guerrilla bands on the Chinese side and regular armies from Western countries. Nevertheless, many Chinese firms have now gradually begun to turn themselves into regular armies, while Western companies are increasingly adopting a guerrilla approach to their battles as China's international competitiveness strengthens.

Corporate control

Corporate headquarters can influence both the marketing strategy of subsidiaries and the performance of these firms, as shown in Figure 5.2. The concept of corporate control, for both wholly foreign-owned and joint venture businesses, embodies two layers of relationships: (1) the (control) relationship within the China business unit between the firm and Chinese partner(s) and (2) the control relationship between the headquarters and the business units. In the case of a joint venture, effective control can be achieved by resorting to majority shareholding or capital-based power (hard) and/or to non-capital resources, such as technology, expertise, skills and capabilities (soft).[91] In terms of the relationship between headquarters and the subsidiaries or business units, control is exercised through (1) the company's organisational structure, such as line reporting, promotion and compensation and (2) resource allocation such as capital investment and knowledge transfer.[92] Some common control mechanisms used by multinationals, classified as either formal and structural or informal and subtle, are shown in Table 5.3.[93]

It has been found that management control has a positive impact on the performance of joint ventures in China.[94] Control can affect the foreign partner's strategy vis-à-vis its subsidiary and determine the extent to which it can modify decisions on adaptation to the local environment, with a resultant impact on the firm's performance.[95]

The management relationship between a firm's headquarters and its China business unit will have a strategic impact on its performance in China. In a global organisational structure, where the headquarters exercises a certain degree of control over business units worldwide in order to maintain a unified global standard in a number of business areas, efficient and effective communications tend to have an effect on the performance of these business units. However, three obstacles have been identified to such communications: (1) geographical distance (including time difference), (2) information distance (lack of knowledge about China at the centre) and (3) cultural distance (misperceptions of China). Since the Chinese business environment is highly changeable, fast

Table 5.3 List of most common control mechanisms[96]

Structural and Formal Mechanisms:
- Departmentalisation or grouping of organisational units, shaping the formal structure.
- Centralisation or decentralisation of decision-making through the hierarchy of formal authority.
- Formalisation and standardisation: written policies, rules, job descriptions, and standard procedures, through instruments such as manuals, charts, etc.
- Planning: strategic planning, budgeting, functional plans, scheduling, etc.
- Output and behaviour control: financial performance, technical reports, sales and marketing data, etc., and direct supervision

Informal and Subtle Mechanisms:
- Lateral or cross-departmental relations: direct managerial contact, temporary or permanent teams, task forces, committees, integrators and integrative departments.
- Informal communication: personal contacts among managers, management trips, meetings, conferences, transfer of managers, etc.
- Socialisation: building an organisational culture of known and shared strategic objectives and values by training, transfer of managers, career path management, measurement and reward systems, etc.

response and adaptation are often essential to success. However, when decisions are to be made at the headquarters, rapid reactions are hardly ever possible.[97] Too high a level of management control from the head office tends to have a negative effect on market orientation at subsidiary levels.[98] Although Uber has not conquered the Chinese market, it has become $5 billion richer with 20 per cent of Didi (worth about $35 billion). This outcome is attributable to its full preparation before it entered China:

> one lesson that Uber China has taken to heart from its Western predecessors is headquarters knows it cannot strategize about China while sitting in the Silicon Valley office. Uber's management values China enough that they give the local team a massive amount of autonomy, and the leadership is among the most-seen Western business leaders in local Chinese events and press. All of these have shown the newer generation of Silicon Valley entrepreneurs galvanized determination to listen, and to adapt, in order to win.[99]

There are many cases in which headquarters have overemphasised corporate standards without adequate attention to local culture, resulting in irreparable damage to the performance of their subsidiaries. eBay's mishap in China is a case in point. Founded in San Jose, California, in 1995, eBay is a US e-commerce multinational with operations in over 30 countries, providing a powerful platform for B2C (business-to-consumer) and C2C (consumer-to-consumer), enabling the sale of goods and services on a local, national and an international basis. In fact, eBay's CEO was the first in Silicon Valley to recognise the potential of China's Internet market, making a remark in 2002: 'With demographics and incredible changes in China, our hypothesis is this could be one of the largest e-commerce markets in the world.'[100] In June 2003, eBay took full control of a major Chinese Internet company, EachNet, as a vessel for entering the Chinese e-commerce market. At the time, eBay's EachNet had a 90 per cent share of China's C2C market. However, the next few years witnessed a dramatic turn of the company from the leading player into insignificance in China. What has brought about the demise of eBay in China? The problem has stemmed from the ill-formed relationship between the headquarters and the China subsidiary: the heads of marketing and technology started to run the show in China. In 2004, the headquarters 'decided to "migrate" the China website to the United States. Instead of hosting the website close to customers in China, it was shifted to the States,'[101] seriously denting the subsidiary's entrepreneurial culture.

> eBay was confident that its global network and experience would ensure EachNet pulled well clear of any competitors. But corporate bureaucracy, worsened by the extended and dysfunctional reporting lines all the way to San Jose, were to smother whatever embers of entrepreneurialism still burned within EachNet in Shanghai. eBay's China adventure, lasting from 2003 to 2006, is today a case study in how not to go about managing a business in a distant market.[102]

A study has identified four types of corporate rigidities that potentially hinder MNCs' ability to respond to market dynamics in China: mind-set rigidity, strategic rigidity, operational rigidity and HRM rigidity.[103] Mind-set rigidity represents a subtle and habitual mental attitude towards the interpretation of and response to actual situations. Consequently, corporate managers tend to cast misconceptions, prejudices, stereotypes and insensitivities into China operations. Strategic rigidity derives from corporate strategic planning system backed up by market information. Because of a relatively long life cycle of planning, it often fails to take complex and dynamic local conditions into consideration or respond to dynamic changes in China's environment. Operational rigidity comes from firm's operating system, involving its speed of decision-making and problem-solving. Many MNCs have a centrally manipulated system that results in a corporate inability to deliver the size or speed of changes that keep up with customers' requirements or ahead of their competitors. The first three types of rigidities can be linked to the final source of rigidity, HRM. Because of mind-set rigidity, a firm may stick to its existing HRM system, which brings about inadequate initiative and input from local staff, leading to strategic rigidity.

Marketing strategy

Two principal dimensions of international marketing strategy are standardisation and localisation or adaptation.[104] The decision on standardisation versus localisation has been a central issue among scholars of both international business and marketing for over 50 years[105] and is at the heart of internationalisation strategy or management.[106] International marketing standardisation refers to the practice whereby a firm's marketing activities are the same or similar across different countries. It applies to either marketing programmes or marketing processes. The former term denotes the marketing strategies, policies and activities of a company, while the latter means the procedures by which a firm makes and implements marketing decisions as well as controls their outcomes.[107] Nowadays, all multinationals tend to apply both standardisation and localisation simultaneously, with a difference of degree in each element of the marketing mix.[108] The degree of localisation is reflected in the effort made by the company to match local customer needs or requirements and is measured by its local market orientation. There are a number of factors that drive the firms' pursuit of a standardisation strategy, including economies of scale, technological uniformity, consistent corporate brand image, convergence of consumer needs, tastes and preferences and the emergence of global market segments.[109] Strong arguments are also articulated in favour of the adaptation/localisation strategy, and local responsiveness is deemed essential to long-term profitability.[110] Essentially, the two strategies involve different strategic focuses: standardisation is cost-driven while localisation/adaptation is market-driven. A school of thought known as 'transnational strategy' advocates that in order to survive and develop in the current global business environment, firms must strive for both cost reduction and local responsiveness.[111]

> In essence, firms that pursue a transnational strategy are trying to simultaneously achieve low costs through location economies, economies of scale, and learning effects; differentiate their product offering across geographic markets to account for local differences; and foster a multidirectional flow of skills between different subsidiaries in the firm's global network of operations.[112]

The corporate decision on standardisation/localisation has a major effect on headquarters-subsidiary relationships within multinationals.[113] The higher the degree of standardisation, the more closely the headquarters is involved or controls the subsidiary's marketing strategy. The relationship between international marketing strategy and performance is underlined by strategic contingency theory, which has been widely accepted in the field of strategic management.[114] The theory, asserting that alignment between environmental factors and a firm's strategies is positively associated with its performance,[115] has been supported by a major empirical study.[116] The external environment generally comprises the factors that influence the company's functioning and strategy, such as industrial dynamism, complexity and munificence, constraints and contingencies.[117] The internal environment consists of factors such as leadership,[118] organisational culture[119] and organisational capabilities.[120]

An examination of China's external environment, as presented above, generally suggests that to achieve effective marketing in China, multinationals must pursue a high degree of localisation to cope with a fragmented, disorderly, fluctuating and diverse market. However, an overreliance on expatriates in multinationals, fuelled by corporate politics, control or culture, has constrained their abilities to materialise effectively localisation strategy. A survey of Chinese employees working multinationals shows that 40 per cent of them believe that 'most senior positions are, and will continue to be, held by expatriates.'[121] On the other hand, a low degree of management localisation gives rise to a limited understanding of the Chinese environment by headquarters, and this in turn fosters a high degree of standardisation, resulting in the potential loss of market opportunities. Nevertheless, as these multinationals become mature, it is to be expected that this paradoxical situation can be addressed. Four recommendations have been made concerning how the headquarters should manage its relationships with its subsidiaries:[122]

- Support for China operations should be established among the top management at corporate headquarters.
- A top executive who is well respected and well connected at headquarters should be appointed in China. Wherever possible, autonomy should be given to China operations.
- Staff at headquarters should regularly visit China to update their knowledge of the local environment and operations.
- Managers in China should be given strategic decision-making power, allowing their operations to be responsive and adaptive to the local market.

As early as 1999, it was found that foreign firms' subsidiaries in China had already become an integral part of their global operations and that their head offices had heavily coordinated their activities, particularly in production and supply. A high degree of standardisation was found to be exercised in branding policy, product line/new product development, product positioning and customer services, while a high degree of adaptation was maintained in distribution channels, advertising and market segmentation.[123]

Managing brand development

A brand is defined by the American Marketing Association as 'a name, term, sign, symbol or design, or a combination of them, intended to identify the goods or services of one seller or group of sellers and to differentiate them from those of competitors'.

> A brand adds dimensions that differentiate the offering in some way from other offerings designed to satisfy the same need. These differences may be functional, rational, or tangible – related to the brand's product performance. They may also be more symbolic, emotional or intangible – related to what the brand presents.[124]

The utilisation of branding and related brand images or logos can be traced back as far as China's Song dynasty (960–1297).[125] One of the earliest-identified outdoor advertisements is a printed poster from the Northern Song period, consisting of a square sheet of paper with a logo in the form of a white rabbit in the centre. Written above this is: 'Quality Needle Shop of Jinan Liu's Family' and below: 'We buy high quality steel rods and make quality fine needles, to be ready for use at home in no time.' On either side are the slogans: 'Identify the White Rabbit as our mark' and 'Please remember White Rabbit'.[126]

In contemporary society, a firm's branding policy is one of the most important elements of its overall marketing strategy, and its brands can play a vital role in establishing its visibility and position in international markets.[127] Building and managing brand equity have become priorities for many companies.[128] Most top performers in China, including both multinationals and domestic companies, have successfully built highly reputable and recognisable brands. However, given the characteristics of the Chinese business environment, managing branding policy is challenging, often involving a high risk. The literature presents the following practical recommendations on building a brand and managing its development.

ADOPT A DUAL BRANDING STRATEGY WHEN LAUNCHING NEW PRODUCTS

When launching new products in China, the simultaneous use of the parent brand name and a sub-brand name tends to result in a greater chance of success. A suggestive brand explicitly communicates a product's benefit, giving rise to a better recollection of an advertised benefit that is consistent with the brand name's connotations. A suggestive sub-brand name enhances consumers' recall of the new product's key benefits and features, while a suggestive parent brand name conveys the benefits of the product category. With a dual branding strategy, a suggestive parent brand name allows the company to add new products with different sub-brand names in the future, while the sub-brand name delivers the message of its core benefits and features. An example is Coca-Cola's successful launch in China of the Minute Maid Orange Pulp juice drink in 2004. The product was launched with two names: the sub-brand name, *Guo Li Cheng*, meaning 'fruit pulp orange', and the parent brand name, *Mei Zhi Yuan*, which is the Chinese brand name for Minute Maid, denoting 'good juice source'. This sub-brand name was suggestive of the key benefits and features of the new product, while the parent brand name was also suggestive, positioning Minute Maid as a juice-based wellness parent brand.[129]

BUY INTO THE MARKET

Many consumer goods multinationals have successfully employed the strategy of buying into 'good enough' segments, because their cost structure is not low enough to compete with local brands; examples are Gillette, L'Oréal, Colgate-Palmolive and Anheuser-Busch.[130]

> Overseas companies are acquiring breweries, or setting up new ones, across the country to widen the reach of their premium brands. Japan's Asahi Group Holdings, which entered China in 1994 and in 2009 bought a stake

in China's Tsingtao Brewery, plans to support local partners to compete at the lower end while it focuses on the high end. It's trying to establish the brand image of its Asahi Super Dry beer by asking local bars and Japanese restaurants to serve it draft-style from kegs, which is less common in China.[131]

Gillette's Duracell division, for instance, lost market share to lower-priced competitors in China throughout the 1990s. By 2002, its market share stood at 6.5 per cent, while a Chinese company, Nanfu, controlled over half the market. Recognising the fundamental cost disadvantage of Duracell compared with Chinese competitors, Gillette's management decided to buy in instead of fighting a hard battle, so in 2003 Gillette acquired a majority stake in Nanfu.[132]

Procter & Gamble, Unilever, Henkel and Kao have between them acquired ownership or control of 13 major Chinese consumer and chemical goods companies in Shanghai, Guangzhou, Beijing and Tianjin. Through M&As and marketing efforts, multinationals have occupied 60 per cent of China's colour TV market, 80 per cent of the shampoo and conditioner market, 68 per cent of the passenger car market, 70 per cent of the lift market, 65 per cent of the colour cathode ray tube market and 90 per cent of the programme-controlled telephone exchange market.[133]

EXPAND SELECTIVELY AND VERTICALLY

Most foreign consumer goods companies tend to focus on the building and extending of their brands for high-income markets, by expanding horizontally and charging premium prices. This strategy has achieved limited success in China. While premium brands owned by foreign companies, for instance, account for more than 30 per cent of all food and beverage consumption in China, only half of these companies can claim to be profitable. The research suggests that the success of premium brands in China is subject to different rules; that is, profitability is driven by both market share and the nature of the brand's product category, with the question of whether the given brand is 'premium' being of little relevance. If a product category mainly comprises premium brands, most of the brands in that category tend to be profitable. On the other hand, if the category mainly consists of value or own-label brands, the profitability of premium brands will be lower across the board.[134]

Chinese luxury consumers have the following characteristics:[135]

- Their purchasing behaviour differs significantly from those of other cultures, with limited brand awareness and loyalty, except for some of the most recognisable brands.[136]
- They tend to be younger and more easily identifiable than those from Western countries.[137]
- Their purchasing motivations are to display their wealth and social status,[138] but they have been shifting to pay attention to intrinsic value, rarity and exclusivity.[139]

DEFINE BRAND IMAGE WITH A CLEAR TARGET CUSTOMER BASE

Although it is recognised that Chinese consumers switch brands frequently and easily,[140] this is not determined by Chinese culture. Instead, two factors are considered responsible for the fickleness of Chinese consumers: first, there are too many brands bombarding the market, making consumer choice of brands difficult; and second, many multinationals fail to do an adequate job of identifying and understanding the market in order to define clearly their target consumer groups. For instance, when General Motors reintroduced its Buick brand to the China market in the early 2000s, it was positioned as appropriate for senior executives and other elites, showing that China's last emperor had a Buick in the 1920s, as did other Chinese leaders such as Sun Yat-sen and Zhou Enlai. This strategy met with immediate success, and GM was soon selling more Buicks in China than in the USA. To take advantage of the rapid growth, Buick then began to sell lower-end models in the $12,000 price range. Sales initially went up as many youngsters were keen to buy into the prestigious brand, but its image was thereby seriously diluted, causing market share to plummet in the first half of 2007. GM was then obliged to discount further in order to attract price-sensitive customers and boost lacklustre sales.[141]

A three-step brand development model has been proposed: acquiring deep customer insights, developing a targeted and compelling value proposition and aligning the company's activities to deliver the desired customer experience.[142] This model suggests that companies should target China's younger generation of consumers, who have similar budgets and needs and who want to become tomorrow's loyal customers and opinion leaders.[143] By doing so, not only will the company gain current sales but, more importantly, it will secure a future market position.

DIFFERENTIATE THROUGH DISTRIBUTION CHANNELS

One way to reduce or discourage cannibalisation is to use distribution channels to differentiate premium products from value-priced variants. Such differentiation can take place in terms of geographic locations or types of retail channels, such as traditional family-run shops, convenience stores, department stores and different shelves within the same outlet.[144] One of the reasons for points of sale becoming an important factor in differentiation is that mass media advertising is not only extremely expensive but also less effective. In 2004, when advertisements were shown on television, for 72 per cent of the time Chinese viewers either left the room or changed channels. In addition, there is a tendency for many Chinese consumers to make up or change their minds about what to buy at the last minute, in the presence of the sales staff. Therefore, sales promotion techniques can be more effective in China than in developed countries, and more effort should be put into retail execution to improve point-of-sale performance. This includes ensuring that well-trained and experienced salespeople are sent to stores and that everything meets the company's requirements in matters such as promised shelf space and packages on display.[145]

Accenture surveyed over a thousand Chinese consumers to understand how they make buying decisions. Based on the survey results, the researchers derived seven core lessons for marketers to develop successful brands in China. The first three lessons involve how to shape brand image and the other four how to communicate the brand message.

Strive to build trust   Trustworthiness is rated by Chinese consumers as the most important factor in deciding a brand. Any brands, regardless of origin, are likely to be tried and accepted, as long as they are perceived by Chinese consumers as being of high quality. Foreign brands still have a more favourable perception in terms of style in some segments.

Link Chinese consumers' values and needs to brands   Brand messages should convince Chinese consumers that the brand provides what they need and value. Different market segments have different needs and values, and some like brands to express social status, aspirations and peer equality, but others like to keep a low profile and avoid ostentatious appearance when they purchase upscale brands.

Show that the company cares about the Chinese people, not just money   The brand should deliver the message that the company owning it cares about people, not just their money. The company should operate social outreach programs to deliver the message that foreign companies are concerned about the Chinese people. In this way, consumers' purchase can make them feel that by buying the product, they are contributing to Chinese society.

Broaden the company's advertising mix   Chinese people are quite interested in the new choices the world may offer. They are exposed to five kinds of advertising media: TV, the Internet, video boards, billboards and kiosks, with websites near the top. This allows companies to use various media to create or enhance brand awareness and loyalty.

Utilise product reviews as PR opportunities   Consumers in China pay much more attention to product reviews than consumers elsewhere in the world do. This makes reviews a cost-free yet effective way to build an image of quality and dependability. About 63 per cent of Chinese consumers evaluate new brands from product reviews in newspapers and magazines, while only 34 to 42 per cent of consumers in other countries use published product reviews in this way.

Give Chinese consumers something good to say about the brand   Research shows that 67 per cent of Chinese consumers become aware of brands from friends and co-workers, while in other countries, only 34 to 52 per cent learn about products from their acquaintances. Nowadays, the discussion of brands in China is often carried out online. Chinese Internet users participate actively in online forums, communities, blogs and social networks. Positive stories will travel fast via these media, having a positive impact on the brand.

Make the brand visible and palpable   It is crucial to allow Chinese consumers to see, try and buy your products. If Chinese consumers are satisfied with a foreign brand, for example, they are more likely to recommend it to friends; 80 or 90 per cent of them will do so, depending on the product category. The buying decisions of Chinese consumers are more influenced by in-store displays and salespeople than those of consumers elsewhere.[146]

Concluding remarks

The concept of strategy is culturally bound. To date no consensus has been reached on its definition in the academic community. The notion originated in the Greek tradition, whereby an ideal goal is set, and then measures are taken to materialise it. This kind of strategic approach developed under the influence of rationality in the Age of Enlightenment, which brought scientific and technological development and economic prosperity to Europe and North America during the eighteenth and nineteenth centuries. It first influenced the conduct of military engagements and has shaped research methodology in the areas of strategy and management since the 1950s. On the whole, it has been successfully applied in the mature and stable environment of the West, but some limitations have also been recognised.

The Western approach to strategy has rarely been successfully applied by Chinese companies, because of differences in culture, organisational structure and decision-making processes. In China, the entrepreneur, founder or business leader, influenced by his or her personal preferences, knowledge, insight or perception, tends to play a dominant role in making strategic decisions.

From a Western perspective, many Chinese companies may be seen as having no strategy in place – no long-term goals or specific steps to achieve such goals. Based on industrial knowledge, personal instinct, insight or cues from the media or literature, Chinese entrepreneurs or business decision-makers identify, create, ride or borrow *shi* to guide their companies' direction. Failing this, many simply follow their competitors.

When developing strategies in China, Western firms can essentially adopt either a *guanxi*-driven orientation in restricted sectors or a market-driven orientation in encouraged sectors. In the latter environment, although *guanxi* can also be important in dealing with suppliers, customers, distributors and government officials, it is not a determinant of success or failure, while in the former, it is crucial. Market-driven strategies in China should take into consideration Chinese contextual factors, including market maturity, consumer and competitor behaviour, marketing infrastructure and government or regulatory influences, all of which differ from those in the West.

Effective marketing by multinationals depends greatly on subsidiaries' flexibility and responsiveness to the market. These are often hampered by the rigidity of corporate structure, resulting in poor responsiveness compared with local firms. No matter how multinationals emphasise agility in policy, it is hard to earn a higher score on this point than their Chinese competitors because of the factors of organisational structure and culture. This handicap may be overcome by maintaining the leadership position in technology and products or simply brand value.

Notes

1   Liu, H. (2015), *The Chinese Strategic Mind*, Northampton, MA: Edward Elgar Publishing.
2   Snow, C.C. and Hambrick, D.C. (1980), "Measuring Organizational Strategies: Some Theoretical and Methodological Problems," *Academy of Management Review*, 5 (4), 527–538.
3   Schendel, D. and Hofer, C.W. (1979), *Strategic Management: A New View of Business Policy and Planning*, Boston, MA: Little Brown.
4   Nag, R., Hambrick, D.C. and Chen, M.J. (2007), "What Is Strategic Management, Really? Inductive Derivation of a Consensus Definition of the Field," *Strategic Management Journal*, 28 (9), 935–955.
5   Aligica, P.D. (2007), "Efficacy, East and West: François Jullien's Explorations in Strategy," *Comparative Strategy*, 26, 325–337.
6   Nag, R., Hambrick, D.C. and Chen, M.J. (2007), "What Is Strategic Management, Really? Inductive Derivation of a Consensus Definition of the Field," *Strategic Management Journal*, 28 (9), 935–955.
7   Learned, E.P., Christensen, C.R. and Andrews, K.D. (1965), *Business Policy: Text and Cases*, Homewood, IL: Richard D. Irwin.
8   Schendel, D. and Hofer, C.W. (1979), *Strategic Management: A New View of Business Policy and Planning*, Boston, MA: Little Brown.
9   Bracker, J. (1980), "The Historical Development of the Strategic Management Concept," *Academy of Management Review*, 5 (2), 219–224.
10 Jemison, D.B. (1981), "The Contributions of Administrative Behavior to Strategic Management," *Academy of Management Review*, 6 (4), 633–642.
11 Van Cauwenbergh, A. and Cool, K. (1982), "Strategic Management in a New Framework," *Strategic Management Journal*, 3 (3), 245–264. Van Cauwenbergh, A. and Cool, K. (1982), "Strategic Management in a New Framework," *Strategic Management Journal*, 3 (3), 245–264.
12 Rumelt, R.P., Schendel, D.E. and Teece, D.J. (1994), *Fundamental Issues in Strategy: A Research Agenda*, Boston, MA: Harvard Press School Press, p. 9.
13 Nag, R., Hambrick, D.C. and Chen, M.J. (2007), "What Is Strategic Management, Really? Inductive Derivation of a Consensus Definition of the Field," *Strategic Management Journal*, 28 (9), 935–955.
14 Aligica, P.D. (2007), "Efficacy, East and West: François Jullien's Explorations in Strategy," *Comparative Strategy*, 26, 325–337.
15 Andrews, K.R. (1971), *The Concept of Corporate Strategy*, Homewood, IL: Richard D. Irwin, p. 28.
16 Bracker, J. (1980), "The Historical Development of the Strategic Management Concept," *Academy of Management Review*, 5 (2), 219–224.
17 Jullien, F. (2004), *A Treatise on Efficacy: Between Western and Chinese Thinking* (J. Lloyd, Translation), Honolulu: University of Hawaii Press, p. 10.
18 Chinese 'visions' tend to be a mixture of 'value' statement and a goal expressed in a qualitative manner.

19 Yang, S.L. (2013), *Huawei Kao Shenme (On What Huawei Relies)*, Beijing: China CITIC Press, p. 20.
20 Liu, H. (2015), *The Chinese Strategic Mind*, Northampton, MA: Edward Elgar Publishing, pp. 93–100.
21 Griffith, S.B. (1963), *Sun Tzu: The Art of War*, translated and with an introduction by S.B. Griffith and Foreword by B.H. Liddell Hart, London: Watkins Publishing, p. 140.
22 Ames, R.T. (1994), *The Art of Rulership*, Albany, NY: State University of New York Press, p. 68.
23 Jullien, F. (1995), *The Propensity of Things: Toward a History of Efficacy in China*, translated by J. Lloyd, Cambridge, MA: Zone Books. Distributed by MIT Press, p. 10.
24 Lau, D.C. and Ames, R.T. (2003), *Sun Bin: The Art of War*, Albany, NY: State University of New York Press, p. 63.
25 Griffith, S.B. (1963), *Sun Tzu: The Art of War*, translated and with an introduction by S.B. Griffith and Forward by B.H. Liddell Hart, London: Watkins Publishing, p. 138.
26 Ibid, p. 142.
27 Clark, D. (2016), *Alibaba: The House That Jack Ma Built*, New York: HarperCollins Publishers, p. 5.
28 Ibid, p. 113.
29 Ibid, p. 5.
30 Ibid, p. 122.
31 Erisman, P. (2015), *Alibaba's World*, New York: Palgrave Macmillan, p. 3.
32 Liu, Y. and Ye, G.S. (2016), *Qushi hongli (The Bonus of Trend)*, Beijing: Cultural Development Press.
33 Liu, H. (2015), *The Chinese Strategic Mind*, Northampton, MA: Edward Elgar Publishing, pp. 108–116.
34 Yip, G.S. and McKern, B. (2016), *China's Next Strategic Advantage: From Imitation to Innovation*, Cambridge, MA: MIT Press, p. 59.
35 Ibid, p. 12.
36 Another version of the quote is: 'Plans are worthless, but planning is everything.'
37 Eisenhardt, K.M. and Brown, S.L. (1998), "Competing on the Edge Strategy as Structured Chaos," *Long Range Planning*, 31 (5), 786–789.
38 Clark, D. (2016), *Alibaba: The House That Jack Ma Built*, New York: HarperCollins Publishers, p. 111.
39 Hout, T. and Michael, D. (2014), "A Chinese Approach to Management," *Harvard Business Review*, 92 (2), 103–107.
40 Griffith, S.B. (1963), *Sun Tzu: The Art of War*, translated and with an introduction by S.B. Griffith and Forward by B.H. Liddell Hart, London: Watkins Publishing, p. 213.
41 Ibid, p. 223.
42 Clark, D. (2016), *Alibaba: The House That Jack Ma Built*, New York: HarperCollins Publishers, p. 173.
43 The Economist (2011), "The Long March of the Invisible Mr Ren," *The Economist*, 2 June 2011.
44 Yang, S.L. (2013), *Huawei Kao Shenme (On What Huawei Relies)*, Beijing: China CITIC Press, pp. 9–10.
45 Holstein, W.J. (2014), "Lenovo Goes Global: China's Most Recognizable Brand Has Plans to Overtake Apple and Samsung," *Strategy + Business*, 76, August, www.strategy-business.com/article/00274?gko=abf3e, retrieved on 25 October 2016.
46 Liu, H. (2015), *The Chinese Strategic Mind*, Northampton, MA: Edward Elgar Publishing, pp. 176–196.
47 China Commerce Yearbook 2007.
48 Bosshart, S., Luedi, T. and Wang, E. (2010), "Past Lessons for China's New Joint Ventures," McKinsey & Company, December. www.mckinsey.com/business-functions/strategy-and-corporate-finance/our-insights/past-lessons-for-chinas-new-joint-ventures, retrieved on 26 September 2016.

49 Ibid.
50 Orr, G. (2014), "A Pocket Guide to Do Business in China," *Commentary*, McKinsey & Company, October, www.mckinsey.com/business-functions/strategy-and-corporate-finance/our-insights/a-pocket-guide-to-doing-business-in-china, retrieved on 28 September 2016.
51 Gronroos, C. (1996), "Relationship Marketing: Strategic and Tactical Implications," *Management Decisions*, 34 (3), 5–14. Gordon, I.H. (1998), *Relationship Marketing*, Toronto & New York: John Wiley & Sons, Canada Ltd. Gummesson, E. (1999), *Total Relationship Marketing – Rethinking Marketing Management From 4P's to 30Rs*, Oxford: Butterworth-Heinemann.
52 Payne, A. (ed.) (1995), *Advances in Relationship Marketing*, London: Kogan Page, p. 31.
53 Gordon, I.H. (1998), *Relationship Marketing*, Toronto & New York: John Wiley & Sons, Canada Ltd, p. 9.
54 Tsang, E.W.K. (1998), "Can *Guanxi* Be a Source of Sustained Competitive Advantage for Doing Business in China," *Academy of Management Executive*, 12 (2), 64–73.
55 The Economist (1996), "The Overseas Chinese: Inheriting the Bamboo Network," *The Economist*, 23 December 1995–January 1996, 79.
56 Yi, L.M. and Ellis, P. (2000), "Insider-Outsider Perspectives of *Guanxi*," *Business Horizon*, January–February, 25–30.
57 Vanhonacker, W.R. (2004), "'When Good *Guanxi* Turns Bad," *Harvard Business Review*, 82 (4), 18–20.
58 Yeung, I.Y.M. and Tung, R.L. (1996), "Achieving Business Success in Confucian Societies: The Importance of *Guanxi* (Connections)," *Organization Dynamics*, 25 (2), Autumn, 54–65.
59 Chua, R.Y.J. (2012), "Building Effective Business Relationships in China," *Sloan Management Review*, 53 (4), 1–7.
60 Graham, J.L. and Lam, M. (2003), "The Chinese Negotiation," *Harvard Business Review*, 81 (10), 82–91.
61 Yang, J.Z. (1998), "Key Success Factors of Multinationals in China," *Thunderbird International Business Review*, 40 (6), 633–668.
62 Hall, E.T. and Hall, M.R. (1990), *Understanding Cultural Differences*, Yarmouth, ME: Intercultural Press.
63 Graham, J.L. and Lam, M. (2003), "The Chinese Negotiation," *Harvard Business Review*, 81 (10), 82–91.
64 Chen, M.J. (2001), *Inside Chinese Business: A Guide for Managers Worldwide*, Boston, MA: Harvard Business School Press, pp. 53–64.
65 Yeung, I.Y.M. and Tung, R.L. (1996), "Achieving Business Success in Confucian Societies: The Importance of *Guanxi* (Connections)," *Organization Dynamics*, 25 (2), Autumn, 54–65.
66 Tsang, E.W.K. (1998), "Can *Guanxi* Be a Source of Sustained Competitive Advantage for Doing Business in China," *Academy of Management Executive*, 12 (2), 64–73.
67 Ibid.
68 Chua, R.Y.J. (2012), "Building Effective Business Relationships in China," *Sloan Management Review*, 53 (4), 1–7.
69 Solbertg, C.A. (2000), "Educator Insights: Standardization or Adaptation of the International Marketing Mix: The Role of the Local Subsidiary/Representative," *Journal of International Marketing*, 8 (1), 78–98.
70 Yan, R. (1994), "To Reach China's Consumers, Adapt to Guo Qing," *Harvard Business Review*, 72 (5), 66–69. Jagersma, P.K. and Gorp, D.M. (2003), "Still Searching for the Pot of Gold: Doing Business in Today's China," *Journal of Business Strategy*, 24 (5), 27–35. Teo, L.L., Piotroski, S.A. and Nunes, P.F. (2007), "Why Winning the Wallets of China's Consumers Is Harder Than You Think" *Outlook (An Accenture's Publication)*, September, 1–12.
71 Stuttard, J.B. (2000), *The New Silk Road: Secrets of Business Success in China Today*, New York: John Wiley & Sons, Inc.

72 Levitt, T. (1983), "The Globalization of Markets," *Harvard Business Review*, May–June, 92–102.

73 Jagersma, P.K. and Gorp, D.M. (2003), "Still Searching for the Pot of Gold: Doing Business in Today's China," *Journal of Business Strategy*, 24 (5), 27–35.

74 Ibid.

75 Lane, K.P., St-Maurice, I. and Dyckerhoff, C.S. (2006), "Building Brands in China," *The McKinsey Quarterly*, 2006 Special Edition, 33–41. Rein, R. (2007), "The Key to Successful Branding in China," *Business Week Online*, 26 September.

76 Roy, A., Walters, P.G.P. and Luk, S.T. (2001), "Chinese Puzzles and Paradoxes: Conducting Business Research in China," *Journal of Business Research*, 52 (2), 203–213. Williamson, P. and Zeng, M. (2004), "Strategies for Competing in a Changed China," *Sloan Management Review*, 45 (4), 85–91.

77 Ibid.

78 A joint venture between Yahoo and Sina.

79 Clark, D. (2016), *Alibaba: The House That Jack Ma Built*, New York: HarperCollins Publishers, p. 163.

80 Fernandez, J.A. and Underwood, L. (2006), *China CEO: Voices of Experience From 20 International Business Leaders*, Singapore: John Wiley & Sons (Asia) Pte Ltd.

81 Clark, D. (2016), *Alibaba: The House That Jack Ma Built*, New York: HarperCollins Publishers, pp. 222–224.

82 Ibid, p. 205.

83 The Economist (2015), "Alibaba: Love on the Rocks," *The Economist*, 17 February 2015.

84 Lopez, L. (2016), "This Is Why Uber Failed in China," *Business Insiders*, 2 August, http://uk.businessinsider.com/why-uber-failed-in-china-2016-8?r=US&IR=T, retrieved on 8 October 2016.

85 Kuo, Y.C. (2016), "3 Great Forces Changing China's Consumer Market," *World Economic Forum*, 4 January, www.weforum.org/agenda/2016/01/3-great-forces-changing-chinas-consumer-market/, retrieved on 28 October 2016.

86 Zheng, A.J. (2016), "Luxury Brands Step Up Shift to Digital in China," *The Wall Street Journal*, 20 June, http://blogs.wsj.com/chinarealtime/2016/06/20/luxury-brands-step-up-shift-to-digital-in-china/, retrieved on 21 November 2016.

87 Orr, G. (2014), "A Pocket Guide to Do Business in China," *Commentary*, McKinsey & Company, October, www.mckinsey.com/business-functions/strategy-and-corporate-finance/our-insights/a-pocket-guide-to-doing-business-in-china, retrieved on 28 September 2016.

88 Daniel Zipser, D., Chen, Y. and Gong, F. (2016), "Here Comes the Modern Chinese Consumer," *McKinsey Quarterly*, March.

89 Kuo, Y.C. (2016), "3 Great Forces Changing China's Consumer Market," *World Economic Forum*, 4 January, www.weforum.org/agenda/2016/01/3-great-forces-changing-chinas-consumer-market/, retrieved on 28 October 2016.

90 Orr, G. (2014), "A Pocket Guide to Do Business in China," *Commentary*, McKinsey & Company, October, www.mckinsey.com/business-functions/strategy-and-corporate-finance/our-insights/a-pocket-guide-to-doing-business-in-china, retrieved on 28 September 2016.

91 Yan, A. and Gray, B. (2002), "Antecedents and Effects of Parent Control in International Joint Ventures," *Journal of Management Studies*, 38 (3), 393–416.

92 Birkinshaw, J. and Hood, N. (1997), "An Empirical Study of Development Processes in Foreign-Owned Subsidiaries in Canada and Scotland," *Management International Review*, 37 (4), 339–364.

93 Martinez, J.I. and Jarillo, J.C. (1989), "The Evolution of Research on Coordination Mechanisms in Multinational Corporations," *Journal of International Business Studies*, 20 (3), 489–514.

94 Ding, D.Z. (1997), "Control, Conflict, and Performance: A Study of U.S. – Chinese Joint Ventures," *Journal of International Marketing*, 5 (3), 31–45. Yan, A. and Gray, B. (2002),

"Antecedents and Effects of Parent Control in International Joint Ventures," *Journal of Management Studies*, 38 (3), 393–416.

95 Ambos, T.C., Andersson, U. and Birkinshaw, J. (2010), "What Are the Consequences of Initiative-Taking in Multinational Subsidiaries?" *Journal of International Business Studies*, 41 (7), 1099–1118.

96 Martinez, J.I. and Jarillo, J.C. (1989), "The Evolution of Research on Coordination Mechanisms in Multinational Corporations," *Journal of International Business Studies*, 20 (3), 489–514.

97 Fernandez, J.A. and Underwood, L. (2006), *China CEO: Voice of Experience From 20 International Business Leaders*, Singapore: John Wiley & Sons (Asia) Pte Ltd, pp. 95–99.

98 Kohli, A.K. and Jaworski, B.J. (1993), "Market Orientation: Antecedents and Consequences," *Journal of Marketing*, 57 (July), 53–70.

99 Kuo, K., Bao, A., Parker, E. and Custer, C. (2016), "Was Uber's China Exit a Failure or a Success?" *Foreign Policy*, 4 August, http://foreignpolicy.com/2016/08/04/was-ubers-china-exit-a-failure-or-a-success-didi-chuxing-sale-chinafile/, retrieved on 8 October 2016.

100 Clark, D. (2016), *Alibaba: The House That Jack Ma Built*, New York: HarperCollins Publishers, pp. 153–154.

101 Ibid, p. 169.

102 Ibid, p. 163.

103 Shenxue Li, S.X., Easterby-Smith, M. and Lyles, M.A. (2008), "Overcoming Corporate Rigidities in the Dynamic Chinese Market," *Business Horizons*, 51, 501–509.

104 Ryans, J.K., Griffith, D.A. and White, S.D. (2003), "Standardizations/Adaptations of International Marketing Strategy: Necessary Conditions for the Advancement of Knowledge," *International Marketing Review*, 20 (6), 588–603.

105 Schmid, S. and Kotulla, T. (2011), "50 Years of Research on International Standardization and Adaptation – From a Systematic Literature Analysis to a Theoretical Framework," *International Business Review*, 20 (2011), 491–507. Katsikeas, C.S., Samiee, S. and Theodosiou, M. (2006), "Strategy Fit and Performance Consequences of International Marketing Standardization," *Strategic Management Journal*, 27 (9), 867–890.

106 Boddewyn, J.J. and Grosse, R. (1995), "American Marketing in the European Union: Standardization's Uneven Progress, 1973–1993," *European Journal of Marketing*, 29 (12), 23–42. Schmid, S. and Kotulla, T. (2011), "50 Years of Research on International Standardization and Adaptation – From a Systematic Literature Analysis to a Theoretical Framework," *International Business Review*, 20 (2011), 491–507.

107 Muhlbacher, H., Dahringer, L. and Leihs, H. (1999), *International Marketing: A Global Perspective*, London: International Thomson Business Press, p. 62.

108 Quelch, J.A. and Hoff, E.J. (1986), "Customizing Global Marketing," *Harvard Business Review*, 64 (3), 69–79.

109 Levitt, T. (1983), "The Globalization of Markets," *Harvard Business Review*, May–June, 92–102. Yip, G.S., Loewe, P.M. and Yoshino, M.Y. (1988), "How to Take Your Company to the Global Market," *Columbia Journal of World Business*, 23, 37–48. Theodosiou, M. and Leonidou, C.L. (2003), "Standardization Versus Adaptation of International Marketing Strategy: An Integrative Assessment of the Empirical Research," *International Business Review*, 13 (2), 141–171.

110 Boddewyn, J.J. and Grosse, R. (1995), "American Marketing in the European Union: Standardization's Uneven Progress, 1973–1993," *European Journal of Marketing*, 29 (12), 23–42. Gupta, A.K. and Govindarajan, V. (2000), "Knowledge Flows Within Multinational Corporations," *Strategic Management Journal*, 21 (4), 473–496. Jensen, R. and Szulanski, G. (2005), "Stickiness and the Adaptation of Organizational Practices in Cross-Border Knowledge Transfers," *Journal of International Business Studies*, 35 (6), 508–523.

111 Bartlett, C.A. and Ghoshal, S. (2003), *Transnational Management: Text, Cases, and Readings in Cross-Border Management* (4th ed.). New York: McGraw-Hill.

112 Hill, C.W.L. (2014), *International Business: Competing in the Global Marketplace*, New York: McGraw Hill Education, p. 399.

113 Shoham, A. (1996), "Marketing-Mix Standardization: Determinants of Export Performance," *Journal of Global Marketing*, 10 (2), 53–73. Subramaniam, M. and Hewett, K. (2004), "Balancing Standardization and Adaptation for Product Performance in International Markets: Testing the Influence of Headquarters-Subsidiary Contact and Cooperation," *Management International Review*, 44 (2), 171–194.

114 Venkatraman, N. and Prescott, J.E. (1990), "Environment-Strategy Coalignment: An Empirical Test of Its Performance Implications," *Strategic Management Journal*, 11, 1–23. Lukas, B.A., Tan, J.J. and Hult, G.T.M. (2001), "Strategic Fit in Transitional Economies: The Case Study of China's Electronic Industry," *Journal of Management*, 27 (4), 409–429.

115 Ginsberg, A.N. and Venkatraman, N. (1985), "Contingency Perspectives of Organizational Strategy: A Critical Review of the Empirical Research," *Academy of Management Review*, 10, 421–434. Lee, J. and Miller, D. (1996), "Strategy, Environment and Performance in Two Technological Contexts: Contingency Theory in Korea," *Organization Studies*, 17 (5), 729–750.

116 Katsikeas, C.S., Samiee, S. and Theodosiou, M. (2006), "Strategy Fit and Performance Consequences of International Marketing Standardization," *Strategic Management Journal*, 27 (9), 867–890.

117 Dess, G. and Beard, D. (1984), "Dimensions of Organizational Task Environments," *Administrative Science Quarterly*, 29 (1), 52–73. Luo, Y. and Peng, M.W. (1999), "Learning to Compete in a Transition Economy: Experience, Environment, and Performance," *Journal of International Business Studies*, 30 (2), 269–296.

118 Maidique, M.A. and Hayes, R.H. (1984), "The Art of High-Technology Management," *Sloan Management Review*, 25 (2), 17–31.

119 Jassawalla, A.R. and Sashittal, H.C. (2002), "Cultures That Support Product-Innovation Processes," *Academy of Management Executive*, 16 (3), 42–54.

120 Moorman, C. and Slotegraaf, R.J. (1999), "The Contingency Value of Complementary Capabilities in Product Development," *Journal of Marketing Research*, 36 (2), 239–257.

121 Schmidt, C. (2011), "The Battle for China's Talents," *Harvard Business Review*, March, 25–27.

122 Fernandez, J.A. and Underwood, L. (2006), *China CEO: Voice of Experience From 20 International Business Leaders*, Singapore: John Wiley & Sons (Asia) Pte Ltd, p. 114.

123 Liu, H. and Pak, K. (1999), "How Important Is Marketing Today to Sino-Foreign Joint Ventures?" *European Management Journal*, 17 (5), 546–555.

124 Kotler, P., Keller, K.L. and Lu, T. (2009), *Marketing Management in China*, Singapore: Pearson Education South Asia Pte Ltd, p. 252.

125 Wang, J. (2008), *Brand New China: Advertising, Media and Commercial Culture*, Cambridge, MA: Harvard University Press.

126 Liu, C.C. (2003), *General History of China* (in Chinese), Beijing: China Drama Publishing House, pp. 646–649.

127 Douglas, S.P., Craig, C.S. and Nijssen, E.J. (2001), "Integrating Branding Strategy Across Markets: Building International Brand Architecture," *Journal of International Marketing*, 9 (2), 97–114.

128 Aaker, D. (1996), *Building Strong Brands*, New York: The Free Press. Keller, K.L. and Lehmann, D.R. (2006), "Brands and Branding: Research Findings and Future Priorities," *Marketing Science*, 25 (6), 740–760.

129 Lam, P.Y., Annie Chan, A., Gopaoco, H., Oh, K. and So, T.H. (2013), "Dual Branding Strategy for a Successful New Product Launch in China," *Business Horizons*, 56, 583–589.

130 Gadiesh, O., Leung, P. and Vestring, T. (2007), "The Battle for China's Good-Enough Market," *Harvard Business Review*, September, 3–13.

131 Business Week (2012), "Foreign Beermakers Raise a Glass to China," *Businessweek*, 23 April, 1.

132 Gadiesh, O., Leung, P. and Vestring, T. (2007), "The Battle for China's Good-Enough Market," *Harvard Business Review*, September, 3–13. Gadiesh, O. and Vestring, T. (2007), "Capturing China's Middle Market," *Wall Street Journal*, 17 November.

133 Qi, X. (2005), "Battles for China's Brands," *Chinese Quality and Brands* (in Chinese), 10, 32–41.

134 Chen, A. and Vishwanath, V. (2004), "Be the Top Pick in China," *Business Times Singapore*, 16 January.

135 Sindy Liu, S., Perry, P., Moore, C. and Warnaby, G. (2016), "The Standardization-Localization Dilemma of Brand Communications for Luxury Fashion Retailers' Internationalization Into China," *Journal of Business Research*, 69, 357–364.

136 Zhan, L. and He, Y. (2012), "Understanding Luxury Consumption in China: Consumer Perceptions of Best Known Brands," *Journal of Business Research*, 65 (10), 1452–1460.

137 Lu, X. and Pras, B. (2011), "Profiling Mass Affluent Luxury Goods Consumers in China: A Psychographic Approach," *Thunderbird International Business Review*, 53 (4), 435–456.

138 Li, G., Li, G. and Kambele, Z. (2012), "Luxury Fashion Brand Consumers in China: Perceived Value, Fashion Lifestyle, and Willingness to Pay," *Journal of Business Research*, 65, 1516–1522. Kapferer, J.N. (2014), "The Artification of Luxury: From Artisans to Artists," *Business Horizons*, 57, 371–380.

139 Kapferer, J.N. (2014), "The Artification of Luxury: From Artisans to Artists," *Business Horizons*, 57, 371–380.

140 Lane, K.P., St-Maurice, I. and Dyckerhoff, C.S. (2006), "Building Brands in China," *The McKinsey Quarterly*, 2006 Special Edition, 33–41.

141 Rein, R. (2007), "The Key to Successful Branding in China," *Businessweek*, 26 September.

142 Crocker, G. and Tay, Y.C. (2004), "What It Takes to Create a Successful Brand," *China Business Review*, 31 (4), 10–15.

143 Rein, R. (2007), "The Key to Successful Branding in China," *Businessweek*, 26 September.

144 Chen, Y.G. and Penhirin, J. (2004), "Marketing to China's Consumers," *The McKinsey Quarterly*, 2004 Special Edition, 63–73.

145 Lane, K.P., St-Maurice, I. and Dyckerhoff, C.S. (2006), "Building Brands in China," *The McKinsey Quarterly*, 2006 Special Edition, 33–41.

146 Nunes, P.F., Piotroski, S.A., Teo, L.L. and Matheis, R.M. (2010), "Seven Lessons for Building a Winning Brand in China," *Strategy & Leadership*, 38 (1), 42–49.

6 Chinese innovation

Innovation distinguishes between a leader and a follower.

– Steve Jobs

Great is the human who has not lost his childlike heart.

– Mencius

Creativity is thinking up new things. Innovation is doing new things.

– Theodore Levitt

Innovation, economic development and competitiveness

Research on innovation forms part of many disciplines of knowledge, such as economics, science, sociology, psychology and management; each has a somewhat different definition and conceptualisation of innovation.[1] The importance of innovation is emphasised by Peter Drucker (1955), who states that

> any business enterprise has two – and only two – basic functions: marketing and innovation ... Innovation can therefore no more be considered a separate function than marketing. It is not confined to engineering or research, but extends across all parts of the business, all functions, all activities.[2]

The Organisation for Economic Co-operation and Development (OECD) defines an innovation as 'the implementation of a new or significantly improved product (good or service), or process, a new marketing method, or a new organisational method in business practice, workplace organisation or external relations.'[3] The concept of a national innovation system (NIS) is often used to explain how knowledge is created and disseminated at national, regional and/or industrial levels within national borders.[4] This concept

> rests on the premise that understanding the linkages among the actors involved in innovation is key to improving technology performance.

Innovation and technical progress are the result of a complex set of relationships among actors producing, distributing and applying various kinds of knowledge. The innovative performance of a country depends to a large extent on how these actors relate to each other as elements of a collective system of knowledge creation and use as well as the technologies they use.[5]

Schumpeter may be regarded as a pioneer of innovation studies. He divides businessmen into managers, landowners, capitalists and entrepreneurs, contending that the sole function of the entrepreneur is innovation.[6] Schumpeter links innovation with industrial development via the concept of creative destruction: innovation is the 'industrial mutation – if I may use the biological term – that incessantly revolutionizes the economic structure from within, incessantly destroying the old one, incessantly creating a new one. This process of Creative Destruction is the essential fact about capitalism.'[7] The successful entrepreneur, in Schumpeter's view, 'practices "creative destruction" of existing markets and competitors and fuels new economic growth.'[8]

> Stanford economist Paul M. Romer carries on in the Schumpeter tradition by showing that technological discoveries are the driving engine of economic growth . . . Ideas build on each other, and are reproduced cheaply. As you add more and more machinery, it delivers less and less additional output. Ideas, on the other hand, especially those embodied in new technology, can continue to add value, well beyond their cost.[9]

An OECD strategy document states:

> Innovation underpins the growth and dynamism of all economies. In many OECD countries, firms now invest as much in the knowledge-based assets that drive innovation . . . These [Internet-related innovations], and other technological changes in fields like bio- and nano-technology and the associated advanced materials, will lead to on-going transformations in the nature of production, jobs, the location of economic activity, and the respective roles of different sectors in the economy.[10]

Technological innovation is found to be a major determinant of success in many industries.[11] It provides opportunities for new products, new markets and new industries,[12] enhancing the competitiveness of national economies;[13] it rapidly changed the nature of competition in the late twentieth century.[14] The competitive advantage of the United States in the global arena is considered to be attributable to its active promotion of technological innovation through high-tech entrepreneurship.[15]

Brown and Eisenhardt (1995) identify two major research streams on innovation.[16] The first examines issues associated with the diffusion of innovations across nations, industries and organisations at a macro level.[17] The second stream concerns the development and marketing of new products or services by an organisation at a micro level. New products or services take several forms, such as the commercialisation of an invention and the upgrading, modification and extension of existing products.[18] The second stream can be further divided into two categories. One involves an examination of all activities that bring new products or services to the market[19] and the other pertains to the firm or strategic business unit as a dimension, examining its entrepreneurial strategic posture.[20]

Innovations themselves can be classified into the following categories:

- Non-technical innovation: those in the service sector such as the sharing of bicycles and electric cars in European cities;
- Innovative concepts: redefining and repurposing prior technology and resources in new ways such as the 'socialist market economy' or 'one country, two systems';
- Innovative ways of doing business and carrying out management, such as O2O (online and offline business) and the digital wallet;
- Process innovation: new ways of manufacturing, delivering or assembling products, with improved efficiency, quality and safety; and
- Technology-intensive innovations: R&D and new product development.[21]

Given that only around 6 to 10 per cent of innovations can be classified as creations or inventions, bringing something completely new to the world,[22] incremental improvements in products/services, processes and positions account for a predominant proportion of innovation and have received considerable attention over the past decade.[23] One type of continuous improvement is the establishment of a strong basic platform or family which can be stretched or modified to extend the range and life of a product/service.[24] Another kind of incremental improvement is the creation of new possibilities to meet articulated or latent needs through a combination of different sets of knowledge. Innovation more often than not takes place through integrating a bundle of knowledge into a configuration.[25]

A firm's leaders need to have an innovation strategy to build and maintain the capacity to innovate. An innovation strategy 'stipulates how their firm's innovation efforts will support the overall business strategy. This will help them make trade-off decisions so that they can choose the most appropriate practices and set overarching innovation priorities that align all functions.'[26] A nation can also have an innovation strategy, as firms do, aligning its innovation efforts to support the national development strategy. There are some important concepts to be clarified.

> Here the distinction is made between science policy, which includes concerns for scientific education and basic research funding (usually at the national level), technology policy, which focuses on creation of strategic or generic technologies (usually at the firm level), and innovation policy, which focuses on technology transfer (usually at the business unit level).[27]

China's national innovation system and capabilities

China has an innovation system that is strongly supported by the government, which embraces the policy of nurturing 'indigenous innovation'. The Chinese NIS is characterised by:

> sustained and growing investment in innovation, strengthening major research institutions and the top 100 universities, funding for commercial research that fits with national priorities, a push for transfer of foreign technology, and gradual reforms to the intellectual property regime. Its goal is clearly to strengthen local companies to succeed against foreign competitors both in China and in overseas markets.[28]

Research has shown that in many ways, Chinese industry is more innovative than is generally recognised.[29] The McKinsey Global Institute identifies four archetypes of innovation: customer-focused, efficiency-driven, engineering-based and science-based. It has been found that China has shown great strength in efficiency-driven and customer-focused innovation, but has underperformed in science- and engineering-based innovation. There are a number of areas to which Chinese companies need to pay particular attention in order to catch up with the West, including enhancing innovation performance in engineering and science, engaging in innovation across more industries and becoming innovation leaders rather than followers.[30]

In certain respects, China has made great strides over the past two decades and has taken a global lead in some areas of engineering and technology, as these few examples illustrate:

- The development of China's drone technology is such that seven out of ten drones in civil use in the world come out of China.
- China has built the tallest, longest, most complex and largest number of bridges in the world.
- On 16 August 2016, China launched the world's first quantum science satellite, part of a large project designed to test the fundamentals of quantum communication in space, placing China at the forefront of this field.
- On 18 August 2016, the world's largest and most technologically complex ship elevator was put into operation to carry vessels over the Three Gorges Dam.
- On 22 September 2016, Shenzhen witnessed the opening of the first national gene bank, the world's largest gene pool, following those built in the USA, Europe and Japan. It will assist in advancing research into genetics, protecting genetic resources and developing China's genetics industry.
- On 24 September 2016, China unveiled the world's largest radio telescope, 500 metres in diameter, surpassing the 300-metre Arecibo Observatory in Puerto Rico.
- In September 2016, China completed the world's longest high-speed rail (HSR) network; at over 20,000 km, it is much longer than the rest of the world's HSR routes combined.

Chinese advances in innovation have also been observed at the micro level, examples being Huawei's Single RAN, TCL's TV set, Tencent's WeChat, Xiaomi's business model and Alibaba's Internet portal, as well as solar-energy and wind-energy technologies and nano/micro biotechnology.[31] Since 2011, China has been the world's second largest publisher of research papers after the United States. In 2012, for instance, Chinese scholars produced 193,733 Science Index Citation papers, representing almost a fivefold increase over the total for 2002.[32] The McKinsey Global Institute (2015) has recognised the 'China Effect' on global innovation:

> China will be a growing source of innovation to serve the needs of an enormous and increasingly demanding consumer market. It is also a logical location for R&D and rapid commercialization of new ideas by global companies – for China, for other emerging markets, and for the rest of the world. Finally, the Chinese model of rapid, low-cost innovation can be applied around the world, potentially disrupting a range of industries.[33]

Building science and technology capabilities: a historical view

To understand Chinese innovation, one needs to look into the Chinese innovation systems. The concept of 'national innovation systems' arose in the 1990s, pioneered by Lundvall[34] and Nelson.[35] Liu and White's paper is identified as the most quoted one that has examined the Chinese NIS,[36] the precursor to which was China's system of science and technology (S&T), originating in the 1950s.[37] Thus, it is necessary to examine China's S&T system and capabilities from a historical perspective.

Science and technology play a significant role in promoting economic development as well as providing companies with strategic advantages.[38] The Chinese government has seen scientific and technological competence not only as an indicator of the country's vitality but also as a determinant of sustained development.[39] China's technological capabilities have evolved from a very low base to a point where it is emerging as a serious international competitor. S&T development has gone through a number of stages, each of which is represented by some landmark changes:

Stage 1 (1949–1955): When the People's Republic of China was founded on 1 October 1949, there were about 30 research institutions and fewer than 50,000 researchers nationwide. Research capabilities at the time were mainly in basic areas such as geology and biology, while modern scientific and technological disciplines were almost nonexistent. Most manufacturing technologies and processes were obsolete. Government policy then emphasised the reliance of economic development on the modernisation of S&T.[40] In November 1949, the Chinese Academy of Sciences (CAS) was established as the main governmental research arm. This was followed by the formation of a number of leading administrative and research bodies, such as the China Association for Science and Technology, the

Ministry of Geology and the China Meteorological Bureau. By 1955 there existed over 840 research institutions nationwide and more than 400,000 people were working in S&T fields.[41]

Stage 2 (1956–1967): In January 1956, the government highlighted science as a matter of policy by calling for a 'March towards Science', signifying the beginning of a systematic approach to S&T development. In the same year, the Planning Commission for Science and Technology was set up and laid out the *Long-Term Plan for S&T Development 1956–1967*. The plan defined 57 major projects that became the foundation for the development of China's new technology in areas such as nuclear physics, electronics, semiconductors, automation, computers, aviation and rocketry, leading to the establishment of a number of industrial sectors. In 1958, China formed the State Commission of Science and Technology and the Commission of Science and Technology for National Defence; these two organisations, together with the CAS, constituted an administrative system for S&T in China.

The formation of this administrative system promoted the growth of S&T capabilities and gradually shaped an S&T development system, consisting of the CAS, universities, research institutes affiliated to industrial ministries, military research institutes and regional institutes. The CAS became the largest centre of comprehensive research primarily concerned with the natural sciences, technological science and high-tech innovation; by 1965 it comprised 104 research institutes employing over 24,000 professional researchers.[42] In 1964, the government first put forward the policy of achieving the modernisation of industry, agriculture, national defence and S&T, that is the 'Four Modernisations'.

In the 1950s the Soviet Union had provided great aid to China's S&T development, including assistance with 156 major industrial projects. In 1960, however, because of major disagreements of policy and principle between the Chinese and Soviet leaderships, the Soviet Union withdrew its approximately 3000 scientists and engineers from China, leaving many projects unfinished and causing great difficulties for Chinese scientists and engineers. China nevertheless managed to overcome this setback and completed a number of major projects in the 1960s. For instance, a subatomic particle, the negative sigma hyperon, was discovered in 1960, and synthetic bovine insulin was developed in 1965. In October 1964, China successfully carried out its first atom bomb test and in June 1967 tested its first hydrogen bomb.[43] By 1965, the number of research institutions had reached 1700, with 2.45 million people working in S&T.

Stage 3 (1966–1976): During the following decade, China underwent the Cultural Revolution, which was a period of stagnation and setbacks in research activity. The work of many research institutes came to a standstill, while many others were even wound up. Numerous universities became dysfunctional and countless scientists, engineers and professors were prosecuted and tortured. With the exception of a small number of special projects such as the hydrogen bomb and China's first satellite, most R&D activities were suspended. The technological gap between China and the Western world thus widened further.[44]

Stage 4 (1977–1994): In March 1978, the then paramount leader Deng Xiaoping directed the adoption of the principle that the modernisation of S&T is the key to realising the modernisation of industry, agriculture and defence, so that 'science and technology is the first productive force.' In 1984, the Patent Law of the People's Republic of China was promulgated, granting inventors the legal right to patent their inventions.[45] In 1985, a reform of the S&T administrative system was carried out. In 1988, the government approved 53 national high-tech development zones. Subsequently, a series of major projects aiming to promote S&T development were launched, including the Spark Programme (supporting projects to produce results quickly in rural areas), the Planning Framework for High-Tech Research & Development (otherwise known as the 863 Programme),[46] the Torch Programme (promoting the commercialisation and internationalisation of high-tech research outcomes) and the Climbing Plan (focusing on the development of basic research areas). The Natural Science Foundation was also founded at this time. These measures resulted in a number of significant S&T achievements, such as the building of an electron-positron collider and the Galaxy supercomputer.

Stage 5 (1995–2003): In May 1995, the notion of 'science and education for a prosperous China' was adopted as a national development strategy. In August 1999, the government held a national conference on technological innovation. The new policy shaped at this conference called for greater initiatives to promote the development, application and commercialisation of high technology and to inculcate a spirit of innovation throughout China.

Stage 6 (2004–present): Since the end of 2004, the Chinese government has engaged in the reform of the S&T system towards the enhancement of the country's ability in 'self-innovation' or 'independent innovation', which is carried out by Chinese institutions and/or enterprises without dependence on foreign organisations.

In 2006, the State Council promulgated the *National Medium- and Long-term Plan for Science and Technology Development (2006–2020)*, signifying that China has taken a concrete step to advance its S&T capabilities. It sets three major objectives:

- Achieving major breakthroughs in targeted strategic areas of technological development and basic research;
- Promoting an enterprise-centred technology innovation system and enhancing the innovation capabilities of Chinese firms; and
- Building an innovation-based economy by fostering indigenous innovation capability.[47]

In the same year, at a national S&T congress, it was proposed that China should develop independent innovation systems with 'Chinese characteristics' and build China as a nation of innovation; thus, independent innovation has become an important element of the national development strategy.[48] In the decade since then, a number of legal documents have followed, laying out legislative foundations for the Chinese NIS:

- In December 2007, the Standing Committee of the National People's Congress promulgated the Law of the People's Republic of China on Scientific and Technological Progress, to improve technology transfer and promote the support of local government for research cooperation between industry and higher education institutions.
- In June 2008, the State Council issued the Outline of the National Intellectual Property Strategy, to strengthen China's capabilities in intellectual property creation, utilisation, protection and management.
- In November 2010, the National Patent Development Strategy (2011–2020) was laid out, to enhance China's capability in patent creation, utilisation, protection and administration through the implementation of the Outline of the National Intellectual Property Strategy issued in June 2008.
- In December 2012, the Central Committee of the Communist Party of China and the State Council issued the Opinions on Deepening the Reform of Scientific and Technological Systems and Speeding Up the Construction of a National Innovation System, to support and foster collaboration and innovation via strategic alliances between industry and higher education institutions by building an R&D platform.
- In May 2016, the Ministry of Science and Technology released the Outline of Innovation-Driven Development Strategy, defining the goals, direction and key tasks for China's innovation development in the next three decades.

The evolving S&T administrative system

The S&T system prior to the economic reforms

Before 1956, because of the limited number of research establishments, research activities were managed through the Chinese Academy of Sciences. With the rising number of research institutions, in 1956, the State Council set up the State Science Planning Commission to coordinate R&D activities nationwide, and this organisation was then merged with the State Technology Commission in 1958 to form the State Science and Technology Commission. In each province and municipality there was a corresponding regional commission for the coordination of local activities.

From the 1950s to the early 1980s, China's planned economic system determined the nature and characteristics of the administration of S&T. The civil system was characterised by vertical administration from the central government through regional branches to research institutions. Horizontal links or inter-actions between research institutions in different systems hardly existed. The mission of research institutions was mainly to serve ministerial authorities and enterprises within their industries. For instance, the Ministry of Metallurgical Industry had its own universities and research institutions, which were mainly engaged in research and education in the field of metallurgy and related tech-nologies and sciences. Most technological development was carried out within the industry. Research institutions received R&D projects and tasks as well as funding from the ministerial governing bodies, to which the results of research were then delivered. Research institutions thus had little autonomy and could neither choose their research projects nor decide how to deal with the results. In 1985, there were over 9100 research institutions in China, of which 5700 were not directly linked to enterprises. In contrast, over 90 per cent of Japanese research organisations were connected with companies.[49]

Knowledge and technology were not commodities and could not be bought or sold in the marketplace. The government owned all the technological break-throughs and innovations and decided how to use them in accordance with central plans. Research was isolated from the marketplace and from industry. It was unnecessary for researchers to consider whether the results of their research were applicable to any production or manufacturing processes; neither did enterprises have views or make suggestions concerning their R&D require-ments.[50] The task of both enterprises and research institutions was to execute government plans. Three major impediments within the S&T research system prior to the economic reform were summed up by a former vice minister of the State Science and Technology Commission:

> First, it had relied too heavily on administrative measures and neglected the role of economic levers in managing S&T activities. Secondly, there had been a tendency to over-develop 'independent research institutes' while neglecting S&T activities within production enterprises . . . And thirdly, there has been excessive rigidity in management and distribution of S&T personnel, the majority of whom tend to spend their entire career in one organization.[51]

China's reform of the S&T system

Since the economic reforms were initiated in December 1978, China's eco-nomic system has been transformed from a planned to a market-oriented one and the overall administrative system concerning S&T development and trans-fer has accordingly undergone various structural changes. In the early 1980s, the government started to emphasise that scientific research should meet the needs of national economic development and that all research institutions should develop their R&D projects by using the mechanism of competition. The specific reform measures can be divided into three significant steps, taken in 1985, 1995 and 1999.

(1) In 1985, the Resolution on the Reform of the S&T System enacted by the Communist Party Central Committee inaugurated a structural reform mainly affecting areas such as changing the funding system and channels, opening up the technology market, promoting the integration of S&T with production, enhancing the ability of enterprises to absorb new technology and reforming the personnel management system. The reform of the funding system was considered among the key factors having a major impact on the development of Chinese technology.[52] Issued in 1985 were the Patent Law of the People's Republic of China and the State Council's Interim Provisions on Technology Transfer, fostering the linkage of universities and research institutions with industry. The year 1988 witnessed the establishment of the first national high-tech development zone in Beijing and the launch of the Torch Programme to promote more high-tech zones. By the end of 1992, 52 national high-tech development zones had been established nationwide, hosting 9687 high-tech enterprises.[53]

> In February 1987, the State Council took a number of major decisions. First, research institutions formally under the administration of central or regional governments were encouraged to join large and medium-sized enterprises and be responsible for their own profits and losses. These enterprises were then to increase their R&D budgets annually and pay for the research carried out by newly attached research institutions. The budgetary allocation from the central government to these now enterprise-related research institutions remained the same. Those institutions remaining under government control, due to their obligations to complete research projects commissioned by central or local government before the reforms, were also permitted to undertake research projects from other sources and make profits.[54]

(2) In 1995 the government announced the Ninth Five-Year Plan for Domestic Economy and Social Development. Emphasis was placed on strengthening the reform of the S&T management system, speeding up the reforms and establishing the mechanism that bound scientific research, development, production and marketing tightly together. The organisational structures of research institutions were to be optimised. Mergers and collaborations between academics, universities and enterprises were to be consolidated. Research institutions whose main activities were in the development of applied technology were to join large industry groups or be converted into high-technology firms. Large and medium-sized enterprises were to be encouraged to run their own technology development centres.[55] In 1996, the State Council issued the *Resolution on the Further Reform of the S&T System during the 9th Five-Year Plan*.

The first two reform steps had the following consequences:

- The vertical administrative relations between the government and the research institutions were weakened, while the horizontal links or interactions among the various institutions, especially between research institutions and enterprises, were strengthened significantly.

- Research institutions gained more autonomy or became completely independent of the government. Now, institutions could receive earnings from the transfer of technology, the provision of consulting services and the development of new products. They now needed to decide what research projects to undertake and how to raise funds for projects and salaries. Thus, both freedom and pressure increased.
- Research institutions were able to undertake cross-sector projects without being bound by the industry to which they belonged. Universities had more opportunities to take part in research and technology innovations sponsored by government and industry. Research institutions no longer relied entirely on the government for R&D expenditure, but could secure research projects and funding through many channels.
- Scientific knowledge and technology were henceforth seen as merchandise to be bought and sold in the marketplace. China has passed and implemented many laws and regulations on marketing the findings of research or innovations, including the Patent Law promulgated in 1985, which was amended further in 2001 to bring it in line with international standards.
- Many scientists and engineers have given up their 'iron-bowl' jobs with SOEs and started up R&D-based businesses. By the end of 2000, the number of R&D-based private businesses had reached 86,000, employing about 5.6 million people and generating a turnover of RMB 1.46 trillion.

(3) In 1999 the government began to implement further reform measures to turn applied research institutions into profit-orientated organisations and to reorganise public-oriented research institutions into different categories. These are regarded as milestones in the optimisation of the scientific and technological system. Over 30 government policies have been issued in order to smooth the implementation of the reform measures. These policies involve budgeting, intellectual property rights (IPRs), incentive shareholding, tax rebate and exemption, welfare, retirement pensions and so forth.

As a result of these measures, applied research institutions have become more market-oriented and service-minded and their creativity and innovative capabilities have been greatly strengthened. Research institutions now take a strategic view of innovation and have maintained a steady investment in research activities. A study of 290 research institutions that were transformed from government-owned to profit-oriented entities has shown that their revenue increased by 52.5 per cent from 1999 to 2001 and their profit by a factor of 2.6.[56] In 2004, applications for patents from those research institutions that had been transformed increased by 22 per cent and the number of applications granted by 43 per cent, among which the number involved in original research rose by 57.7 per cent. In 2005 these research institutions acquired substantial research funds from the market, and the revenues received from their technology transfer or know-how grew by 20 per cent.[57]

The reorganisation of public research institutions has also led to significant progress, in that research areas have been optimised and research capabilities have been enhanced. The budget for public-oriented research has also been increased markedly. For instance, the Ministry of Land and Resources has four departments which own 98 research institutions. After the restructuring which began in 2001, 29 of these (28.4 per cent) remained as non-profit organisations, while the other 69 institutions were merged either with universities or with other public organisations. Since then, employment and promotion have been based on competition, and outstanding researchers enjoy priority support.[58]

Two major reforms of China's S&T system in 2000 have achieved notable success. Firstly, China developed a system of peer-reviewed and merit-based competitive funding for basic research and for evaluating S&T results, which has the potential to fuel more innovative and world-class research efforts at Chinese universities and research institutes. Secondly, China planned to open its major S&T projects to international participation and encourage its scientists to participate in foreign research programmes, such as those under the European Union (EU) Fifth Framework. China has concluded S&T cooperation agreements with 96 countries.[59]

Chinese innovation indicators

Ultimately, a nation's international competitiveness in S&T will be manifested through its economic micro-entities – its enterprises. As a result of a series of reforms of China's S&T or innovation systems and the implementation of the government's S&T policies and strategies, the capabilities of Chinese enterprises for innovation have been significantly enhanced.

Some difficulties in measuring a country's innovation have been recognised: (1) gauging or quantifying some innovation activity, such as the talent and motivation of researchers and (2) defining or measuring certain inventions and innovation categories across countries with consistent definitions and measurements.[60] However, a number of measures have been considered good proxies for national innovation performance.

R&D budget and spending

In 1995 China's spending on R&D was 0.5 per cent of GDP, and it averaged only 0.7 per cent during the 1990s, while that of OECD countries averaged 2.3 per cent between 1981 and 1996. This indicates inadequate spending on R&D activities in China before 2000,[61] but it increased to 1.42 per cent in 2006 and 2.05 per cent in 2014. China's R&D spend in 2006 exceeded, for the first time, that of Japan, Britain, Germany and France, making China the world's second-highest R&D spender after the USA.[62] Indeed, China is forecast to overtake the USA on R&D spending in 2022. However, its expenditure as a share of GDP, known as R&D intensity, remains lower than that of other major economies, whose R&D intensity ranges from 3 to 4 per cent, although the gap is narrowing. In 2014, with a growth rate of 9.9 per cent over the previous year, China spent $203.7 billion on R&D.[63] Its R&D spend grew from just 5 per cent of global R&D investment in 2005 to about 20 per cent from 2009 to 2014, ahead of the EU (19%) and Japan (10%), but behind the USA (28%).[64]

A PwC study has shown that from 2007 to 2015, China's imported R&D spending increased by 79 per cent, from $25 billion to $44 billion, as it closed in on the USA as the largest country for imported R&D. The top five countries from which China imported R&D were the USA (41%, with a growth rate of 141%), Japan (21%), Germany (10%), Switzerland (7%) and South Korea (6%), with the rest of the world accounting for 15%. Multinationals have rated strategic reasons higher than cost advantage when justifying the transfer of R&D functions to China. The most frequently cited factors and the percentage responses were:

- Proximity to China's high growth market (71%);
- Proximity to China's key manufacturing sites (59%);
- Proximity to key suppliers (54%);
- Lower development costs (53%);
- Access to technical talent (39%);
- Easer place from which to export to the rest of the world (33%);
- Experienced labour market (30%); and
- Reliability of project execution (26%).[65]

Patents

The word 'patent' originates from the Latin *patere*, meaning 'to lay open', or to make available for public inspection. The World Intellectual Property Organization (WIPO) describes a patent as

> a legal document granting its holder the exclusive right to control the use of an invention, as set forth in the patent's claims, within a limited area and time by stopping others from, among other things, making, using or selling the invention without authorization ... The term of a patent is generally twenty years from the filing date of the patent application.[66]

Patents are a form of intellectual property right, other forms including trademarks and copyright. The US Patent and Trademark Office grants three basic types of patent: utility patents, design patents and plant patents. Utility patents include the invention of new and useful processes, machines, manufactures, compositions of matter, or any new and useful improvement thereof.

The Chinese Patent Law also specifies three types of patent: invention patents, utility model patents and design patents. By 'invention' is meant new technical solutions proposed for a product, a process or the improvement of one or a combination of these, while 'utility model' denotes new technical solutions put forward for the shape and structure of a product, or the combination thereof, with practical usefulness. An invention patent lasts for 20 years from the date of filing and a utility model patent 10 years.

Following the promulgation of the 1985 patent law in China, it took 14 years and 9 months for the number of patent applications to reach one million, a further 4 years and 2 months for the second million, then 2 years and 3 months for the third. The total number of patent applications made in 2006 was 573,000, an increase of 20.3 per cent over 2005, while the total number granted was 268,000, a rise of 25.2 per cent.[67] According to WIPO, the total number of patents filed in 2014 was 2.7 million. In the same year, the number of patent applications received by the China Patent and Trademark Office was 928,177, the highest of all countries, followed by the USA (578,802), Japan (325,989) and Europe (152,662). Notably, the total filings in China surpassed the combined total of these other three patent offices. In total, 233,000 applications filed in China were granted.

In the international patent system, the Patent Cooperation Treaty (PCT) helps applicants who seek patent protection internationally. The PCT assists patent offices in their patent granting decisions and facilitates public access to technical information associated with the applications. Applicants can be granted simultaneous protection for an invention in numerous countries by filing one international patent application under the PCT. China's applications through the PCT have shown a strong trend of growth. In 2015, China filed 29,800 PCT applications, up 16.8 per cent over the previous year, as the only country which has maintained a two-digit growth in PCT applications worldwide, ranking third in the world after the USA and Japan. In 2015, Huawei led the world's PCT application rankings, with 3898 applications, followed by the US multinational Qualcomm with 2442 filings and another Chinese company, ZTE, with 2155 filings. Huawei has maintained the top global position since 2013.

R&D researchers

The number of qualified researchers involved in innovation can be an indicator of a nation's innovative capability, in that R&D activity and output can be influenced by teamwork and researchers' talent and aspiration.

In 2012, China ranked first in the world in R&D personnel for the fifth consecutive year, with the number of R&D personnel amounting to 3.247 million FTE or 29.2% of the world's total. On the other hand, although Japan and Russia are two major powers in terms of the human resources in S&T research, their percentage in the world in R&D personnel has been constantly declining, falling to 7.8% and 7.5% respectively in 2012.[68]

In addition, there are annually about seven million university graduates, plus two million who acquire university degrees from distant learning programmes and further education institutions.[69] China awards as many as 30,000 doctorates annually.[70] Although the number of researchers per capita is significantly lower in China than in the USA or Europe, the number of engineering graduates from Chinese universities is seven times higher than in the USA. It is noted that the quality of Chinese engineers and graduates is generally considered lower than in developed countries, but one positive indication is that about 12 per cent of Silicon Valley's start-ups have been founded by Chinese immigrants, contributing 17 per cent of US global patents.[71]

Science parks and incubators

Since the mid-1980s, there has been a rapid development of science parks and technological centres worldwide, greatly facilitating technological innovation and transfer from university research labs to industry.[72]

> China is seeing rapid development in more than 130 high-tech parks and independent innovation demonstration zones. These parks and zones, accounting for less than 1% of China's territory, account for nearly 40% of R&D investment by all the country's enterprises, as well as 32.8% of revenue from sales of new products.[73]

Therefore, the number of science parks and incubators can be seen as representing a kind of innovation capability. China has 115 university science parks and more than 1600 technological business incubators, housing over 80,000 enterprises with 1.7 million employees. However, there has been the recognition that some of these parks and incubators have not functioned as fully as those in the West.[74]

Investment in basic research

Basic research involves theoretical development and experimentation that are aimed at advancing knowledge of natural phenomena without considering immediate practical applications.

There has been a structural weakness in the distribution of R&D expenditure in China among basic research, applied research and experimental development. From 1995 to 1998, the respective average shares of R&D expenditure in these categories were 5 per cent, 25 per cent and 70 per cent respectively.[75] In many developed countries such as the United States and Japan, the share of basic research is generally more than 20 per cent, and even the Czech Republic, Korea and India conduct a significantly higher proportion of basic research than China. China's spending on basic research has been about one-fifth of that of Switzerland and a little more than one-third of the Indian figure.[76] In 2014, the situation remained more or less the same, and only 4.7 per cent of China's total R&D spending was on basic research.[77] China's investment in basic research has ranged from 1 per cent to 7 per cent; in contrast, the figure is about 15 per cent in the USA. Furthermore, there has been considerable doubt about the quality of China's basic research.[78] To some extent, this pattern has to do with the influence of the Chinese (pictographic) language, which has shaped a philosophy that emphasises simplicity and practicality. Historically, China has witnessed the development of a large number of inventions such as materials, machines and techniques, including gunpowder, the compass, printing and the seismograph, but has had no science that involves basic research.[79] Indeed,

> what is called Chinese classic science and technology is, in fact, technology rather than science. For instance, agronomy, military science, medicine, and arts and crafts were relatively developed in ancient China, while there was almost no development of theories of pure natural science that were independent of practical application.[80]

China's venture capital industry

The level of development of its venture capital (VC) industry can be a good indicator of a nation's innovation capability. Research by Michael Porter of Harvard Business School indicates that a nation's competitiveness depends on its capability to innovate, which relies on four attributes: factor conditions, demand conditions, related and supporting industries, and firm strategy, structure and rivalry.[81] The availability of venture capital is an important part of related and supporting industries, becoming an advantageous factor for US national competitiveness.[82] In China, VC began in the government sector in the mid-1990s, followed by university VC; the late 1990s saw the entrance of corporate VC and foreign VC. Over the past decade, China's average VC investment has been $5 billion, placing China as the world's third largest VC market after the USA ($35 billion) and Europe ($7 billion).[83] However, China is witnessing a rapid change in the development of its VC industry. In the past three years,

> Venture Capital investment in China-based internet companies has skyrocketed. In 2012, VC investment value of China-based businesses was just 55% of that of US-based companies; however, in 2015 China became the premier location for early-stage internet investment with USD $20bn of deals (compared with USD 16bn in the US).[84]

Innovation in China's enterprise sector

Empirical research has confirmed that corporate R&D is positively correlated with a company's productivity, earnings and stock price.[85] In China, there are three types of R&D establishment: enterprises, (government-run) R&D institutions and universities. Before 2000, China's enterprise sector was a weak player in the Chinese NIS in comparison with R&D institutions and universities. First, R&D spending was extremely low, at an estimated total of $1.1 billion in

1995, which was 1.1 per cent of American firms' R&D expenditure, 1.3 per cent of the Japanese figure and 3.6 per cent of that of German companies. Second, Chinese enterprises lagged behind in technological innovation. Between 1996 and 1999, although Chinese enterprises filed over 50 per cent of China's total patent applications, their share of the patents actually granted was lower than that of R&D institutions and universities.[86] Over the past decade, Chinese companies have increased their R&D spending by more than 3000 per cent.

In 2014, about 64,000 Chinese enterprises were engaged in R&D activities, accounting for 16.9 per cent of China's total enterprises, up 2.1 per cent over the previous year. Those classified as designated-scale enterprises[87] numbered 48,000, amounting to 12.6 per cent, a 1 per cent increase over the previous year. With 363,300 R&D researchers, up 7.6 per cent over the previous year, the designated-scale enterprises had R&D spending of RMB 925.4 billion (about $151.2 billion) and an R&D intensity (R&D spending/total sales) of 0.84 per cent. The number of patents filed by such firms was 24,000, a growth of 17.1 per cent over the previous year.

Since the mid-2000s, great changes have taken place in terms of the role of enterprises in the national innovation system. In 2005, Chinese enterprises were not only the major source of R&D funds, accounting for 67 per cent of the total, but also the leading performer of R&D activities, amounting to 68.4 per cent in China.[88] This suggests that other sources of funds were partly channelled to the enterprise sector. A survey study has shown that the Chinese government exerts a great influence on Chinese high-tech firms and their performance.[89]

Between 2002 and 2005, in terms of patent applications filed, the Chinese enterprise sector accounted for about 65 per cent of the total number among universities, R&D institutions and other organisations. In particular, the number of applications granted to the enterprise sector made up over 52 per cent of the total, well ahead of the contribution of the second most important player, the higher education sector.[90] In 2014, Chinese enterprises filed 48,500 invention patent applications, amounting to 60.5 per cent of total applications, up 13.6 per cent over the previous year; the number of invention patent applications granted was 92,000, representing an increase of 15.7 per cent over the previous year and accounting for 56.5 per cent of the total invention patents granted. The total of enterprise R&D spending was RMB 710.4 billion (about $116.1 billion), accounting for 76.89 per cent of total R&D spending. Enterprises based in Hong Kong, Macao and Taiwan spent RMB 85.2 billion ($13.9 billion), representing 9.2 per cent, while foreign-funded enterprises spent RMB 130 billion (about $21.2 billion), making up 14 per cent.[91]

China's innovative drive and imperative

Four factors, known as the 4Cs, have been identified as the drivers of Chinese innovation: customers, culture, capabilities and cash. *Customers* refers to the in-depth knowledge of customers that Chinese enterprises have gained to respond to their needs and wants, while the huge and dynamic Chinese market creates a powerful force that underlies intensive competition and the rapid growth of Chinese companies. *Culture* denotes the role of the government, entrepreneurial drive and the vision of Chinese business leaders. The Chinese government has had a clear ambition to make China technologically independent and a grand strategy to create an indigenous innovation ecosystem, with other necessary supportive strategies that have helped Chinese companies to meet customer needs through innovation. *Capabilities* means the innovative ability that Chinese companies have developed to compete domestically and internationally, gaining advantages in some particular areas while showing some weaknesses in others. *Cash* signifies the profitability of Chinese companies in domestic markets, which provides the funding, together with government financial support, to make inroads into international markets and compete with multinational corporations.[92]

Research undertaken by the McKinsey Global Institute has shown that from 1985 to 2015, China's average annual GDP growth was 9.4 per cent, while two forces have been identified as driving this growth: a constant inflow of new labour and enormous investment in housing, infrastructure and industrial capacity. However, these forces are waning. The supply of China's ample labour force will soon peak and decline, as a result of ageing. A long decline could persist and reduce its size by 16 per cent by 2050. A fall has already taken place in macroeconomic returns on fixed asset investments: 60 per cent more capital is now required to produce one unit of GDP in China than was the case, on average, from 1990 to 2010. China's further investment is also constrained by its debt, which accounts for 282 per cent of GDP, exceeding the debt-to-GDP ratios of the USA and Germany.[93]

Without these two forces to drive growth, China will have to resort more to innovation to improve productivity. Research indicates that in order to sustain 5.5 to 6.5 per cent growth rates until 2025, innovation is so crucial that it would need to make a contribution up to 50 per cent of GDP growth.

> Improving innovation performance would have additional benefits – helping China's transition to a more balanced, consumption-driven economy by expanding the service sector and providing more high value-added jobs. Rising productivity is also critical for creation of the well-paying jobs that can raise living standards and employ a growing urban population.[94]

Competitiveness of Chinese innovation

McKinsey researchers have identified the strengths and weaknesses of Chinese companies' innovativeness. In the category of consumer-focused industries, Chinese companies have gained some degree of advantage. For instance, China has captured 36 per cent of global revenues in the appliances sector and 15 per cent in Internet services and software. Chinese companies have learned to tailor their products to the needs of Chinese consumers, providing them with good value for their money. The huge market size helps companies to materialise the commercialisation of new ideas on a large scale quickly.

In the category of efficiency-driven industries, Chinese companies have also shown a certain degree of edge. For instance, in the solar panel industry, Chinese companies account for 51 per cent of global revenue, and in the textile industry, for 20 per cent of global revenue. Chinese companies have derived their strengths from China's role as the world's factory. Their manufacturing capacity enables them to carry out process innovations that involve cost-cutting, quality improvement and shortening time to market. These companies have also moved up the value chain, developing more technology-intensive and knowledge-based products and flexible manufacturing systems to attain responsiveness with competitive cost.

Although Chinese companies have enjoyed some degree of success in engineering-based industries such as high-speed trains (41% of global revenue), wind turbines (20%) and communications equipment (18%), many have not been competitive internationally, such as China's auto industry (8% of global revenue). Particularly in the category of science-based innovation, China has a long way to go to catch up with the West, examples including specialty chemicals, semiconductor design and branded pharmaceuticals. To date, none of these Chinese industries has more than 12 per cent of global revenue. A major cause of China's inadequacy in these industries is their characteristically long lead times for new discoveries and commercialisation.[95]

Chinese companies benefit from the support of a government that emphasises indigenous innovation, underscored in its recent five-year plan.

> Chinese authorities view innovation as critical both to the domestic economy's long-term health and to the global competitiveness of Chinese companies. China has already created the seeds of 22 Silicon Valley-like innovation hubs within the life sciences and biotech industries. In semiconductors, the government has been consolidating innovation clusters to create centers of manufacturing excellence.[96]
>
> The recent Chinese National Patent Development Strategy highlights the country's plans through 2020, including seven strategic industries positioned for growth: biotechnology, alternative energy, clean energy vehicles, energy conservation, high-end equipment manufacturing, broadband infrastructure and high-end semiconductors.[97]

Despite its innovation drive, its strengths in customer-focused and efficiency-driven innovation and government support, China faces significant challenges to achieving its aim of becoming an innovation-led nation by 2020. The government promotes innovation in China primarily through substantial investment in R&D, the expansion of higher education and the training of skilled workers, without adequately utilising market forces and the open exchange of ideas; it remains to be seen whether this top-down approach will work.[98] *The Economist* has observed: 'Chinese firms can innovate. But its government has not yet learned to distinguish between helpful support and counter-productive meddling.'[99]

Some weaknesses of Chinese companies have also been noted:

> several basic skills are at best nascent within a typical Chinese enterprise. Pain points include an absence of advanced techniques for understanding – analytically, not just intuitively – what customers really want, corporate cultures that don't support risk taking, and a scarcity of the sort of internal collaboration that's essential for developing new ideas.[100]

Yip and McKern identify ten major ways in which Chinese companies have conducted innovations differently from Western multinationals:[101]

- *Having a greater focus on local customer needs and requirements*: Western technology-based companies tend to allow their technologically superior capabilities to dominate in their innovation, without paying sufficient attention to customer needs or requirements. By contrast, with limitations in technology, Chinese companies have to focus more on customer needs, while their competent low-cost R&D capabilities enable them to respond to customer needs swiftly.
- *Accepting 'good enough' standards*: Many Chinese business and individual customers are willing to buy low-cost, fit-for-purpose, 'good enough' products. Western companies usually need to change the complexity of their products to make them 'good enough', with increased costs, while most Chinese enterprises tend to start from serving low-end markets, building up, not down, to meet 'good enough' standards. Once successful, they then move up into the 'good enough' segments to compete with the multinationals.
- *Undertaking incremental rather than radical innovation*: Most Chinese companies have inadequate technical capabilities compared with their Western counterparts; thus, they tend to pursue incremental innovation, improving product design, cost, operational processes or time to market, rather than making a radical technological change. Incremental innovation can often result in disruptive innovation in some niche markets, without being noticed by existing competitors, posing threats to Western multinationals.
- *Being willing to cater for special needs*: Chinese companies are willing and able to cater for any needs. This willingness derives partially from their ability to develop and build products or variants at a low cost and partially from their knowledge of customer needs and requirements by being close to them.
- *Enjoying access to a large number of researchers*: With a large pool of engineers and scientists in China, Chinese companies can afford to employ many researchers for R&D activities at a limited cost. In so doing, Chinese companies are able to break down an innovation process and assign a large team to different steps of innovation, with an accelerated innovative process. Western companies are constrained by the cost of researchers if they take this course.
- *Having the environment in which researchers work harder*: Chinese business leaders and entrepreneurs tend to foster a Chinese tradition in their companies,

making their R&D employees work longer hours than those in the West. This gives Chinese companies something of an advantage over their Western counterparts.

- *Having faster and less formal innovation processes*: Speedy action is advocated as part of Sun Tzu's teachings, being embedded in Chinese stratagem culture.[102]

> Chinese companies do everything faster than multinational corporations. We have heard this again and again from representatives of Chinese and Western companies. We have found that Chinese companies are motivated to innovate in a much faster way, while multinationals are constrained by elaborate, formal processes imposed by headquarters.[103]

- *Undertaking fast trial and error – failing fast but learning*: Chinese companies are more willing to go through fast trial and error, 'because the fast-growing Chinese markets are more forgiving than slow-growing markets in developed countries . . . This trial-and-error approach fits in well with the Chinese culture of pragmatism.'[104]
- *Experiencing more intervention by the boss*: Chinese companies tend to be run by quasi-emperors, each of his own corporate empire, as a result of Confucian influence. '"Autocratic" and "intervening" are two adjectives often used to differentiate Chinese bosses from Western ones.'[105]
- *Forging closer ties with government*: The Chinese government still has a stronger influence on businesses than do Western governments, so Chinese companies have closer relationships with the government than their Western counterparts. The Chinese authorities, national and/or local, can often provide support, particularly financial support, to innovators.

The McKinsey Global Institute makes these predictions and suggestions:

> In the next ten years the 'China effect' on innovation will be felt around the world as more companies use China as a location for low-cost and rapid innovation. The overall China effect could be disruptive, bringing large-scale yet nimble innovation to serve unmet needs in emerging markets and produce new varieties of goods and services for advanced economies. Around the world consumers could benefit from better goods at lower prices.[106]

A recent study has identified the factors that are conducive to innovation in China:

- An embracing of the entrepreneurial spirit,
- A strong sense of market orientation,
- A large pool of research talent from different fields,
- A strong and comprehensive manufacturing base,
- A strong motivation for successful commercialisation,

- A culture of executing R&D projects with speed and agility,
- A high level of Internet adoption and sophistication,
- A keenness to conduct experiments and
- Fierce competition among Chinese firms.[107]

The study also underlines some impediments to China's innovation:

- A high level of bureaucracy,
- A hierarchical societal structure,
- Rampant corruption hampering the quality of R&D activity,
- A weak spirit of commitment to teamwork,
- A weak capacity for system integration,
- Censorship and information control,
- Acute short-termism and
- A low level of investment in basic research.[108]

China's open innovation

With the emergence of digital and Internet technology, small and medium-sized businesses have witnessed an acceleration of improvement in price and performance, potentially becoming a serious threat to large incumbent businesses, with major business disruption from outside the realm of traditional competitors. The fact that core component technology becomes ever smaller, cheaper and better provides opportunities for start-ups to launch disruptive innovations. As a countermeasure, many large companies have engaged in a new approach to R&D known as open innovation (OI).[109]

Chesbrough's 2003 paper is considered to have inaugurated research into OI,[110] which he defines as

> the use of purposive inflows and outflows of knowledge to accelerate internal innovation and expand the markets for external use of innovation, respectively. Open innovation is a paradigm that assumes that firms can and should use external ideas as well as internal ideas, and internal and external paths to market, as they look to advance their technology.[111]

Following this pioneering work, a large number of research topics have been examined in the OI literature, including the direction of knowledge flows; the forms of openness such as alliances, joint ventures or networks; the parties involved such as suppliers, users, competitors or communities; and the influences on OI performance.[112] Open innovation has been widely practised in developed economies, but in China it is at a relatively early stage of adoption. The annual report on the OI initiatives of the world's 150 largest companies shows that from 2009 to 2013, three-quarters of non-Chinese companies were engaged in OI, but among the 24 Chinese companies in these 150, less than half were involved in OI.[113]

In traditional R&D activities, a company develops new technology, products and services internally with strict confidentiality, giving rise to a surprising effect on competitors when the innovative product is launched. In OI, without full ownership of technical solutions, the company has less control and confidentiality, but gains a much speedier product development, with reduced risk and lower costs. Each company shares its research problems with stakeholders such as universities, customers, suppliers and competitors, in order to find partners who can deliver effective solutions.

The actors that can influence China's innovation ecosystem include foreign companies, government agencies, universities, institutes, consultancy firms, suppliers and customers. In China, most companies, both Chinese and foreign multinationals, commonly utilise three approaches to open innovation, collaborating (1) with universities and research institutes, (2) with suppliers or customers in the business value chain and (3) with technical providers or buyers. Despite the OI concept being similar to those used in Europe and the USA, practices in China have differed as a result of influencing factors such as culture, institutions, technological development and markets.[114]

Research indicates that it is important for multinationals to become embedded in China's national innovation mainstream in order to benefit from R&D projects brought about by universities and institutions, through open innovations, with the potential to attract funding and work closely with suppliers, customers and start-ups. The following strategic recommendations apply to an MNC seeking to participate in this system; it should:

- Set up an action plan to increase the reputation of the company's R&D organisation in the local ecosystem and show the benefits to China of collaboration;
- Adjust the company's local business based on an understanding of the national government strategy and priorities for China's innovation;
- Become better informed and accepted by local stakeholders, such as industry experts, local researchers and officials through connection and engagement with them;
- Develop knowledge and experience of dealing with local authorities;
- Offer assistance to small and medium-sized Chinese companies when needed and work with partners to grow together with them;
- Differentiate the company's position from those of competitors in the field;
- Apply for initial project funding from local governments before making proposals to the central government;
- Work closely with partners who have established long-term and consistent collaborations; and
- Team up with other MNCs and representative associations in lobbying the various levels of government.[115]

How OI has been developed and practised in China can be illustrated by taking Haier as a case study, as presented in Box 6.1.

Box 6.1   Innovation in the Haier Group

Background

Haier's predecessor was the Qingdao Refrigerator Plant, which was officially renamed the Haier Group in December 1992. After a new general manager (the current CEO) was appointed in 1984, a series of measures were taken to improve enterprise efficiency, discipline and quality control and to develop a market-driven and innovative culture, as a result of which the company's performance was greatly improved. It then started to pursue internationalisation from 1995 onwards, investing in manufacturing facilities in the USA, Japan, New Zealand and numerous other Asian countries.

In 1984, Haier had sales of $1.24 million and employed 600 people. In 2015, its sales of RMB 188.7 billion (about $28.3 billion) accounted for 10 per cent of global market share, its profit was RMB 18 billion (about $2.7 billion) and it had been the world's largest manufacturer of household appliances for seven consecutive years. By 2015, Haier had 5 R&D centres (in Japan, New Zealand, Europe, the USA and China), 66 trading companies, 24 industrial parks, 143,330 sales outlets and over 80,000 employees worldwide. Exporting to North America, Europe, the Middle East, Asia and Africa, the company serves customers in over 100 countries and regions. Its product range consists of over 15,100 models in 96 categories.

With continuous innovation at the core of its corporate culture, Haier's cumulative number of patent applications exceeded 16,000 by the end of 2014, with a portfolio of over 9000 patents granted, including 480 PCT patents. The company has over 4800 registered trademarks in over 190 countries and regions.[116]

Haier's corporate strategy has gone through five stages: brand building (1984–1991), diversification (1991–1998), internationalisation (1998–2005), global branding (2005–2012) and networking (2012–2019), as shown in Figure 6.1.[117]

Haier's ZZJYT

As can be seen from Figure 6.1, Haier adopted an organisational form called ZZJYT, an abbreviation of *zhi zhu jing ying ti*, denoting self-organising work units, which represented a major stride for organisational innovation in the company. Under this system, specially selected employees from three functions – design, manufacturing and marketing – work together directly with customers. First to be appointed is a ZZJYT manager, who then selects a team of 10 to 20 members, consisting of people from different functional roles. All ZZJYT activities are interlinked by internal

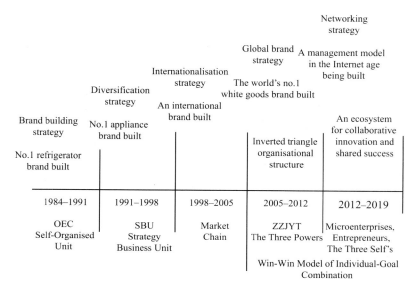

Figure 6.1 Haier – stages of five corporate strategies

contracts, and talent is selected through Haier's internal labour market. Afforded profit and loss responsibility and accountability, ZZJYTs have autonomy in recruiting and firing employees, setting internal working rules, determining bonus distribution and making operational decisions as microenterprises. ZZJYT managers provide resources and guidance to their team members to serve customers.

This organisational form represents an attempt by Haier to avoid the potential impact of innovation disruption. It provides Haier's top management the opportunity of noting early warning signs of disruption so that it can respond swiftly with countermeasures. Working in the same ZZJYTs, R&D and marketing people meet regularly, particularly when new products are developed.[118] As a result of adopting the ZZJYT organisational form, 'the company has become a giant business incubator. By introducing market mechanisms into its research and development (R&D) processes, Haier is able to generate a flow of disruptive new technologies and convert them into commercial products.'[119]

Haier's open innovation

Figure 6.1 indicates that Haier has entered the fifth stage of corporate strategy, networking, and has embraced OI as part of its business strategy. Haier can be considered China's champion of open innovation, which accounts for half of its innovations. Haier began to explore the idea of OI in the 1990s, and the Haier Open Innovation Centre (HOIC) was established in 2009. 'Its mission is to explore external technologies and solutions from around the world for all its business units.'[120]

Haier's basic approach to OI is that 'the world is our R&D centre', referring to zero-distance innovation and sustainable innovation among global users, manufacturers and innovation resources. Haier's goal for OI is to build an innovation ecosystem in which global resources and users participate and continuously produce products of exponential technology.[121]

Figure 6.2 shows how the HOIC works within Haier's OI system. The HOIC is mainly operated by two teams: the Technology to Business (TTB) and Global Resource Integration (GRI) teams. The TTB team is responsible for collecting innovation needs from each business unit, while the GRI team identifies external technologies that might be used to meet those needs. Receiving technical needs from the TTB team, the GRI team reaches out to potential technical providers through its global technology searching partners. The search network not only connects Haier's five R&D centres, located in Germany, Japan, China, the USA and New Zealand, but also reaches out to innovators in other countries, such as Israel, South Korea and the UK. In addition, the GRI recommends technologies with potential to meet future needs of business to the business unit teams, which are responsible for the evaluation and acceptance of candidate technologies.

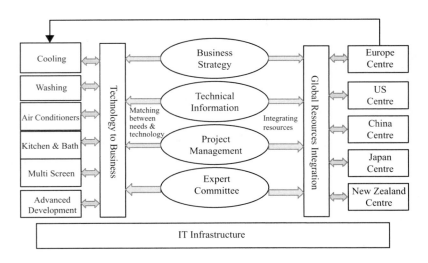

Figure 6.2 The structure of Haier's Open Innovation Centre

The HOIC has four major supporting teams: a business strategy team, a technical information team, a project management team and an expert committee. Since 2009, the HOIC has helped Haier's business units to adopt over 300 technologies.[122]

As a major step towards materialising OI, Haier has developed the Haier Open Partnership Ecosystem (HOPE) platform. Developed by the HOIC, HOPE connects a growing global network of technical partners and resources. By 2014, it had approximately 200,000 registered users. Also used by third parties, the platform enables the company to surmount development bottlenecks, to find technological solutions rapidly and efficiently and to bring leading-edge products to the market more quickly.[123]

About 30 external companies pay to use Haier's platform. Users post research questions in the form of cases and seek potential solutions from over 370,000 registered problem solvers, who range from individuals to large global corporations, including Dow Chemical, Bayer and Honeywell. On average, 150–200 cases are posted each year.

> Reflecting the unique economics of the Chinese market and industry structure, Haier's strategic goal is to achieve 'zero-distance' between global users and innovation partners, allowing customers, suppliers, entrepreneurs and other stakeholders to initiate and collaborate on product innovation.[124]

Haier's Air Cube, launched in 2014, is an exemplary case where the platform created the world's first intelligent air quality control device. This innovative product is protected by 40 design patents and 22 invention patents and was generated by collaboration among 128 internal and external experts and researchers from eight countries through the HOPE platform. Having consulted with over 9.8 million users worldwide over a six-month period, the team addressed 122 criticisms of the product and developed a solution providing consumer satisfaction.[125]

Priorities for innovators in China

In order to enhance innovation performance, McKinsey researchers have recommended seven priorities for innovators in China:[126]

(1) Developing deeper knowledge of Chinese consumers. Alibaba is an exemplary company which has grown rapidly within a short period of time into a world-class player in the field, because its founder, Jack Ma, has a deep understanding of Chinese consumers. His knowledge of the constraints of the Chinese distribution system and banking sector has enabled him to build platforms for B2B, B2C and C2C businesses, a logistics platform

and an escrow payment device, Alipay. On this point, Chinese companies run into different problems from those of their Western counterparts. Chinese companies' understanding of consumers is primarily based on each researcher's personal experience, rather than systematic knowledge developed by employing marketing research techniques. Western companies, despite having marketing research competence, tend to have difficulty in balancing standardisation and adaption, often leaning towards the former. Expatriate-run China centres and R&D centres impose limitations on their abilities to understand Chinese consumers.

(2)   Inculcating a culture of risk taking. Undertaking innovation is unavoidably accompanied by failures, requiring researchers to be willing to take risks. China's Confucian environment is not conducive to a risk-taking attitude or action. To overcome this barrier, it is suggested that risk be transferred from individual innovators to teams, where shared accountability and community support are more tolerable and acceptable.

(3)   Seeking partnership with Chinese universities. It has been recognised that Chinese universities are now equipped with some of the best researchers in certain fields of science, who have graduated from top Western universities. There are two major forms of collaboration between Chinese universities and Western multinationals: project-based collaboration to resolve specific research problems and joint innovation collaboration frameworks with long-term agreements.[127]

(4)   Protecting intellectual property rights as a core part of innovation culture. Although great progress has been achieved in cracking down on IPR violations in China, IPR theft, including reverse engineering and the copying and sale of parts or products, remains a major concern. Companies should incorporate IPR protection into their internal codes of conduct and ethical policies. It is suggested that if Chinese employees of multinationals are appreciated and valued as part of a broad global entity, they will be less likely to violate IPRs behind the company's back.

(5)   Promoting a cooperative working environment. Chinese culture does not encourage teamwork or collaboration among employees. Companies must find ways to surmount this hurdle in order to make progress in innovation.

(6)   Tapping into the pool of a young generation of talent. An increasing number of young Chinese graduates and high-tech start-ups are reshaping corporate culture and individual mind-sets. They can be good assets for multinationals. However, research shows that multinationals tend to focus their attention on experienced Chinese recruits, while a high percentage of Chinese high-tech companies are keen to hire technically adept Chinese youngsters.

(7)   Retaining local talent. Most multinationals have pinpointed the formidable challenges of recruiting and retaining talent in China, making talent management a top priority in China. This issue is discussed in detail in the next chapter.

Notes

1 Burgelman, R.A. and Sayles, L.R. (1986), *Inside Corporate Innovation*, New York: The Free Press. Tang, H.K. (1998), "An Integrative Model of Innovation in Organisations," *Technovation*, 18 (5), 297–309.

2 Drucker, P.F. (1955), *The Practice of Management*, London: Heinemann, pp. 35–38.

3 OECD and Eurostat (2005), *Guidelines for Collecting and Interpreting Innovation Data*, Oslo Manual (3rd ed.), Paris: OECD, p. 46.

4 Lundvall, B. (1992), *National Systems of Innovation: Toward a Theory of Innovation and Interactive Learning*, London: Pinter. Nelson, R.R. (1993), *National Innovation Systems: A Comparative Analysis*, Oxford: Oxford University Press. OECD (1997), *National Innovation Systems*, Paris: OECD. Edquist, C. (1997), *Systems of Innovation: Technologies, Institutions and Organizations*, London: Pinter. Freeman, C. (1987), *Technology Policy and Economic Performance: Lesson From Japan*, London: Pinter. Freeman, C. (1995), "The 'National System of Innovation' in Historical Perspective," *Cambridge Journal of Economics*, 19, 5–24. Saxenian, A. (1994), *Regional Advantage: Cultural and Competition in Silicon Valley and Route 128*, Boston, MA: Harvard University Press.

5 OECD (1997), *National Innovation Systems*, Paris: OECD.

6 Schumpeter, J.A. (1934), *The Theory of Economic Development*, Cambridge, MA: Harvard University Press, p. 132.

7 Schumpeter, J.A. (1950), *Capitalism, Socialism, and Democracy*, New York: Harper, p. 83.

8 Ettlie, J. (2012), *Managing Innovation*, Oxford: Taylor & Francis, p. 8.

9 Ibid.

10 OECD (2015), *OECD Innovation Strategy 2015: An Agenda for Policy Action*, Meeting of the OECD Council at Ministerial level, Paris.

11 Zahra, S.A. and Covin, J.G. (1993), "Business Strategy, Technology Policy and Firm Performance," *Strategic Management Journal*, 14 (6), 451–478. Oviatt, B.M. and McDougall, P.P. (1994), "Toward a Theory of International New Ventures," *Journal of International Business Studies*, 25 (1), 45–64. Price, R.M. (1996), "Technology and Strategic Advantage," *California Management Review*, 38 (3), 38–56.

12 McCarthy, D.J., Spital, F.C. and Lauenstein, M.C. (1987), "Managing Growth at High-Technology Companies: A View From the Top," *Academy of Management Executive*, 1 (4), 313–322. Tidd, J., Bessant, J. and Pavitt, K. (2005), *Managing Innovation: Integrating, Technological, Market and Organizational Change*, Chichester: John Wiley & Sons.

13 Porter, M.E. (1990), *The Competitive Advantage of Nations*, New York: Free Press. Oviatt, B.M. and McDougall, P.P. (1994), "Toward a Theory of International New Ventures," *Journal of International Business Studies*, 25 (1), 45–64. Price, R.M. (1996), "Technology and Strategic Advantage," *California Management Review*, 38 (3), 38–56. Zahra, S.A. and Covin, J.G. (1993), "Business Strategy, Technology Policy and Firm Performance," *Strategic Management Journal*, 14 (6), 451–478.

14 Bettis, R.A. and Hitt, M.A. (1995), "The New Competitive Landscape," *Strategic Management Journal*, 16 (Special Issue), 7–19.

15 Dowling, M.J. and McGee, J.E. (1994), "Business and Technology Strategies and New Venture Performance: A Study of the Telecommunications Equipment Industry," *Management Science*, 40 (12), 1663–1677.

16 Brown, S.L. and Eisenhardt, K.M. (1995), "Product Development: Past Research, Present Findings, and Future Directions," *Academy of Management Review*, 20 (2), 343–378.

17 O'Neill, H.M., Pouder, R.W. and Buchholtz, A.K. (1998), "Patterns of Diffusion of Strategies Across Organizations: Insights From the Innovation Diffusion Literature," *Academy of Management Review*, 23 (1), 98–114.

18 Zirger, B.J. and Maidique, M.A. (1990), "A Model of New Product Development: An Empirical Test," *Management Science*, 36 (7), 867–883.

19 Ibid.

20 Zahra, S.A. and Covin, J.G. (1993), "Business Strategy, Technology Policy and Firm Performance," *Strategic Management Journal*, 14 (6), 451–478.

21 Haour, G. and von Zedtwitz, M. (2016), *Created in China: How China Is Becoming a Global Innovator*, London: Bloomsbury Information Ltd, pp. 21–22.

22 Ettlie, J. (1999), *Managing Innovation*, New York: John Wiley & Sons.

23 Figueiredo, P. (2002), "Does Technological Learning Pay Off? Inter-Firm Differences in Technological Capability-Accumulation Paths and Operational Performance Improvement," *Research Policy*, 31, 73–94. Tidd, J., Bessant, J. and Pavitt, K. (2005), *Managing Innovation: Integrating, Technological, Market and Organizational Change*, Chichester: John Wiley & Sons.

24 Rothwell, R. and Gardiner, P. (1985), "Invention, Innovation and Re-Innovation and the Role of the User," *Technovation*, 3, 176–186.

25 Henderson, R. and Clark, K. (1990), "Architectural Innovation: The Reconfiguration of Existing Product Technologies and the Failure of Established Firms," *Administrative Science Quarterly*, 35, 9–30. Tidd, J., Bessant, J. and Pavitt, K. (2005), *Managing Innovation: Integrating, Technological, Market and Organizational Change*, Chichester: John Wiley & Sons.

26 Pisano, G. (2015), "You Need an Innovation Strategy," *Harvard Business Review*, 93 (6), 44–54.

27 Tidd, J., Bessant, J. and Pavitt, K. (2005), *Managing Innovation: Integrating, Technological, Market and Organizational Change*, Chichester: John Wiley & Sons, p. 99.

28 Yip, G.S. and McKern, B. (2016), *China's Next Strategic Advantage: From Imitation to Innovation*, Cambridge, MA: MIT Press, pp. 26–27.

29 Woetzel, J., Chen, Y., Manyika, J., Roth, E., Seong, J. and Lee, J. (2015), *The China Effect on Global Innovation*, Seattle: McKinsey Global Institute, McKinsey & Company, http://www.mckinseychina.com/wp-content/uploads/2015/07/mckinsey-china-effect-on-global-innovation-2015.pdf Yip, G.S. and McKern, B. (2016), *China's Next Strategic Advantage: From Imitation to Innovation*, Cambridge, MA: MIT Press.

30 Woetzel, J., Chen, Y., Manyika, J., Roth, E., Seong, J. and Lee, J. (2015), *The China Effect on Global Innovation*, Seattle: McKinsey Global Institute, McKinsey & Company, http://www.mckinseychina.com/wp-content/uploads/2015/07/mckinsey-china-effect-on-global-innovation-2015.pdf

31 Yip, G.S. and McKern, B. (2016), *China's Next Strategic Advantage: From Imitation to Innovation*, Cambridge, MA: MIT Press, pp. 10–12.

32 Qiu, J. (2015), "Safeguarding Research Integrity in China," *National Science Review*, 2, 122–125.

33 Woetzel, J., Chen, Y., Manyika, J., Roth, E., Seong, J. and Lee, J. (2015), *The China Effect on Global Innovation*, Seattle: McKinsey Global Institute, McKinsey & Company, http://www.mckinseychina.com/wp-content/uploads/2015/07/mckinsey-china-effect-on-global-innovation-2015.pdf

34 Lundvall, B. (1992), *National Systems of Innovation: Toward a Theory of Innovation and Interactive Learning*, London: Pinter.

35 Nelson, R.R. (1993), *National Innovation Systems: A Comparative Analysis*, Oxford: Oxford University Press.

36 Chen, A.H., Patton, D. and Kenney, M. (2016), "University Technology Transfer in China: A Literature Review and Taxonomy," *Journal of Technology Transfer*, 41, 891–929.

37 Zhou, Y. and Liu, X. (2016), "Evolution of Chinese State Policies on Innovation," in Y. Zhou, W. Lazonick, and Y. Sun (eds.), *China as an Innovation Nation*, Oxford: Oxford University Press, pp. 33–67.

38 Buffa, E.S. (1984), *Meeting the Competitive Challenge*, Homewood, IL: Dow Jones-Irwin. Price, R.M. (1996), "Technology and Strategic Advantage," *California Management Review*, 38 (3), 38–56.

39 Larson, C.F. (2001), "China Moving on Many Fronts to Boost S&T and Innovation," *Research Technology Management*, 44 (2), 2–4. World Bank Institute (2001), *China and*

the Knowledge Economy: Seizing the 21st Century, Washington, DC: WBI Development Studies.

40 Gould, S (ed.) (1961), *Science in Communist China*, Washington, DC: American Association for the Advancement of Science.

41 Ma, H. (1982), *Encyclopaedia of Chinese Modern Economy* (in Chinese), Beijing: Chinese Social Sciences Press, p. 539.

42 The CAS now has 5 academic divisions, 108 scientific research institutes, over 200 S&T establishments and over 20 affiliated institutions, including a university and a graduate school, as well as 5 information centres. It has made major contributions to China's S&T development in many areas such as biology, aviation and aerospace, nuclear physics, computing, lasers, semiconductors and various new materials.

43 The interval between the first atom and hydrogen bombs for China was two years and eight months, while it took seven years and three months for the United States, four years and three months for Russia, and four years and seven months for Britain to move from one stage to the other.

44 Ma, H. (1982), *Encyclopaedia of Chinese Modern Economy* (in Chinese), Beijing: Chinese Social Sciences Press, p. 540.

45 Chen, A.H., Patton, D. and Kenney, M. (2016), "University Technology Transfer in China: A Literature Review and Taxonomy," *Journal of Technology Transfer*, 41, 891–929.

46 The 863 Programme was proposed by a group of eminent Chinese scientists in response to US President Reagan's 'Star Wars' Plan and the European High-technology Research and Development Programme (Eureka) and was approved by the State Council.

47 Yoshida, P.G. (2007), "Rising China Faces Challenges to National Innovation Goals," *Research Technology Management*, 50 (6), 2–5.

48 Ma, H. and Wang. M.K. (2006), *2006 中国经济年鉴 (Almanac of China's Economy 2006)*, Beijing: Almanac of China's Economy Publishing House.

49 Simon, D.F. (1989), "China's Drive to Close the Technological Gap: S&T Reform and Imperative to Catch Up," *The China Quarterly*, 119, Special Issue: The People's Republic of China After 40 Years, 598–630.

50 Zhong, X.W. and Yang, X.D. (2007), "Science and Technology Policy Reform and Its Impact on China's National Innovation System," *Technology in Society*, 29, 317–325.

51 Simon, D.F. (1989), "China's Drive to Close the Technological Gap: S&T Reform and Imperative to Catch Up," *The China Quarterly*, 119, Special Issue: The People's Republic of China After 40 Years, 598–630.

52 State Science and Technology Commission (1987), *Guidelines to China's Science and Technology Policy – White Paper on Science and Technology No. 1* (in Chinese), Beijing: International Academic Publisher.

53 Zhong, X.W. and Yang, X.D. (2007), "Science and Technology Policy Reform and Its Impact on China's National Innovation System," *Technology in Society*, 29, 317–325.

54 Development Research Centre of the State Council (1987), *Almanac of China's Economy 1987*, Beijing: Almanac of China's Economy Publishing House.

55 Development Research Centre of the State Council (1995), *Almanac of China's Economy 1995*, Beijing: Almanac of China's Economy Publishing House.

56 Xue, M.Q., Ma, H. and Wang, M.K. (2003), *Almanac of China's Economy 2003*, Beijing: Almanac of China's Economy Publishing House, p. 462.

57 Ma, H. and Wang, M.K. (2006), *2006 中国经济年鉴 (Almanac of China's Economy 2006)*, Beijing: Almanac of China's Economy Publishing House, p. 511.

58 Xue, M.Q., Ma, H. and Wang, M.K. (2003), *Almanac of China's Economy 2003*, Beijing: Almanac of China's Economy Publishing House, p. 462.

59 Yoshida, P.G. (2007), "Rising China Faces Challenges to National Innovation Goals," *Research Technology Management*, 50 (6), 2–5.

60 Haour, G. and von Zedtwitz, M. (2016), *Created in China: How China Is Becoming a Global Innovator*, London: Bloomsbury Information, p. 24.

61 OECD (2003), *China in the World Economy: An OECD Economic and Statistical Survey*, London: Kogan Page, p. 196.

62 Wolff, M.F. (2007), "OECD Ranks China No. 2," *Research Technology Management*, 50 (3), 8.

63 Ministry of Science and Technology (2015), 2014 年全国科技经费投入统计公报 (*Statistical Report of 2014 Chinese National Science and Technology Spending*), Ministry of Science and Technology, www.most.gov.cn/tztg/201511/t20151124_122460.htm, retrieved on 16 October 2016.

64 UNESCO (2015), *UNESCO Science Report: Towards 2030*, Paris: UNESCO Publishing.

65 Jaruzelski, B., Schwartz, K. and Staack, V. (2015), "Innovation's New World Order," *Strategy+Business*, 27 October, www.strategy-business.com/feature/00370?gko=e606a, retrieved on 28 October 2016.

66 WIPO (2007), *WIPO Patent Drafting Manual*, Geneva: The World Intellectual Property Rights Organization.

67 Planning Department of the Ministry of Science and Technology (2007), "Results of China's Patent Statistical Analysis in 2006" (in Chinese), *Statistical Report on Science and Technology*, 405 (14), The Ministry of Science and Technology, http://www.most.gov.cn/kjtj/201506/t20150630_120408.htm, p.1.

68 Chinese Academy of Science and Technology for Development (2013), *National Innovation Index Report 2013*, Beijing: Scientific and Technical Documentation Press.

69 Manufacturing Research Group of the China Economic Times (2016), *Major Findings of Chinese Manufacturing: Towards Mid and High Sectors*, Beijing: China CITIC Press, p. XI.

70 Woetzel, J., Chen, Y., Manyika, J., Roth, E., Seong, J. and Lee, J. (2015), *The China Effect on Global Innovation*, Seattle: McKinsey Global Institute, McKinsey & Company, http://www.mckinseychina.com/wp-content/uploads/2015/07/mckinsey-china-effect-on-global-innovation-2015.pdf, retrieved on 27 October 2016.

71 Haour, G. and von Zedtwitz, M. (2016), *Created in China: How China Is Becoming a Global Innovator*, London: Bloomsbury Information, pp. 34–35.

72 Sunman, H. (1987), "Science Parks, Technopoles and Innovation Centres: The European Experience," *International Journal of Technology Management*, 2 (1), 142–145. Quintas, P., Wield, D. and Massey, D. (1992), "Academic – Industry Links and Innovation: Questioning the Science Park Model," *Technovation*, 12 (3), 161–175. Liu, H. and Jiang, Y.Z. (2001), "Technology Transfer From Higher Education Institutions to Industry in China: Nature and Implications," *Technovation*, 21, 175–188.

73 World Economic Forum (2016), *China's Innovation Ecosystems*, White Paper, World Economic Forum, August 2016, http://www3.weforum.org/docs/WEF_GAC_On_China_Innovation_WhitePaper_2016.pdf, retrieved on 27 October 2016.

74 Haour, G. and von Zedtwitz, M. (2016), *Created in China: How China Is Becoming a Global Innovator*, London: Bloomsbury Information, pp. 38–39.

75 OECD (2003), *China in the World Economy: An OECD Economic and Statistical Survey*, London: Kogan Page, p. 196.

76 Zhang, Y.L and Sun, S.Y. (2005), *Report on the Development of Chinese Enterprises* (in Chinese), Beijing: Enterprise Management Publishing House, p. 32.

77 The Ministry of Science and Technology (2015), *2014 年全国科技经费投入统计公报 (Statistical Report of 2014 Chinese National Science and Technology Spending)*, Ministry of Science and Technology, www.most.gov.cn/tztg/201511/t20151124_122460.htm, retrieved on 16 October 2016.

78 Ibid, pp. 39–40.

79 Liu, H. (2015), *The Chinese Strategic Mind*, Northampton, MA: Edward Elgar Publishing, pp. 52–77.

80 Zi, Z.Y. (1987), "The Relationship of Chinese Traditional Culture to the Modernization of China: An Introduction to the Current Discussion," *Asian Survey*, 27 (4), 442–458.

81 Porter, M.E. (1990), "The Competitive Advantage of Nations," *Harvard Business Review*, March–April, 73–91.

82 Ibid.
83 Haour, G. and von Zedtwitz, M. (2016), *Created in China: How China Is Becoming a Global Innovator*, London: Bloomsbury Information, p. 84.
84 Birtwhistle, T. (2016), *The Rise of China's Silicon Dragon*, PwC's Experience Centre, www.pwc.com/my/en/assets/publications/1605-the-rise-of-china-silicon-dragon.pdf, retrieved on 9 November 2016.
85 Deng, Z., Lev. B. and Narin, F. (1999), "Science and Technology as Predictors of Stock Performance," *Financial Analysis Journal*, 55 (3), 20–32.
86 OECD (2003), *China in the World Economy: An OECD Economic and Statistical Survey*, London: Kogan Page, pp. 200–202.
87 The designated-scale enterprises are those that have an annual sales of RMB 20 million (about $3.3 million).
88 Ministry of Science and Technology (2006), "Science and Technology Statistical Data 2006," *China Science & Technology Statistical Data Book* (in Chinese), Beijing: The Ministry of Science and Technology.
89 Liu, H., Liu, H. and Jackson, P. (2011), "China's High-Tech Firms: Strategic Patterns and Performance," *Journal of Global Business and Technology*, 7 (2), 1–13.
90 Ibid.
91 Ministry of Science and Technology (2016), *2014年我国专利统计分析 (2014 Chinese Patent Statistical Analysis)*, The Ministry of Science and Technology, www.most.gov.cn/kjtj/, retrieved on 18 October 2016.
92 Yip, G.S. and McKern, B. (2016), *China's Next Strategic Advantage: From Imitation to Innovation*, Cambridge, MA: MIT Press, pp. 4–5.
93 Woetzel, J., Chen, Y., Manyika, J., Roth, E., Seong, J. and Lee, J. (2015), *The China Effect on Global Innovation*, Seattle: McKinsey Global Institute, McKinsey & Company, http://www.mckinseychina.com/wp-content/uploads/2015/07/mckinsey-china-effect-on-global-innovation-2015.pdf
94 Ibid.
95 Roth, E., Seong, J. and Woetzel, J. (2015), "Gauging the Strength of Chinese Innovation," *McKinsey Quarterly*, October, www.mckinsey.com/business-functions/strategy-and-corporate-finance/our-insights/gauging-the-strength-of-chinese-innovation, retrieved on 24 October 2016. Woetzel, J., Chen, Y., Manyika, J., Roth, E., Seong, J. and Lee, J. (2015), *The China Effect on Global Innovation*, Seattle: McKinsey Global Institute, McKinsey & Company, http://www.mckinseychina.com/wp-content/uploads/2015/07/mckinsey-china-effect-on-global-innovation-2015.pdf
96 Orr, G. and Roth, E. (2012), "A CEO Guide to Innovation in China," *McKinsey Quarterly*, February, www.mckinsey.com/global-themes/asia-pacific/a-ceos-guide-to-innovation-in-china, retrieved on 23 November 2016.
97 Lange, J. (2015), "Chinese Firms Pour Money Into U.S. R&D in Shift to Innovation," *Reuters*, 21 June 2015, www.reuters.com/article/us-usa-china-investment-insight-idUSKBN0P10KD20150621, retrieved on 28 October 2016.
98 Chan, J. (2015), "China's Innovation Paradox," *Perspectives: Policy and Practice in Higher Education*, 19 (1), 23–27.
99 The Economist (2015), "Calibrating Chinese Creativity," *The Economist*, 11 July 2015, www.economist.com/news/business/21657376-sceptics-exaggerate-some-industries-chinese-firms-are-innovative-calibrating-chinese, retrieved on 21 November 2016.
100 Orr, G. and Roth, E. (2012), "A CEO Guide to Innovation in China," *McKinsey Quarterly*, February, www.mckinsey.com/global-themes/asia-pacific/a-ceos-guide-to-innovation-in-china, retrieved on 23 November 2016.
101 Yip, G.S. and McKern, B. (2016), *China's Next Strategic Advantage: From Imitation to Innovation*, Cambridge, MA: MIT Press, pp. 75–99.
102 Liu, H. (2015), *The Chinese Strategic Mind*, Northampton, MA: Edward Elgar Publishing, p. 117.

103 Yip, G.S. and McKern, B. (2016), *China's Next Strategic Advantage: From Imitation to Innovation*, Cambridge, MA: MIT Press, p. 88.

104 Ibid, p. 90.

105 Ibid, p. 92.

106 Woetzel, J., Chen, Y., Manyika, J., Roth, E., Seong, J. and Lee, J. (2015), *The China Effect on Global Innovation*, Seattle: McKinsey Global Institute, McKinsey & Company, http://www.mckinseychina.com/wp-content/uploads/2015/07/mckinsey-china-effect-on-global-innovation-2015.pdf

107 Haour, G. and von Zedtwitz, M. (2016), *Created in China: How China Is Becoming a Global Innovator*, London: Bloomsbury Information, p. 171.

108 Ibid.

109 Nunes, P. and Downes, L. (2016), "At Haier and Lenovo, Chinese-Style Open Innovation," *Forbes*, 26 September, www.forbes.com/sites/bigbangdisruption/2016/09/26/at-haier-and-lenovo-chinese-style-open-innovation/#62ad095c4bb5, retrieved on 25 November 2016.

110 Chesbrough, H. (2003), "The Era of Open Innovation," *Sloan Management Review*, 44 (3), 35–41.

111 Chesbrough, H. (2006), "Open Innovation: A New Paradigm for Understanding Industrial Innovation," in H. Chesbrough, W. Vanhaverbeke and J. West (eds.), *Open Innovation: Researching a New Paradigm*, Oxford: Oxford University Press, 1–12.

112 Ibid. Dahlander, L. and Gann, D.M. (2010), "How Open Is Innovation?" *Research Policy*, 39 (6), 699–709. Huizingh, E.K.R.E. (2011), "Open Innovation: State of the Art and Future Perspectives," *Technovation*, 31 (1), 2–9. Gambardella, A. and Panico, C. (2014), "On the Management of Open Innovation," *Research Policy*, 43, 903–913.

113 Nunes, P. and Downes, L. (2016), "At Haier and Lenovo, Chinese-Style Open Innovation," *Forbes*, 26 September, www.forbes.com/sites/bigbangdisruption/2016/09/26/at-haier-and-lenovo-chinese-style-open-innovation/#62ad095c4bb5, retrieved on 25 November 2016.

114 Yip, G.S. and McKern, B. (2016), *China's Next Strategic Advantage: From Imitation to Innovation*, Cambridge, MA: MIT Press, pp. 167–169.

115 Ibid, pp. 194–195.

116 Wang, Y., Teng, D.H., Huang, C., Wang, J.G. and Wan, X.M. (2015), "Haier: Pioneering Innovation in the Digital World," *WIPO Magazine*, August, www.wipo.int/wipo_magazine/en/2015/04/article_0006.html, retrieved on 27 April 2016.

117 The Haier Group: "Haier – 5 Stages of Strategic Development," Qingdao: The Haier Group, www.haier.net/cn/about_haier/strategy/

118 Fischer, B., Lago, U. and Liu, F. (2015), "The Haier Road to Growth," *Strategy+Business*, 27 April, www.strategy-business.com/article/00323?gko=c8c2a, retrieved on 27 April 2016.

119 Wang, Y., Teng, D.H., Huang, C., Wang, J.G. and Wan, X.M. (2015), "Haier: Pioneering Innovation in the Digital World," *WIPO Magazine*, August, www.wipo.int/wipo_magazine/en/2015/04/article_0006.html, retrieved on 27 April 2016.

120 Yip, G.S. and McKern, B. (2016), *China's Next Strategic Advantage: From Imitation to Innovation*, Cambridge, MA: MIT Press, p. 199.

121 The Haier Group: "The Basic Idea of Haier's Open Innovation," Qingdao: The Haier Group, www.haier.net/en/research_development/rd_System/, retrieved on 21 November 2016.

122 Yip, G.S. and McKern, B. (2016), *China's Next Strategic Advantage: From Imitation to Innovation*, Cambridge, MA: MIT Press, pp. 199–200.

123 Wang, Y., Teng, D.H., Huang, C., Wang, J.G. and Wan, X.M. (2015), "Haier: Pioneering Innovation in the Digital World," *WIPO Magazine*, August, www.wipo.int/wipo_magazine/en/2015/04/article_0006.html, retrieved on 27 April 2016.

124 Nunes, P. and Downes, L. (2016), "At Haier and Lenovo, Chinese-Style Open Innovation," *Forbes*, 26 September, www.forbes.com/sites/bigbangdisruption/2016/09/26/

at-haier-and-lenovo-chinese-style-open-innovation/#62ad095c4bb5, retrieved on 25 November 2016.

125 Wang, Y., Teng, D.H., Huang, C., Wang, J.G. and Wan, X.M. (2015), "Haier: Pioneering Innovation in the Digital World," *WIPO Magazine*, August, www.wipo.int/wipo_magazine/en/2015/04/article_0006.html, retrieved on 27 April 2016.

126 Orr, G. and Roth, E. (2012), "A CEO Guide to Innovation in China," *McKinsey Quarterly*, February, www.mckinsey.com/global-themes/asia-pacific/a-ceos-guide-to-innovation-in-china, retrieved on 23 November 2016. rr, G. and Roth, E. (2013), "China's Innovation Engine Picks Up Speed," *McKinsey Quarterly*, June, www.mckinsey.com/business-functions/strategy-and-corporate-finance/our-insights/chinas-innovation-engine-picks-up-speed, retrieved on 23 November 2016.

127 Yip, G.S. and McKern, B. (2016), *China's Next Strategic Advantage: From Imitation to Innovation*, Cambridge, MA: MIT Press, pp. 199–200.

7 Chinese Internet-based business

We are all now connected by the Internet, like neurons in a giant brain.
– Stephen Hawking

Invisible threads are the strongest ties
– Friedrich Nietzsche

We are more closely connected to the invisible than to the visible.
– Novalis

China's new economy and new perspectives on business

Few books on Chinese business include a chapter on Internet-based business or e-commerce, unless it discusses China's e-commerce marketing in particular; therefore, readers may naturally wonder why such a chapter would be necessary. The short answer is that Chinese Internet companies have become increasingly important players in China's B2B (business to business), B2C (business to consumer) and C2C (consumer to consumer) markets, as formidable competitors that have not only carved up the Chinese Internet market, but have potential and ambition to eat into global market share. The founder of JD.com or Jingdong Mall, a leading Chinese e-tailer which ranked 366 in the Fortune Global 500 in 2016, has made the following projections: (1) in the next 10 years, there will be a number of Chinese e-tailers whose sales will have reached billions and even trillions of US dollars, (2) in 20 years or less, the world's largest e-tailer will be Chinese and (3) JD.com will be one of the largest retailers in the world.[1]

Historically, there have been technological forces that have fundamentally changed the ways in which goods are produced and distributed, resulting in an exponential increase in productivity and economic growth, and transforming people's lives worldwide. Any transitional period between one state of the world and the new world created by transformative technology is known as an industrial revolution. The First Industrial Revolution was characterised by the utilisation of water and steam power to mechanise production. The Second occurred with the introduction of electricity to power mass production. The Third involved the application of electronics and information technology to automate production.

> Now a Fourth Industrial Revolution is building on the Third, the digital revolution that has been occurring since the middle of the last century. It is characterized by a fusion of technologies that is blurring the lines between the physical, digital, and biological spheres. . . . The Fourth is evolving at an exponential rather than a linear pace. Moreover, it is disrupting almost every industry in every country. And the breadth and depth of these changes herald the transformation of entire systems of production, management, and governance.[2]

Chinese Internet-based businesses have grown faster and with greater momentum than those in the West, overtaking or incorporating traditional industries, with a trend to grow into the international business arena. Although Chinese Internet businesses began by learning from or imitating American Internet giants, including Amazon, Google, eBay, Yahoo, Uber and Facebook, these Chinese companies have recast themselves into different species and managed to outdo their American counterparts, fending off their potential inroads into China's e-commerce markets.

The development of Internet-based industry has been strongly supported by the Chinese government. At the 12th National People's Congress in 2013, Chinese prime minister Li Keqiang introduced the Internet Plus (Internet + traditional industry) policy, whose objective was to 'integrate mobile Internet, cloud computing, big data and the Internet of Things with modern manufacturing to encourage the healthy development of ecommerce'. On 4 July 2015 the State Council issued its *Guiding Opinions on Actively Promoting the 'Internet Plus' Action Plan*, stating the aim to achieve rapid, high-quality economic growth and industrial development. In line with Chinese government policy, China's economy is moving towards becoming one characterised by Internet Plus, with far-reaching implications for international businesses.

Many business leaders and entrepreneurs have failed to recognise the strategic and managerial implications of Internet-based business. The Internet has been seen as a domain of sophisticated and complicated technology or simply a marketing tool, which should be dealt with by marketing professionals. Jack Ma, the founder of Alibaba, has identified a five-stage evolutionary process which many business leaders and entrepreneurs of traditional enterprises have undergone while failing to follow the tidal wave or *shi* of Internet Plus:

(1) Failing to see: These traditional enterprises simply did not see that the Internet was about to make an impact on their existing businesses.
(2) Disdaining Internet-based business: They witnessed the emergence of the Internet, but believed that it was a children's game without future prospects, compared with traditional businesses which were on solid ground.

(3) Failing to understand: They were unable to figure out how TV companies could sell their products at prices lower than production costs, why taxi companies would subsidise passengers' fares or why some e-laundry companies were willing to collect a large pack of dirty washing for a much lower price than offline laundry shops.
(4) Failure to follow: They saw that Internet companies had started to take away their market share, so tried to incorporate the Internet into their own businesses, but failed to catch up with the pioneers.
(5) Acting too late: It was soon too late to do anything about incorporating the Internet into their existing business; they lost their businesses completely to the newcomers and had to close them down.[3]

In the autumn of 2016, I ran a workshop on doing business in China, as part of which I took the participants, executive MBAs from a major business school, on a visit to a leading Chinese Internet company that offers a platform for B2C and O2O (online to offline) businesses, with offline shopping malls nationwide. Having listened to an introduction to the company by a vice president and visited one of its shopping malls, some students commented that they had never seen anything like what this company was doing; it was an eye-opening experience. Some participants even approached the company to learn more about its business after the end of the workshop.

Internet Plus and m-commerce (mobile commerce), whereby goods and services are bought and sold using wireless handheld devices, will increasingly penetrate many parts of the Chinese economy and society, rewriting the rules of the game in most industries. Textbooks in many subject areas at business schools will need to be rewritten, because the existing theories and models of traditional industry will have been rendered irrelevant or obsolete by e-commerce.

Nobody is certain what will happen in terms of the real impact of e-commerce on traditional industry. In 2012, receiving an award for his business achievements on a China Central Television programme, Jack Ma conveyed good news and bad news to captains of China's retail industry: the good news was that e-commerce companies might not succeed in replacing all offline retailers, but the bad news was that they would certainly supplant most of them.[4] In the introduction to the Alibaba Annual Report 2015 as executive chairman of the group, he predicts that within ten years, over 50 per cent of China's consumption will be conducted online.[5] The founder of Suning Commerce Group, a leading Chinese retailer, has made similar predictions regarding the influence of e-commerce on traditional industry: The Internet will pervade all walks of life like the air itself, so all industries and enterprises must be connected via the Internet. No future retailer will be able to operate offline only, nor indeed online only; they must all integrate online with offline.[6]

Internet Plus and m-commerce are making classic strategic and management theories inapplicable to the new economy and society, requiring new concepts and models to guide students of business and management as well as practitioners. Anyone who aspires to leadership must understand, ride, borrow and create this *shi*. We have already seen that those who have failed to follow it, such as Nokia, Kodak and many other companies, have gone out of business.

There are three specific factors that necessitate the inclusion of this chapter:

(1) The Internet is a catalyst and strong force (*shi*) that has brought about and continues to create fundamental changes in business, society and technology, no matter whether one likes or understands it. It has already spawned a large number of business giants worldwide, caused the close-down of numerous businesses and created many others, including small and medium-sized ones. It is rewriting the rules of the game in the worldwide business arena.

(2) Despite the importance of the Internet and its impact on business, technology and society, e-business volumes have accounted only for about 15–20 per cent of global business. This means that there are still a large proportion of business leaders who have failed to understand it or act on it.

(3) Although Chinese companies are latecomers to e-business compared with those in Western developed economies, they have quickly got themselves into the game, surpassed many of their US counterparts and taken their place in the top league. China is already the world's largest online shopping market; a number of Chinese Internet companies are neck and neck with their US counterparts, catching up in technology and business size.

This chapter discusses what Chinese Internet-based business means in an economy and society that are undergoing fundamental changes, explains why Chinese online companies have, to date, developed much faster than in the rest of the world, analyses the strengths and weaknesses of Chinese companies and explores how Western companies might take advantage of this tidal wave or *shi*. In addition, readers may get some inspiration about how they could develop their own Internet Plus businesses.

The nature of 'connection' and e-commerce development in China

The concept of 'connection' or 'criss-cross circulation network' is embedded in Chinese culture, affecting its social, economic, health, transportation and military systems. China's policy of 'One Belt, One Road' seeks in essence to lay the foundations of global economic development through 'connections'.[7] As a Chinese saying goes, 'building the road is the first step to becoming rich'. From the viewpoint of Chinese medicine, the human body is criss-crossed by a network of 'meridians', which must be unimpeded for one to stay in good health.

In September 2016 China hosted the G20 Summit in the city of Hangzhou, Zhejiang Province. This was the first time that such an important meeting had taken place in China and also the largest international meeting that had ever been chaired by China, involving G20 members' heads of state or government, invited guests and representatives of international organisations such as the World Bank and the International Monetary Fund. The G20 countries account for 90 per cent of global GDP and 85 per cent of world trade. This was a historic milestone in terms of China's political and diplomatic impact on the world, with far-reaching economic and social implications. The theme and agenda of the G20 meeting set by the Chinese government reflected Chinese thinking. In the past, for instance, G20 meetings had tended to deal with current economic crises, whereas the Chinese government chose to focus on economic development as a way of easing global economic difficulties.

Beijing, Shanghai, Guangzhou, Tianjin and Shenzhen are classified as the first tier of Chinese cities, while Hangzhou is in the second tier. This classification is based on the degree of economic development and the services that each city provides to its surrounding region or neighbouring cities. One might wonder why such an important meeting was held in Hangzhou, rather than a first-tier city. The answer can be found from the summit theme laid out by Chinese president Xi Jinping: 'Toward an innovative, invigorated, interconnected and inclusive world economy'.

The world economy is currently characterised by a shortage of innovation, invigoration and momentum, while China's proposed economic direction may be what is needed to reconfigure the global economy. Not only is the global Internet giant Alibaba located in Hangzhou, but the city also represents what the summit theme was intended to achieve. Among other factors, Hangzhou is first and foremost where about one-third of China's e-business websites are headquartered, including the world's largest B2B platforms, the world's largest online retail platforms and the world's largest online payment platforms. Jack Ma decided to place Alibaba's headquarters in Hangzhou because he believes it embraces the innovative spirit, supports privately owned companies and is the home of many Internet talents. Attracted by its status as providing the most inclusive and tolerant business environment, all major Chinese e-business companies have established their bases there, examples being JD.com, Tencent and Baifubao, Baidu's online payment company. Most interestingly, Cisco has also located its China headquarters in Hangzhou, the first foreign company in the Global 500 to do so. Hangzhou can be seen as China's Silicon Valley for Internet companies.

Hangzhou is one of the most interconnected cities in the world. The Internet has increasingly become the driver of global economic development, connecting and interacting with different parts of the world. In November 2014, the neighbouring town of Wuzhen hosted the first World Internet Conference (WIC), where the global development of Internet business was discussed. The conference attracted top Internet scientists, developers, entrepreneurs, business leaders and international statesmen from over 100 countries as well as representatives of top high-tech companies including Microsoft, Samsung, Qualcomm, Alibaba, Baidu and Tencent. Since then, the WIC has become an annual event. On 16 November 2016, the third WIC opened in Wuzhen with the theme of 'Innovation-driven Internet development for the benefit of all – Building a community of common future in cyberspace'. Discussions at the conference focused on five main topics: the Internet economy, Internet innovation, Internet culture, cyberspace governance and global Internet cooperation. Wuzhen has become a global centre of Internet business.

At the Sixth Plenum of the 18th Communist Party of China Congress held in October 2016, President Xi Jinping set out the national cyber-development strategy, with the aim of building the nation into a strong cyber power. The amazing achievements which Chinese companies have made within a short spell of time reflect the nature of the strategic priority which the Chinese government has set and the compatibility between connectedness and Chinese culture. Therefore, it is essential for foreign companies to understand the nature and trends of Internet business in China and to anticipate its forthcoming impact on the global marketplace, ensuring their strategic readiness to meet the associated challenges.

In 2013 China overtook the United States to become the world's largest online retail market. A 2016 report by AT Kearney establishes China as the world's undisputed leader in e-commerce. In 2015, China's online sales of $672 billion accounted for 15.9 per cent of the country's total sales, compared with 7.3 per cent in the USA. With a 42 per cent annual growth in 2015, China's online share is projected to reach 30 per cent by 2018. Alibaba, with its major online retail platforms, Taobao and Tmall, handled more transactions than eBay and Amazon combined.

> China's November 'Singles Day' drew more sales than Black Friday, Thanksgiving, and Cyber Monday combined in the United States. Mobile commerce grew 140 percent to $334 billion, or roughly half of all online sales (compared to 22 percent in the United States). The rapid rise of e-commerce has turned China into a leading innovator in mobile payments. Alibaba's pioneering Alipay has more than 400 million registered users, Tencent's WeChat Pay has seamlessly integrated e-commerce and messaging with payments, and Apple Pay entered early in 2016.[8]

At the end of 2015, China had 690 million Internet users and 700 million smartphone owners,[9] ensuring favourable demand conditions and providing a national competitive advantage.[10] Of the world's top ten Internet companies in 2015, six were American and four Chinese: Google/Alphabet (USA, $373 billion), Alibaba (China, $233 bn), Facebook (USA, $226 bn), Amazon.com (USA, $199 bn), Tencent (China, $190 bn), eBay (USA, $73 bn), Baidu (China, $72 bn), Priceline.com (USA, $63 bn), Salesforce.com (USA, $49 bn) and JD.com (China, $48 bn). The Chinese Internet market is primarily dominated by Chinese companies.

A major development in China is the emergence of m-commerce. Each Chinese Internet user spends an average of 3.5 hours per day on a mobile device. More than 150 million Chinese consumers browse Alibaba's Taobao app daily. It has been noted that 'online luxury sales rose by 20% in 2015, nearly three times faster than the broader luxury market. Mobile is particularly important.

Searches for luxury brands conducted on smartphones are nearly twice those done on a desktop, and rose 44% in 2015.'[11]

Changing the rules of the Internet-based business game

How has Internet Plus changed the ways in which business is carried out, leading to the inevitable need to modify the models of strategy and marketing? These changes stem from how consumers receive, expose and process information about products and services and how companies interact with consumers:[12]

The customer rules

Although customer orientation has been advocated and practised in all market economies, many traditional companies have approached it half-heartedly or paid it only lip service, because of the perceived high cost of market or customer orientation. Because of the asymmetry of market information in traditional societies, consumers had difficulty in directly comparing options before making purchase decisions. In an e-commerce society, since shoppers are presented with the full range of products and brands, together with prices and customer ratings, without having to visit a shop, street or mall, companies have little choice but to deliver their products on customers' terms. With extensive options on shopping and delivering, consumers are greatly empowered. Free registration and timely and free delivery become normal. Companies have to be truly customer-oriented, giving all customers what they need and want. Customers now dictate what to deliver where, how and when.

Mass production and marketing are giving way to customised service. Consumers have an ever wider choice of products, while the costs of marketing and inventory have been greatly reduced. Consumers can put forward their own ideas about product design and functions. It is easy for an individual to call up a group of friends to influence a company's design, production and marketing decisions. China's Xiaomi is an example of a company which gets ideas about its product designs from its customers and upgrades its products on a weekly basis.

Time online

It is highly probable that a new word, 'onlinisation', indicating the status of being online or connected by the Internet, will be accepted soon. Smartphone users tend to remain online all the time, except when they sleep, with about 16 hours per day of browsing and reading various apps. They are exposed to market information much more rapidly, in much greater volume and with much more impact than non-users. While they are doing something else, they may receive information about products or services, scan apps and respond to those that interest them. More importantly, they are able to locate shops, restaurants, garages, removal services and so forth by using the location-based services, which meet their needs and wants more conveniently.

Fragmentation

The ways in which consumers receive information are fragmented: they may get information while they are waiting for friends, eating dinner or travelling in buses; they may conveniently look at their smartphones and use apps like WeChat and Weibo in China to browse relevant information.

The information that consumers receive has also become fragmented: Few now systematically scan newspapers, magazines, television channels, conferences or gatherings to gather information. Most find what they need and want from the mobile Internet, which is dictated by the way in which they receive information.

Furthermore, consumers' needs and wants are fragmented: their buying decisions may be triggered by messages or comments within social networking groups accessed via smartphones; in China such groups are quite common and active. For instance, there are groups interested in particular themes such as children's education, health care, military affairs and traditional Chinese culture; there are high school or university-based alumni groups; there are also professionally associated groups, such as in architecture, law, pharmaceuticals, consultancy, management and strategy; and there are simple friendship-based groups. People are bombarded daily with all kinds of information from these different groups, influencing their buying motivations and decisions.

Marginalisation of central locations

In the past, when making strategic decisions for retail business, the unhesitating advice would be 'location, location, location'. Any retail business would generally find it desirable to occupy a central location where large crowds would gather, walk, stroll and shop. This no longer holds in an Internet-based economy, where the viability and sustainability of e-tailing business is determined by the density of web traffic, that is the number of user visits or hits on the website per time unit, which is equivalent to footfall in a high street shop. For PC Internet businesses, Web traffic is everything; the name of the game is to collect hits or visits and allocate them. To enjoy a high volume of traffic is equivalent to being located in the centre of a busy town. In China, the three major Internet platform companies with the heaviest Web traffic are Baidu, Alibaba and Tencent, commonly known as BAT.

Disintermediation

In the past, in many service environments, intermediaries or agents were necessary to link customers with service providers, in order to achieve wide coverage and distribution efficiency. The Internet economy shortens the distance between consumers and manufacturers, which deal directly with their customers or use a single distributor with a simplified organisational structure, leading to a reduction in channel costs. Many service companies can be contacted directly by customers through their websites, from which the location of the service company can be easily found. In the case of the mobile Internet, many companies have adopted an Internet Plus format, acting as the intermediaries themselves, with their own apps.

Global reach

Having gained greater control of channels and more influence on product choice and design, consumers can nowadays purchase global brands outside their home countries while sitting at home. They expect the familiar experience of well-known brands at local prices. Traditional companies can have access to a much larger market without being hurt by regional economic downturns and with much lower transaction costs. They can deal with global and local customers simultaneously, with a flexible supply chain management system.

Impact of e-commerce on traditional industry

To understand the impact of e-commerce on traditional industry, it is necessary to exclude the Internet factor first and go back to the basic process of business, which consists of three parts: value creation, value communication and value utilisation, as shown in Figure 7.1.[13] No matter in what kind of society people live, a business needs to create value, generally including the design and production of goods, then to communicate the value to potential users, involving exchanges of information, cash and goods between sellers and buyers; finally, the value embedded in the goods must be utilised by the consumers, whose satisfaction is affected by the functions of the goods, their personal experience and the extent to which the goods match each user's personality.

With the introduction of e-commerce, the business process has been restructured. Figure 7.2 shows a model of the business process in which e-commerce plays a part.[14] The Internet business has first penetrated and reconfigured the value communication step.

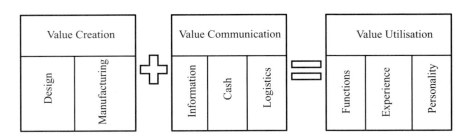

Figure 7.1 A model of traditional business process

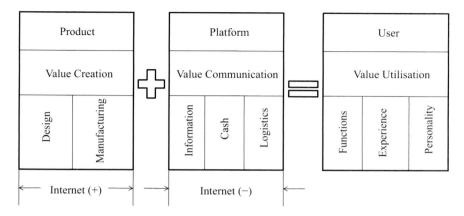

Figure 7.2 Two ways of Internet development: plus versus minus

In a platform business, buyers are situated on one side and sellers on the other, with zero distance between them. In this setting, there is no longer any role for traditional media such as television, radio, newspapers, billboards and direct mail, with their related communication modes such as advertising, sales promotion and public relations, since information can be communicated instantly, making these traditional services obsolete. E-commerce has restructured the media and advertising industries, forcing them to work with Internet companies to find ways of adding value in the new environment. For instance, with a decline in printed advertising revenues, many newspapers have either experienced closures and layoffs or gone online. In July 2009, it was reported that in the first half of that year in the USA alone, '105 newspapers have been shuttered. 10,000 news-paper jobs have been lost. Print ad sales fell 30% in Q1 '09. 23 of the top 25 newspapers reported circulation declines between 7% and 20%.'[15]

Let us take Alibaba as an illustrative example. Its Taobao and Tmall are plat-form businesses, which do not hold any inventory but provide services for other buyers and sellers to conduct transactions through these platforms. The difficulty in starting up a platform company is to get enough buyers on one side and sellers on the other; the number of buyers and sellers has to reach a 'critical mass' for the business to be viable and profitable. Many platform com-panies have failed because they have failed to attract enough buyers and sellers or sufficient Web traffic. Alibaba has survived and prospered because, apart from the important factor that Jack Ma's strategic mind has worked its magic, it has acquired investment from venture capital companies to help Alibaba to sustain the transitional period until it has attained the required critical mass. Most suc-cessful Internet Plus companies have been supported by venture capital com-panies, but there are many Internet entrepreneurs who have failed to reach the point of critical mass, leading to the early demise of their ventures.

Taobao consists of nine million storefronts run by small traders or individuals. Attracted by the site's huge user base, these 'micro merchants' choose to set up their stalls on Taobao in part because it costs them nothing to do so. Alibaba charges them no fees. But Taobao makes money – a lot of it – from selling advertising space, helping promote those merchants who want to stand out from the crowd.[16]

The essential role of e-commerce in the new business environment can be summarised as two parts: Internet Plus and Internet Minus, as shown in Figure 7.3. In a particular industry, at the stage of value creation, e-commerce has changed the landscape of industry by connecting users to manufacturers without any added cost, shaping how the industry is organised. This is seen as the '+' role played by e-commerce and hence is shown by the 'yang' side of the yin-yang symbol in Figure 7.3. At the stage of value communications, e-commerce reduces the distance and barriers between buyers and sellers, making communications more effective and efficient, as expressed on the 'yin' side in Figure 7.3.

The traditional retail industry has followed in the footsteps of the media industry, undergoing an increasing number of closures of retail shops worldwide. In January 2016, Walmart, the world's largest retailer, announced the closure of 269 stores and had already shut down 9 per cent of those in China. By 2016

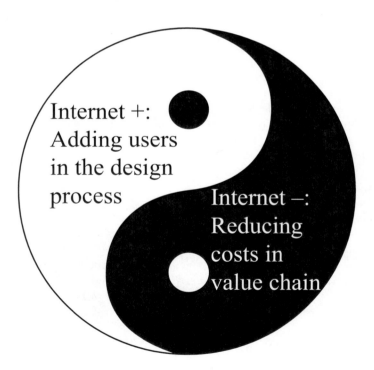

Figure 7.3 The role of e-commerce in users' value

a number of luxury retail stores had closed outlets: Louis Vuitton closed eight (but opened another two), Gucci closed five, Burberry two and Prada four. A 2016 report by Bain & Company states:

> Over the last four years, the country's e-commerce marketplace has grown at an annual rate of approximately 37 percent and generated revenues of nearly RMB 4 trillion, making China the world's largest e-commerce market. . . . Conversely, hypermarkets, which redefined China's retailing environment over the past decade, registered their first-ever drop in 2015, losing 0.2 percent value in the urban FMCG [fast-moving consumer goods] market as traffic dropped by 4.6 percent and volume per household sank by 4.7 percent. Super/mini stores didn't fare much better; growth plummeted from 9.5 percent to 4 percent last year.[17]

The primary role that e-commerce has played in retail business is that it eliminates the cost which is generated from the asymmetry of information between sellers and buyers. For instance, Alibaba's Taobao allows an individual or a business to open an e-shop on its website free of charge. On the other side, a potential buyer can open an account to search or browse products based on the criteria of price, credibility and popularity. The buyer is able to see the same product offered by different sellers, including individuals or retailers. By the end of 2011, Taobao had about 500 million registered users and 60 million hits daily, with over 800 million listed products. On Singles Day, 11 November 2016, the transaction value on Alibaba's Tmall reached RMB 120.7 billion (about $17.8 billion).

E-commerce has also exerted a significant impact on China's inefficient banking industry, putting great pressure on it to reform. The sector has been dominated by the 'Big Four': the Industrial and Commercial Bank of China (ICBC), Bank of China, the Construction Bank and the Agricultural Bank of China, controlling 70 per cent of the market. Traditionally, these banks offered low rates of interest, sometimes even lower than the rate of inflation. It was Alibaba's Yu'e Bao, an online mutual fund launched in 2013, that first upset the balance of China's stagnant financial service industry.

> Alibaba set no limits on the amount customers could deposit. Not only were the rates it offered much higher than the bank – as much as two percentage points higher – but Yu'e Bao allowed customers to make withdrawals at any time without penalty. . . . By February 2014, Yu'e Bao had attracted over $93 billion from 809 million investors, more than the combined total accounts of all other money managers in China.[18]

Having operated for only ten months, Yu'e Bao ranked the world's fourth largest money manager, following closely behind the American fund giants Vanguard, Fidelity and J.P. Morgan. With access to the complete trading history of its customers, Alibaba is in a far better position than traditional banks to evaluate individual credit risk. The company has subsequently also launched other financial services, including an Internet-only bank known as MYbank, wealth management, peer-to-peer (P2P) lending and insurance.

Three models of Internet business

The emergence of Internet business eliminates the distance between buyers and sellers. The elimination of distance between users and manufacturers gives rise to C2B relationships, eliminating the distance between online and offline brings about O2O business and the elimination of distance between users engenders C2C business. Figure 7.4 shows these three models of Internet business.[19]

Consumer to business: C2B denotes that the product design and manufacturing are dictated by consumers; more often than not, the purchase is completed before the product is made, with specific requirements for the company to design and manufacture it. Thus, fundamental changes have to take place and market orientation has to be wholeheartedly adopted, notwithstanding concerns regarding its cost compared with a production or sales orientation. In the context of Internet business, because of the elimination of information asymmetry, any inadequacies in terms of product design or functions will be quickly noted and penalised. Furthermore, with Internet connections, designs predominantly based on customers' suggestions can be easily carried out without incurring significant costs. China's Xiami, a major smartphone company, has successfully implemented such an approach.

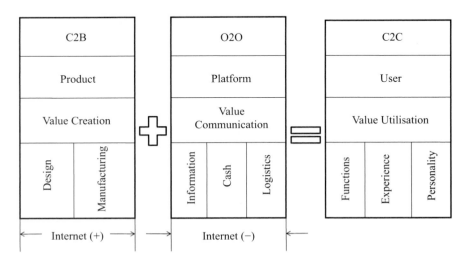

Figure 7.4 Three Internet-based business models: C2B, O2O and C2C

Online to offline: The **O2O** type of business integrates online businesses with offline physical (bricks and mortar) stores; it utilises online business to undertake marketing and communications, and offline to provide consumers with a physical experience before they make a purchase. Companies with integrated online and offline setups can gain loyal customers by providing them with such experience on their terms. There are two kinds of O2O businesses, that is 'Internet +' and '+ Internet'. The first starts up as a pure Internet business; following the successful development of its online business, it expands into the offline space with physical shops or malls. China's Jingdong Mall (JD.com), one of the largest e-tailers in the world, is such a company and has become the industry standard in China, with the best ratio of quality to price. The second kind originates with an existing physical retailer that develops Internet businesses to be integrated with its offline stores. Examples are Tesco, Walmart and China's Suning Commerce Group, one of the largest retailers in China, with 1600 stores around 700 cities in mainland China, Hong Kong and Japan; all of these firms have successfully incorporated online business with their existing offline ones.

Customer to Customer[20]: **C2C**, which is also known as consumer to consumer or peer to peer (P2P),[21] indicates the business involving the creation of trade between large numbers of fragmented sellers and buyers through C2C platforms. It was pioneered in the USA by eBay in 1995; since then, numerous platform companies have followed suit.

> Companies such as eBay, Etsy, and Airbnb allow thousands of sellers to experiment with prices, selling mechanisms, and advertising strategies. Finance platforms such as Prosper and Kickstarter use a variety of public good mechanisms to enable individuals to collectively fund loan or project investments. Labor markets such as Upwork and TaskRabbit allow buyers to run small-scale procurement auctions for specialized tasks. Businesses such as Instacart and Uber use centralized mechanisms to assign workers to jobs, but these mechanisms also rely on market forces.[22]

The essence of C2C business development is disintermediation, allowing fragmented individuals or suppliers to find buyers at minimum cost without going through intermediaries. China's C2C lender Ppdai.com, founded in 2007, was among the first online platforms in the country to offer C2C unsecured loans. By the end of 2015, about 12.1 million users had registered, with a 98 per cent geographical coverage of the country. It is unquestionably the market leader in China.

The first step in a Ppdai.com transaction is taken by a prospective borrower, who specifies the desired amount to be borrowed and supplies materials such as financial credentials, credit references or a credibility report to establish his or her credibility with potential lenders; the borrower also specifies an acceptable rate of interest on the loan. If enough lenders are willing to accept these terms and to lend the sum requested between them, the transaction can be completed.

The competitiveness of Chinese e-commerce companies

The Internet is a product of US science and technology during the Cold War. Concerned about the possibility of a nuclear war, the US government sought ways to maintain communications within its military complex. Considering the vulnerability to enemy attack of any centrally located communication system, the Rand Corporation worked on the idea of a communication system with neither a central location nor a central authority and which would continue to work in chaotic situations. During a nuclear-war scenario, information would find its way, without fixed routes, to its destination. The earliest form of such a system was known as ARPANET, its nodes being formed by the high-speed supercomputers of the time. The first such node was installed at the University of California in 1969 as part of a military project, then later separated from the ARPANET to follow its own developmental path. The ARPANET evolved exponentially into several different communication networks, one of which was the Internet, which began to be widely used in the USA in the mid-1980s.

Among the pioneering Internet companies in the USA, Yahoo and Amazon were both founded in 1994; in the same year in China, the first Internet connection with the USA was established for the purpose of academic exchange. eBay, which was founded in 1995, has unquestionably become the market leader in C2C and B2C businesses and embodies an e-commerce model that has been imitated by many followers, including Chinese Internet companies. In 1997, three Chinese Internet companies made their debuts: Sohu, NetEase and Stone Rich Sight, the predecessor of Sina.com; these may be considered to constitute the first generation of Chinese Internet companies. It is, however, the second generation that can truly be said to have worked Internet miracles: Baidu dominates the search market, connecting people with information, Alibaba the e-commerce market, linking people with merchandise, and Tencent the messaging market, networking between people. Each of these giants controls a different sector of the Internet market.

China's Internet economy has developed at surprising speed and gathered great momentum. Chinese Internet companies may have started as latecomers, copying the US pioneers, but the latter can now be said to be learning from their erstwhile imitators.

> China's tech industry – particularly its mobile businesses – has in some ways pulled ahead of the United States. Some Western tech companies, even the behemoths, are turning to Chinese firms for ideas . . . The shift suggests that China could have a greater say in the global tech industry's direction . . . China's largest internet companies are the only ones in the world that rival America's in scale.[23]

The emergence of the Internet appears to be an invaluable natural endowment, delivering what China needs desperately, in that (1) the Internet makes up the areas which have been severely underdeveloped or inadequate in China, such as traditional retailing, banking and organisation; (2) it fully utilises a unique Chinese natural resource, its huge population, which provides the scale to nourish e-commerce, where the greater the number of users, the stronger is the advantage that an Internet company can gain; and (3) it is intrinsically compatible with Chinese culture. Each of these factors is now explained in turn.

(1) Before the e-commerce era, China's retail industry had struggled; few Chinese retailers were competitive against foreign retail giants such as Walmart and Carrefour. This impediment arose partially from the Chinese inability to organise large-scale businesses requiring seamless coordination and teamwork, and partially from the outlandishly high cost of urban land, making large-scale retailing uncompetitive without the compensation of efficient value chain management.

> Jack [Ma] has likened e-commerce to a 'dessert' in the United States, whereas in China it is the 'main course.' Why? Shopping in China was never a pleasurable experience. Until the arrival of multinational companies like Carrefour and Walmart, there were very few retailing chains or shopping malls. Most domestic retailers started as state-owned enterprises (SOEs). With access to a ready supply of financing, provided by local governments or state-owned banks, they tended to view shoppers as a mere inconvenience.[24]

In China, a large proportion of government income has come from land, which often accounts for as much as a quarter of its fiscal revenue. Having the power to decide the price of land, the government depends on taxes and fees in relation to the selling of land. On one hand, existing retail businesses struggle for profitability, and any successful offline retailer is more than likely to face a rent increase when its lease is up for renewal, driving its business online. On the other hand, traditional retailers are reluctant to invest in marketing, customer service, human resources and logistics, producing a vicious circle in which offline retailing performs less and less well.

The underdevelopment of the traditional retail industry in China means that online is often the only place for Chinese shoppers in small and medium-sized cities to buy certain foreign brands, while these brands are easily available from both traditional retailers and e-retailers in developed economies. In particular, Alibaba's Taobao and Tmall host more than 80 per cent of e-commerce transactions in China, allowing consumers to buy goods from different retailers via a single account with Tmall or Taobao. It is more than likely that

> China is now a more advanced economy than most richer countries. And that would be in the sense of having leapfrogged retail development, missing out much of the stage of bricks and mortar based retailing. This isn't unusual, it comes under the heading of perhaps path dependence in

economics, possibly even of technological drag . . . Just as late adoption of a technology can allow you to leapfrog, so adoption too early can lock you into a less than optimal technology.[25]

In e-commerce, the absence of rental cost makes a major difference in cost/price competitiveness, attracting the interest of a great many shoppers. On the other hand, the abundant and inexpensive human resources consisting of the logistics part of e-commerce make the overall costs and thus prices of merchandise competitive. For instance, in a big city, a shop will deliver a bottle of water to a consumer without a significant addition to the price, while a package can be delivered within 24 hours at a cost of one US dollar. Furthermore, the inefficient banking system has made it difficult for many Chinese consumers to acquire credit cards, whereas goods can be easily purchased through the Taobao or Tmall platforms using an e-payment system such as Alibaba's Alipay, which can be secured without difficulty.

In China, most Internet companies have taken the form of 'Internet +', that is a company has started from an online business, then taken over traditional businesses or built new offline shops to outdo existing offline retailers. This type of development entails more innovation, creating disruption, commotion or demolition of the retail industry. Taobao, Tmall and JD.com are cases in point. In contrast, US Internet businesses take the form of '+ Internet', whereby traditional retailers have incorporated online business to work with their offline ones, without major interruption or destruction of the existing retail industry. Among the top 25 US Internet companies, 18 are traditional brick-and-mortar retailers that have built their online arms over the past five years, including Walmart, Apple, Macy's, Nordstrom, Target, Gap and Neiman Marcus.

(2) As explained previously, in e-commerce, where a business is set up has an insignificant impact on its performance, location being peripheral; instead, Web traffic or visits will determine the viability of the e-business: the greater the number of visits, the lower the cost and the higher the profit. Web traffic is equivalent to the number of visitors to the business, reflecting the economies of scale. For instance, the cost of developing a website or an app remains the same no matter how many people visit or use it, while the scale makes a big difference to the marginal yield. This is why it would be difficult for a small country to develop a globally competitive platform business.

> Manufacturing industry is based on making physical products, whereas the Internet industry depends on communications, with a unified language underlying the successful development of the industry. The USA has a population of 300 million and English is its common language, laying the foundation for its Internet industry. Although the EU has about 500 million inhabitants, its linguistic fragmentation presents a significant barrier to the development of Europe-wide Internet business. Given its population of over 1.3 billion with a common

written language, China is well positioned to recoup its investment in the Internet industry.

(3) In many consumer and industrial goods industries in China, foreign brands either dominate or play a substantial part. However, in China's e-commerce market, major US Internet companies have failed to gain a strategic foothold. Alibaba and JD.com have established themselves among the largest e-business players in the world. While Expedia sold its majority share in eLong.com to Ctrip.com, the leading Chinese online travel agency, eBay's acquisition of EachNet went badly: it started with 90 per cent of China's market share, but this declined to only 10 per cent three years later. Having spent about $1 billion in China's e-hailing taxi market, Uber ended by withdrawing from the Chinese market to become a minority shareholder in Didi. Facebook and Twitter have yet to work out ways of entering the Chinese market.

Since communications, not tangible products, underlie Internet business, the branding effect, which is rated highly by Chinese consumers, is immaterial. A product bought from eBay's platform does not give a Chinese consumer more brand value than its price, nor does the use of Google for a job search make the user more proud. Without the attraction of flashy foreign brands, Chinese consumers simply go for the platforms that provide the best value for money. US Internet subsidiaries have failed in China because either ideas or standardisation operations have been imposed from their headquarters on local operations, making them uncompetitive against Chinese Internet companies, examples being eBay and Yahoo. In other words, Internet business is also cultur-ally bound in China; success or failure depends to a great extent on how well the company satisfies consumers' special needs and wants.

Operating on the pattern of Internet Plus business, firms are required to develop or adopt new management thinking, organisational culture and struc-ture, and human resource management, while the *yin-yang* doctrine embedded in Chinese culture imposes much less of a barrier to Chinese firms compared with the difficulty that their Western counterparts have in overcoming the inertia of existing rigid business structures.

Alibaba: the tiger in China's Internet jungle

Since many readers may be unfamiliar with the development and operation of Chinese e-commerce, it will be helpful to examine the case of Alibaba, China's leading Internet player.

> Alibaba has a much greater impact on China's retail sector than Amazon does in the United States. Thanks to Taobao and its sister site, Tmall, Ali-baba is effectively China's largest retailer. Amazon, by contrast, only became one of the top ten retailers in America in 2013.[26]

The Alibaba Group was founded by Jack Ma, a former English teacher, in 1999. Its debut on the New York Stock Exchange in 2014 was the world's largest ever IPO, raising $25 billion. At the end of 2015, having 34,000 employees, 350 million active buyers in its marketplace and tens of millions of small and medium-sized businesses operating on its platforms, the group generated RMB 2.44 trillion (about $354 billion) GMV.[27] Meanwhile, with over 289 million monthly mobile active users and RMB 1 trillion ($145 billion) annual mobile GMV, Alibaba is also unquestionably the world's number one mobile Internet company.[28] The company's competitive advantage is underpinned by three pillars, also known as Alibaba's 'iron triangle': e-commerce, logistics and finance,[29] as shown in Figure 7.5.

The e-commerce pillar

Alibaba's e-commerce business consists of two arms: (1) Business-to-business, including Alibaba.com, 1688 and AliExpress; (2) business-to-consumer (Tmall. com) and consumer-to-consumer (Taobao.com). Alibaba.com, an English-language e-commerce platform, was founded by Jack Ma in 1999, with the aim of helping small and medium-sized businesses to find customers and suppliers without the need for costly intermediaries. It is now the world's largest B2B online platform for global wholesale trade, linking millions of buyers and

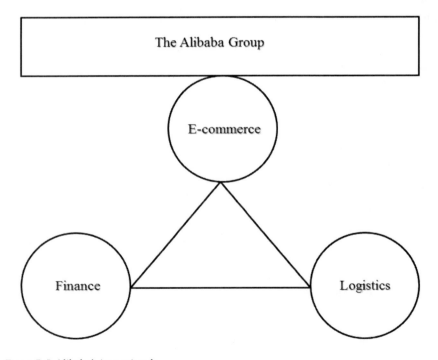

Figure 7.5 Alibaba's iron triangle

suppliers all round the world. Sellers on the site offer all kinds of products, including health and beauty, apparel, electronics, agriculture and food, industrial parts and tools. In the same year, Alibaba introduced a Chinese-language portal, 1688.com, for domestic B2B trade, connecting domestic wholesalers with domestic retailers. In Chinese, '1688' is pronounced '*yao liu ba ba*', which sounds like 'Alibaba'. Noticing a gap in the online wholesale market between Alibaba.com and 1688.com for low-quantity trading, Jack Ma then launched AliExpress.com, allowing smaller international buyers to purchase small quantities of goods from Chinese wholesalers online at wholesale prices.

Taobao was founded in 2003 to offer a C2C marketplace for small businesses and individual entrepreneurs to conduct business in Chinese-speaking regions and elsewhere. Taobao, literally meaning 'digging for treasure', is now China's largest C2C online shopping platform.

> You can buy pretty much anything on Taobao – China's version of eBay and its biggest online trading platform. The only catch is you need to be able to read and write Chinese. By geographical default, Taobao is a made-in-China bonanza where you can snap up everything from inconspicuous everyday items like clothes and furniture to more incongruous things such as wedding flip-flops – for the casual bride – or a bouncy castle in the shape of the sinking Titanic.[30]

There are tens of millions of shop-fronts run by small businesses or individuals, who are attracted to the site by its vast user base and the fact that setting up operations costs nothing. Although Alibaba does not charge its platform users any fees, Taobao still makes substantial money from selling advertising space to those merchants who are keen to stand out against other sellers on the website.

Apart from Taobao's customer-orientated actions, Jack Ma has also relied on the deployment of two main stratagems to enhance its chance of success. First, the Taobao website was launched with the maximum of secrecy, which blinded not only its competitors but also Alibaba's own employees who were not involved in the Taobao project. Second, its chief competitor eBay was misled, failing to note the arrival of a new rival who was about to disrupt the industry. Jack Ma commented on eBay's reaction to Taobao before the product launch: 'eBay didn't consider us their rival. They didn't even think that we could be their rival. They thought, We haven't even heard about Alibaba. Such a strange name. Chinese all know what tao bao means, foreigners don't.'[31]

Introduced into the market in 2010, Tmall.com is a B2C platform that allows brands to sell their goods and services directly to consumers in the Chinese-language regions, including mainland China, Taiwan, Hong Kong and Macau. In Chinese, the site's name is pronounced '*tian mao*', meaning 'sky cat'; its black cat logo contrasts with Taobao's alien doll. Taobao can be compared to the largest garage sale in the world, while Tmall is equivalent to the largest flashy shopping mall. The companies that have established stores on the platform range from luxury brands such as Estee Lauder, Burberry, Zara, Calvin Klein and Hugo Boss to purveyors of consumer goods such as Sainsbury's, Macy's and Costco. 'Unlike Taobao, which is free for buyers and sellers, merchants pay commissions to Alibaba on the products they sell on Tmall, ranging from 3 to 6 per cent depending on the category.'[32] In 2015, Tmall generated $136 billion GMV for Alibaba, hosting 50,000 storefronts with over 70,000 brands. Tmall and Taobao account for about 80 per cent of Alibaba's total sales.[33]

In February 2014, Alibaba launched Tmall Global, with the aim of encouraging major foreign brands to enter China's e-commerce market. As a cross border e-commerce platform, Tmall Global is based in Hong Kong, attracting the particular interest of those foreign brands that do not already have a presence in the market. It is the largest B2C platform that links foreign merchants with Chinese consumers by allowing foreign brands to set up an e-storefront on the platform, so that Chinese consumers can have direct access to brands. Tmall Global mainly targets and serves high-end customers.

Any merchant who wants to sell on Tmall must be a legal entity, an organisation, an official manufacturer or a registered brand, providing goods or services to end consumers. When opening an e-store on Tmall, the merchant needs to present all appropriate documentation to establish reliability, genuineness and the existence of the entity. This process is intended to eliminate the risk of unprincipled sellers with products of dubious quality trading on Tmall. Alibaba pledges that all goods on Tmall are official and authentic.

Nevertheless, the counterfeiting of goods remains a serious problem in China and a challenge to Alibaba. In May 2016, the company was suspended from the International Anti-Counterfeiting Coalition because a number of top brands withdrew from the group with concerns about counterfeit products being sold on its platforms. Despite the suspension, Alibaba continues to crack down on counterfeit goods and to work with governments, industry partners and brands in this effort. There is a realisation that combating counterfeiting is a complex industry-wide issue; it is technically difficult for Alibaba to prevent the sale of counterfeit goods, since it serves as a platform for sellers rather than as a manufacturer or merchant.[34] However, in a 2016 article in the *Wall Street Journal*, Jack Ma made his position clear:

> Counterfeit goods are absolutely unacceptable, and brands and their intellectual property must be protected. Alibaba is only interested in supporting those manufacturers who innovate and invest in their own brands. We have zero tolerance for those who rip off other people's intellectual property.[35]

The logistics pillar

In 2009, Jack Ma started the tradition of Singles Day as an unofficial Chinese holiday celebrating single people, to promote sales on its B2C platform Tmall. Known as the 'bare sticks holiday' in Chinese, based on how it looks numerically, Singles Day was initiated in the 1990s by university students in China, as a counterpart to the Western Valentine's Day. It is now the world's largest online shopping festival: $14.3 billion worth of goods were sold in 24 hours in 2015, rising to $17.8 billion in 2016. All of this would have been impossible without an efficient logistics system. This year, the logistics company founded by Alibaba as its major shareholder, Cainiao, facilitated the delivery of 657 million packages, involving 1.7 million couriers and postal workers from 5000 warehouses to Chinese and international customers worldwide. Cainiao is one of the three pillars of Alibaba's success.

After two years of planning and discussion with potential consortium partners, a new company, Cainiao Network Technology Co. Ltd, was launched in 2013, with Alibaba owning 48 per cent of its shareholding. Cainiao – whose name has the connotation of 'rookie' in Chinese, implying that one needs to continually learn and grow – is designed to manage the creation of a nationwide express logistics platform, China Smart Logistics Network. The platform links a network of logistics providers, warehouses and distribution centres in order to attain higher efficiency in China's logistics industry.

> By investing in Cainiao, Alibaba aims to lock in vital relationships with its logistics partners while finding outside investors to fund the expansion of the networks themselves. Cainiao neither owns the physical infrastructure of the networks nor employs the personnel who make the deliveries. Those assets are contributed by the consortium's members and partners, allowing Alibaba to pursue an 'asset–light' strategy.[36]

Cainiao works with 15 strategic logistics partners through China Smart Logistics, including SF Express, Shentong, Zhontong, Yuantong and Shanghai Yunda, as well as the Yintai Group and Fosun International. They jointly operate 1800 distribution centres, over 97,000 delivery stations and 20,000 Cainiao collection spots. In 2014, the delivery partners employed 1.5 million personnel in over 600 cities and 31 provinces. Having started to expand into the countryside, Cainiao now facilitates home delivery services in over 1200 rural locations nationwide.

The finance pillar

In 2004, Taobao had 4.5 million registered users and 4.9 million products were transacted, with a monthly GMV of RMB 160 million (about $26 million). In 2013, there was an average loss of $293 per person as a result of Internet fraud in the USA, whose financial system is well established. Given the underdeveloped financial system in China, fraud was a much more serious problem for e-commerce there than in the USA. Shoppers were not comfortable about making payment before the goods were received, while sellers were worried about not being paid if the goods were delivered first. Jack Ma realised the gravity of this impasse, believing that it would be imperative to resolve the Internet payment hurdle before China's e-commerce could take off. In late 2004, there were over 100 million Internet users, but few were willing to use e-commerce because of the problems of trust, payment and logistics. A study at the time found that 42.3 per cent of Internet users were concerned about security in e-commerce and 36.8 per cent about after-sales service.[37]

Alibaba's answer to the payment problem was the launch in 2014 of Alipay, a third-party online payment platform with an escrow service, whereby the buyer makes the payment to Alipay, which holds it until the buyer confirms receipt of the goods with satisfaction, then releases it to the seller. Alipay was well suited for China's underdeveloped banking system, under which few consumers held credit cards, while there was a high level of distrust between buyers and sellers. Today, Alipay has become the leading third-party payment service, with a 58 per cent share of China's online payment market.

> Alibaba websites account for more than one-third of its revenues, but other sites also rely heavily on Alipay to process their online payments. People use Alipay to make money transfers, top up their cell phone accounts, and make cashless purchases using bar codes at retailers and restaurants, like KFC. Twenty percent of all Alipay transactions involve paying for utilities, such as water, electricity, and gas bills. Customers can also buy train tickets, pay traffic fines, or purchase insurance using Alipay, making it the de facto currency of an increasingly digital China.[38]

Having over 450 million users, Alipay has dominated China's online payment market, processing 153 million online transactions per day and $369 billion of Chinese online spending in 2015. Because of China's limited use of credit cards, unlike the USA where it is widespread, hundreds of millions of consumers have turned to smartphone apps including Alipay, making China the largest mobile-payment market in the world. In 2015, mobile transactions in China reached $235 billion, moving ahead of the $231 billion in the USA.

Alipay was later separated from Alibaba, becoming the largest asset of a domestic company under Jack Ma's control. The separation was in response to concerns that new regulations might affect its ability to be licensed for payments. Foreign-owned finance companies would have less opportunity to secure a licence than domestically owned ones, while Alibaba is registered overseas with foreign investors. Alipay accounts are linked to bank accounts in various Chinese banks, where users can transfer money to Alipay to pay bills, buy movie tickets or even hire a fake boyfriend for a social occasion. Internationally, Alipay is accepted by over 80,000 merchants in 70 countries.[39]

Alipay has become part of an umbrella holding company, Ant Financial, which also operates a money-market fund known as Yu'e Bao and an online bank called MYbank. Taking its name, Ant, from its roots in facilitating small merchants to sell their goods through Alibaba, Ant Financial has over 450 million active users. Both Ant Financial and Alibaba are controlled by Jack Ma.

> Alibaba has brought in a roster of state financial institutions as investors in Ant Financial. The $740 billion sovereign wealth fund China Investment Corp. and the country's national social security fund are now among its biggest shareholders after Ant Financial began introducing outside investors. Ant

Financial's latest round of fundraising gives it a roughly $60 billion valuation after it was previously valued at about $45 billion last year [2015].[40]

In 2004, in an effort to enhance communications between buyers and sellers, Alibaba created a personal computer-based instant messaging tool on Taobao, known as Aliwangwang, enabling online buyers to interact with sellers, authenticate products and bargain prior to purchase. Once buyer and seller have made a deal, Alipay as the escrow payment service provides consumer confidence in dealing with small merchants. After the transaction is concluded, the customer rates the vendor and releases payment. Aliwangwang has over 50 million users, making it the second largest instant messaging tool in China.

Summary

The emergence and development of Alibaba have crystallised the application of the Chinese strategic mind to Western technology and management. When the Internet and e-commerce began taking shape in the USA in the mid-1990s, Jack Ma, among others, foresaw the forthcoming Internet wave in China and the world. Shunning planning in favour of learning by doing, he started Alibaba in 1999, after a number of futile attempts to start up a business. The factors underlying his persistence in pursuing his dream are intrinsically embedded in Chinese culture.

(1) Ever since he initiated his venture, Jack Ma has had a vision that is in line with Tao: connecting small and medium-sized businesses worldwide and making Alibaba a world-class Internet business. In addition, he has followed Tao principles by showing great care for his colleagues and employees, concern for China's environment and a determination to crack down on counterfeiting.

(2) His actions are guided by Chinese strategic thinking, particularly the principles of yin and yang embedded in the *I Ching* and holism. He has often utilised the yin-yang symbol to illustrate his strategic ideas and has adapted his businesses to the environment whenever necessary, like water flowing to its destination over or round any barriers it encounters. For instance, to overcome the impediments of China's financial environment, where the availability of credit cards and confidence in credit tools have both been limited, he launched an escrow product, Alipay, essentially laying the foundation for the success of e-commerce in China. In addition, the development of Alibaba's logistics pillar, AliExpress and Aliwangwang reflects uniquely Chinese holistic thinking.

(3) Jack Ma's personality, passion and emotional intelligence have also played an important part in Alibaba's success. He has been nicknamed 'Jack Magic',[41] indicating his personal impact on the company. He has been recognised to have the ability to connect, attract and motivate other people, getting talents to work alongside him. In particular, his iron will has allowed him to bounce back from the various failures that he has experienced.

Box 7.1 examines the case of another Chinese twenty-first-century e-business success: Qijia.

Box 7.1   Qijia

Background

Qijia was founded by Huajin Deng on 11 March 2005 and is now the leading vertical e-business platform in home decoration, furniture and decorative products in China.

The company's name, Qijia, is derived from one of the Confucian Four Books, *The Great Learning*, with the meaning of putting one's home in order or harmony.

In 2014 Qijia had 33.4 per cent of market share in the vertical e-business platform business; in 2016, its sales network served 180 cities, with over 10 million users. It had over 40,000 brands, suppliers and service providers and 25,000 designers registered, providing customers with professional furnishing consultation and overseeing after-sales service.

Corporate management

Corporate Mission/Goal[42]: Provide customers with the best home decoration solutions.

> Management Philosophy: Serving customers sincerely with dedication to service.
> Management Focus: Cost, detail, efficiency and determination.
> Corporate Culture:
>
> > **Thankful**: Serving customers unreservedly with gratitude;
> > **Creative**: Embracing change with passion for service;
> > **Practical**: Focusing on the corporate mission with practicality;
> > **Respectful**: Being respectful of ourselves and others.

Key products and services

(1) In 2007, Qijia started to provide decorating services based on customer requirements. As a platform company, Qijia has to rely on third-party decorating companies to deliver these services. Therefore, it must address a major customer concern: 'What if my home decoration is completed and paid for, but the quality is not satisfactory?' In response, it launched a form of escrow service known as Qijia Bao, somewhat similar to Alibaba's Alipay. The decorating process is divided into five stages; after the completion of each stage, the work is inspected by professionals who are certified by authoritative

---

bodies and only if they approve it is 20 per cent of the total payment released. In this way, customer confidence and satisfaction are assured.

(2) Furniture and building materials are high-value products. No matter how perfect and beautiful online pictures might be, customers will not feel comfortable unless they can see and touch them. When people buy online based on photos, they will quite often return the goods. Customer experience has become a key issue for e-business in the industry. In 2008, Qijia addressed this by becoming an O2O platform company, offering an extensive offline display space, where customers can see, touch and feel the products in which they are interested, boosting their confidence and comfort before they place orders online. The O2O model is shown in Figure 7.6. The consumer experiences the goods in an offline mall, then places an order via the platform, which subsequently processes it. Upon completion of the transaction, the consumer can log in to Jia.com to rate and provide feedback on the goods and services received and to seek service support. Qijia has established offline malls in major cities nationwide. Each such space generally consists of three halls: one where customers can buy all kinds of building materials needed for house decoration; a furniture hall, displaying dining room, bedroom and living room furniture; and a brand sales space, where famous brands are displayed with huge discounts.

(3) In China's building material and home decoration markets, consumers once commonly encountered the following problems after making payment: the materials were not delivered on time; the wrong materials were received and the seller failed to dispatch the right

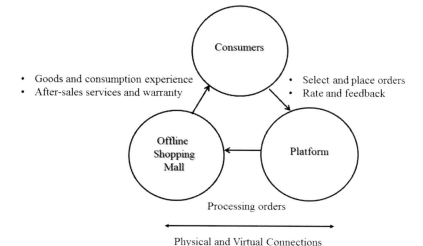

Figure 7.6 Qijia O2O (online to offline) model

ones in time; the quantities delivered differed from those ordered; the materials received were different from what the consumer saw on display; counterfeits were delivered, but the seller refused to acknowledge this; and materials were damaged during the decoration process, but the contractor did not attend to it. To compound the consumers' woes, there have not been any industrial or government regulations to adjudicate on these disputes, putting those who wanted to undertake a home decorative project at risk of major disappointment.

In early 2014, Qijia introduced a financial product known as Qijia Wallet, similar to Alibaba's Alipay, as the answer to the above problems. The Wallet is a free platform for customers' payment and financial services; as a form of escrow service, it has the functions of topping up, making payment and transferring money. With this instrument, the customer first makes the payment to Qijia Wallet, and then the seller dispatches the goods ordered; only when the customer is satisfied with the goods received is an instruction sent to Qijia Wallet to release the payment.

(4) In 2015, Qijia launched a new business platform: a total house decoration solution, also known as House Decoration 2.0, providing one-stop shopping in home decoration. Redefining standards for Internet decoration platforms, it integrates design, construction and building materials. Figure 7.7 shows how the total house decoration business model works.

- Qijia selects and trains designers to reach a high standard and utilises virtual reality technology to produce designs. A company designer first meets the customer and provides free consultation and sketches, then selects a third-party designer of good reputation and expertise on behalf of the customer. About 250,000 designers are registered on the Qijia platform.

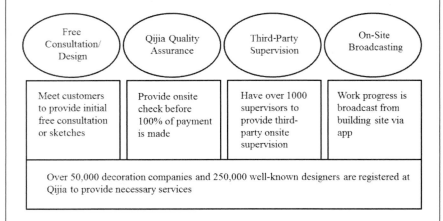

Figure 7.7 Qijia house decoration services

- Qijia selects construction teams for its customers based on 480 standard procedures, monitoring construction work through an enterprise resource planning (ERP) system to provide quality assurance. There are about 50,000 decoration companies available to be chosen to undertake construction work.
- The Qijia platform uses an F2C (factory to consumer) supply chain, where top brands can be ordered directly from factories with excellent quality/price value.
- Once a contract is signed, there are no top-up fees, which are often applied in traditional decoration business.
- Qijia provides an escrow payment system whereby the customer makes the payment to Qijia, which will not release it to the construction team until it has inspected the building work as being to its satisfaction.
- The construction work is monitored and inspected by experienced supervisors through five stages and broadcast through an app to which the customer has access.
- Qijia provides a five-year warranty for plumbing and electric power systems and a two-year warranty for other work.

Figure 7.8 shows a series of measures taken by Qijia to provide customers with quality assurance and value.

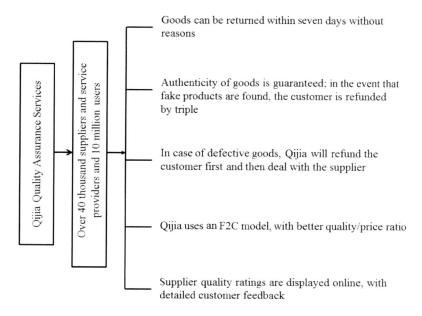

Figure 7.8 Qijia's quality assurance and value

Concluding remarks

Internet business occupies a unique position in China for four reasons:

(1) Traditional industry is inefficient and poorly organised, while e-business companies, particularly platform businesses, have connected traditional companies with hundreds of millions of customers without additional cost. It appears that the development of e-commerce is an answer to China's backward industries such as retail and banking.
(2) There is compatibility between e-commerce and Chinese culture, in that the process of developing e-business requires great flexibility and adaptability in linking people, goods, cash and information together, while the *yin-yang* doctrine embedded in Chinese culture provides fertile ground for e-commerce to grow.
(3) The size of the population is positively correlated with the conduciveness of e-commerce; the larger the better, as it reduces the unit cost for Internet developers. China's huge population affords Chinese Internet companies a natural competitive advantage. This is also why it is difficult for small countries to develop competitive platform businesses.
(4) The Chinese government has strongly supported the industry by creating a business environment that is conducive to e-commerce. In particular, increasingly embracing Internet thinking and practices, the government strongly promotes the development of Internet Plus as a matter of policy nationwide.

China's favourable environment for e-commerce has spawned a large number of entrepreneurs who have the qualities needed in Internet pioneers, such as vision, benevolence, courage, self-confidence, decisiveness and perseverance. They have, within a short period of time, built world-class Internet giants including Baidu, Alibaba, Tencent, Jingdong and more.

The rise of China's e-commerce has amplified the distinctiveness of Chinese business compared with the norms of Western strategy and management. In the environment of an Internet-based economy, Western strategic and organisational theories will be even wider of the mark if applied to China or by Chinese companies, requiring new theoretical guidelines and academic studies. Academic disciplines such as strategic management, general management, marketing, human resource management and economics all need to take the changes in industrial configuration into consideration and incorporate the impact of e-commerce in new theories and frameworks.

Notes

1 Liu, Y. (2015), *Hulianwang + zhanlueban: Chuantong qiye, hulianwang zhaitimen (The Internet + Strategy Assessment: Traditional Enterprises, the Internet Is Kicking at Your Door)*, Beijing: China Overseas Chinese Publishing House, p. 155.
2 Schwab, K. (2015), "The Fourth Industrial Revolution," *Foreign Affairs*, 12 December, www.foreignaffairs.com/articles/2015-12-12/fourth-industrial-revolution, retrieved on 9 October 2016.

3 Wang, J.B. and Peng, D. (2016), *Internet +: Self-Overthrow, Reorganization, Management Evolution and Transformation of Traditional Businesses*, Beijing: China Machine Press, pp. 39–40.

4 Liu, Y. (2015), *Hulianwang+zhanlueban: Chuantong qiye, hulianwang zhaitimen (The Internet + Strategy Assessment: Traditional Enterprises, the Internet Is Kicking at Your Door)*, Beijing: China Overseas Chinese Publishing House, p. 127.

5 Ma, J.Y. (2015), "Letter From Executive Chairman Jack Ma," *Alibaba Group 2015 Annual Report*, Alibaba Group, http://ar.alibabagroup.com/2015/letter.html, retrieved on 21 November 2016.

6 Liu, Y. (2015), *Hulianwang+zhanlueban: Chuantong qiye, hulianwang zhaitimen (The Internet + Strategy Assessment: Traditional Enterprises, the Internet Is Kicking at Your Door)*. Beijing: China Overseas Chinese Publishing House, p. 142.

7 There may be an underlying political agenda on the part of the Chinese government, to reduce political conflict and create a harmonious society among different countries.

8 Ben-Shabat, H., Moriarty, M., Kassack, J. and Torres, J. (2016), "Global Retail Expansion at a Crossroads," 2016 Global Retail Development Index™, AT Kearney, www.atkearney.com/consumer-products-retail/global-retail-development-index/full-report/-/asset_publisher/oPFrGkbIkz0Q/content/global-retail-expansion-at-a-cross roads/10192, retrieved on 20 November 2016.

9 McKinsey & Company (2016), "The CEO Guide to China's Future," *McKinsey Quarterly*, September 2016, www.mckinsey.com/global-themes/china/the-ceo-guide-to-chinas-future, retrieved on 9 November 2016.

10 Porter, M.E. (1990), *The Competitive Advantage of Nations*, New York: Free Press. According to Porter, a nation's competitiveness depends on its industrial capacity for innovation and upgrade, depending in turn on four broad attributes: factor conditions, demand conditions, related and supporting industries, and firm strategy, structure and rivalry. China's demand conditions in the Internet sector advantage Chinese e-commerce companies.

11 Zheng, A.J. (2016), "Luxury Brands Step Up Shift to Digital in China," *The Wall Street Journal*, 20 June, http://blogs.wsj.com/chinarealtime/2016/06/20/luxury-brands-step-up-shift-to-digital-in-china/, retrieved on 21 November 2016.

12 The following are described mainly based on what has happened in China, but they may have implications in Western countries as well.

13 Liu, Y. (2015), *Hulianwang+zhanlueban: Chuantong qiye, hulianwang zhaitimen (The Internet + Strategy Assessment: Traditional Enterprises, the Internet Is Kicking at Your Door)*. Beijing: China Overseas Chinese Publishing House, p. 55.

14 Ibid, p. 61.

15 Dumpala, P. (2009), "The Year The Newspapers Died," *Business Insider*, 4 July. www.businessinsider.com/the-death-of-the-american-newspaper-2009-7?IR=T, retrieved on 15 November 2016.

16 Clark, D. (2016), *Alibaba: The House That Jack Ma Built*. New York: HarperCollins Publishers, p. 5.

17 Bain & Company (2016), *China Shopper Report 2016*, 28 June, Bain & Company, www.bain.com/about/press/press-releases/china-shopper-report-2016.aspx, retrieved on 15 November 2016.

18 Clark, D. (2016), *Alibaba: The House That Jack Ma Built*, New York: HarperCollins Publishers, p. 20.

19 Liu, Y. (2015), *Hulianwang+zhanlueban: Chuantong qiye, hulianwang zhaitimen (The Internet + Strategy Assessment: Traditional Enterprises, the Internet Is Kicking at Your Door)*, Beijing: China Overseas Chinese Publishing House, p. 77.

20 They are also known as consumer to consumer or peer to peer (P2P).

21 Plouffe, C.R. (2008), "Examining 'peer-to-peer' (P2P) Systems as Consumer-to-Consumer (C2C) Exchange," *European Journal of Marketing*, 42 (11/12), 1179–1202.

22 Einav, L., Farronato, C. and Levin, J. (2016), "Peer-to-Peer Markets," *The Annual Review of Economics*, 8, 615–635.

23   Mozur, P. (2016), "China, Not Silicon Valley, Is Cutting Edge in Mobile Tech," *The New York Times*, 2 August, www.nytimes.com/2016/08/03/technology/china-mobile-tech-innovation-silicon-valley.html?smid=tw-nytimes&smtyp=cur, retrieved on 28 August 2016.

24   Clark, D. (2016), *Alibaba: The House That Jack Ma Built*, New York: HarperCollins Publishers, p. 8.

25   Worstall, T. (2015), "Extraordinary Number: Jack Ma Claims That Alibaba Handles 12% of All Chinese Domestic Purchasing," *Forbes*, 14 October 2015, www.forbes.com/sites/timworstall/2015/10/14/extraordinary-number-jack-ma-claims-that-alibaba-handles-12-of-all-chinese-domestic-purchasing/#436883095468, retrieved on 21 November 2016.

26   Clark, D. (2016), *Alibaba: The House That Jack Ma Built*, New York: HarperCollins Publishers, p. 4.

27   GMV, i.e. gross merchandise volume, is a term used to indicate total sales value in online retailing for merchandise sold through a particular marketplace over a certain timeframe.

28   Zhang, D.Y. (2015), "Letter From CEO Daniel Yong Zhang," *Alibaba Group 2015 Annual Report*, Alibaba Group, http://ar.alibabagroup.com/2015/letter.html, retrieved on 21 November 2016.

29   Clark, D. (2016), *Alibaba: The House That Jack Ma Built*, New York: HarperCollins Publishers, p. 5.

30   Rowe, D. (2016), "The 10 Strangest Things on Taobao, China's Biggest Online Trading Platform," *Time*, 22 September 2016, http://time.com/4502415/taobao-china-ebay-weirdest-strangest-items/, retrieved on 21 November 2016.

31   Clark, D. (2016), *Alibaba: The House That Jack Ma Built*, New York: HarperCollins Publishers, p. 163.

32   Ibid, pp. 6–7.

33   Ibid, p. 7.

34   Zhang, M. and Zuo, M. (2016), "Alibaba Presses on in Crackdown on Fake Goods After Suspension From Anti-Counterfeiting Group," *South China Morning Post*, 16 May, www.scmp.com/news/china/economy/article/1945547/alibaba-presses-crackdown-fake-goods-after-suspension-anti, retrieved on 21 November 2016.

35   Ma, J.Y. (2016), "Counterfeit Goods Have No Place on Alibaba," *The Wall Street Journal*, 22 June, www.wsj.com/articles/counterfeit-goods-have-no-place-on-alibaba-1466635312, retrieved on 21 November 2016.

36   Clark, D. (2016), *Alibaba: The House That Jack Ma Built*, New York: HarperCollins Publishers, p. 16.

37   Wang, L.F. and Li, X. (2014), *Chuan buxie de ma yun (Ma Yun Who Wears Canvas Shoes)*, Beijing: Union Publishing Co. Ltd.

38   Clark, D. (2016), *Alibaba: The House That Jack Ma Built*, New York: HarperCollins Publishers, pp. 18–19.

39   Wu, K. and Osawa, J. (2016), "Alipay Mobilizes for World-Wide Expansion," *The Wall Street Journal*, 1 November, www.wsj.com/articles/alipay-mobilizes-for-world-wide-expansion-1477930366, retrieved on 21 November 2016.

40   Wu, K. (2016), "Things to Know About China's Ant Financial," *The Wall Street Journal*, 26 April, http://blogs.wsj.com/briefly/2016/04/26/5-things-to-know-about-chinas-ant-financial/, retrieved on 21 November 2016.

41   Clark, D. (2016), *Alibaba: The House That Jack Ma Built*, New York: HarperCollins Publishers, p. 23.

42   As explained in Chapter Five, in Western companies, mission and goal are separate, providing different levels of guidance to the company. In China, however, there is no such distinction.

8   The war for talent

The key for us, number one, has always been hiring the smartest people.

– Bill Gates

The people are the most important element in a nation; the spirits of the land and grain are the next; the sovereign is the least.

– Mencius

He will win whose army is animated by the same spirit throughout all its ranks.

– Sun Tzu

The nature of talent management in China

The domain of human resource management (HRM) is considered to cover three subfields: micro HRM (MHRM), strategic HRM (SHRM) and international HRM (IHRM).[1] MHRM, including HR policy and practice, comprises two dimensions: (1) the management of individuals and small groups, such as recruitment, selection, training and development, performance evaluation and remuneration, and (2) the management of work organisation and systems of employee voice.[2] SHRM is defined as 'the pattern of planned human resource deployments and activities intended to enable an organisation to achieve its goals,'[3] involving HRM's alignment with the firm's strategy. IHRM deals with companies' HRM in the context of international business. The nature of HRM in China dictates that it is SHRM that covers IHRM. In the West, HRM as an academic discipline is well established conceptually and empirically;[4] how people are managed in companies is found to have a positive impact on their competitiveness and performance.[5]

Since the late 1990s, a widely used term has been talent management (TM), which was first referred to by McKinsey & Company in their report *The War for Talent*. 'TM is said to be critical to organisational success, being able to give a competitive edge through the identification, development and redeployment of talented employees.'[6] Concerning the nature of talent management, four perspectives are identified in the literature: (1) exclusive-people: those who have the competencies to contribute to organisational performance;[7] (2) inclusive-people: this perspective regards everyone in the organisation as potentially having talent and sees the managers' task as tapping their talent to make a difference to the firm's performance;[8] (3) exclusive-position: from a viewpoint of a talent identification process, each talented person takes a position to which he or she is uniquely suited in order to make a strong contribution to organisational performance;[9] and (4) social capital: de-emphasising the role of an individual, this perspective takes a contingent position on TM, seeing the contribution of talent as dependent on social environmental factors such as teams, cultures, leaderships and networks.[10]

Needless to say, human resource management or talent management is of paramount importance to any business, any culture or any nation. However, given how business is conceived, strategised and organised in China, the qualities of the key individual in a Chinese organisation play a much more important role in determining the survival and development of business than in many other cultures, as the key individual shoulders a much heavier organisational load than in Western companies, where organisational structure takes a large portion of the weight. In China, individual entrepreneurs make strategic decisions, and these are implemented by divisional managers who rely on other employees through 'leadership', with limited effective organisational procedures and rules to guide them. In the West, by contrast, because of well-developed bureaucratic organisational structures, strategic implementation can rely on following standard procedures and rules, while managers only need to deal with exceptional circumstances. For instance, McDonald's and KFC do not need to employ the most creative and talented managers to run their businesses successfully, as long as management recruits can follow the organisational procedures which specify what needs to be done and how. Therefore, the quality of strategic implementation in the West can often be better than that in China, as manifested by better Western business management and organisation. Western managers just need to follow procedures to execute decisions, while their Chinese counterparts often alter or divert decisions in the process of strategic implementation, resulting in better or worse outcomes. In other words, management tends to be undertaken by individuals in China, while in the West, it is supported by a well-structured organisational system; this is commonly referred to as people-based management in China versus rule-based management in the West.

A number of factors have made HRM in China extremely challenging: (1) recruitment, retention and compensation play a more critical role in the effectiveness of securing and retaining talent in China than in the West; (2) there has been a limited supply of competent professionals in China, because China's business educational system generates a limited supply of the kind of talented people needed by Western standards, in terms of experience, knowledge and skills, both professional and managerial; (3) the rapid growth of foreign companies in China has created a huge demand for qualified professionals; (4) in order to attract talented people, Chinese companies have raised their offers to make them comparable to those of multinationals; and (5) Chinese skilled professionals and middle managers tend to have high mobility and high expectations.[11]

> They [Chinese employees] have the mentality that a better opportunity is always waiting just around the corner. It is very difficult to be loyal to one organization when they frequently receive new job offers with a substantial salary increase and a flamboyant job title. Besides, there is the perception among those who stay that they are somehow punished for their loyalty.[12]

The war for talent has become the nature of competition for human resources since foreign businesses began to gain a foothold in China.

A 2012 survey of HR professionals undertaken by PricewaterhouseCoopers (PwC), one of the world's largest providers of professional services to MNCs, headquartered in London, asserts that

> less than 10% of Chinese candidates are suited to work in a foreign company in nine selected occupations: engineers, finance workers, accountants, quantitative analysts, generalists, life science researchers, doctors, nurses and support staff. One reason cited is that Chinese education focuses more on theory than practical experience, and graduates have little experience working on projects or teams.[13]

A McKinsey survey of senior executives of multinationals also shows that 77 per cent of respondents referred to the difficulty in attracting qualified managers in China, while 91 per cent identified a high turnover of employees as their top TM challenge.[14]

A 2016 PwC survey of CEOs in 83 countries further highlights the ever-increasing importance of HRM in their business development:

> 72% of CEOs are concerned about the availability of key skills, particularly with 48% planning to increase headcount in the coming year. And it explains why by far the most CEOs (75%) say that a skilled, educated and adaptable workforce should be a priority for business in the country where they're based.[15]

The identification and management of talented people has, since antiquity, been a topic of keen interest to the authors of various Chinese classics, such as *Zizhi Tongjian* (*Comprehensive Mirror for Rulers*), *Twenty-Four Histories, Tso Chuan* and the *Analects of Confucius*. Despite the existence of a huge body of literature associated with what could broadly be called 'talent management' in China, this body of knowledge has never been crystallised or systemised in the way that it has in Western countries. Instead, it has become an art form, where it falls to individuals to decide how to interpret and utilise the knowledge to their advantage. The identification and management of talented people often involves the adoption of stratagems to achieve the desired effect.

Research shows that the role of HRM in China has gone through three stages:[16]

(1) Early 1980s – mid-1990s: Prior to the economic reform of the early 1980s, China's planned economic system dictated that labour was treated as merely a factor of production similar to land and capital. Until the mid-1980s, the Chinese public were unfamiliar with the term 'HRM'. Seen as a tool of managing and controlling costs, the personnel departments of Chinese state-owned enterprises (SOEs) dealt mainly with administrative orders and routine office work, such as personnel evaluation, payment and personal file management. Since the market system was not fully functional in China's economy, personnel management lacked the mechanisms of effective incentives and employment competition.

(2) Mid-1990s – late 1990s: From the mid-1990s onwards, Chinese enterprises and government agencies began to apply and implement HRM as part of personnel management practices. They implemented HRM functions including recruitment, remuneration, performance appraisal and improvement of professional skills. Some incentive schemes were put into practice, such as an annual salary system, which represented a major advancement in Chinese HRM.[17] Since the market system remained underdeveloped, there were many limitations in HRM.

(3) Late 1990s – 2012: During this period, HRM reform was deepened, a strategic role was added and HRM practices were further developed. The labour market underwent strong growth, with the labour law being fully implemented. HRM in both governmental and business organisations was practised with more effectiveness, becoming a significant part of corporate management. Taking on the new role of SHRM, the HRM department became involved in corporate development. Seen as a core resource, HRM began to embrace a 'people orientation', adopting practices with personnel evaluation, performance assessment and incentive remuneration at their heart.

The development of Internet business has also exerted great pressure on the role of HRM, sharpening the need for its transformation. A 2016 survey by Deloitte of 7000 senior executives and HR leaders across 130 countries has shown that Western HR managers are contemplating two fundamental questions: (1) how they can help business leaders and employees to make the transition towards a 'digital mind-set', that is managing, organising and leading change by digital means, and (2) how HR itself can revolutionise HR processes, systems and organisations, with new digital platforms, apps and methods of delivering services. The findings indicate that

> 74 percent of executives identified digital HR as a top priority, and it will likely be a major focus in 2016. The trend is moving rapidly: 42 percent of companies are adapting their existing HR systems for mobile, device

delivered, just-in-time learning; 59 percent are developing mobile apps that integrate back office systems for ease of use by employees; and 51 percent are leveraging external social networks in their own internal apps for recruitment and employee profile management.[18]

In the areas of B2B, B2C and C2C businesses, Chinese companies have raced against Western ones and have managed to catch up and run almost abreast of the leading US companies. However, it remains to be seen whether Chinese companies are able to utilise digital means to manage and organise their businesses effectively, since orderly, efficient organisation has always been a cultural weakness of Chinese firms. Whatever the potential impact of technology on management and organisation, it cannot overshadow the role of people. Brian Moynihan, CEO of Bank of America, has stated: 'Even with all the new technology, people skills are actually more important now. Whether it's providing day-to-day services in our bank branches or managing our data analytics: it's all about people.'[19]

Talent management: the West versus China

HRM as part of corporate management and organisation follows strategy which is influenced, among other factors, by national culture, particularly cognition.

> HRM is seen as an essentially American concept, finding its fullest exemplification in non-unionized multinational firms, and overlapping with practices found elsewhere in enterprises in capitalist economies. Most HRM theories derive from a non-universal tradition of scientific rationality, meritocracy, individualism and short-termism.[20]

Research suggests that US management theories may not be applicable to European and Asian countries.[21] In other words, although there seems to be a strong adoption of Western HRM theories and practices in China, there remains a core part of Chinese HRM that needs adaptation. In many cases, what really makes Chinese employees tick lies in Chinese tradition. For instance, it is known that Huawei has spent a huge sum to introduce a Western HRM system: certifying systems for professional qualifications from the Hay Group and an incentive system from Towers Perrin. As effective as it has been seen publicly, Huawei's HRM has been characterised as 'three highs': high pressure, high performance and high pay. However, what has sustained the stability and viability of Huawei's HRM system lies in Chinese tradition: the Middle Way.[22] The adoption of methods based on Mao Zedong's Yanan Rectification Movement has also played a vital part.[23]

> Another tactic Mr Ren copied from Mao is ideological education. In the early years, he had employees sing revolutionary songs. Even today, the thousands of new recruits hired every year undergo a six-month course

that includes two weeks of cultural induction on the Shenzhen campus and an internship on the ground, for instance helping to set up base stations. This is when new Huaweians are supposed to acquire the 'wolf spirit' which is said to drive the firm on.[24]

A metaphor may shed light on this point. Western and Chinese HRM may be likened to a tall, strong Western man and a medium-built, medium-weight Chinese man. In the West, technology enables tailors to make warm, soft, comfortable, wear-resistant clothes. Now the Western man has too many outfits and decides to sell one to a Chinese man. With his new suit, the Chinese man may appear to gain a new face and image, but to keep himself warm, comfortable and healthy, he has to wear home-made underclothes beneath the 'foreign outfit'.

There is a huge body of extant literature examining how Chinese companies have practised or incorporated Western HR theories and practices.[25] Indeed, research efforts have tended to focus primarily on the application of Western theories and frameworks; while these are undoubtedly important, it should be recognised that equally crucial are the principles embedded in Chinese tradition that have been employed in successful Chinese companies or by Chinese elites. It is the purpose of this chapter to summarise the basic principles, teachings or doctrines on talent identification, attraction and retention in Chinese tradition. Offering an introduction to Chinese HRM practices will not make them more scientific or effective, but it is hoped that it will help readers to understand Chinese ways of thinking about and executing HRM, with a view to adapting their own HRM or managing Chinese employees more effectively.

Figure 8.1 displays figuratively the relationship between Western HRM theories and practices, which is systematically structured, developed and utilised, while Figure 8.2 depicts the Chinese system of talent management as seemingly unstructured and artistic. In the West, SHRM as a discipline has gradually become mature and well systemised over the past three decades, but the fundamental idea emerged as early as the 1920s.[26] In each sub-field of SHRM, theories have been established on empirical grounds, as shown in Figure 8.1. Each arrow represents a subject within SHRM, such as HRM strategy and policy, IHRM, industrial relations, leadership development, employment and employee relations, training and development, talent and reward management, performance management, cross-cultural management and managing equality and diversity.

In China, by contrast, ideas, thinking and principles are quite rich, with an accumulated span of over two millennia, and are discoursed in various historical, political and military writings. However, unlike HRM in the West, they have not developed into a number of well-established systems, as principles and policies have differed markedly under the reigns of various emperors. A ten-year research project on historical talent management in China from the Spring and Autumn period (771 BC) to the Qing dynasty (1911) have identified 48 schools of thought and 52 types of policies and practices on talent

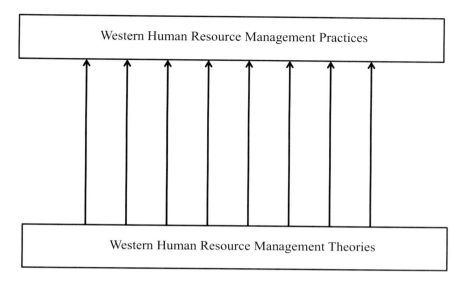

Figure 8.1 Western HRM theories and practices

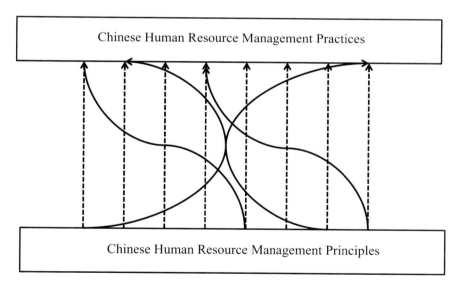

Figure 8.2 Chinese HRM principles and practices

management.[27] It can be said that there exist different schools of thought, under the guidance of which the practices of HRM become an art, rather than a science, as expressed in Figure 8.2, whose curved lines indicate that diverse schools of thought touch on multiple aspects of HRM, each with its own emphasis. In antiquity, the extent of an emperor's achievement depended mostly on how he identified, utilised and treated or rewarded his ministerial underlings. It can be said that Chinese history is a history of the war for talent; whoever identified, selected and utilised people with the right competencies and skills won the nation. The following are a few examples:

- In the late third century BC, the Qin state launched a series of military campaigns against six other major states, Wei, Chu, Qi, Han, Zhao and Yan; by the end of 221 BC, Qin had unified most of these and founded the Qin dynasty. Such a great feat was made possible by a number of well-known civil and military officials who helped the kings of the Qin state with legal systems, strategies, policies and military prowess. Among the most distinguished are Shang Yang, Bai Qi, Fan Ju, Li Si, Wang Jiang and Wang Peng.
- The West Han dynasty was founded and developed by Liu Bang, known as Emperor Gao of Han, who overthrew the Qin dynasty. Liu Bang's success was attributable to his ability to employ a number of capable counsellors and advisors, including historically renowned figures such as Xiao He, Han Xin, Cheng Ping and Zhang Liang. Therefore, the empire enjoyed great prosperity for over two centuries before it fell into decline.
- The early Tang dynasty was ruled for 23 years by Emperor Li Shimin, under whom it witnessed a period of historic economic success known as the Prosperity of Zhenguan. Some of the major contributory factors include his willingness to seek and act upon the views of others, some of which were often against his initial intention and will. He even appointed a former enemy known as Weizheng as one of his ministers and allowed him to openly argue with or criticise him for any inappropriate behaviour and policy, because Weizheng had the intellectual strength and moral courage to do so.

Chinese HRM principles and wisdom

This section provides a summary of ancient Chinese wisdom on HRM, citing various philosophers, certain historical classics and the ideas and ways of thinking of diverse dynasties.

Value and position of human resources

Humanism is at the heart of Chinese tradition in terms of talent management. In China's political sphere, emphasis has always been placed on people, who are considered the foundation of the nation. As a Chinese saying goes, 'the humane man has no one to oppose him'. Among the resources and tools for governing a country, human beings have been accorded the highest value. Lao Tzu says: 'Therefore, the Sage is good at helping men; For that reason there is no rejected (useless) person. He is good at saving things; For that reason there is nothing rejected.'[28] This means that there are no useless people, as everyone can be useful according to his or her talent, and there are no useless things; all things can be utilised. In other words, everyone has talent and an enlightened leader knows how to recognise and utilise it. Thus, the ability to identify and employ the talented becomes a vital criterion for being a good leader.

The question arises as to what the criteria of 'talent' should be. Generally, organisations often use the following: university degrees, professional qualifications, special expertise, previous positions, achievements, honours or titles and work experience. As far as the value of talent to a company is concerned, none of these is relevant if the person cannot bring any value to the company or create value for it, no matter how impressive his or her curriculum vitae. A person's talent can be a double-edged sword: it may create or indeed destroy value for a company, depending on how the person's value fits with that of the company. More often than not, an unscrupulous talented person can do much greater damage to a company than those who are less talented. Among the major tasks of an HRM department should be to ensure that employees' value and talent match those of the company and/or to instil corporate value in the talented.

Confucius is among the earliest sages to have emphasised the importance of human talent in running a country well; he writes in the *Analects*: 'Shun[29] had five officials and the Empire was well governed. King Wu said, "I have ten capable officials." Confucius commented, "How true it is that talent is difficult to find! The period of Tang and Yu was rich in talent."'[30] Shun governed a peaceful and prosperous nation before the dynastic era, and King Wu created a dynasty which lasted for 800 years. Both attributed their praiseworthy outcomes to their employment of capable officials, while Confucius reiterated the crucial role of talent. As early as the third century BC, Emperor Qin Shihuang enacted the Way to Be an Official, a law whose underlying principle was virtue. The law stipulated 'five merits': a virtuous official must be loyal and respectful, honest and free of slander, discreet at work, benevolent and deferential.[31]

The key to making everyone useful is to provide open and fair opportunities in recruitment and selection. Lao Tzu writes: 'But the way of Heaven is impartial; It sides only with the good man.'[32] In the West, this principle is strongly held and widely practised, whereas in China, although its importance has been recognised since antiquity, there is still a long way to go before talented people can enjoy fair and open opportunities, because the *guanxi* factor still plays a part in one way or another in talent management.

The dyad of virtue and talent has been at the core of TM for millennia. Of these two, virtue is accorded greater importance because an immoral talented person can do more harm than a less capable virtuous one. Confucius says: 'I set my heart on the Way [Tao], base myself on virtue, lean upon benevolence for support and take my recreation in the arts.'[33] In Confucius' view, his action follows Tao as the direction, develops virtue as the basis, relies on benevolence for support and utilises skills to set him free. On the whole, he sees virtue as going hand in hand with talent, with virtue underlying talent.

Talent management and types of people

In Chinese tradition, people are classified into categories based on their possession of virtue in order to utilise them to the best of their abilities:

(a) *Xian chen* (XC) and *neng li* (NL): In Chinese history, XCs are those whose virtue exceeds their talent,[34] while NLs are those whose talent overshadows their virtue.[35] XCs have limited capabilities but are highly moral, loyal, sincere, hardworking, punctual, honest and selfless. They are committed to their work and take an orderly approach, with little creativity or adaptability. They may not be suitable for a leadership position that requires ingenuity, creativity or analytical ability, but can be excellent executors.

   The NL concept is a uniquely Chinese phenomenon, as virtuous behaviour is observed and measured mostly outside the person's official position. For instance, a capable, creative and ingenious man successfully performs difficult work, sometimes at the expense of others' toil and feelings, while outside his work he leads an unprincipled personal life, perhaps engaging in prostitution or gambling and disrespecting his family. By Chinese standards, this person is talented but not virtuous. In antiquity, such people were quite useful for politicians and officials to get certain kinds of things done, becoming an important part of the resource pool. In today's business environment, one's moral dimension can have a major impact on one's career development, particularly if one is considered for a high position.

(b) *Junzi* and *xiaoren*: *Junzi* denotes a superior man or gentleman with high moral standards, while *xiaoren* means a small or petty person.[36] In the words of Confucius, 'The gentleman understands what is moral. The small man understands what is profitable.'[37] 'The gentleman gets through to what is up above [moral principles]; the small man gets through to what is down below [profit].'[38] 'The gentleman seeks [room for improvement or occasion to blame], he seeks within himself; what the small man seeks, he seeks in others.'[39] 'While the gentleman cherishes benign rule, the small man cherishes his native land. While the gentleman cherishes a respect for the law, the small man cherishes generous treatment.'[40] 'The gentleman never deserts benevolence, not even for as long as it takes to eat a meal. If he hurries and stumbles one may be sure that it is in benevolence that he does so.'[41]

   The two classifications are by nature in the ethical domain, not involving talent, but can provide guidance to talent management. A *junzi* behaves strictly according to a high moral standard, with integrity and honesty, whereas a *xiaoren* is amoral and entirely driven by the goal of profit, which he pursues by fair means or foul. From a *yin-yang* perspective, a person can be both *junzi* and *xiaoren*, depending on when and how he or she does things. A fundamental HRM principle is that one should cultivate *junzi* and shun *xiaoren*, particularly in the sphere of civil service and leadership positions. This classification is specific to the Chinese context, in that for over two millennia, in China's underdeveloped legal system, public institutions or private organisations have had to rely on individuals' morality to regulate the extent to which they act according to the public interest. Under a well-developed legal system, *xiaoren's* behaviour is constrained and restricted in its harmfulness. A talented *xiaoren* can still be useful for certain functions or jobs, but should be in a setting where the rules and regulations are in good order.

Talent identification and selection

In the West, a number of scientific methods and tools are used by companies for the identification and selection of candidates to match certain job specifications. An aptitude test is generally used to measure candidates' ability to perform critical thinking, to solve problems and to learn and apply new information. A personality test is employed to evaluate the behavioural patterns and traits that will influence candidates' workplace performance. A skills test is utilised to gauge their abilities in relation to job specifications. In addition, multinationals work closely with Chinese universities, through sponsorships, guest lectures and scholarships, to gain early access to promising graduates, use internal referrals to identify potential candidates and conduct 360-degree interviews to ensure a culture fit.

By contrast, as far as the selection of personnel for senior positions is concerned, most Chinese private companies still rely to a great extent on the 'soft' judgement embedded in Chinese tradition, rather than Western 'hard, scientific' assessment. In Chinese history, the identification and assessment of talent have been highly valued and well documented, becoming an art of innate personal capabilities. Two examples vividly illustrating the ability to identify talented people are Zeng Guofan's assessment of character through observation and Bole's judging of horses.

Zeng Guofan's observation of character

Zeng Guofan (26 November 1811 – 12 March 1872) was an outstanding statesman, military commander and Confucian scholar of the last Qing dynasty. He identified and promoted two other prominent Chinese statesmen and military leaders, Zuo Zongtang (also known as Tso Tsung-t'ang in the West) and Li Hongzhang (aka Li Hung-chang). He was known as having a penetrating eye for talent identification and selection. Here is a story about how he discerned people's character with great precision by simple observation.

One day, Li Hongzhang brought three final candidates for an important position to be interviewed by Zeng Guofan, who had just finished his lunch and who took a stroll, as was his habit, while they were waiting. When he returned, Li invited Zeng to meet the finalists, but to Li's surprise, Zeng said that this would not be necessary, because he had already made up his mind by observing them while he was strolling. He explained: 'The first person is simple and honest, because he kept his head down, not daring to look at me as a senior officer; he is suitable for a job that does not require much creativity and resourcefulness. The second person is insincere, as he showed me great reverence when he first saw me, but soon afterwards, he began looking round; he should not be appointed. The third person remained upright and motionless, with his eyes fixed straight ahead; his career path will be comparable to ours. He can be appointed to an important position.' They eventually turned out to be what Zeng had predicted. The third person, Liu Mingchuan, later became a famous provincial governor of Taiwan.

How was Zeng able to discern the moral character of these men within such a short time? Apart from his consummate skills, he benefited from the fact that the candidates did not know that they were being interviewed or observed, so made no effort to disguise the true nature of their character. Zeng proved to be an effective general, not because of his commandership or ingenuity but because of his competence in talent management. Over a period of 20 years, he selected and recruited over 400 officials, of whom 33 reached ministerial level and 47 the level below this, making him one of the best talent identifiers in China. He was admired and praised by Mao Zedong.

Bole judging horses

The classic Chinese tale of 'Bole judging horses' is often used to imply a superior judge of (particularly hidden) talent, reflecting Chinese views of the nature of talent and its recognition. During the Spring and Autumn period (770–476 BC), there was a horse tamer named Sun Yang who had an exceptional ability to judge horses, earning the sobriquet of Bole, the god of horse tamers in Chinese mythology. In ancient China, whoever acquired horses of superior quality would gain a huge advantage over his opponents in warfare. The vital role of horses in warfare determined the high value afforded to equine physiognomy; 'the judging of horses was early recognized as a special art.'[42]

One day, the king of Chu summoned Bole and told him that if he could find a beautiful *chollima* (a fabled horse with magical staying power, able to run a thousand miles), he would be rewarded handsomely. Bole responded: 'Rest assured that I will find the best horse under heaven for you, my King, but as chollima are rare, we can only hope to secure one by luck, needing time and effort to find it. Please be patient, my King.'

Bole travelled throughout China, unable to find a horse to his satisfaction, but despite the hardships he endured and his lack of success in his quest, he was convinced that there would be a magical horse somewhere waiting to be found, to fulfil the king's desire. So he continued searching for a long period of time; he looked everywhere, but without success. Eventually, he decided to return home and admit to the king that he had failed.

On his way back, Bole saw a horse pulling a cart overloaded with salt approaching a hill. The horse looked clumsy and as thin as a skeleton. Despite the severe whipping that the carter gave it, the horse could not climb the hill and had to stop for breath after every step. Bole ran towards the cart and as he approached, he felt his heart beating heavily in his chest. He raised his head and looked the horse straight in the eye. As an adept of equine physiognomy, he had a natural sympathy with the creature, whose skeletal frame brought tears to his eyes.

At that very moment, the horse seemed to be connected with Bole in spirit. It raised its head and gave a long and strident neigh, which echoed loudly around the valley. Bole stroked the horse's back and covered it with his own jacket, as if he sensed its pain and grievance. Taking out a bag of gold nuggets, Bole beseeched the carter to sell the horse to him. The man's eyes widened in astonishment at this insane offer. To him, the horse was nothing but trouble: it was extremely clumsy, hopelessly unable to learn anything, even very basic skills, feeble and restless, often causing damage by bumping into things. He had felt extremely unlucky to own such a horse. Now this fool was willing to buy it from him and pay in gold! Without hesitation, he took the payment and walked away grinning.

But his delight was not half as great as that of Bole, who had finally found a chollima that had happened to fall into the hands of an ignorant salt-trader. He said to the horse, 'It is God's will to let you be found; your grievance has not gone unnoticed by God.' The chollima seemed to understand this and raised his head, giving another long, loud neigh.

Bole took the chollima to present it to the king of Chu. Upon seeing the condition of the beast, the king was as surprised as the carter had been. He supposed that being lazy, Bole had probably found a horse randomly to fool him. Angrily, he said: 'Bole, because I believed that you were capable of judging horses, I sent you to find a chollima. Having gone for so long a time, you brought back a horse which seems to have difficulty walking. How can you possibly expect it to run a thousand miles?'

Bole responded: 'Your Majesty, it is indeed a chollima. However, its previous owner treated it badly by giving it inferior food, starving it, whipping and scolding it and making it pull carts. If you allow it to rehabilitate with rest and good food, in less than half a month, it will return to its original form, becoming a magical horse.'

The king remained dubious, but ordered the supposed chollima to be tended carefully in the royal stables. Just as Bole had said, the horse soon became a strong, handsome chollima. It served the king with distinction for many years, carrying him to countless battles.

These two examples reflect some general aspects of talent management in China:

(1) Finding the most talented is an art, with certain principles to be followed. It often requires special insight and perceptiveness to recognise talent. Students of art may learn some basic skills and principles at art school, but those who become outstanding artists must be able to call on innate gifts and perceptivity, bolstered by long practice. Business leaders should be HRM artists; when they come across a human chollima, they should be able to recognise the talent before them. Jack Ma, the founder of Alibaba,

has proved to be a Bole by his personal success in building and cultivating an effective HR team as well as being a successful entrepreneur and leader.

(2) The greatest talents are often disguised or hidden, unintentionally or unconsciously, needing to be discovered, nurtured and modified. However, most current HRM policies tend to focus on people with proven talent, while too little attention is paid to tapping hidden resources of talent. The Chinese government, for instance, has implemented a 'Thousand Talents Programme' to recruit superlative professors and researchers. Such a programme relies on the talented to come forward to be assessed by the recruitment institutions, which presents a number of challenges to its success: (a) If an applicant is already a first-rate researcher, he or she would normally have a well-paid and supported position elsewhere and be less likely to come forward to go through the ordeal of an assessment process; (b) if the talented, for some reason, decide to take advantage of the programme, the existing members of staff at the recruiting institutions often see the candidates as their rivals, so they may either make the recruitment more difficult or become less supportive, in order to defend the status quo; and (c) the programme does not allow the discovery of 'emerging' talent, leaving a talent pool waiting to be tapped.

Two scenarios are likely to be successful. The first is where a candidate is identified and approached by the recruitment institution, which offers a reasonable package, including research support facilities, funding and care for personal well-being. Alternatively, the candidate may have already earned a first-class reputation and may not gain any substantial advancement from the recruiting institution or make any significant call on its resources, but the institution may benefit from its new association with the reputed candidate.

A special case of talent management in China is that of the founders of Vimicro Corporation, a leading video technology supplier serving the market for networked video applications. In the 1990s, as part of a government effort to develop integrated circuit technology essential to China's information industry, Chinese officials identified three US PhD graduates as suitable researchers for China, as they all had knowledge of chip technology and experience of working in Silicon Valley. A vice minister at the Ministry of Information Industry (MII) went to the USA in person to invite them to participate in the development of Chinese chip products. To bypass China's daunting bureaucratic system, a deputy mayor of Beijing personally assisted the returnees to set up Vimicro, within 24 hours, backed by the MII's investment of much-needed funds. The three founding members became shareholders by virtue of their intellectual property rights. In 2001, two years after its foundation, the company successfully released its first chip product, a world-leading CMOS digital image processing chip. In November 2005, Vimicro became the first NASDAQ-listed Chinese chip company, raising $87 million from its IPO. This case shows how talented people were identified, recruited and supported, leading to the achievement of expected performance: developing China's chip business.

Identification through observation

Observation is an important part of the talent identification process in Chinese tradition. The following are a number of aspects on which Chinese leaders tend to focus in their observation:

(1) Personal interests such as reading, ambition and hobbies. These may reveal a person's vision and career path. Some like to read literary works that provide readers with inspiration, wisdom and useful knowledge. For instance, from a young age, Mao Zedong liked to read Chinese histories and classics, making him believe that Chinese tradition offered a unique contribution to the world and could share half of the world with Western tradition.[43]

(2) One's social circle. This follows the logic that 'everyone is defined by his or her friends.' If a candidate socialises with a group of *junzi*, it is likely that he or she is a *junzi*, as it is unusual for *junzi* and *xiaoren* to commingle.

(3) Attitude towards favours. In ancient China, before the final appointment was made, a candidate would be tempted by favours such as a piece of gold bar, as a test of his attitude. Nowadays, in China, before finalists are decided, the CEO of the recruiting company often invites them to a luxury buffet lunch to observe how they eat, talk or behave.

(4) Integrity. A candidate is often given a task to observe the extent to which he or she would deliver what is agreed on. There are many people who easily make promises without being able to deliver on them. For instance, in order to impress one's superiors, one may promise to complete a project in five months, but then fail to achieve this. This is an indication of low integrity, a bad quality for HRM. Tests are often undertaken to observe those who show an excessive obedience to their leaders, which is considered a relatively undesirable HR quality.

(5) Lifestyle. Candidates are observed for how and where they spend money and with whom. Moral behaviour has consistency; one may pretend to be decent in some respects, but it is difficult to hide a lack of decency in others. For instance, Ren Zhengfei, the founder of Huawei, has continued to live thriftily, still using the things he used when he served in the army, despite having become seriously rich.

(6) The kind of people recommended for promotion. Cultivated people will ignore personal bias and focus directly on the candidates' merits. Some narrow-minded people will tend to recommend those who are loyal to them, rather than basing their recommendations on overall morality and competencies. For instance, if a potential candidate for promotion has justifiably criticised his or her superior for something that has not been done properly, the superior may not recommend that person for promotion, even though he or she is highly talented and moral. This 'superior' is not considered suitable for being a leader. Generally, a successful business leader tends to be a Bole, particularly in the context of China, as exemplified by Liu Chuanzhi of Lenovo, Ren Zhengfei of Huawei and Jack Ma of Alibaba, because the team members on whom they have relied have become cornerstones of their business success.

Utilisation of talent

Since Chinese management is individual-based, rather than rule-based, the utilisation of talent is closely associated with the leader's conscience, philosophy, vision and wisdom. Therefore, traditionally, how talented people are used is not a simple HRM issue. A despotic leader tends to utilise the less talented, with more emphasis on obedience and loyalty, whereas career-orientated, visionary or upright leaders disregard any personal biases, focusing instead on a combination of morality and talent, allowing the talented to materialise their value and ambitions. It should be pointed out that nowadays all companies of decent size in China have appropriate policies and procedures for selection, recruitment, training, reward and compensation for medium-level or lower managerial positions. However, when it comes to the appointment of top positions, the preferences, background and character of key individuals play an important part.

The utilisation of talent cannot be separated from training, which for top executives tends to be done through practice; as the saying goes, practice is the best training. For instance, Liu Chuanzhi of Lenovo identified and appointed Yang Yuanqing as vice president of Lenovo at the age of 31 and CEO of Lenovo at 36. In a Confucian society, where respect for seniority is still a norm, Liu has audaciously provided Yang with the arena where he could apply his talent, allowing him to be 'trained' in practice and proving his worthiness.

The effectiveness of utilising talent lies in three words: position, trust and appropriateness. Mencius once referred to 'giving the worthiest among them places of dignity and the able offices of trust'. This means that those of high moral worth should be appointed to positions of symbolic importance, such as chairman of the board of directors, while the capable should be relied on to get things done, by appointing them as CEOs or divisional directors, for example. Trust is a uniquely Chinese category because of the culture of low trust in society. A particularly apposite Chinese saying urges that one should 'never doubt the person you hire; never hire the person you doubt.' If you have decided to appoint someone, you should let the person fulfil his or her duties without casting any suspicion on him or her. If you cannot do so, you should not give the position to the person. Appropriateness means that there should be a match between the position and the appointee's capability, implying the utilisation of both one's talent and the position. Often it is necessary to create a position in order to use a particular talent.[44]

Case study 1: HRM in Alibaba

The previous chapter discussed details of Alibaba's 'iron triangle' of e-commerce, logistics and finance, which can be seen as the framework of the Alibaba edifice. In this section, we examine the foundation of this edifice, with a focus on Alibaba's HRM system and practices. Figure 8.3 is a figurative depiction of the structure of the Alibaba Group, comprising its strategic foundation (its HRM system and Jack Ma's strategic mind) and its framework (the iron triangle).

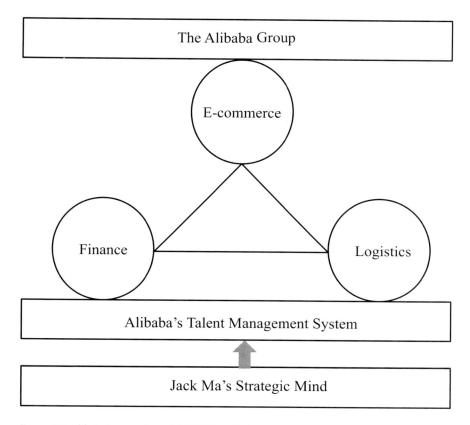

Figure 8.3 Alibaba's strategic and HRM foundation

Jack Ma's strategic mind

In 2015, Hong Liu developed a framework for the Chinese strategic mind, including the idiosyncratic factors of Tao, *shi*, stratagem, Chinese dialectic, competitor orientation and agility.[45] The following is a brief summary of how Jack Ma's strategic mind is reflected in practice.

When he launched the Alibaba business venture, Jack Ma set out its vision in the phrase: 'We don't want to be number one in China. We want to be number one in the world.'[46] This broad vision provides an unmistakable direction for the company, allowing it to be equipped with wings to fly.

At the outset, Jack Ma laid out a blueprint to build a company that would last for 102 years, at least.[47] An implementation of this blueprint means that the company will not only grow rapidly but operate in a steady, risk-controlled way.

Jack Ma's initial mission was to 'help millions of Chinese factories find an outlet overseas for their goods.'[48] He was breaking new ground and entering what has turned out to be a land of opportunity.

He is open-minded and unselfish. When the CFO, Joe Tsai, asked him for a list of people to be considered as the shareholders of Alibaba, Jack Ma listed all 18 people who had worked with him from day one, including a number of his students. It is this quality that enables him to attract and retain talent.[49]

Alibaba's management philosophy has been: 'Customer first, employees second, and investors third.'[50] Putting customers and employees ahead of investors and the company itself is in line with the ethos of Tao.

SHI

Jack Ma has made it clear on several occasions that the company's success has not relied on strategy, technology or money.[51] It has ridden the tidal wave or *shi* of the Internet, taking a leading role in doing so, combined with the visionary ambition of connecting small and medium-sized companies around the world.

At an initial stage of Alibaba's operations, few were aware of the company's name. In order to create *shi*, making the company known to the outside world, Jack Ma organised a conference in 2000, just one year after the founding of Alibaba, under the title, 'Forum for Swordsmanship at the West Lake'. The theme and title of this forum were inspired by a story entitled 'Forum for Swordsmanship in the Hua Mountain', about a gathering of the best swordsmen under Heaven, written by the 74-year-old martial arts novelist, Jin Yong. This renowned author was among the high-profile figures invited to the Alibaba forum, others being successful entrepreneurs such as the founders of Sohu, NetEase and 8848, the Canadian ambassador, the British consul general and more than 50 high-level representatives of MNCs in China. Altogether, over a thousand people attended the forum, which proved to be a successful *shi*-creation event; since then, the name of Jack Ma has been firmly attached to China's IT industry and Alibaba's brand has become widely known.[52] In this way, Jack Ma borrowed the *shi* of Jin Yong, an icon and household name in China, to attract participants, creating *shi* for Alibaba through the participation of many distinguished guests.

Alibaba's iron triangle represents *shi* in three areas, e-commerce, finance and logistics, which are likened to snowballs rolling down a high hill, starting small and becoming bigger and bigger. To use another metaphor, these three pillars support each other, creating a solid framework for the rapid growth of the Alibaba empire.

STRATAGEM

Jack Ma has been a keen reader of Chinese classics such as *The Water Margin* and of Jin Yong's martial arts novels, including *The Legend of the Condor Heroes* and *Demigods and Semi-Devils*. His ethos for running Alibaba has been strongly inspired by the underlying philosophy and spirit of these novels.[53] He is also versed in Mao Zedong's selected works. His reading has infused him with knowledge of stratagem. For instance, Jack Ma allowed the Taobao project, a major competitor to eBay's EachNet in China, to be developed secretly; when the battle began, eBay did not know the identity of its chief opponent.[54]

Jack Ma has applied a strategy popularised by Mao Zedong during the Chinese civil war, 'the encirclement of cities from the countryside', which has also been utilised by other Chinese companies such as Haier and Huawei. In this context, 'countryside' denotes not physical locations but a large number of small websites, versus the large websites which eBay had bought out by using its financial strength, intending to block any competitors from emerging. In any event, these small websites have brought advertising revenues and Web traffic to Alibaba, forming a virtuous cycle.[55]

In 2004, eBay made a further investment of $100 million in China to boost its marketing effort, while Jack Ma decided to reduce Alibaba's marketing budget by two-thirds, in order to focus on product development. This decision was based on Mao Zedong's guerrilla warfare strategy:

> The enemy approaches, we retreat.
> The enemy halts, we move in.
> The enemy tires, we attack.
> The enemy retreats, we pursue.[56]

eBay's use of its huge marketing budget represents the approach of an opponent, to which Alibaba responded by retreating, letting the opponent educate the market. Once the market had become mature, Alibaba's products would be ready to take advantage of its maturity.[57]

CHINESE DIALECTIC

When competition between eBay and Alibaba started, they were considered unequal opponents, with eBay overwhelming Alibaba. The war between them lasted for three years, from 2003 to 2006. The balance of power was so uneven that eBay never saw Alibaba as a worthy opponent. Adopting a Chinese dialectic perspective, Jack Ma stated that 'eBay may be a shark in the ocean, but I am a crocodile in the Yangtze River. If we fight in the ocean, we lose – but if we fight in the river, we win.'[58] Embracing Chinese dialectic, Jack Ma was emboldened to challenge a much stronger and more powerful opponent. The outcome of the war is that Alibaba's platforms now dominate China's e-commerce market, whereas eBay has become an insignificant player in China.

The development of Alibaba itself, particularly the iron triangle, reflects a holistic view. At the time, the barriers to e-commerce were not just the users or the market, but more importantly, the ability to deliver and consumers' security concerns. Alibaba has had to engage in three different areas of business to succeed in e-commerce, and each one of these areas has become a profit centre for the group. Alibaba's financial arm, Ant Financial, and logistics arm, Cainiao, have gone far beyond just serving e-commerce customers, penetrating a number of other service areas in society.

COMPETITOR ORIENTATION

Competitor orientation means that Alibaba has been inspired by its competitors' ideas, but not their ways of operating, simply because these would not work in China; if they had, Alibaba would not have existed. Jack Ma had to infuse e-commerce with a large number of Chinese elements to make it work in China. Alibaba's competitor orientation in this case is reflected in its concentration of its attention and resources to outdoing eBay in China, with its secrecy, PR effort and strategic detours, in other words, its stratagems.

AGILITY

Agility is in the blood of Chinese business, and Alibaba is no exception, as shown by the speed at which Alibaba has developed its e-commerce, finance and logistics pillars. A former vice president of Alibaba has used the metaphor of being 'as fast as a rabbit but patient as a turtle.'

> Entrepreneurs need to work on two different tracks at the same time. On the one hand, they should orient their vision to the long term, like Jack's 102-year company. But on the other hand, they need to move aggressively and quickly day-to-day. The two tracks help keep the company balanced between long-term vision and short-term action.[59]

The Alibaba HRM system

A cornerstone of the Alibaba edifice is its HRM system, as Figure 8.3 makes clear. A saying of Zhu Geliang, an incarnation of wisdom in China, illuminates the nature of business success: Man does what he can, God does what he will. Just as Bole needed luck (or divine intervention) to find his chollima, the presence of Joe Tsai on the Alibaba board was a godsend for Jack Ma, as he is seen as indispensable to Alibaba's success.

Joe Tsai studied economics and East Asian studies at Yale College and took a law degree at Yale Law School. Having worked briefly for a New York law firm, Sullivan & Cromwell, he joined Investor AB, a Swedish investment bank, in Hong Kong, as CEO of Venture Capital, Asia. Jack Ma met him for the first time when he represented Investor AB to discuss a venture capital deal; negotiations lasted for four days without success. However, a positive outcome of this failure was that Joe Tsai made the audacious decision to join the start-up of Alibaba, despite having to give up his million-dollar salary for a meagre income of RMB 500.

Joe Tsai's decision to leave a well-paid job in Hong Kong for a start-up in Hangzhou surprised many people, including his wife. He explained himself thus:

> I saw something in Jack. Not just the vision, the sparks in his eyes. But a team of people, his loyal followers. They believed in the vision. I said to myself, if I am going to join a group of people, this is the one. There is a clear leader, the glue to the whole thing. I just felt a real affinity to Jack, I mean who wouldn't.[60]

The importance of Joe Tsai to Alibaba cannot be overemphasised:

- Appointed as CFO, Joe Tsai registered an offshore company, making Alibaba ready to receive venture capital investment.
- He incorporated the company, specifying the percentages of shareholding and responsibilities of 18 shareholders, without any ambiguity or controversy at a later stage.
- He played a vital role in persuading Goldman Sachs, a world-class investment bank, to invest in Alibaba, a start-up, in 1999.
- He twice refused offers from Softbank, allowing Alibaba to get a much better deal for investment prices.
- He was instrumental in having Alibaba.com listed on the Hong Kong Stock Exchange in 2007 and in forging a number of mergers and acquisitions, as part of Alibaba's strategic restructuring.

Jack Ma has acknowledged that Joe Tsai is the kind of talented person he has always sought. The philosophy of Zhu Geliang cited above would suggest that this kind of talent cannot be found by man but has to be given by God; it was fate or destiny which led Joe Tsai to appear and join Alibaba.[61] This could not be further from the truth; just like the chollima that Bole found, the key to finding the long-sought miracle worker was mutual attraction.

To prepare Alibaba for international expansion, Jack Ma was once obsessed with 'international talent', believing that to become one of the top ten websites in the world, the company must have world-class talents. He decreed that anyone in a top position must have been educated in Europe or the USA for at least three years or have five to ten years of overseas work experience. He formed a 'super' management team consisting of MBA recruits from top US business schools such as Harvard and Stanford. However, none of these super-talented people delivered satisfactory performance. For instance, one vice president of marketing prepared a marketing budget for the second half year of about $12 million, while Alibaba only had $5 million, and then tried to persuade Jack Ma to accept his plan by talking about strategy and planning, without considering any of the practical problems.

After some time, Jack Ma recognised the problems of overseas elites and expressed a sceptical view of Ivy League MBAs: they have unrealistically high expectations, they are incapable of teamwork and they could spend a year doing nothing but talking about who should be CEO. Eventually, he had to let 95 per cent of the MBA recruits go, as he later explained:

> These professionals were indeed quite competent at management. They were just like aircraft engines, very powerful but not suitable for tractors. They were extremely good at management theory and all their decisions sounded quite reasonable, but once you put them into practice, they were all wrong. My company was not ready at that time to accommodate these people.[62]

This realisation caused Jack Ma to review his approach to talent management and reverse his policy of recruiting elite people exclusively from top business schools. He understood that start-ups cannot rely solely on overseas talent, but should train homegrown human resources. From then on, he started to pay close attention to the identification and training of internal talent, deciding that top posts would be filled mainly by the promotion of internal candidates. When he was asked whether, during the process of business development, the company should endeavour to search around for talents to form an elite management team or focus on internal training and promotion, his answer was:

> Start-ups should avoid relying on all-star management teams or working with those who have already achieved great success in start-up. During the start-up period, you should find people to form a team: not successful yet, but craving success; they should be ordinary and cooperative and should have shared values. Once your business has grown to a certain extent, you may employ the talented to benefit investment and market development.[63]

Jack Ma places great emphasis on the role of teamwork, and once proudly presented his top team known as the Four Os: himself as CEO, Joe Tsai as CFO, John Wu (the inventor of the Yahoo search engine) as CTO and Savio Kwan (with 25 years of experience in GE and BTR) as COO. For instance, as COO, Savio Kwan has also made a marked contribution to the company: he rationalised Alibaba's international operations by scrapping a futile joint venture in South Korea and scaling back the company's presence in Silicon Valley; he let many of the higher-paid foreign employees go and replaced expensive advertising campaigns with word-of-mouth marketing; and having increased domestic hiring, he rapidly expanded the company's sales team to focus on the promotion of fee-paying services.[64]

Alibaba is very careful to cultivate a corporate culture that emphasises putting the customer's interest ahead of its own. Employees are encouraged to be informal at work and to shoulder personal responsibility, undertaking or delegating tasks without waiting for orders from their superiors. Complaining is discouraged.

Jack Ma has borrowed ideas and terminology from Jin Yong's novels, to provide a sense of realism. From *Demigods and Semi-Devils*, he has been inspired by the Nine Swords of Dugu and the Six Meridian Divine Swords, with which he links corporate values. Thus, the Nine Swords of Dugu represent collective wisdom and effort, mutual learning, quality, simplicity, passion, open-mindedness, innovation, focus, and service and respect, while the Six Meridian Divine Swords denote customer priority, teamwork, embracing change, sincerity, commitment and dedication.

> Measuring how employees live up to the Six Vein Spirit Sword is the job of Alibaba's human resources department, which plays a critical role, overseeing the hiring of twelve thousand people in one year alone … HR at Alibaba has tremendous power over promotions and hiring. With its constant emphasis on culture and ideology, people at Alibaba refer to HR informally as the "Political Commissar" (*zheng wei*). The HR department also oversees extensive training, with manuals of more than one thousand pages for new employees and a sophisticated database, matching performance closely with promotions and pay raises.[65]

To summarise, Alibaba's successful development is inseparable from Jack Ma's vision and his ability to recognise and secure talented people who share his values. Although he has made mistakes in his HRM philosophy and policy, he has learned quickly from his misjudgements and rectified his HRM decisions. This case shows that some special talents may not be found by laborious searching; instead, a business leader needs to be clear about what kind of talent would fit with the company and be able to recognise such talent if it appears. The way in which the company has developed its corporate culture has been unique, having much to do with Jack Ma's personal interests, but it has worked. The company's HRM policy and practices reflect a combination of standard HRM procedures and practices with the leader's ethos and preferences.

Case study 2: HRM in Huawei

Hong Liu has developed a framework for Huawei's strategic mind and its implementation system, leading to an enhanced performance outcome.[66] Figure 8.4 presents an adapted model of Huawei's strategy formation and implementation, in relation to its HRM system. It indicates that the firm's HRM policy and practices underpin its strategy formation and implementation system; the quality and types of executive recruits can have a direct effect on how corporate strategy is formulated and implemented. A good starting point is Huawei's decision-making system, particularly related to HR evaluation and promotion.

With advice and guidance from IBM consultants, Huawei has adopted an organisational structure consisting of seven divisions: market and service, strategy and marketing, product and solution, operation and delivery, finance, policy

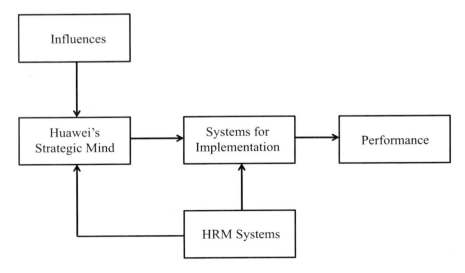

Figure 8.4 Huawei's strategy and implementation system

and cooperation, and human resources. An executive management team (EMT) comprising the head of each division is the decision centre in Huawei. The chair of the EMT is occupied for six months by each committee member in turn. The company is run by a system of three rotating CEOs.

The selection and promotion of senior executive positions are based on a system of separation of powers, under which nomination, approval and veto are independent of one another. Under this system, business units nominate candidates for promotion, the HRM department evaluates them and the Committee of the Chinese Communist Party can exercise its veto if it has sound reasons. The performance assessment mechanism takes account of (1) performance results and behaviour in key incidents, (2) performance-based contracting and (3) position-related qualifications. This system effectively protects the company's HRM decisions from the effects of the cronyism and nepotism embedded in Chinese culture.[67]

The HRM edifice model

Since it was founded, Huawei has developed a model of HRM in the form of the edifice depicted in Figure 8.5, with three layers of foundation and four pillars, supporting effective communication, with resultant competitive advantage as the roof. At the base of the edifice are laid out the company's vision and strategic objectives, above which are its corporate culture and values, then appointment and qualification management.[68]

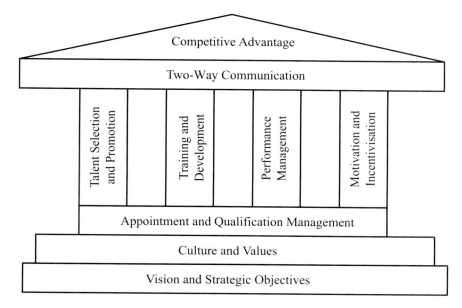

Figure 8.5 Huawei's HRM structural model

The four pillars are talent selection and promotion, training and development, performance management, and motivation and incentivisation. In essence, the four pillars involve the selection, development, utilisation and retention of talent. Building four solid pillars requires effective two-way communication between the HRM function and the talented people. When all of these steps are undertaken appropriately, a competitive edge can be gained. In the view of Ren Zhengfei, Huawei's HRM system is unique compared with other companies, making a strong contribution to the company's performance.

The company's HRM system is closely tied with its core value, that in everything it does the company must serve its customers to its best ability. The founder has instilled a corporate culture that treats customers with religious reverence, as if they were gods. Huawei's entire business process is built on this principle, from R&D to manufacturing, products, marketing and corporate culture.[69] Therefore, its HRM policies are geared to measuring and assessing how well its employees serve its customers, involving value creation, assessment and distribution. Each department or individual is evaluated according to the value they create and to how this should be distributed among departments or individuals and on what criteria. Huawei's employee evaluation covers five points: attitude towards work, ability to work independently, performance, adaptability and potential, and management capability. The criteria for evaluation are (1) shared value, (2) the challenges of target and objectives and (3) present and potential capability.[70]

In 2012, the company changed the basis of its profit-sharing policy from shareholding to value contribution. Under this new HR policy, all organisations and individuals receive financial rewards on the basis of their value creation and performance. Service/logistics departments participate in profit sharing through their services to business units. This policy has four characteristics:

- It has strengthened the support of service/logistics departments for business units and increased their efficiency, linking their performance with its consequences.
- It has increased remuneration elasticity and connected the interests and values of organisations and individuals to their performance, enhancing the effectiveness of employee incentivisation.
- It reflects the company's customer orientation policy, based on customer satisfaction and experience.
- It is a bottom-up reward system, with greater emphasis on rewarding the lower levels of organisational units.[71]

Drastic HRM measures

Huawei was founded in 1987, and by 1996 the company had firmly established a strategic foothold in the industry, with sales of RMB 150 million. Its marketing department was a major contributor to this early success, but instead of being rewarded handsomely, all heads of marketing, including regional directors and office directors, were in February 1996 required to submit two documents to the corporate centre: a critical review of work done in 1995 and a letter of resignation.

A top executive of Motorola based in China later commented on this episode, noting that marketing was an area of high mobility, where it was extremely difficult to recruit and train regional directors. The directors concerned had recently proved themselves to be good performers. If they had been headhunted, they would have taken many customers with them when they departed. This was a 'big bang' event, involving all regional marketing directors and office directors, without any prior experience or testing. It could only be imposed by Ren Zhengfei, as an ex-military man, showing great guts and risk-taking. His move turned out to be a success and resulted in great cohesion and morale-building.[72]

After a month of open competition for managerial positions and management evaluation of candidates, 30 per cent of employees and contributors to the company had left their original positions. During the campaign, the marketing department put out a slogan: 'The birds surviving fire are phoenixes.' Some members of the department wrote articles with titles such as 'Responsibility is heavier than Tai Mountain' and 'Don't tell me that I don't care,' indicating that marketing staff had started to reflect on past marketing approaches, to reject them and to prepare themselves for marketing in a new era.[73]

Ren Zhengfei believed that the decision to demand group resignation was more of a morale-booster than anything else, signifying the company's connection with the international marketplace. It promoted the reorganisation of the company, involving a changeover of management, without demoralising the managers who had just stepped down. Once the marketing department had been restructured, the reorganisation of the rest of the company would be automatically initiated and implemented. Without the change of management personnel, the internationalisation strategy could not be put into effect.

In fact, the group resignation of the marketing department was just the starting point for a company-wide restructuring programme, with the aim of driving the whole organisation towards market orientation and international connection. It laid the foundation for IBM consultants to help Huawei build an integrated product development (IPD) system. A major barrier to the installation of such a system is the reallocation of power; the group resignation programme in marketing was aimed at managers throughout Huawei, to prepare them psychologically to accept an organisational revolution. In 1997, 70 IBM consultants moved into Huawei to work on the IPD system.

In October 2007, 11 years after the first group resignation, Huawei put on another show of collective resignation involving 6687 employees, including Ren Zhengfei himself. Internal company policy dictates that anyone employed by the company for over eight years must resign and has six months in which to reapply for a job. If the application is accepted, a new contract valid for one to three years will be signed. Those who are qualified will have the same level of remuneration as before. Most old employees have shares in the company, and the company holds these for them for six months and then cashes them in for any employee whose contract is not renewed.

The earlier group resignation drew attention only within the industry, making international competitors feel pressurised, as they believed that if a business leader could orchestrate such a magnificent show with success, such a person's leadership and team fighting spirit would be formidable and his company would sooner or later catch its rivals. However, the second group resignation became a hot media topic both domestically and internationally, and was closely scrutinised by the All-China Federation of Trade Unions. Condemnation was rife on the Internet.

Why did Ren Zhengfei initiate such radical and risky reform? By 2007, Huawei had outperformed all of its rivals except Ericsson and Cisco. However, a shake-up of the industry had taken place in 2006, whereby Alcatel merged with Lucent Technologies, Nokia with Siemens and Sony with Ericsson, which acquired Marconi. This increased competitive pressure on Huawei. On the other hand, Ren Zhengfei was greatly concerned that Huawei's initial success had made many employees so well off that they had become indolent. The Law of Labour Contracts, soon to be promulgated by the Chinese government, stipulates that if an employee has worked for a company for ten years or has renewed a fixed-term contract twice, he or she can become a permanent employee of the company. This conflicts with Huawei's HR remuneration policy, which is based on employees' responsibilities and contribution, rather than on length of service. The beneficiaries of this policy were those who assumed most responsibility, worked hardest and made the strongest contributions to the company's performance; those who rested complacently on their laurels were urged to make changes, while those old employees who had become lazy were made redundant. The reform measure was intended to prepare employees to be ready for the expansion of international business.

All resignation applications, including Ren Zhengfei's, were accepted by the board of directors, which beseeched Ren Zhengfei to stay on as CEO. Of the 6687 employees who resigned, 6581 had their contracts renewed, 38 retired by choice or on health grounds, 52 left the company voluntarily to seek for greater space of career development and 16 departed because of their poor performance (but compensated without resentment)s. A large number of mid- and high-level posts were reshuffled, some post holders being promoted and some demoted, while numerous competent youngsters were appointed. Despite the scale of change in HRM, the process passed without significant conflict, under the gaze of the All-China and the Guangdong trade union federations, which sent inspectors to scrutinise employee-employer relations. All appears to have gone smoothly and calmly at Huawei.[74]

Mao Zedong's Yanan Rectification Movement inspired the Huawei HRM practice of 'criticism and self-criticism', which was formerly heavily utilised within the CPC. Mao invented this tool of social transformation, whose aim was to cast off organisational laziness and complacency and to energise the CPC and nation.[75] In adopting this approach, Huawei primarily emphasised self-criticism and de-emphasised mutual criticism, which was prone to causing friction within the company. Self-criticism became a core value of Huawei, intending to keep its employees upbeat and energetic in a tough competitive environment. Ren firmly believes that the achievement of long-term organisational stability and sustainability at Huawei will depend on its ability to exercise self-criticism and embrace the Middle Way.

Huawei has executed this practice for 20 years. Everyone from top managers to ordinary employees is required to attend monthly 'democratic-life meetings', where they talk about their own shortcomings, with an analysis of their causes. Colleagues may help an individual to identify the causes of his or her failings, without engaging in exaggeration or personal attack and without becoming emotional. Surprisingly, this practice has not caused friction within the organisation, but reinforced the unity of its 150,000 employees; nor has it generated spurious obedience to senior management, but maintained the personality of each individual. Huawei has achieved its objective of keeping the organisation energised, by means both of Ren's personal involvement in the movement as the top leader and of the exercise of the Middle Way, without anyone becoming extreme.[76]

HRM in China from an MNC perspective

In China, no matter how the environment differs from that of the West, the basic tasks of human resources management are the same as anywhere else: recruitment, retention and compensation. With MNCs in mind, Fernandez and

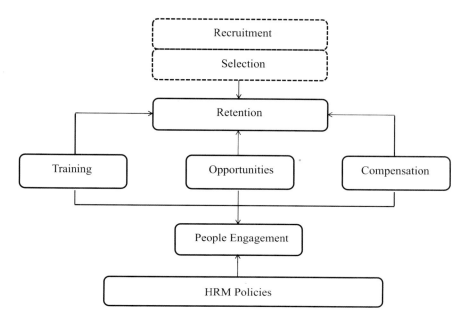

Figure 8.6 A HRM model for MNCs in China

Liu have developed an HRM model, with a focus on its application in China, as shown in Figure 8.6.[77]

Beginning at the top of the figure, the first two steps are recruitment and selection, followed by retention, with three proposed methods: training, career opportunities and compensation. These measures generate the effect at the next stage of engagement, characterised by 3Ss: stay, say and strive. Engaged staff will stay with the company, speak out and say positive things about it, while striving to the best of their ability to perform well. Finally, companies must have transparent and consistent HR policies.

Companies should first define the types of employees that they require, and then send signals to the target groups. One way for MNCs to attract the right candidates is to leverage their brands. Confucianism dictates that Chinese people value the image of an organisation with which they are affiliated; reputable brands make them feel proud and confident. Those companies whose brands are less well known should concentrate on building a brand image among their target candidates. They may form partnerships with Chinese universities through joint research programmes, offer scholarships and internships to college students and donate relevant teaching equipment.

To enhance the effectiveness of the next step, retention, three HR methods are proposed: training, career opportunities and compensation. Compensation alone is not enough to retain employees, so other incentive methods are needed. Since education is valued in Chinese culture, training can often become a powerful tool to keep employees, who should be made to understand that training is an investment, not a reward. Specific measures should be taken to work with employees on their career development plans, making them feel confident of their future in the company. Fair and transparent HR policies should be in place to make Chinese employees feel respected, valued and positive about working for a foreign multinational.

China's HR market has been hectic and challenging ever since the country opened its economy to foreign investment. Although the absolute supply of talent has increased dramatically in the last ten years, identification, selection and retention have become even more difficult. These four complementary strategic recommendations are worth following:

(1) Regenerating employment branding efforts. Despite encountering fierce competition for talent from Chinese companies, MNCs still have a competitive edge over them. They should sustain this by communicating more effectively with the labour market on their overall stability, their commitment to China and their attention to individual career development.

(2) Creating international rotation as part of job specifications. Research reveals that high-potential Chinese professionals who have signed contracts with MNCs aspired to being posted, at some point, to company headquarters. In response, companies could create long-term international projects involving job rotation, whereby Chinese professionals would take a short-term headquarters post, while corporate leaders might also spend some time in China.

(3) Making smart counteroffers. Many Chinese domestic companies approach experienced technical talent and executives of Western multinationals with offers of dramatic pay increases. It is often necessary to make counteroffers, and this can be challenging. It is suggested that those who have received an offer might automatically get a pay increase of, say, 20 per cent.

(4) Acting like a local company. If a company has become sufficiently localised, it can accommodate itself very well to local talent requirements and thus achieve a better retention rate.[78]

Concluding remarks

The management of human assets, or talent management as it is now known, has been at the core of Chinese politics, military affairs and commerce since antiquity. Military victories have always been associated with eminent generals, while enlightened sovereigns have been assisted by exceptional counsellors and ministers. The same is true today of China's business warfare. Lenovo's founder, Liu Chuanzhi, has famously stated: 'The management of a company in essence is the management of people.'

The topic of the war for talent has been addressed in countless books and articles; this modest chapter has highlighted the major differences between

Chinese and Western HRM practices and has explored some important characteristics of Chinese HRM. Although the HRM practices of medium-sized and large companies in China contain a high proportion of standard or scientific elements, each successful company has a unique core part that is distinctly company-specific and often associated with the application of Chinese tradition. The identification and selection of top management team members and the cultivation of a corporate ethos in successful Chinese companies entail more components of art than science, with Chinese culture playing a vital part.

The role of talent in a company is relative, in that there is no best talent, only the best-suited talent. It is possible to identify talent made prominent by qualifications and external recognition, but if a person's values do not fit with those of the company, he or she cannot contribute to the company's value creation and thus cannot be considered a worthwhile talent from the company's point of view. An unfitted talent can even cause damage to the company. Alibaba's experience shows that high-flyers and those who have already achieved notable success in entrepreneurial firms may not be suitable for involvement in start-ups. The essential nature of talent management in China is to identify, select and train talents to fit with corporate culture, so that they can make significant contributions to company performance.

The effectiveness of talent management is associated with the company's (the founder's or the CEO's) Tao, in three respects: (1) the company has a far-sighted vision grounded in a deep understanding of the industry or *shi*; (2) the top person occupies the high moral ground and acts as a magnet for talent; and (3) the top management grasps the essence of HRM in the company. For instance, Jack Ma's vision and personal morality-based charisma have attracted the talent that Alibaba needs, while Huawei links its HRM with employees' value creation, which serves as the basis for HR rewards and promotion.

Corporate culture is the soul of a company, binding employees together with cohesion and synergy. An essential task of HRM is to cultivate and strengthen the corporate culture. However, each company has to find its own way of instilling a culture which is associated with the founder's ethos and values.

Notes

1 Boxall, P., Purcell, J. and Wright, P.M. (2007), "Human Resource Management: Scope, Analysis and Significance," in P. Boxall, J. Purcell and P.M. Wright (eds.), *The Handbook of Human Resource Management*, Oxford: Oxford University Press, pp. 1–16.
2 Lewin, D. and Mitchell, D.J.B. (1992), "Systems of Employee Voice: Theoretical and Empirical Perspectives," *California Management Review*, 34 (3), 95–111.
3 Wright, P.M. and McMahan, G.C. (1992), "Theoretical Perspectives for Strategic Human Resource Management," *Journal of Management*, 18, 295–320.
4 Ibid. And see Lengnick-Hall, M., Lengnick-Hall, C., Andrade, L. and Drake, B. (2009), "Strategic Human Resource Management: The Evolution of the Field," *Human Resource Management Review*, 19 (2), 64–85.

5 Crainer, S. (1995), *The Financial Times Handbook of Management*, London: Pitman Publishing, p. 258. Huselid, M.A., Jackson, S.E. and Schuler, R.S. (1997), "Technical and Strategic Human Resource Effectiveness as Determinants of Firm Performance," *Academy of Management Journal*, 40, 171–188. Wright, P.M. and Gardner, T.M. (2003), "The Human Resource-Firm Performance Relationship: Methodological and Theoretical Challenges," in D. Holman, T.D. Wall, C.W. Clegg, P. Sparrow, and A. Howard (eds.), *The New Workplace: A Guide to the Human Impact of Modern Working Practices*, Wiley, pp. 311–328.

6 Iles, P., Chuai, X. and Preece, D. (2010), "Talent Management and HRM in Multinational Companies in Beijing: Definitions, Differences and Drivers," *Journal of World Business*, 45, 179–189.

7 Morton, L. (2005), *Talent Management Value Imperatives: Strategies for Execution*, New York: The Conference Board. Iles, P., Chuai, X. and Preece, D. (2010), "Talent Management and HRM in Multinational Companies in Beijing: Definitions, Differences and Drivers," *Journal of World Business*, 45, 179–189.

8 Buckingham, M. and Vosburgh, R. (2001), "The 21st Century Human Resources Function: It's the Talent, Stupid!" *Human Resource Planning*, 24 (4), 17–23. Iles, P., Chuai, X. and Preece, D. (2010), "Talent Management and HRM in Multinational Companies in Beijing: Definitions, Differences and Drivers," *Journal of World Business*, 45, 179–189.

9 Huselid, M., Beatty, R. and Becker, B. (2005), "'A Players' or 'A Positions'? The Strategic Logic of Workforce Management," *Harvard Business Review*, 83 (12), 110–117. Iles, P., Chuai, X. and Preece, D. (2010), "Talent Management and HRM in Multinational Companies in Beijing: Definitions, Differences and Drivers," *Journal of World Business*, 45, 179–189.

10 Groysberg, B., Nanda, A. and Nohria, N. (2004), "The Risky Business of Hiring Stars," *Harvard Business Review*, May, 1–8. Iles, P., Chuai, X. and Preece, D. (2010), "Talent Management and HRM in Multinational Companies in Beijing: Definitions, Differences and Drivers," *Journal of World Business*, 45, 179–189.

11 Schmidt, C. (2011), "The Battle for China's Talents," *Harvard Business Review*, March, 25–27.

12 Fernandez, J.A. and Liu, S.J. (2007), *China CEO: A Case Guide for Business Leaders in China*, Singapore: John Wiley & Sons (Asia), p. 36.

13 PwC (2012), *Human Resources and Talent Management*, PwC, www.pwchk.com/web media/doc/634868463816378457_iic_ch5.pdf, retrieved on 12 December 2016.

14 Orr, G. and Roth, E. (2012), "A CEO Guide to Innovation in China," *McKinsey Quarterly*, February, www.mckinsey.com/global-themes/asia-pacific/a-ceos-guide-to-innovation-in-china, retrieved on 23 November 2016.

15 PwC (2016), "Redefining Business Success in a Changing World CEO Survey," *19th Annual Global CEO Survey*, January 2016, www.pwc.com/gx/en/ceo-survey/2016/landing-page/pwc-19th-annual-global-ceo-survey.pdf, retrieved on 12 December 2016.

16 Zhao, S.M. and Du, J. (2012), "Thirty-Two Years of Development of Human Resource Management in China: Review and Prospects," *Human Resource Management Review*, 22, 179–188.

17 Deng, T. and Liu, X. (2007), "Meander of Chinese Human Resource Management," *The Human Resource*, 18, 18–26.

18 Bersin, J., Solow, M., Wakefield, N. and Walsh, B. (2016), "The New Organization: Different by Design," *2016 Global Human Capital Trends Report*, Deloitte University Press, https://www2.deloitte.com/content/dam/Deloitte/global/Documents/Human Capital/gx-dup-global-human-capital-trends-2016.pdf, retrieved on 12 December 2016.

19 PwC (2016), "Redefining Business Success in a Changing World CEO Survey," *19th Annual Global CEO Survey*, January 2016, www.pwc.com/gx/en/ceo-survey/2016/landing-page/pwc-19th-annual-global-ceo-survey.pdf, retrieved on 12 December 2016.

The war for talent 311

20 Li, Y. (2013), *Traditional Chinese Thinking on HRM Practices*, London: Palgrave Macmillan, p. 2. Guest, D. (1992), "HRM: Its Implications for Industrial Relations and Trade Unions," in J. Storey (ed.), *New Perspectives on HRM*, London: Routledge, p. 12.
21 Hofstede, G. (1993), "Cultural Constraints in Management Theories," *Academy of Management Executive*, 7, 81–94.
22 Liu, H. (2015), *The Chinese Strategic Mind*, Northampton, MA: Edward Elgar Publishing, pp. 188–189.
23 Ibid, p. 195.
24 The Economist (2011), "The Long March of the Invisible Mr Ren," *The Economist*, 2 June 2011.
25 Ngo, H.Y., Lau, C.M. and Foley, S. (2008), "Strategic Human Resource Management, Firm Performance, and Employee Relations Climate in China," *Human Resource Management*, 47 (1), 73–90. Zheng, C. and Lamond, D. (2009), "A Critical Review of Human Resource Management Studies (1978–2007) in the People's Republic of China," *International Journal of Human Resource Management*, 20 (11), 2194–2227. Zhao, S.M. and Du, J. (2012), "Thirty-Two Years of Development of Human Resource Management in China: Review and Prospects," *Human Resource Management Review*, 22, 179–188.
26 Kaufman, B. (2001), "The Theory and Practice of Strategic HRM and Participative Management," *Human Resource Management Review*, 11 (4), 505–533.
27 Miao, F.L. (2015), *Zhongguo yongren shi (History of Talent Management in China)*, Beijing: Chinese Communist Party History Publishing House.
28 Lin, Y.T. (1976), *The Wisdom of Taotse* (A translation of *Tao Te Ching*, edited and with an Introduction by Lin Yutang), New York: The Modern Library, p. 156.
29 One of the five ancient emperors before the dynastic periods.
30 Lau, D.C. (1979), *Confucius: The Analects*, translated with an introduction by D.C. Lau, London: Penguin Books, p. 95.
31 Liu, Q.L. (2014), *Zhonghua quanzhi (Chinese Power and Wisdom)*, Beijing: Union Publishing House, p. 31.
32 Lin, Y.T. (1976), *The Wisdom of Taotse* (A translation of *Tao Te Ching*, edited and with an Introduction by Lin Yutang), New York: The Modern Library, p. 308.
33 Lau, D.C. (1979), *Confucius: The Analects*, translated with an introduction by D.C. Lau, London: Penguin Books, p. 86.
34 Gao, L. (2013), *Renchai (Human Assets)*, Beijing: Chinese Youth Publishing House, p. 51.
35 Ibid, p. 60.
36 Ibid, p. 69.
37 Lau, D.C. (1979), *Confucius: The Analects*, translated with an introduction by D.C. Lau, London: Penguin Books, p. 74.
38 Ibid, p. 128.
39 Ibid, p. 135.
40 Ibid, p. 73.
41 Ibid, p. 72.
42 Creel, H.G. (1965), "The Role of the Horse in Chinese History," *American Historical Review*, 70 (3), 647–672.
43 Ren, Z.G. (2013), *Wei Shen Mo Shi Mao Zedong? (Why Is Mao Zedong?)*, Beijing: Guang Ming Daily Publisher, p. 81.
44 Gao, L. (2013), *Renchai (Human Assets)*, Beijing: Chinese Youth Publishing House, p. 295.
45 Liu, H. (2015), *The Chinese Strategic Mind*, Northampton, MA: Edward Elgar Publishing.
46 Clark, D. (2016), *Alibaba: The House That Jack Ma Built*, New York: HarperCollins Publishers, p. 212.

47 Erisman, P. (2015), *Alibaba's World*, New York: Palgrave McMillan, p. 217.
48 Clark, D. (2016), *Alibaba: The House That Jack Ma Built*, New York: HarperCollins Publishers, p. 99.
49 Wang, L.F. and Li, X. (2014), *Chuan buxie de ma yun (Ma Yun Who Wears Canvas Shoes)*, Beijing: Union Publishing Co. Ltd, pp. 50–51.
50 Clark, D. (2016), *Alibaba: The House That Jack Ma Built*, New York: HarperCollins Publishers, p. 218.
51 Ibid, p. 5.
52 Wang, L.F. and Li, X. (2014), *Chuan buxie de ma yun (Ma Yun Who Wears Canvas Shoes)*, Beijing: Union Publishing Co. Ltd, pp. 85–87.
53 Clark, D. (2016), *Alibaba: The House That Jack Ma Built*, New York: HarperCollins Publishers, pp. 29–35. Wang, L.F. and Li, X. (2014), *Chuan buxie de ma yun (Ma Yun Who Wears Canvas Shoes)*, Beijing: Union Publishing Co. Ltd, p. 84.
54 Clark, D. (2016), *Alibaba: The House That Jack Ma Built*, New York: HarperCollins Publishers, p. 163.
55 Wang, L.F. and Li, X. (2014), *Chuan buxie de ma yun (Ma Yun Who Wears Canvas Shoes)*, Beijing: Union Publishing Co. Ltd, pp. 119–120.
56 Salisbury, H. (1985), *The Long March: The Untold Story*, New York: Palgrave Macmillan, p. 129.
57 Wang, L.F. and Li, X. (2014), *Chuan buxie de ma yun (Ma Yun Who Wears Canvas Shoes)*, Beijing: Union Publishing Co. Ltd, p. 120.
58 Erisman, P. (2015), *Alibaba's World*, New York: Palgrave Macmillan, pp. 110–111.
59 Ibid, pp. 219–220.
60 Clark, D. (2016), *Alibaba: The House That Jack Ma Built*, New York: HarperCollins Publishers, p. 100.
61 Wang, L.F. and Li, X. (2014), *Chuan buxie de ma yun (Ma Yun Who Wears Canvas Shoes)*, Beijing: Union Publishing Co. Ltd, p. 50.
62 Ibid, p. 88. Author's own translation.
63 Wang, L.F. and Li, X. (2014), *Chuan buxie de ma yun (Ma Yun Who Wears Canvas Shoes)*, Beijing: Union Publishing Co. Ltd, p. 89. Author's own translation.
64 Clark, D. (2016), *Alibaba: The House That Jack Ma Built*, New York: HarperCollins Publishers, p. 142.
65 Ibid, p. 34.
66 Liu, H. (2015), *The Chinese Strategic Mind*, Northampton, MA: Edward Elgar Publishing, pp. 176–196.
67 Yang, S.L. (2013), *Huawei Kao Shenme (On What Huawei Relies)*, Beijing: China CITIC Press, pp. 155–156.
68 Zhou, L.Z. (2016), *Huawei zhexue (Huawei's Philosophy)*, Beijing: China Machine Press, pp. 213–214.
69 Tian, T. and Wu, C.B. (2012), *Xia yige dao xia de hui bu hui shi Huawei? (Is Huawei the Next One to Fall?)*, Beijing: China CITIC Press, pp. 25–26.
70 Zhou, L.Z. (2016), *Huawei zhexue (Huawei's Philosophy)*, Beijing: China Machine Press, p. 214.
71 Ibid, pp. 214–217.
72 Tian, T. and Wu, C.B. (2012), *Xia yige dao xia de hui bu hui shi Huawei? (Is Huawei the Next One to Fall?)*, Beijing: China CITIC Press, pp. 200–201.
73 Yang, S.L. (2013), *Huawei Kao Shenme (On What Huawei Relies)*, Beijing: China CITIC Press, p. 58.
74 Tian, T. and Wu, C.B. (2012), *Xia yige dao xia de hui bu hui shi Huawei? (Is Huawei the Next One to Fall?)*, Beijing: China CITIC Press, pp. 204–208.
75 Liang, K. (2004), "The Rise of Mao and His Cultural Legacy: The Yan'an Rectification Movement," *Journal of Contemporary China*, 12 (34), 225–228.

76 Tian, T. and Wu, C.B. (2012), *Xia yige dao xia de hui bu hui shi Huawei? (Is Huawei the Next One to Fall?)*, Beijing: China CITIC Press, pp. 170–171.
77 Fernandez, J.A. and Liu, S.J. (2007), *China CEO: A Case Guide for Business Leaders in China*, Singapore: John Wiley & Sons (Asia), pp. 37–41.
78 Schmidt, C. (2011), "The Battle for China's Talents," *Harvard Business Review*, March, 25–27.

Epilogue

This is a book that offers its readers a comprehensive and systematic body of knowledge of Chinese business. It has taken a holistic perspective, intending to achieve a balance between the academic and practical, between theory and practice and between traditional and current (Internet-based) industry. One major difference between Western and Chinese strategic thinking is that in a conflict situation, Western opponents are prone to emphasise the need for strength, while the Chinese tend to rely on wisdom, specifically stratagem. Following the same logic, Western readers may naturally conclude that they may take the point that to understand Chinese business it is necessary to take a holistic perspective, but they may prefer to study the writings of experts in each different discipline, reading up on Chinese philosophy, history, military studies, e-commerce, innovation and HRM, for instance, in order to get the best knowledge of each field. This may sound reasonable, but it is infeasible.

It is neither necessary nor doable, since going through huge volumes of disciplinary literature takes a great deal of time and effort; in most cases, it would be difficult to link the literature on history, military studies and philosophy, for instance, to business practice. Many Western businesspeople are likely to be daunted by the ordeal of reading extensively on Chinese philosophy and history or even Chinese HRM. Even in business-related fields, such as Chinese e-commerce, innovation and HRM, readers may find that specialist writings entail too much knowledge to be relevant to business practice. In other words, the nature of knowledge aggregation and integration in this book reflects the Middle Way; in each disciplinary area, some fundamental knowledge is summarised, integrated and linked to business practice. The Middle Way as a core Confucian value represents gold standard behaviour and crystallises Chinese wisdom, benefiting readers with optimal knowledge of Chinese business. Confucius has made it abundantly clear that the Middle Way is the highest standard of moral virtue in the ethical realm; Huawei has relied on it to achieve rapid and steadfast business development in the business sphere. It is hoped that this approach can help readers make great strides in knowledge acquisition in the academic world.

Many Western and Chinese academics and practitioners have taken the general view that Chinese companies should learn or adopt Western scientific management philosophy and methods, because this would greatly improve their competitiveness; therefore, a main task of business academics is to help Chinese companies with the Westernisation of management.

As a general assessment, Western management is much more scientific and efficient, and Chinese companies should learn as much as possible from the West. However, management and organisation follow strategy, which is influenced, among other factors, by culture, particularly cognition, history and philosophy. Chinese culture dictates that strategy and organisation in China are by nature individual-based; strategy is formed mostly on the basis of the judgements and decisions of key individuals, while organisations are managed by individuals at different levels. Western management is characterised by 'hardness', that is the bureaucratic structures and systems which are compatible with Western strategic planning approaches, whereas Chinese management is by comparison 'soft', relying on malleable and flexible organisational structures and systems which are attuned with Chinese incremental strategic approaches. Therefore, when introducing Western management into Chinese organisations, an appropriate blend of hardness and softness is needed to provide resilience and stability. In general, the less the human factor is involved, the more appropriate is the scientific management approach. For instance, in the area of HRM, the complete adoption of a Western system without any adaptation is unlikely to be successful, whereas in manufacturing and innovation systems, a high degree of Westernisation may work efficiently and effectively. Similarly, when a Western company operates in China, its management systems may also need to incorporate some elements of Chinese softness, particularly in the area of HRM.

Chinese individual-based (vs. Western rule-based) strategic and management systems have innate advantages and disadvantages, depending on the key individual of the organisation or nation. A major characteristic of this system is that it allows a decision to be made rapidly to get things done, without going through a prolonged decision-making process. A special case of a nation that illustrates this is Singapore, whose late eminent leader Lee Kuan Yew turned a third-world nation into a first-world one; under his outstanding leadership, a small nation rose to play an influential role in international, particularly Asian, affairs, while in other countries where a dictator has ruled, the results have mostly been disastrous. A business example is Huawei, which was built on Ren Zhengfei's personal charisma, vision and insight; his leadership has created and developed a strategy and management system bolstered by Western firms, such as IBM, the Hay Group and Towers Perrin, which has enabled Huawei to expand into different business fields with effectiveness and momentum. An exemplary case is that, having established its firm leadership position in the telecommunication networking industry, Huawei has expanded rapidly into the smartphone business; despite being a latecomer, it has gained a strategic foothold and is now the world's number three player, with potential for further progress. One of its major hurdles is the blocking of its entry into the US market, the largest in the world. Improving its international competitive position will depend on whether it can overcome this hurdle.

Huawei is not typical, however; behind every successful Chinese company, there are countless ones that have failed, as a result of individual blunders or weak organisational support. Thus, while a number of Chinese Internet-based companies such as Alibaba, Baidu, Tencent and JD.com have risen to prominence within a short period of time, the Chinese industrial landscape is littered with the corpses of Internet start-ups; there are plentiful examples of bankrupt e-commerce companies in retail, catering, tourism, automotive dealerships, education, finance, health care, real estate, community service, beauty, wedding services and many other areas. To revive the metaphor of Chinese companies as canoeists paddling downstream, only a minority reach the mouth of the river, while most capsize, hit rocks or become becalmed in stagnant backwaters.

Technology and related areas such as innovation and Internet business have traditionally been the forte of Western companies and major sources of income for them. The rise of Chinese competitors has changed this region of the business landscape in two ways: (1) they have driven out of business those Western companies that do not have sustainable technology and (2) they have forced some of those companies that used to earn excessive profits to reduce their prices, leading to non-profitability. Chinese companies are often seen as eliminators of excessive profits, with Western companies as their victims.

In the areas of engineering-based and science-based research, Chinese companies may have a long way to go to catch up with Western companies because of cultural factors, while in customer-based and efficiency-based research, they tend to run faster and hit the target more often. When Chinese companies find themselves disadvantaged technologically in international competition, their holistic cognitive instinct drives them to come up a package that has a better value/price ratio. Internet-based business is a case in point, where Chinese companies have focused on how to deliver value to customers, while Western companies have emphasised technology and efficiency; for instance, eBay migrated its China platform to the USA to achieve standardisation and efficiency, failing to deliver better value to Chinese customers. In engineering and science research, Chinese companies may follow Mao's dictum: concentrate all your resources on destroying your enemies one by one. This has worked in the past, for some companies (e.g. Huawei) and in some areas (e.g. military technology). Whether this approach will work more widely or not, allowing Chinese companies to catch up gradually with Western ones, remains to be seen.

China has a culture of using stratagems, reflecting the Chinese people's conflict-prone history, where the survivors were often those who were best able to outsmart their opponents. A Chinese saying suggests that clever persons may become the victims of their own cleverness. For over four millennia, Chinese society has been subject to innumerable clashes, restrained and brutal, military and non-military, within families and between families, and internal and international. Influenced by the Confucian Middle Way or moderation, historically, Chinese people have generally refrained from aggression into other countries, and this has become one of the conditions that have prevented China from falling into the same trap as other empires, such as the Roman and Byzantine, which consumed their resources through aggressively international expansion. Chinese stratagem culture, however, tends to give rise to an innate instability within any Chinese organisation once it becomes sizeable, so that Chinese combatants have often been defeated not by their opponents, but by their own internal conflicts. The ultimate source of strength in a successful Chinese organisation, be it a commercial company or the nation itself, is its exceptional leader, one who has the magnetic force to hold it together and the wisdom to guide it. This person is the soul of the nation or company. If a foreign company sees a Chinese one as a major competitor and wishes to study its strategy and management, it must analyse the leader's strategic mind and management philosophy, rather than focusing on its organisational behaviour and decision-making, as is often done in the West.

For Western companies to be viable and sustainable in China, they must have a few prerequisites in place: (1) offerings, that is products of superior quality or embedded in advanced technology, brands and knowledge or know-how concerning business processes or management and organisation; (2) mechanisms to deal effectively with Chinese stakeholders including customers, consumers, suppliers, competitors and government agencies; and (3) the human resources required to undertake operations in China.

(1) Offerings: To get its competitive offerings to the Chinese market, a foreign company must maintain an effective innovation system, rolling out products that its Chinese competitors cannot match. In many engineering-based or high-tech industries, Western companies have remained one step ahead of Chinese companies, which then attempt to find ways to catch up or neutralise their technological advantage. For instance, in 2014, China's luxury passenger car market was dominated by foreign brands – BMW, Mercedes-Benz, Audi, Volvo, Land Rover, Lexus, Porsche, Cadillac, Infiniti and Jaguar – because of their superior technology and brand reputation.

(2) Mechanisms of delivery: Superior offerings may not guarantee foreign firms' success in China. They have to deal with customers so that their offering is understood and their innovative products or services accepted, probably involving essential adaptations; with government agencies to meet necessary regulatory requirements; with suppliers if local sourcing is required; and with local distributors if these are required. All of these involve only (strategic) execution or simply effective management. The more concerned a company is with strategy, the less likely it is to be adaptive to the local market, as the strategic plan has to be followed to the letter. The key to success lies in having a flexible organisational structure and getting details right.

(3) Human resources underpin the second prerequisite and part of the first. A foreign company must have the right people to understand and communicate with stakeholders. It is often said that in China the war for business is in essence a war for human resources. Those companies that employ the right talent have already won a major campaign in that war.

Research into the performance of Chinese organisations should be conducted within a holistic perspective. An organisation should be seen as an organic entity like a human body. Strategic management can be likened to the brain, marketing to the heart, HRM to the liver and operations to the lungs. An organisation that performs well is like a body in good health: each field (or organ), be it strategy (brain), marketing (heart) or HRM (liver), should make a major contribution to the firm's performance (good health). Indeed, if a person is fit and well, he or she should have vigorous organs all round. However, if a person is unwell, one should not always attribute the cause to one organ, as is often the case in Western academic fields. For instance, researchers may find that ineffective marketing has caused a company to underperform and conclude that marketing is solely responsible for its poor performance. However, ineffective marketing (heart malfunction) may be caused by inadequate HRM (liver disease), just as the liver affects blood flow in the human body and an unhealthy liver can result in cardiac symptoms. Therefore, to study Chinese business effectively, a holistic perspective is essential, and this requires a cross-disciplinary study design involving collaboration between researchers in different fields. However, this is by no means an easy task, as in most academic journals, such an initiative is unacceptable: Western analytical thinking requires researchers to focus on a very narrow 'research gap' to make a contribution. Only one scenario would make it possible: where a research foundation or university allocates funds to initiate such a research project.

Chinese organisational systems, including the government, are individual-based; rational and stable mechanisms of leadership succession have yet to be established. For two millennia, the nation has been under the rule of a sovereign or an emperor, who has selected his successor. Since the founding of the People's Republic of China, this pattern has essentially remained the same. The political system really depends on the supreme leader of the Communist Party of China (CPC), his or her leadership skills and personal charisma, which are built on the leader's experience, connections, knowledge and personality. Mao Zedong was the first paramount leader of the CPC, followed by Deng Xiaoping. The system has three intrinsic weaknesses: (1) if a CPC leader is unprincipled or incompetent, the party and nation risks falling into a certain degree of chaos; (2) if the leader is benevolent and competent, but his (or, in principle, her) support is not as strong as the opposition to him, his position may be insecure; and (3) when the CPC leadership goes through a transition, there tends to be a high level of uncertainty within party and nation. For instance, after Mao Zedong passed away, the CPC and the nation underwent a short period of uncertainty, involving a power struggle between the Gang of Four, who were Mao's close allies, and the new generation of leaders, including Hua Guofeng, whom Mao Zedong had personally selected as his successor. Hua's team utilised military means to consolidate his leadership, having the Gang of Four arrested, sentenced and imprisoned. Despite Hua's official position as the top CPC leader, however, he did not have the kind of experience, knowledge and connections or the strength of support of Deng Xiaoping, who soon supplanted Hua as de facto leader of the CPC. It turned out that Deng's vision, experience, knowledge and resolution were just what China needed, steering the economy onto a fast track of development.

In 2013, Xi Jinping took over the leadership of the CPC and has since used his experience, connections (political and military) and knowledge to consolidate his position within the party. Under his leadership, China has enjoyed political and economic stability, providing an environment that is attractive to businesses both domestic and international. He is a pro-business leader and willing to listen to the voice of business, becoming a supporter of Chinese industry. However, when Xi Jinping's term comes to an end, China will probably go through a period of uncertainty again. He was born in 1953 and his background naturally suits him for his position of leadership. It is hard to visualise a person with the character, experience, connections (support) and knowledge to emerge from the Chinese succession pool with that charisma and magnetism. Unless, before he steps down, Xi Jinping can establish a system that is characterised by the separation of powers with checks and balances under the constitution, uncertainty will characterise China's business environment. Any international business should be prepared for all possible eventualities.

No matter what happens politically and economically in China, though, we can be sure that the country will long continue to wield great influence in the international arena, by virtue of its sheer size and what Chinese people want most as a kind of *shi*: stability and prosperity. Therefore, in the foreseeable future, most Western businesses, large or small, will have to do business, directly or indirectly, with Chinese companies. Time and effort invested in learning Chinese business can be well spent.

Index

Note: Tables and figures are indicated by an *italic* page number.